Indian Reserved Water Rights

Legal History of North America

Legal History of North America

General Editor
  Gordon Morris Bakken, *California State University, Fullerton*

Associate Editors
  David J. Langum, *Samford University*
  John P. S. McLaren, *University of Victoria*
  John Phillip Reid, *New York University*

Indian Reserved Water Rights

THE *WINTERS* DOCTRINE IN ITS SOCIAL AND
LEGAL CONTEXT, 1880s–1930s

John Shurts

University of Oklahoma Press : Norman

Library of Congress Cataloging-in-Publication Data

Shurts, John, 1956–
    Indian reserved water rights : the Winters doctrine in its social
and legal context, 1880s–1930s / John Shurts.
        p.   cm. — (Legal history of North America ; v. 8)
    Includes bibliographical references and index.
    ISBN 0–8061–3210–8 (cloth)
    ISBN 0–8061–3541–7 (paper)
    1. Water rights—Milk River (Mont. and Alta.)—History.   2. Indians of
North America—Montana—Claims—History.   3. Water development
projects—Milk River (Mont. and Alta.)   4. Water rights—West (U.S.)
5. Indians of North America—West (U.S.)—Claims.
    I. Title.   II. Series.
    KF8210.N37S55   2000
    346.7304'32—dc21   99–43558
                                                                                        CIP

Indian Reserved Water Rights: The Winters *Doctrine in Its Social and Legal
Context, 1880s–1930s,* by John Shurts, is Volume 8 in the Legal History of
North America series.

2 3 4 5 6 7 8 9 10

For Lin

Contents

Maps

Acknowledgments

In 1908, in *Winters v. United States,* the Supreme Court affirmed a lower court ruling that the Gros Ventre and Assiniboine Indians and the United States had reserved rights to water in the Milk River for the Fort Belknap Indian Reservation in Montana based on an 1888 treaty between the United States and these Indians. Out of this decision has come what is known as the *Winters,* or Indian reserved water rights, doctrine. Reserved water rights have played an important if controversial role in the West ever since. This is the first in-depth historical study of the *Winters* litigation and the early use and development of the doctrine.

The debt I owe to Donald Pisani is too large to pay. First, readers will note the many citations to Professor Pisani's articles and books. Nobody has done more to lay bare the historical developments in western water law. I gleaned important insights on Indian water rights from Don's published work as well as the unpublished material he let me see. As described in the text, in many ways I feel this book builds on a foundation he has begun. Second, a number of years ago I sent Don a research paper to see if I could interest him in commenting. From him I received not only wonderful comments but also the beginning of lively, friendly, and always useful correspondence that has helped shape my thinking. Third, readers will also note the many citations to documents in the records of the National Archives in Washington, D.C. I did not have to make a trip to the District to get these documents. It turns out that Don has, over the years, microfilmed the water law and water policy material in the relevant files of the Department of Interior, Bureau of Indian Affairs, Bureau of Reclamation, Justice Department, and more. Don simply shipped me box after box of roll after roll of microfilm, which I could view and copy in the comfort of the University of Oregon Law Library. Everyone in the field that has heard this story has shook his or her head and murmured that I cannot possibly know how fortunate I have been. I know. Thank you, Don.

Professor Richard Maxwell Brown is the other person to whom I owe the most in developing this book. As anyone who knows him would agree, Professor Brown is incredibly knowledgeable in the basic "facts" of history and in the various analytical methods for organizing those facts. More important is how accessible and amenable he has been in sharing that knowledge when asked. Professor Brown also achieved the difficult balance of allowing me complete freedom in developing the project as a dissertation while providing just the right guidance, criticism, and support. And he has to be one of the kindest and most courtly gentlemen ever. I am honored to have been his last graduate student.

Professors Jeff Ostler, Jim Mohr, Matthew Dennis, and Daniel Pope deserve thanks for reading and commenting on a draft of this study. They mean much more to me, however, as teachers who became friends with whom I have shared many enjoyable hours talking about history and that which is not history. I also want to thank Jim Mooney and James O'Fallon of the University of Oregon Law School for their review of drafts and other assistance, especially to Professor Mooney for many years ago introducing me to the work of Willard Hurst.

Three other people gave generously of their time and expertise to read the entire draft and provide detailed comments. I am especially grateful for the time John Volkman, my colleague at the Northwest Power Planning Council, devoted to my drafts even while pursuing his own masterful study of Columbia River water policy for the Western Water Policy Review Commission. Another Council colleague, John Harrison, who knows more Montana history than I ever will, provided careful substantive and editorial checks. Professor Michael Blumm's willingness to read and critique the draft and encourage the project in other ways is just the latest example of his many years of help to me and other scholars, and lawyers working on natural resource issues.

Thanks are also due to Kazuto Oshio, Lloyd Burton, and Jeanne Whiteing for their comments on conference papers that helped frame the ideas developed here. I also acknowledge the debt I owe to the excellent scholarship of Norris Hundley on *Winters* and on water history in general. I still remember the thrill of finding out that Professor Hundley was in audience for, and enjoyed, one of my conference presentations. Also in the audience at that conference, and asking tough questions, was Emily Rader, a graduate student at the University of Southern California, who is working on what should be a most useful study of the San Luis Rey River reservations in southern California. Emily and I later formed a Western History Association conference panel on Indian water rights and now enjoy a mutually supportive friendship. It was at this later conference that I met Shelly Dudley, a historical analyst for the Salt River Project and graduate student at Arizona State University, who was finishing a master's thesis on the water rights conflict at the Gila River Indian Reservation. Shelly shared with me not only the thesis but also her imposing research files and skills. I also wish to acknowledge the help and friendship over the years of fellow graduate students (now professors) Laurie Mercier and Jay Taylor.

I am thankful for the assistance of research staff at various institutions, including Brian Shovers at the Montana Historical Society, Jean Howard and Eric Bittner at the Rocky Mountain branch of the National Archives in Denver, and especially Laura McCarthy and June Justice of the Seattle branch of the archives. Thanks are also due to a number of reference assistants at the Knight Library and Law Library at the University of Oregon. The University of Oregon provided important financial assistance through a research fellowship and teaching fellowships.

Also reading the manuscript were Gordon Bakken, editor of the University of Oklahoma Press's Legal History of North America series, and Charles Wilkinson and David Langum. I am grateful for their insights and especially for their enthusiasm for the study. A big thank you goes to Barbara Siegemund-Broka for a wonderful editing job and for saying such nice things about the substance. Thanks are also due to John Drayton, Randolph Lewis, Sarah Nestor, Sarah Iselin, and other editors and staff at the University of Oklahoma Press.

Stephen Sasser and Bobbe Fendall of the Northwest Power Planning Council produced the original versions of the maps of the Milk River valley and Uintah reservation area. I appreciate their willingness to put up with my endless tinkering and the resulting revisions. Thanks are also due to the Council members for allowing me the time to work on this project while also working for the Council, and especially to Council members Ken Casavant and John Etchart for their personal interest in and support of my academic work.

In reflecting on my journey in the pursuit of law and history I cannot ignore the great if indirect influence on my thinking and goals of three wonderful people. It would be misleading to say that I was not interested in studying history until I had Patricia Nelson Limerick for a teacher; but nobody before or since has made history come alive for me like she did, and so I do not think I would have pursued it so avidly without her influence. I do know I would not have entered into the serious study of history at the University of Oregon at the time I did except that George Drake (my favorite undergraduate history professor at Colorado College and subsequently Grinnell President) told me in 1989 to quit whining about ending up on a path that kept me from studying history. He pointed out the obvious—I could still study history at the University of Oregon while keeping my hand in resource law work. Most important, I never spent a better two years than as the law clerk for a great water judge, former Justice George Lohr of the Colorado Supreme Court. I am honored to have become his friend and by the interest he has shown in my academic work.

My parents, Nelson and Suzanne Shurts, were a little bit amazed that I embarked on graduate studies in history the way I did, but they have always been loving and supportive of the strange things I have chosen to do. I appreciate more than they will ever know that they traveled to Eugene to watch one of the high points along the way, the defense of this study as a dissertation. My father also slogged through the draft and provided useful insights into what made sense and what did not. Russell Shurts has always pulled me along the right path, as a big brother should.

Patricia Shurts did not type the manuscript or even read it, and the ins and outs of the *Winters* doctrine have receded in her memory as the gardens grow, her landscape inclinations overwhelming the legal. Patty remains the most fascinating, intelligent, and wonderful person I have ever known, with ways of thinking and living that cut deeply into the commonplaces of what the rest of us will accept in thought, culture, and life. I would dedicate this work to her if not for what I have to say in the last paragraph. As for Sam, he might be a great historian someday, although he thinks he wants to be a chemist. These days he is just hoping Dad will get some things off his plate soon and be home more often to play.

Our family and the world lost a special person in October 1974 with the death of my beloved and beautiful sister. It is funny what things come to mind at times like that, but I told myself then that if I ever wrote a book I would dedicate it to her. It seemed (and seems) a pitifully small response to the enormity of the loss, but it was one thing I thought I could do to preserve her memory beyond our own minds and hearts. This book may be my only opportunity, and I mean to take advantage of it: This is dedicated to the loving memory of Linda Susan Shurts.

JOHN SHURTS

Eugene, Oregon

*Indian Reserved
Water Rights*

Introduction

What has come to be known as the *Winters* doctrine, or the Indian reserved water rights doctrine, arose out of litigation in Montana just after the turn of the twentieth century. The Winters case itself began in 1905 when public-land settlers upstream of the Fort Belknap Indian Reservation in northern Montana diverted all the water in the drought-reduced Milk River to irrigate their hay and other crops, something they believed they had the right to do under Montana law. The United States government sued the settlers in federal district court in Montana to protect whatever rights to water were held by the people downstream on the reservation. The federal judge in Montana, William H. Hunt, ruled in favor of the United States and the residents of the reservation. He based his decision on an interpretation of an 1888 agreement (supplemented by an 1896 agreement) between the United States and the Gros Ventre and Assiniboine people. The 1888 agreement reserved for these Indians the reservation lands along the Milk River out of a much larger tract ceded to the United States. Although the 1888 agreement said nothing explicit about reserved water rights or about water rights in general, Judge Hunt held that the agreement reserved water in the Milk River to accomplish the purposes of the reservation, especially to irrigate the reserved lands. The court determined that the reservation had an immediate need of 5,000 miner's inches of water, close to the entire natural flow of the river at that time and place. The court enjoined the settlers from diverting that amount and putting it to beneficial use on their own lands, as they were doing pursuant to the laws of the State of Montana.

The federal appeals court in San Francisco affirmed the ruling in 1906, and the Supreme Court followed suit in 1908 in the relatively famous decision of *Winters v. United States*. In these years (1907 and 1908), the same lower federal courts further explained and applied this reserved rights doctrine in a water dispute arising on the Blackfeet Indian Reservation, also in northern Montana and also involving the same 1888 agreement, a case known on appeal as *Conrad Investment Company v. United States*. As the courts developed the reserved rights doctrine in the various stages of the *Winters* and *Conrad Investment Company* decisions, they made clear that the Indians' rights to water were not limited to amounts then needed or then in use on the reserved lands, in contrast to water rights established under the western state law system of prior appropriation. The measure of the reserved right was whatever water was now needed or might become necessary in the future from the streams and rivers flowing on or adjacent to the reserved lands to allow Indian peoples to lead successful lives on these lands as "pastoral and civilized people," at least to make the lands "productive and suitable for agricultural, stock raising and domestic purposes." The non-Indians settlers upstream of the reservation could not perfect a private right to water in the Milk River that might be needed to fulfill the purposes of the reservation.[1]

The book first examines the course of the *Winters* litigation itself, placing that litigation in its legal context, in the local context of water development efforts and ideas in the Milk River valley just after the turn of the century, and in the broader national context of Indian and water policy at the same time. The *Winters* decision has been treated as an anomaly, an unwelcome intrusion into western water law and the activities of non-Indians along the Milk River. Using litigation records, contemporary legal information, reservation records, other government documents, and newspaper accounts, I explain to the contrary how the litigation and its outcome fit well within the existing legal context and into on-going efforts at water development in the Milk River valley.

The second part of the book examines the life of the *Winters* doctrine in the first decades after its formation, primarily through a case study of water rights conflict and litigation at the Uintah and Ouray Indian Reservation in Utah, but placing that litigation in a broader context as well. Here again I hope to reverse the usual understanding. Rather than being ignored or squashed by antagonistic forces, *Winters* had a lively existence in those years, as a tool of lawyers, government officials, and others interested in Indian and non-Indian water issues. These uses of *Winters* had real impacts on water allocation decisions, including impacts partially favorable to the long-term interests of western Indians, although a precise understanding of those impacts requires careful consideration of the dynamics of particular water disputes.

Winters and the reserved rights doctrine took shape in the shadow of, and to a great extent in opposition to, on-going developments in Indian policy and western state water law. How the *Winters* doctrine emerged, developed, and survived in this harsh social and legal context is one of my main themes. With regard to Indian policy, historians have described the first decades of the twentieth century as the most coercive and vicious phase of the allotment and assimilation process, during which non-Indians were most rapacious and successful in stripping western Indians of control over land and other resources and subjecting Indians to state law and the market economy. The Supreme Court's 1903 decision in *Lone Wolf v. Hitchcock,* five years before the Court's *Winters* decision, gave support to this effort, holding that Congress could force the individual allotment of tribal land and the sale of unallotted land without the consent of the members of the tribe, unilaterally abrogating a treaty that required such consent.[2]

The *Winters* decisions and the early development of the reserved rights doctrine had important links to the allotment policy. Moreover, *Winters* can be reconciled with *Lone Wolf* in the technical terms of the doctrine of federal Indian law. But the *Winters* decisions also stand in opposition to this general Indian policy in fundamental ways. The place of *Winters* in the context of resource loss and assimilation is complicated. There are elements to the *Winters* litigation, the decisions and the doctrine, elements both conscious and inadvertent, that run counter to what historians document as the fundamental, on-going process by which the various Indian peoples lost control of their resource base and the economic, cultural, and legal autonomy associated with that base, becoming more vulnerable to forced dependence and assimilation. The Indians in the Supreme Court's decision in *Lone Wolf,* corresponding to the basic patterns of Indian policy at the time, are described as weak wards of the government, incapable of control over their land and destinies in a modernizing world controlled by a different culture. In *Winters,* the same people are depicted as in "command of the land and the waters," sufficiently capable to have legal and functional control of their property, in a collective, tribal capacity if they so chose, and to decide how to reserve and use that property to react and adapt to changing circumstances. The ways in which people developed and used the reserved rights doctrine in the first decades after its development did not undermine this basic foundation, surviving with the doctrine into the current social and legal context.

Winters also directly contradicted the developments of western state water law, at least on the surface. By 1905, all of the western states had adopted (in whole or in part) some form of the prior appropriation system for determining rights to and allocating water. State prior appropriation law defined a right to water by the amount of water actually diverted from the river and put to beneficial use, and rights so determined were held and implemented (at least in theory) by a strict chronological priority (first-in-time, first-in-right). More precisely, the core elements or principles of the prior appropriation system could be characterized as (1) privatization of water by means of individual, vested property rights; (2) a first-in-time, first-in-right priority allocation, which meant that people who came late to a watercourse for water had to yield to those who had come previously, who drew first in times of shortage; (3) the divorce of water, rights to water, and use of water from strict relation to the land that lies along its course; (4) measurement solely in terms of a diversion of a specified amount for a beneficial, productive, present use; and (5) state and local control under state law, a property rights system administered primarily by locally situated state administrative officials and local state courts. In the late nineteenth and early twentieth centuries, important participants in western development, politics, and law elevated the prior appropriation system beyond legal choice to the realm of law determined by nature or even divine providence.[3]

The reserved rights doctrine could hardly have conflicted more with the official elements and doctrine of the prior appropriation system: The reserved rights doctrine described in the *Winters* and *Conrad Investment Company* decisions allowed for an inchoate, unquantified, flexible reservation of water. Reserved rights were based on historical occupancy, intention, and agreement, not on diversion and use. Reserved rights established on this basis mostly predated any other rights on the watercourse. Reserved water did not have to be used or needed at present to preserve rights to it. Reserved rights served and were defined by their relationship to specific, reserved lands along the watercourse. The amount of water represented by reserved rights was uncertain, as the rights were to be "measured" by what water it might take to serve generally described purposes, and that amount could increase over time.

And, finally, reserved rights were part of federal law and could be declared and enforced by federal courts. The supremacy of federal law and treaties meant, of course, that water in a watercourse subject to *Winters* rights could not be securely appropriated by non-Indian farmers and town developers under state law. Many westerners who were affected by or heard about the *Winters* decisions expressed outrage at what one labeled a "monstrous" doctrine. In light of this reaction, one issue explored here is how and why *western* lawyers and judges from the mainstream western economic and legal culture created the reserved rights doctrine in the period 1905 to 1908, on behalf of western Indians no less. Another issue explored is how what has appeared to some to be a weakly established reserved rights doctrine continued to survive its early decades despite being so fundamentally at odds with western water law and the supposed social, economic, and ideological underpinnings of that law, especially indicated by the number and the vehemence of attacks launched against the reserved rights doctrine.

One answer this study posits is that the prior appropriation system itself was not nearly as dominant, or universally supported, or as productive of desired outcomes as has been supposed. Legal theories supporting water rights for an Indian reservation outside of the realm of the state law of prior appropriation were well within the legal mainstream of 1905 Montana. Just as important, certain non-Indian settlers, irrigators, and other water users and people interested in economic development, who might be thought to be beholden to the prior appropriation system, were finding the system an obstacle to their plans or dreams for economic development. They found they could make use of the way the *Winters* decisions interfered with the prior appropriation system to serve their own interests, a dynamic central to the reaction to the *Winters* litigation itself. Also, legislators, executive branch policymakers, administrators, lawyers, and others, including important western interests, could deflect and transform the conflict over the reserved rights doctrine into a broad vision of what could be called Indian reclamation that matched the general reclamation vision in the West.

As anyone interested in water rights issues or the affairs of American Indian communities knows, effective control over and use of significant amounts of water by western Indians did not follow in the wake of the *Winters* decisions. Other studies have described how the doctrine's promise of federal Indian water rights and water use was undone by a combination of forces: westerners who were hostile to Indians and wedded to state law systems of water rights; conflicted and indifferent reactions from the Department of the Interior and the Department of Justice; a hostile Reclamation Service; a politically weak Bureau of Indian Affairs, inclined for a number of reasons to try to perfect Indian rights to water under state law while attempting to transform, through an impossible policy, western Indians into individual property-owning, small-tract farmers; politically and economically weak Indian tribes, unable to exercise sovereign powers over water and little interested in the way the federal government was trying to direct their use of water; an ambiguous Supreme Court opinion in *Winters;* and a powerful union of western and federal non-Indian interests that directed private and public money toward water development in favor of non-Indians and against Indians.[4] The end result is a sense that the *Winters* doctrine appeared and then disappeared, that it lay dormant until resurrected by the Supreme Court in the *Arizona v. California* decision in 1963, when it became a significant part of modern water disputes in the West and of the more effective assertion of Indian sovereignty.

This picture is partly inaccurate. It tends to obscure the ways in which people *did* understand and make use of the *Winters* doctrine in the first decades after the decisions. Rather than being ignored or unknown, what I find is that *Winters* was well known and often used by lawyers, government officials, members of Congress, and others interested in water issues involving Indians and non-Indians alike. And, as noted above, these uses of the *Winters* doctrine had real effects on water allocation decisions, including effects at least partially favorable to the long-term interests of western American Indians, although understanding precisely what those impacts were (or were intended to be) requires careful consideration of the dynamics of particular water disputes, in and out of litigation. The people most active in creating, understanding, and using the *Winters* doctrine in the decades studied here were western non-Indians. Western residents in the dominant culture never presented a monolithic front in favor of the prior appropriation system and state law and antagonistic to reserved rights and federal law, despite the rhetoric then and later of westerners loyal to their state law systems.

This book explores not just the particular course of the *Winters* doctrine and Indian water rights, as important and dynamic as that subject is. It also explores the role of *Winters* in a largely misunderstood contradiction within the dominant culture in the West. Many people superficially pledged allegiance to or went along with the prior appropriation system while doing whatever they could, and taking advantage of whatever they could, to escape some of its key features and reserve water and watersheds for coordinated and comprehensive economic development. *Winters* and the reserved rights doctrine were not always as contradictory and threatening as has been supposed precisely because they could be understood within this context and could even be, on occasion, an opportunity for non-Indians seeking to further their own similar aims. This dynamic may explain the most about how and why the reserved rights doctrine not only survived but was actively used, considered, and applied in water disputes, and yet why the central purpose of the doctrine—that is, to ensure control and use of water for American Indians—was never significantly realized.

Western American Indians were by far the least active participants in the work of *Winters* in the years studied here, despite the obvious fact that *Winters* was about Indian water rights and despite the Supreme Court's view of Indians in the original *Winters* decisions as active participants in command of the water. For just one example, discussed in detail below, in 1916 the United States filed suit against non-Indian water users in Utah to assert and protect the reserved water rights of the Uintah reservation, relying primarily on the *Winters* decisions. The litigation remained active for fifteen years as the federal court supervised the allocation of water in this area into the early 1930s. Yet the Ute Indians, residents of the Uintah reservation, were entirely absent in the litigation records, except in collective reference. No actor in the litigation or individual named or described in the court records was a Ute Indian living on the reservation or a member of any other Indian nation. I found no reference or statement in the records of the court or the records of the Office of Indian Affairs (commonly known as the Indian Office—the agency that would later become the Bureau of Indian Affairs) indicating that the residents of the Uintah lands were even consulted about or informed of the litigation, its progress, or its outcome. Presumably some communication did occur at that level, but even so, the Indians' effective participation in or influence on the litigation appears to have been exceedingly minor.

This is not an isolated example. I made an effort to uncover, for the years studied, how much Indians knew of the *Winters* doctrine, how they integrated the doctrine into their preexisting understandings of water and rights to water, and how they made use of the doctrine. *Everything* I found is noted in the pages that follow; the incidents are few. I do not doubt that Indians had a greater awareness of the nature, meaning, and possibilities of the *Winters* doctrine than I have found, but Indian people were rarely present (or, if present, were generally silent or silenced) whenever and wherever the *Winters* doctrine actually arose in litigation, legal analysis, negotiation, policy formation, policy administration, and the allocation and administration of water. It is not simply a matter of the views of Indians being excluded from the government's records, and it certainly does not mean that western Indians at the turn of the century did not produce or directly induce anything in writing. From these same records I could say a great deal about what the Indian residents of various reservations thought and did about the government's Indian land policies, as expressed in petitions, correspondence, tribal council resolutions, actions described in agency reports, and so forth. The same is not true of the water rights issues. One likely reason for this disparity is that the reserved water rights doctrine originated in the government's policy to transform western Indians into small-tract irrigation farmers, a transformation that did not interest many western Indians, to say the least. This is not to say that the Indians did not have their own needs for water and problems with access to water, but it may explain why those interests did not coincide as much as might be thought with the government's pursuit in these years of reserved water rights for reservations.

Thus despite the fact that what was involved was a doctrine about Indian water rights, the uses of and debates over *Winters* in these years are of primary importance for what they tell us about the non-Indian culture's complex relationship to water and water rights. An understanding of *Winters* has significant implications for the modern field of American Indian history, but this study is not Indian history itself. If it must be labeled, this is a study in environmental, legal, and western history that focuses on issues also of major importance to American Indian history. A topic that still needs to be explored is how western Indian peoples allocated and used water, conceived of rights to water, and understood and used the American laws of water, and how these actions and understandings changed over time.

The *Winters* doctrine and Indian reserved water rights have become an important and controversial part of modern water disputes in the West. For this reason, much has been written in the last twenty-five years on the *Winters* doctrine, especially in the fields of law and political science. Although outside the scope of this study, it is important to note the explosion of interest in reserved water rights that occurred in the legal community following the revival of the *Winters* doctrine in the 1960s and 1970s. The 1980s and 1990s have seen Indian reserved water rights asserted with even greater force, especially in official water rights adjudication proceedings. In contrast to the first few decades following

the *Winters* decision, Indian peoples have been primary actors in asserting these rights in modern times, with the assistance of the federal
government. The prospect of expensive litigation and uncertain outcomes
has led Indian groups, the federal government, state and local governments, private water users, and others to focus heavily on negotiating
agreements to confirm and quantify reserved rights, agreements that
Congress is asked or will be asked to ratify. In the usual situation, a
particular Indian nation is asked by the other parties to relinquish its
indefinite and potentially expandable reserved rights in return for a
clearly described right to a definite, quantified amount of water, plus an
amount of money or an agreement for assistance in bringing water to
reservation lands, or both. Whether these negotiated agreements will
allow American Indians to use (or market) significant amounts of
water, or whether the agreements represent simply another stage in a
long history of efforts to force native peoples to cede rights to valuable
resources, is unknown at this time.[5]

   This situation has prompted the development of a large literature
on the *Winters* doctrine. Some of these writings have included useful
historical information or context, yet on the whole the literature has
tended to ignore, misstate, or obscure the historical origin, development, context, use, and impact of the doctrine. This may be because the
Winters doctrine of the first thirty years is not the *Winters* doctrine of
today. People looked for the modern *Winters* doctrine in the past and
did not find it, and thus tended to assume that it had no useful or active
life until the 1960s and 1970s. I aim here to recapture some of that past
and put it in context.

   There has been no book-length or in-depth historical study of the
Winters doctrine. Norris Hundley and Donald Pisani, prominent western
historians who have focused their careers on water issues, have written
excellent journal articles on the subject, exposing some of the basic
issues and events surrounding the decisions and use of the doctrine.
Both emphasized the ways in which Indian water rights faced and were
squashed by antagonistic forces. As will be seen, I differ with each on a
number of points, including on how active a life *Winters* actually had in
its early years and on the meaning of that life, even as I agree with them
(one could not disagree) that the doctrine did not result in significant
water use or actual control of much water by American Indians in this
period.[6] In a less-noted article, Michael Massie published a useful
account of the *Winters* litigation itself, the Fort Belknap reservation
context of that litigation, and the impact of the decision on the reservation.[7] I also have my disagreements with Massie's analysis and expand

significantly the description of the local Milk River valley context here. Historians have otherwise largely ignored the subject, with at best peripheral references, sometimes incorrect, in various water and Indian histories.[8]

Legal scholars, legal practitioners, journalists, and others outside the historical field have written reams about the reserved rights doctrine (mostly law journal articles or chapters in law books), primarily tracing doctrinal developments or the progress of litigation or settlement efforts (especially the most recent developments) or narrowly discussing the legislative developments that worked to prevent theoretical rights from becoming actual water in use.[9] The latter subject was most ably discussed in one of the two books on the subject with any significant historical content, *Command of the Waters: Iron Triangles, Federal Water Development, and Indian Water* by Daniel McCool, a political scientist, and published in 1987. McCool ably documented how a powerful "iron triangle" of western irrigation and development interests, officials in the Bureau of Reclamation, and congressional committees with control over Reclamation appropriations assured that federal development capital went to non-Indian rather than Indian water projects, which were served by a far weaker triangle of corresponding interests and officials.

The other book of note is Lloyd Burton's 1991 *American Indian Water Rights and the Limits of the Law*. Burton sketched briefly the origin and development of the *Winters* doctrine and then examined recent case studies of water conflicts, settlement negotiations, agreements, and dispute-management methods, most of which focused on the Southwest. Burton's work is an excellent example of the concept of "bargaining in the shadow of the law," the way in which the certainties and uncertainties of law and legal doctrines affect the way people structure their relationships to each other and to resources and rights even in the absence of litigation. This study could be considered a complement to Burton's book and to this particular field of jurisprudential research, as I intend to show that water allocation actions, disputes, decisions, and settlements in the first third of the century were influenced by not only what was known about the *Winters* doctrine but also by what was not known.[10]

The existing literature on the subject paves the way and points to the need for this historical study focused on the reserved rights doctrine. The sources for my analysis have come mostly from the records of the federal government—federal court records; official congressional documents; documents, letters, and reports compiled by congressional committees; and reports, documents, and correspondence from the Office of Indian Affairs, the Reclamation Service (the name at the time for what became the Bureau of Reclamation), the Department of the Interior, and the Department of Justice. These records are, of course, the best source for official actions and attitudes, but they are also surprisingly full of letters and reported comments from less official actors (and descriptions of their actions). Other primary sources include state court records, statutes and other legal and policy records; law reviews and the writings of legal scholars and practitioners of the day; writings by others interested in water rights, uses, and policy; and newspapers, especially the Milk River valley papers at the time of *Winters*.

PART I

Winters v. United States

Litigation, Decisions, and Context

Central to the nineteenth-century relationship between the people of the United States and the Indian peoples of North America were the demands placed by non-Indians on Indians for land cessions and for a particular form of economic and cultural transformation. It is precisely these demands that set the stage for the litigation that resulted in what is known as the *Winters* doctrine, or Indian reserved water rights doctrine—ironically so, as the Supreme Court's decision in *Winters v. United States* and the resulting doctrine have become central to modern Indian efforts to retain and control natural resources important to economic and cultural autonomy.

Another set of relationships that had nothing to do with the Indians may have shaped the *Winters* litigation and its outcome as much (or more) than the non-Indian demand for Indian land and cultural transformation: the demands for water of the upstream and downstream non-Indian farming and ranching settlers in the Milk River valley in Montana, demands greater than the natural flow of the river at irrigation times, especially in drought years. The *Winters* decision reserved a significant portion of the natural flow of the river for the residents of the Fort Belknap Indian Reservation and enjoined the upstream settlers from diverting that water. This altered the balance of power among non-Indian water users, serving the interests of downstream settlers who hoped to persuade upstream users to support a basinwide project to reserve, store, and allocate the springtime runoff flood waters of the Milk.

 Cession

CHAPTER 1

Prelude to the Winters *Litigation*

Land Cession and Reservation Agreements, Non-Indian Settlement, and Irrigation

The *Winters* decisions turned primarily on the meaning of a land cession/reservation agreement negotiated in 1887 between representatives of the United States, on the one hand, and the Gros Ventre and Assiniboine people in northern Montana, on the other, an agreement approved in 1888 by Congress. This agreement was but one in a series of land cession agreements over the last half of the nineteenth century involving the various Indian peoples in Montana, albeit one of the most important and complete of that series.

In the 1851 Treaty of Fort Laramie and an 1855 treaty involving the Blackfeet and other Indian groups, the United States and participating Indian groups in the Northern Plains and Rocky Mountains recognized and reserved as an Indian homeland the northern half of what would later become the Territory and then State of Montana. Over the next thirty years demands for land by non-Indian settlers and encroaching settlements by non-Indians on the reserved lands led to conflict with the Indian residents, which in turn led the federal government to seek and obtain additional treaties and agreements that whittled away significant pieces of the Indians' territory. Most important before 1887 was a land cession/reservation agreement in 1873, approved by Congress in 1874, that now described the portion of Montana Territory north of the south bank of the Missouri River and east of the Rocky Mountains as the area set apart "for the use and occupancy of the Gros Ventre, Piegan, Blood, Blackfoot, River Crow, and such other Indians as the President may, from time to time, see fit to locate thereon." While the 1873 agreement officially recognized one large, all-encompassing reservation, at this time (and increasingly over the next decade), certain Indian groups were understood to be linked to different lands and agency outposts within the larger reservation. The Gros Ventres and certain groups of the Assiniboines controlled lands around the Fort Belknap agency midway along the Milk River and were understood to be within the orbit of that agency.[1]

The process of non-Indian encroachment and settlement on Indian lands followed by demands for additional land cessions continued after 1874. In the late 1880s the government and people of the United States began a new effort to radically reduce the land base of these native peoples. Negotiations in 1886 and 1887 led to three land cession/reservation agreements with the Indians in northern Montana east of the Rockies. These agreements completed the transfer to the United States of millions of acres and reserved for the Indians three parcels of land in far northern Montana—what became known as the Blackfeet, Fort Belknap, and Fort Peck reservations. Congress approved the three agreements in 1888. One of the three agreements, executed with the Gros Ventre and Assiniboine peoples around Fort Belknap, reserved for these Indians the Fort Belknap Indian Reservation, consisting of approximately 600, 000 acres south of and adjoining the Milk River.[2]

The Indian peoples who signed or were affected by these land cession agreements had a variety of interrelated motives and reasons for being involved, from sheer force and duress, to being "included" in agreements they never consented to or understood, to economic necessity, to more complicated combinations of acquiescence to severe pressures and efforts to retain a measure of autonomy under rapidly changing circumstances. The non-Indian people involved in provoking and negotiating these land cession agreements also acted for a variety of interrelated motives, dominated by an insatiable desire to free more land for non-Indian settlement. Non-Indians perceived that the Indian land was not being used appropriately—was going to waste—because the Indians did not use and settle the land as intensively as the non-Indians would. The non-Indians also perceived the land as relatively empty and available for transfer and settlement because the Indian populations of these lands had decreased over the decades, in some cases dramatically, primarily due to diseases. Non-Indians also sought to make official the on-going and, to them, inevitable encroachment on reservation lands, and they sought to clear the path for railroad development to link the East with the developing West Coast. And perhaps more important than any factor other than the basic desire for land for settlement, non-Indians purposely sought to reduce the Indians' land base in order to undermine the subsistence practices of the Indian peoples. This, it was hoped, would force the Indians, in order to survive, to transform themselves into a small-farmer agrarian society resembling the ideal that the non-Indian society had for itself in the settlement of the West.

The transformative intentions of the people of the United States underlying the Fort Belknap agreement are clear from its general provisions. The federal courts in *Winters* later construed the agreement as intending settlement on the reservation to begin the real process of transforming the Gros Ventre and Assiniboine people from a relatively nonsedentary, primarily hunting and trading economy to the way of life of the non-Indian farming and ranching settlers in the West. This transformation was to yield fixed, year-round residences, irrigated farming (eventually on privately and individually owned small, allotted tracts), livestock grazing, and other aspects of the dominant American civilization that might develop over time.[3]

A close examination of the 1888 agreement (and a subsequent 1896 agreement) illustrates the greater policy and cultural context outlined above. The 1888 Fort Belknap agreement began with a preamble that stated that the land then reserved for various Indians in Montana (the 1874 reservation) was "wholly out of proportion to the number of Indians occupying the same, and greatly in excess of their present or prospective wants." Thus, "the said Indians are desirous of disposing of so much thereof as they do not require, in order to obtain the means to enable them to become self-supporting, as a pastoral and agricultural people, and to educate their children in the paths of civilization." The *Winters* courts later relied heavily on this statement of intent in the preamble to understand the purposes for which the Indians and the government might reserve water or rights to water.

The provisions that followed the preamble fell into three categories—land reservation, land cession, and compensation. Article 1 began with a statement of the land reserved, providing that the "permanent homes" of "various tribes or bands" of Indians would be the reservations described at the end of the agreement. The agreed-to boundaries of the Fort Belknap reservation were then attached to the agreement. Important for the later *Winters* litigation would be the fact that the northern boundary of the reservation was described as extending to "the middle of the main channel of Milk River."

Turning to the land cession provisions, article 2 then provided that the Indians "cede and relinquish to the United States all their right, title, and interest in and to all the lands embraced within" the 1874 reservation "not herein specifically set apart and reserved." Article 6 added the caveat that any Indian who had "settled upon and made valuable improvements upon" any of the land ceded could apply to the land office to have allotted to him or her up to 160 acres of the land and a lesser amount per child. The secretary would then issue a patent for the land, to be held in trust for twenty-five years. Given the timing of the agreement—1887, the same year as the General Allotment Act (the Dawes Act), discussed below—it is interesting and surprising that the agreement does not contain a general plan or mechanism for allotment of the reserved lands. Finally, article 7 added that the president could grant rights-of-way for railroads, highways, and telegraphs across the reserved lands when "the public interests require," at a compensation to be fixed by the secretary of the interior "and by him expended for the benefit of the Indians concerned."

Article 3 stated the "consideration" or compensation for the lands ceded. Compensation was not in the form of a direct cash payment, nor in the form of money, goods, or land set aside under the control and direction of the Indians ceding the land. This was by no means a real estate deal between equal parties exchanging land for cash or an equivalent in value. Instead, for the Fort Belknap Indians the federal government agreed to "expend annually, for the period of ten years . . . under the direction of the Secretary of Interior," $150,000

> in the purchase of cows, bulls, and other stock, goods, clothing, subsistence, agricultural and mechanical implements, in providing employees, in the education of Indian children, procuring medicine and medical attendance, in the care and support of the aged, sick and infirm, and helpless orphans of said Indians, in the erection of such new agency and school buildings, mills, and blacksmith, carpenter, and wagon shops as may be necessary, in assisting the Indians to build houses and inclose their farms, and in any other respect to promote their civilization, comfort, and improvement.[4]

Article 7 further provided that the cost of the official survey of the reservation was to come out of this fund. Article 4 added that when "in the opinion of the President" it was not necessary to spend the stated annual amount "in carrying out the provisions of this agreement," the surplus was to be placed in the Treasury to the credit of the Indians and used to extend the benefits stated after the annual installments expired. Finally, and most telling, Article 5 *required* the secretary to show preference in the spending of what was in theory compensation belonging to all the tribal members to benefit those people most interested in making the desired cultural transformation:

> In order to encourage habits of industry, and reward labor, it is further understood and agreed, that in the giving out or distribution of cattle or other stock, goods, clothing, subsistence, and agricultural implements, . . . preference shall be given to Indians who endeavor by honest labor to support themselves, and especially to those who in good faith undertake the cultivation of the soil, or engage in pastoral pursuits, as a means of obtaining a livelihood, and the distribution of these benefits shall be made from time to time, as shall best promote the object specified.[5]

Irrigation is not explicitly mentioned in the agreement, but drawing implications from the express terms of the 1888 agreement, the United States negotiators acknowledged in a report to the commissioner of Indian affairs at the close of the treaty negotiations that implementing the agreement would involve the development of irrigated agriculture, although the negotiators did not state what they thought this would mean for rights to water. The negotiators discussed irrigated agriculture as part of a larger discussion of the way in which the agreement to live on the reduced lands would force the Indians to turn to "stock-raising" and "agricultural pursuits," as the Indians "can never become self-supporting in any other way." The negotiators explained that the physical conditions of the reserved lands would allow the Indians to succeed in these efforts, in that "[t]he lands selected for [the Indians] are as good, if not the best, for agricultural purposes in all that region of country, being well watered and susceptible of irrigation at a small cost. They are also admirably adapted to stock-raising."[6]

The agreement said nothing specific about reserving water, water rights, irrigation, or the development of irrigation improvements. Thus most commentary on the later *Winters* decisions has stated that the courts "implied" a reservation of water in the 1888 agreement through the agreement's statement of agrarian purposes and its reservation of land for those purposes, which would be defeated if water were not also reserved by implication. As will be discussed more fully below, the U.S. attorney who handled the *Winters* litigation for the government, Carl Rasch, denied that a reservation of water was merely "implied" in the agreement or that the trial court understood the reservation of water as implied. Rasch argued that the agreement expressly reserved water for the reservation by describing the reservation boundaries as extending to the middle of the river, especially when that description was considered

in context of the rest of the agreement and the historical and legal circumstances of the Indians' prior control over land and water in northern
Montana. It can be argued that the *Winters* decisions from the various
levels of the federal courts were in accord with Rasch's views. In truth,
the terms of the agreement were such that it could be argued that the
agreement contained an express reservation of water, an implied reservation of water, or no reservation of water, and all positions were later
argued.

I have not uncovered what any of the Indians involved in or
affected by the 1888 agreement thought or said about the agreement's
relationship to water and irrigation or generally about the agreement
itself and its various provisions. U.S. Attorney Rasch later constructed
an argument for his brief to the Court of Appeals, based apparently on
nothing but his imagination and his general knowledge of the situation
on the land in 1887, as to how the Gros Ventre and Assiniboine negotiators must have thought about the agreement and water:

> Can there be any question as to how these Indians must "naturally"
> have understood the treaty of 1888? Why, at that time, not a drop of
> the waters of the stream was or had ever been taken from its channel
> by a white man for any purpose. The entire stream was then and
> always had been a part of the Indian country, and a part of the
> Indian's reservation theretofore occupied by them. They and their
> fathers, from time immemorial, had seen the waters of the stream
> flow down past and through their reservation in abundance, and at
> no time had they known or seen the channel of Milk River other than
> as a flowing, living stream. When the extent and area of the new
> reservation was determined and defined by treaty and agreement,
> one half of the stream was specially, particularly, and carefully
> reserved as a part and portion of the reservation, and while at that
> time the Indians may have not made use of much, if any, of the
> waters for irrigating purposes, they knew that the very object and
> purpose which actuated them in consenting to a diminution of their
> territorial domain, to-wit: "to obtain the means to enable them to
> become self-supporting as a pastoral and agricultural people,"
> required the use of those waters to enable them to accomplish those
> very objects and purposes. *With all of these things before them, it
> would be preposterous to assume that they understood their bargain with
> the Government in any other way than that there was secured and
> reserved to them the flowing, living stream as they had always known
> and seen it.*[7]

As will be noted in another context below, this is one of a few statements, if not the only statement, associated with *Winters* and the
reserved rights doctrine in these early years that characterized reserved
water rights as relating broadly to a reservation of or rights to a stream
or river flowing in a natural, predevelopment condition as a general
sustaining element of the life of the surrounding land and people—in
which the Indians reserved to themselves not just water for irrigation or
stock watering or some other specific economic pursuit that would
advance them materially, but instead "the flowing, living stream as they
had always known and seen it."

Rasch's rhetoric may in fact resemble how at least some of the Gros
Ventre and Assiniboine people did conceive of their relationship to the
waters of the Milk River and the other streams of the reservation at the
time of the 1888 agreement, if historian Michael Massie's brief attempt
to recover that understanding, based mostly on anthropological studies,
is correct. (I have not uncovered anything to indicate that the Assiniboine and the Gros Ventre peoples of the Fort Belknap reservation held
different views about the human relationship to water, even while
aware that the cultural traditions of the two peoples were not the same.)
A complex and intertwined spiritual and physical relationship between
humans and the nonhuman world, including land, water, rivers,
mountains, plants and wildlife, has been shown to be central to many
American Indian cultural traditions, and so one might expect that the
Indians of northern Montana had a broader, more complex living
relationship with the streams and other waters in the area than purely
considerations of use, ownership, and production. Massie concluded
from his review that water "performed significant social and economic
functions" in the lives of the Indian peoples in this semi-arid region,
especially in the way in which the waters sustained the land in order to
feed their horse herds and the animals they hunted and, by late in the
nineteenth century, began to herd. River valleys were also the place
these peoples settled for protection from the worst of winter conditions,
and the river valley places of settlement became identified with the life
and history of the people. Moreover, rivers and other places of water
were important ceremonially, in that the large gatherings for ceremonies such as the Sun Dance required a significant source of water. It
may be that these ceremonies, so essential for the peoples' identity with
each other, the land, and the cosmos, became in part associated with the
waters at which the people gathered, and so the peoples' lives and
identities became associated and intertwined with the flowing, living
streams.[8]

The most in-depth study of the relationship between a western American Indian nation and water that I could find is Joanna Endter's 1987 inquiry into the traditional understandings of water among the Utes who ended up on the Uintah reservation in eastern Utah. Endter noted that the Utes followed a "subsistence round" of hunting, fishing, and gathering in the arid and semi-arid Great Basin and mountain lands of Utah, Colorado, and New Mexico, staying close to sources of waters, from rivers to springs, "where they could obtain food from the fish that lived in, the plant life that grew beside, and the game which congregated around the water." Especially well-watered areas, such as nearby major rivers such as the Green, White, and lower Sevier, were the location of the more permanent, year-to-year habitations of these peoples. "Rights" to make use of water depended mostly on historical identity and occupancy, that is, on the fact that people used the water because they had lived in that area and used that water for a long time.

The Utes conceived of water in terms more fundamental than simply the physical and subsistence characteristics of it. According to Endter, water was one of the two dominant symbols in the Ute spiritual universe, the other being the sun or fire. Nature was a "repository and source" of spiritual force or power, and the "dominant dichotomy of forms in which power appears" was dry/hot and wet/cool. Water had the power to provide and sustain all life—a power both physical and supernatural. Water played an important role in ceremonies, especially in the Sun Dance and sweats. Endter concluded:

> The way Utes conceived of and treated water corresponded to their spiritual beliefs and view of the world. Utes considered water as something which was animate, hence imbued with spirit. It was very sacred to them inasmuch as they believed that water was a source of supernatural power that could heal and cleanse. The special purpose of water was to provide life for all things. Certain springs or lakes which were thought have special healing power or were used for ceremonial purposes were especially sacred to Utes. Utes taught that water was to be respected, preserved, and left free flowing so that it could continue to sustain all living things along its path. There were strong cultural ethics to share water with other people and with all other forms of life, to treat it carefully when using it, and to take only as much as one needed. Special customs and traditions were observed in the way in which water was used.[9]

I realize it is inappropriate to assume that the cultural traditions of the Utes can be automatically applied to any other American Indian people, even to people such as the Gros Ventres and the Assiniboines that shared so many subsistence and environmental characteristics with the Utes (a hunting-and-gathering subsistence mode on the western semi-arid plains) and who incorporated versions of the same ceremonial traditions, such as the Sun Dance. But Endter's analysis did uncover traditions and understandings that are similar to what has been written about the cultural traditions of the Fort Belknap Indians, especially as they stand in contrast to the cultural traditions of the non-Indian settlers. She described a basic set of principles and attitudes that can be assumed here to be relatively common to the different peoples, sufficient at the least to support Rasch's conclusion that the Fort Belknap Indians would have understood that the 1888 agreement, which described a reservation that included the river (and, obviously, the other streams on the reserved lands), "secured and reserved to them the flowing, living stream as they had always known and seen it."

If the 1888 agreement said little about water—again, with the caveat that to some, including the Indians, it may have said much about water—a subsequent Fort Belknap land cession agreement in 1895, approved by Congress in 1896, did mention irrigation, scarcity of water at the reservation, and the implications of that scarcity for land use. Again, however, the agreement did not explicitly describe the Indians' *rights* to water in any legal sense. Commentary on the *Winters* decisions usually focuses on the 1888 agreement alone, probably because so did the Supreme Court. But the lower federal courts, especially the district court, also relied on the 1896 agreement in determining the rights to water for the reservation, essentially as an aid to interpreting the earlier agreement.

In the 1896 agreement, the Fort Belknap Indians sold to the United States about 20,000 acres at the southern edge of the reservation desired by non-Indians for mining and grazing. As compensation, the United States agreed to spend $360,000 for certain purposes over four years following the end of the ten years of expenditures described in the 1888 agreement. The 1896 agreement described a set of items or purposes for which the money could be spent that roughly corresponded to the list in the 1888 agreement, although this time the description explicitly included sums to be expended "in assisting the Indians . . . to irrigate their farms," a provision later emphasized by the district court as indicating a constant intent from 1887 to reserve water for irrigation. The 1896 agreement also included a provision that expressed the official understanding of the United States and the Indians as to the appropriate relationship, at this place and time, of water conditions, suitable land use, and allotment:

> As the scarcity of water on this reservation renders the pursuit of
> agriculture difficult and uncertain, and since the reservation is well
> adapted to stock raising, and it seems probable that the main reliance
> of these Indians for self-support is to be found in cattle raising, it is
> agreed that during the existence of this agreement no allotments of
> land in severalty shall be made to them, but that this whole
> reservation shall continue to be held by these Indians as a communal
> grazing tract, upon which their herds may feed undisturbed; and that
> after the expiration of this agreement the land shall continue to be so
> held until such time as a majority of the adult males of the tribes shall
> request in writing that allotment in severalty shall be made of their
> lands.[10]

I have not found any explanation as to how and why this specific provision ended up in this agreement. At face value it illustrates a common
understanding of the Indians and the government as to the most
appropriate land use and land-holding arrangement under the specific
circumstances at the time. It may indicate that the Fort Belknap Indians
were especially vigilant and successful at this time in resisting the twin
pressures dominant in federal Indian policy at the turn of the century—
crop agriculture and allotment. It also indicates an awareness as to the
experiences non-Indian settlers were having in using land in the Milk
River valley by the mid-1890s, an issue discussed below.

The 1896 agreement most clearly reflected what the Fort Belknap
Indians and the Fort Belknap agency personnel had learned about the
reservation lands by the mid-1890s. The reservation superintendents
tried to promote crop farming, but the Indians preferred stock-raising—
of horses and cattle—which they (and others, including agency personnel) saw as more likely to be successful and which the Indians were
better able to incorporate into traditional subsistence and cultural traditions than crop agriculture. Some of the Fort Belknap Indians tried to
pursue stock-raising (and farming) in the arid, lower valleys of the Milk
River, but many others decided to pursue this calling in the better-
watered stream valleys and meadows of the mountainous areas in the
southern part of the reservation. What little crop farming was taking
place was mostly at the direct behest of the superintendent, near the
agency along the river. Attempts at farming crops confirmed what had
already been the conventional wisdom—irrigation would have to be a
necessary element of a successful farming operation. The Indians and
agency personnel also discovered that significant stock-raising operations were not going to be successful without irrigation. "Seasons of

drought" proved the limiting factor on the land; the area suffered from
dry periods that left the land unable to produce enough vegetation to
sustain over time stock herds of the size necessary to serve the reservation's population. The Indians needed to cultivate hay to feed the
stock, and significant hay production required irrigation.[11]

To promote irrigation for both reasons—crop farming and hay
production—the Office of Indian Affairs, at the request of the reservation superintendents, persuaded Congress in the 1890s to allocate money
to build an irrigation system. Work on an irrigation system began in
1889 to supply water for domestic and agricultural needs, although
most of the construction work took place in the latter part of the 1890s.
The irrigation system developed by 1905, apparently in four different
units, irrigated 5,000 acres of vegetables, grains, and hay with water
from the Milk River and from certain streams in the interior. Agency
officials estimated at the time that at least 30,000 acres were susceptible
of irrigation from the Milk River, and they hoped to expand the system
to that size as soon as possible. The reservation superintendents ignored
the legal formalities of state water rights for the developing irrigation
system until 1898. In that year, Superintendent Luke Hays filed a claim
with the state for 10,000 miner's inches of water out of the Milk River to
supply the irrigation system for the reservation. He filed for the rights
in his own name, not even in his capacity as superintendent for the
reservation, let alone in the name of the Indians or the United States.

While the successful development of canals in the Milk River valley
convinced some Indians to focus on crop-raising, most still resisted
farming crops and continued to focus on stock-raising and on hay
production for stock. By 1905 the Fort Belknap Indians directly farmed
about half the 5,000 irrigated acres, most of it in hay and a significant
portion of it not in the lower valley and not watered from the Milk
River. Personnel from the agency school and non-Indian farmers who
had access to Indian lands farmed the other half of the irrigated
acreage, all of it in the Milk River valley. (How and why non-Indian
farmers had access to Indian lands is discussed below.) At times the
superintendents would continue to push the Indians toward farming
grain; at other times they would declare that hay production and cattle
were the only viable agricultural activities, although the Fort Belknap
superintendents in the 1900s, beginning with William Logan in 1902,
focused as much on hay production for the market as for Indian cattle.
It is clear that the constant policy shifts and pressures tended to
undermine the Indians' transition to and development of a competitive
cattle operation. Even so, the irrigation developments had an impact on

the material lives of the Fort Belknap Indians. As Michael Massie explained:

> By 1905, the tribal livestock industry had greatly expanded, and the reservation sold thousands of pounds of beef to surrounding communities and to the nearby Great Northern Railroad. The irrigation system made possible this dramatic increase in cattle production. The people used the water to grow large fields of hay, thereby supplementing the food supply of the cattle. As a result of these higher yields in farming and stockraising, the Fort Belknap economy became more stable throughout the 1890s and the 1900s.
>
> Despite this growth, the Indians experienced mixed economic results. The agents' insistence upon farming impeded the full development of the stock industry. Since cattle represented the only possible means of gaining financial independence in an arid region, this hindrance prevented the reservation from reaching self-sufficiency. Nevertheless, economic activity did increase due to the construction of the irrigation system.[12]

Massie's account may give a false impression of the level of economic activity at this time and of the strength of the livestock industry on the reservation. Poverty and government subsistence assistance were still the central facts of economic life at the reservation in 1905. He does, however, appear to be correct about the apparent trends and direction of economic development, and the importance of the irrigation system in that development. That is why the gathering momentum of economic activity was disturbed not just by the agents' interference but also in 1905 by threats to the water supply for the reservation's irrigation system.

Unfortunately for those interested in irrigation on the reservation, the non-Indian settlers on the surrounding lands in the Milk River valley had not been idle spectators. The headwaters of the Milk River are on the eastern side of the Rocky Mountains near the Canadian border, part of the Blackfeet Indian Reservation then and in what is now Glacier National Park. The river flows northeast and soon enters into Alberta, Canada. It flows east through Canada just north of the border for approximately one hundred miles before it reenters Montana at about the middle of the state's northern boundary, northwest of Havre. The Milk then moves southeast to the Havre area, turning east to flow for nearly two hundred miles before joining the Missouri between Glasgow and Wolf Point (just downstream of the Fort Peck Dam), passing through or near the towns of Havre, Chinook, Harlem (across the river from the Fort Belknap reservation), Dodson (just after the reservation), Malta, Saco, Hinsdale, Vandalia, Tampico and Glasgow (see map 1). References here to the "Milk River valley" mean that portion of the Milk after it reenters the United States.

What made the Milk River valley attractive for settlers in the 1890s was the combination of public land available for settlement following the land cession agreements in 1888 and the completion of the Great Northern railroad track along the north bank of the Milk River in 1890. Cattle ranchers and crop farmers took up the public lands, while merchants and other town developers created or enlarged a number of towns throughout the Milk River valley, including Havre and Chinook upstream of the Fort Belknap reservation, Harlem just across the river from the northern boundary of the reservation, and Malta, Saco, Hinsdale, Vandalia, and Glasgow below the reservation. The stockmen and farmers developed irrigation systems and began diverting substantial amounts of water from the Milk River and putting the water to beneficial use on their fields, filing water rights claims under first the territorial and then the state prior appropriation laws. Some of the most significant diversions of water were by cattlemen irrigating hay fields in the Havre and Chinook areas in the upper end of the valley, where the Milk River reenters the United States after its brief sojourn in Canada. After 1900, irrigators downstream of the Havre-Chinook area, including water users at and adjacent to the reservation, began noticing diminished river flows available for irrigation due to a combination of increased diversions and drought conditions. With the onset of more severe drought conditions in 1904 and 1905, upstream diversions from the Milk River resulted in an essentially dry river at the Fort Belknap reservation at the time of spring irrigation.

One other dynamic is important: non-Indians not only took control of lands ceded by the Indians in 1888, they also made inroads on the reservation lands themselves. The sale of mining and grazing lands represented by the 1896 land cession agreement is but one example. More important for this study, beginning in the late 1890s the reservation superintendents, following policy authorizations from the central office, began leasing reservation lands to non-Indian cattlemen. What were granted most were short-term grazing permits or leases, allowing the holder to run cattle on the reservation pastures. The records are a bit murky, but at least in the first decade of the twentieth century, and perhaps before, some these leases began allowing the lessees to irrigate and produce hay and other crops. Whether all or most of these production rights were associated with grazing permits, or whether

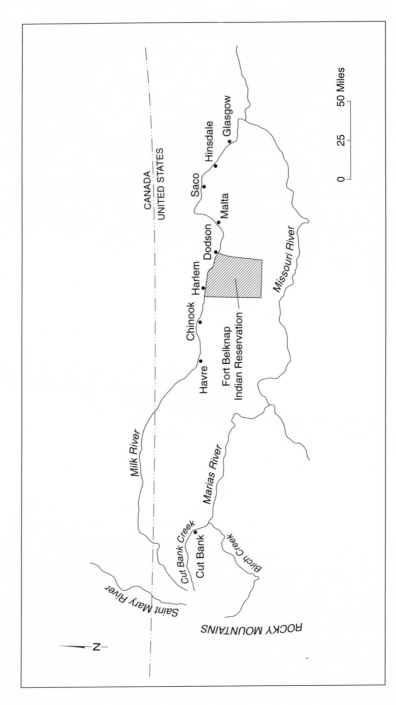

Map 1. Milk River valley, Montana

significant numbers of non-Indians were actually receiving separate leases to farm that were not connected to grazing permits, is unclear. In addition, a few non-Indian men married Indian women and began farming irrigated lands on the reservation. This is why by 1905 non-Indian farmers controlled an important if apparently small portion of the reservation lands irrigated from the Milk River, and had effective control over larger areas through grazing leases. The superintendents used the money from the leases to purchase supplies and subsistence food for the agency and the Indians and to pay wages to Indian laborers on reservation projects. The superintendents also encouraged the Fort Belknap Indians to work for wages for the ranchers on and off the reservation. Most important, in 1905, the year the *Winters* litigation began, Superintendent Logan began a campaign to attract people connected to the sugar beet industry to sign long-term leases for large tracts of reservation land (offering at least 5,000 to 10,000 acres right at the beginning) for the irrigated production of sugar beets with Indian labor, while at the same time trying to convince a sugar company to construct a sugar beet processing operation on reservation lands. Logan did try to convince Indian farmers to plant sugar beets, but as his plans evolved, the Fort Belknap Indians were slated to participate in this operation primarily as wage laborers on the sugar beet farms and in the refinery. Another development in the years around the litigation stemmed from the fact that non-Indian ranchers and farmers in the vicinity of the reservation desired more than the opportunity to lease reservation lands. They began efforts to convince the federal government—especially Congress and the Indian Office—to sell to the non-Indians the reservation lands that were most suitable for irrigation, arguing that the Indians were wasting their productive potential.

The records indicate that the superintendents consulted at times with the Fort Belknap residents about the leasing program and other schemes to promote the use of reservation lands by non-Indians. At times a significant number of the Indians supported the leasing program for the income it produced, especially the short-term grazing permits that did not interfere with grazing uses by the Indians. It is also clear that at times the Indian residents protested and resisted the leasing of reservation lands (especially long-term leases) and the other parts of the economic development program, as diverting their lands and labor to the benefit of the non-Indian cattlemen, farmers, and businesses and to the detriment of the Indian cattle operations. Logan and his successors did approve some significant if short-term leases that allowed for sugar beet cultivation. But the Indians opposed long-term sugar leases for sugar beet production of the magnitude envisioned by Logan, which combined with financing and market problems and the competition from other parts of the valley to be the site of sugar beet production to thwart plans to make sugar beet leasing and processing a significant part of the reservation economy. Another source of conflict between the Indians and the superintendent developed from the fact that Logan himself owned cattle and a cattle ranch west of the reservation, and he grazed his cattle on the reservation, although he made clear to anyone who inquired that he paid the same grazing fee as other lessees.[13]

The fact that non-Indians controlled areas of irrigable land and had other rights to reservation land in 1905 is important in part because it raises the issue of whether they—the non-Indian farmers and grazers and business interests on the reservation—were the intended beneficiaries of the government's lawsuit in the *Winters* case, not the Indians. The one person who has before now looked deepest into the relevant documents and the local context of the litigation, Michael Massie, became convinced of this point. He stated in his 1987 article that the Indians understood how the depletion of the water in the river could undermine their developing economic foundation, and so they asked superintendent Logan to make an effort to restore the supply. But Logan and others would have ignored this plea "if the reservation whites had not supported the tribes' demands." Because Logan believed that non-Indian leasing and ownership of reservation land was, in Massie's words, "the key to the tribes' eventual assimilation into the dominant society," "the need of the reservation whites for a dependable water supply was the determining factor in Logan's request to uphold the tribes' water rights to the Milk River." Looking at the litigation and the events that followed, Massie concluded:

> Even though the Assiniboines' and the Gros Ventres' social and financial needs influenced the federal government's decision to sue the Montanans, the decisive pressure to restore the flow of the Milk River came from the white reservation ranchers and agent Logan. Thus, Fort Belknap's conquest in the Supreme Court battle was more a victory for the whites' motives than for the Indians' desires.[14]

The documents do not really support this conclusion, at least not directly or as so simply stated. Archival records from the reservation contain no correspondence between Superintendent Logan and lessees or other non-Indian users of reservation lands discussing the initiation of the water rights lawsuit; there are no letters in which the non-Indian farmers on the reservation lands requested the federal government to initiate the water rights suit or in which they stated their support for the litigation, and no letters from Logan to these non-Indian farmers stating or implying an intent to pursue the litigation for their benefit. Nor did the letters between Logan and his Indian Office superiors, or between Logan and U.S. Attorney Rasch, express or imply that the purpose of the litigation was to secure a water supply to benefit the non-Indian farmers on the reservation.

Rather, Logan usually conceived of the direct beneficiary of the water as the land and its potential as irrigated farmland, and the indirect beneficiary as the Indians, with the result (he hoped) being greater economic development of the reservation and its Indian residents. He focused less on who would be the immediate users of the land, whether Indian residents or non-Indian farmers or Indians as laborers for non-Indian lessees. Because of his interest in productive reservation leases as part of his overall program, the needs of the non-Indian farmers and grazers on the reservation lands clearly would have been important to Logan. He also felt that increasing the reservation's economic status in these conventional terms would redound to the benefit of the non-Indian community in Harlem, and vice versa. In other words, Logan was interested in at least four related things at the same time, which he did not see as inconsistent: (1) leasing reservation land to non-Indians for grazing and cultivation purposes as a significant part of his economic development scheme for the reservation; (2) trying to make irrigation farmers (and grazers who made use of irrigated hay production) out of as many Indians as possible, and wage laborers on commercially viable irrigated agricultural plots out of the others; (3) recovering and protecting the water supply for the reservation to facilitate these efforts; and (4) promoting the economic development of the region by non-Indians (which presumably also supported his own economic situation, too—perhaps an additional interest to note). Those interests presumably combined into a desire on Logan's part to press for the water rights suit in part to serve the interests of non-Indians on the reservation, which Logan could easily have squared with his understanding of his responsibilities toward the Indian residents. And certainly the non-Indian farmers on the reservation lands and in the surrounding area cared most for their own long-term interests and not the Indians'. Thus a community of interests among Logan and the non-Indian farmers on the reservation lands and in the vicinity could have created mutual support for the water rights litigation, even if, as will be noted, Logan's correspondence and other statements about the litigation focused only on protecting the interests of the reservation land for the Indians.[15]

Much more important, but ignored or only briefly mentioned by
those who have written on the *Winters* litigation, was that non-Indian
farmers in the Fort Belknap area and further downstream inde-
pendently recognized ways in which the *Winters* litigation could serve
their interests, an issue discussed further below. It is sheer speculation to
ask whether Logan and others in the federal government would have
ignored the water supply plight of the Indians in 1905 but for the
presence of non-Indians farming the reservation lands. What can be
said is that the context of the litigation included the fact that a successful
suit to keep water in the Milk River until it reached the reservation
could benefit, for a number of reasons, the non-Indians who were
farming lands in the vicinity of the reservation or downstream—not
just those who were farming lands on the reservation or wanting to
farm lands on the reservation. Widening the context in this way
indicates why a successful suit on behalf of the Indians could be seen as
beneficial to non-Indian people in the valley, a discussion that will
follow an examination of the water law context and then the litigation
itself.

CHAPTER 2

Legal Context of the Litigation

The Prior Appropriation System and Possibilities in the Law of Water in Montana in 1905

What sparked the filing of the *Winters* litigation in July 1905 was the combination of severe drought conditions and upstream diversions, resulting in an essentially dry Milk River at the Fort Belknap reservation at the time for the spring irrigation of the reservation lands. Reservation Superintendent Logan raised the alarm within the federal government and persuaded other federal officials to file a lawsuit in federal court in Montana against the upstream irrigators to protect what Logan felt were the reservation's superior rights to water. Primarily as the result of Norris Hundley's examination of the *Winters* litigation in a 1982 article, the standard analysis of the specific legal context and events of the *Winters* litigation has become as follows: As the lawsuit began, the water law that everyone expected would be the focus of and would govern the suit was the Montana state law of prior appropriation. Logan and U.S. Attorney Carl Rasch believed when they first filed the suit that the reservation had a state law appropriation claim superior to the upstream irrigators, only to discover (to their horror) that this was not true. Only as a result of scrambling to find a legal theory that could bring some water to the reservation did Rasch develop the treaty rights claim, as just one of a number of alternative theories and not even Rasch's favorite, which the federal judge in Montana latched on to in direct conflict with the prior appropriation system and to the surprise of all concerned.[1]

There is some truth to the standard story, enough to require an explanation of the state law prior appropriation system and its role in the development of the *Winters* doctrine. In reality, however, the dynamics of the prior appropriation system in the Milk River valley in 1905 were of little importance to the actual course of the *Winters* litigation, while the effects of the allocation of water in the Milk River under the prior appropriation system actually led certain downstream non-Indian irrigators and boosters to have an ambiguous, even supportive, response to the *Winters* decision. The standard story assumes too much about the dominance of the prior appropriation system. In Montana in 1905 it was not at all certain that the state law prior appropriation system would or should govern the water rights of the reservation, even under Montana law, let alone under federal law. Any competent attorney for the federal government—and U.S. Attorney Rasch was quite competent—would have known going into the litigation that the law allowed for various ways to conceive of the reservation's legal rights to water, most of greater benefit to the reservation than the prior appropriation system. Rasch recognized that if he could succeed in proving a superior claim to water for the reservation under the state law prior appropriation system, then limiting the reservation's claim within the confines of the state law would be a politic maneuver. Once it was clear that a state law claim was not going to be successful, Rasch was free to pursue more fruitful theories outside of state law that he already knew about and was inclined to emphasize anyway. Analyzing the water law context in Montana in 1905 is necessary in order to recapture that sense of possibility, and to dispel any notion of a legal context dominated by the state law of prior appropriation.

PRIOR APPROPRIATION SYSTEM

The history of the prior appropriation doctrine is, as those fond of the doctrine are inclined to stress, "a fascinating chapter in the story of the growth of American laws and institutions."[2] At least from the time of Walter Webb's *The Great Plains* in the 1930s until quite recently, most historians and especially legal scholars have told the story that the doctrine developed in response to and as an adaptation to the limited availability of water in the arid West. They did so even as the formative details of the story they told seemed to have little to do with aridity. Most everyone agrees that the western priority system for allocating natural resources to individual users first developed in the mining areas of the West. The story, in simplified form, went like this: Rather than share access to the mineral resources, which would have contradicted the very idea of reducing a limited amount of gold to as much personal profit as possible, the miners were jealously competitive. To avoid completely disabling conflict, and to figure out how to deal with mining rights to what was, after all, still public land, the miners developed and enforced a first-in-time, first-in-right system for allocating mining claims, just as squatters for decades had allocated public lands ahead of government sale and survey—a particularly appropriate method of allocation considering that most of the claims were on public land and there was no way to obtain fee simple title to the property in an orderly fashion. And just as there was only so much gold to mine, there was only so much water available to wash the gold from the gravel and river beds. Moreover, the water and the mining areas were not always and necessarily together physically. Most important, none of the miners held private title to the land, which was the critical element for determining water rights under the traditional, common law riparian rights doctrine prevalent in the water-rich East, in which rights to water were attached to and shared by landowners along a watercourse. Having to build a practical water law structure out of these elements, the miners developed and enforced a simple system of first-in-time, first-in-right with regard to the water, borrowing from the land allocation practices. They divorced the water from the land bordering the watercourse and connected the water instead to diversion and use. They protected the first user of water from later takers and forbade anyone not actually using the water from claiming any rights to it. At times of scarcity, shortages were not shared equally—those who were first received their needs in full while later appropriators went without. The local courts agreed to enforce the system developed by the miners, and the federal government agreed to defer to and support the system as well. People coming later to the arid West for other purposes—particularly for irrigated farming—found the legal doctrine already in place and useful for their purposes, and so they adapted it to their circumstances. On this set of facts, Webb especially but also others before and after asserted that people were being forced to adapt their legal institutions to the different physical conditions they found in the arid West.

Webb was greatly influenced by the writer of one of the two prominent legal treatises on western water law at the turn of the century, Clesson Selwyne Kinney. Kinney was a competent legal analyst as well as a fanatic for irrigation on the order of William Ellsworth Smythe—a turn-of-the-century writer and leader of the arid-land irrigation movement. Kinney's analysis of the development of the appropriation system in the West began with the concept of irrigation;

he basically ignored the mining camp part of the story. To Kinney, what aridity demanded of the American people as they moved west was irrigation, if they were going to be able to continue the American farming economy and culture. The common law riparian rights doctrine did not facilitate irrigation of the type required in the truly arid West, in Kinney's view. And thus aridity also demanded the abandonment of the riparian rights system in much of the West. People in the West then developed the appropriation system to fill the vacuum, fashioning the core concepts and particular elements of the system (which differed among the states) to allow for irrigation while also addressing a number of other concerns and opportunities. Kinney did not link aridity and the elements of the prior appropriation system itself; he argued only that aridity required irrigation and a legal system that allowed for irrigation, which the common law riparian rights doctrine did not. The subtleties of Kinney's analysis and Webb's sophisticated elaboration of it were soon lost, especially in the legal field and in the minds of western developers and boosters—the prior appropriation system in all its glory had been shown by experts to be determined by nature. These are the people Moses Lasky lampooned in 1929 as those who seemed to believe the doctrine was "an unchangeable rule of natural law" required by some "brooding omnipresence in the sky."[3]

A revisionist approach to this legal transformation could be traced to the 1977 analysis by legal historian Morton Horwitz of the other water law doctrine—the riparian doctrine of the East. In *The Transformation of American Law, 1780–1860,* Horwitz explained that eastern legislatures and courts altered the riparian system over the first half of the nineteenth century to allow for the use of water in emerging industry. In *The Great Plains,* Webb had stumbled upon (again, through Kinney) the same process of redefinition in the riparian system when he examined how and why the riparian system that developed in Kansas and other parts of the western plains in the middle of the nineteenth century looked different from the traditional riparian doctrine, especially in the way the doctrine could accommodate the diversion of water from a watercourse for the purpose of irrigation for commercial agriculture. Webb argued that the legal transformation was due to human adaptation to the local physical circumstances of aridity. He may have missed the fact that the form the riparian doctrine took in Kansas was but a local manifestation of a national transformation of the riparian doctrine to make it suit the needs of an emerging market capitalist society.

At least partly provoked by Horwitz's efforts, Donald Pisani, Donald Worster, Charles McCurdy, and others—especially Pisani— have persuasively argued that the prior appropriation system developed in the same context and along parallel lines. The doctrine's origins and contours had more to do with a shift to a modern, intensive, capitalistic approach to the exploitation of resources—especially modern forms of mining and commercial, irrigated farming—than it did with an adaptation forced by conditions of aridity. Just as important, this was a system particularly useful for private uses of public lands, as it was impossible for the water users to determine water rights by resort to the riparian doctrine, based as that doctrine was on the rights inherent in land ownership. This is not to dispute that conditions of aridity could provoke a different approach to the allocation of water than is practicable in wetter places. But the particular form of the western prior appropriation system had little or nothing to do with aridity and everything to do with the particular economic needs of the first people in nineteenth-century America with a desire to apply scarce capital in the exploitation, for market profits, of promising but untested natural resources on public lands distant from central markets. In particular, there was nothing inherent in conditions of aridity that required that control over water be transferred to private individuals, or that water be allocated on a strict priority basis.[4]

Historical experience indicates that the privatization of rights to water based only on present use and priority—essential elements of the prior appropriation doctrine—was not the only way to use water in the arid West, even for irrigated farming. To begin with the obvious, various indigenous peoples lived successfully in western North America for centuries without the doctrine. Most of these societies had little or no irrigated agriculture or extensive river diversions. Those who did cultivate crops and irrigate, mostly in the Southwest, built and communally shared irrigation works and water, sharing especially in times of shortage without obvious notions of temporal priority.

Historical studies of water allocation in the Spanish and then Mexican communities in the Southwest indicate an approach more similar to the indigenous systems than to the prior appropriation system, or at the least fundamentally different than the prior appropriation system. The Spanish/Mexican system may have allowed individuals and groups to divert and use water on lands away from the watercourse, as did the prior appropriation system. But waters were ultimately controlled and allocated by the central and regional governments, which delegated effective allocation and control responsibilities largely to local communities and community officials, leaders, and judges, people who understood water primarily as a community resource. The system did not include exclusive, irrevocable, individual control of the resource or a priority system. Shortages and conflicts over water were resolved not by an appeal to rights and priority but by a conscious attempt to conciliate disputing claimants while serving the overall good of the community, often through an attempt to allocate water to as many claimants as possible and to share the benefits and burdens of relative or absolute scarcity. No allocation of water was irreversible.

Within Anglo-American culture, some of the early American explorers or boosters of the arid lands such as John Wesley Powell (southwestern survey engineer and explorer), William H. Emory, and William Smythe believed in the necessity of some form of communal development and of sharing water, water works, and other resources if Americans were to live successfully in the region. The Mormon community in Utah established itself on just such a basis. Some have argued that the Mormon patterns of use were a historical antecedent to the prior appropriation system in that the Mormons tied the privilege to water to beneficial use. But the early Mormons practiced cooperative irrigation, believed that all property was held and managed for the benefit of the community, and did not surrender control of the resource to individual private effort and a priority allocation decision.[5]

Most important, Donald Pisani has identified a great number of western settlers, miners, politicians, writers, lawyers, and judges active in mainstream society from the formative years of the western states (especially in the 1850s to the 1880s but also beyond) who were comfortable working with and preferred other water allocation systems, many of whom denounced the development of the prior appropriation system as a giveaway of something valuable to the people and as tending toward unfair, private monopolization of a precious resource. (Pisani has even wonderfully complicated the mining-camp part of the creation story by showing that the development of prior appropriation concepts closely correlated with and facilitated the development of hydraulic mining operations. He shows that the first wave of miners made use of a number of preexisting and reworked legal traditions, including practical variations of the riparian doctrine.) These people worked and argued instead for adherence to the common law riparian system or to an appropriation-type system that featured greater degrees of social or governmental control or ownership and, especially, equitable sharing of the resource in times of shortage. The central thesis of Pisani's book on nineteenth-century water law and policy is *fragmentation*—meaning in his case a West never unified into a homogenous view of the proper system and program for water allocation. The "victory" of the prior appropriation system was always a contested and contingent affair. Pisani has viewed the conflict over the prior appropriation system as largely a nineteenth-century phenomenon, and he has stated that by 1900 the prior appropriation system in general was dominant on the land and in the minds of westerners, even if the various states had developed different forms of that system. And whether or not the prior appropriation doctrine was really the only way to develop the West, many irrigators, farm and town developers, boosters, and western politicians thought and said that it was. Many states in the arid West wrote at least some elements of the prior appropriation doctrine into their state constitutions as something that could never be denied to the people. People who had established, by use, rights to appropriated water had a strong belief in the absolute security of their rights to that water. They invested time and money on that expectation. Perhaps just as important, state and local officials, boosters, and early settlers also relied on the expectation that unappropriated waters would be available for others to privatize and put to use in this way. In this way the arid states believed they had a basis for economic development, at least to the physical limits of the water supply.[6]

It would be a mistake to assume, however, that the conflict over the doctrine and its impact went away in the twentieth century. Debate and conflict over the prior appropriation doctrine continued, and many of the central concerns with the system remained while new ones were added. The language or terms of this debate did shift in the twentieth century, however. Rather than contest the prior appropriation system as an invalid, insurgent doctrine, some people in the West began to argue that the doctrine in its most classic form was passé, appropriate to "frontier" conditions perhaps, but no longer serving the needs of still growing but more complex societies. The prior appropriation system was in need of court and legislative reform to allow for broader, more comprehensive, fair, and efficient economic development, which was not necessarily achieved by a theory that protected first users, however inefficient, up to the full amount of their historic use, or that allowed the ad hoc creation of absolute and inflexible private rights to unappropriated water.[7]

As will be explained in more detail below, *Winters* was but one aspect of what I call a largely ignored contradiction in the West in this period, in which many people superficially supported or worked within the prior appropriation system while doing whatever they could, and taking advantage of whatever they could, to escape some of the system's key features and in essence to reserve water and watersheds for more coordinated, comprehensive, and broadly based economic development. The most obvious effort was the great federal investment in irrigation that began in 1902 with the Reclamation Act. The federal government used its authority under the act—often at the urging of westerners wishing for the broadest possible development of their communities— to "reserve" from immediate, private appropriation a watershed or a volume of water that could be dedicated for coordinated and comprehensive development of a specified area of land via a federally developed irrigation project. This water would be used by farmers on individually owned, relatively small-tract farms participating in commercial irrigated agriculture, through water delivery contracts with the Reclamation Service that had essentially equal priority. Characteristic of the federal government in the West, the Reclamation Act tried to have it both ways, to work with federal *and* state law. The act created a structure whereby the federal government would try to (1) reserve the available land and, if possible, water in an area; (2) organize, finance, and construct irrigation facilities; and (3) then turn the rights to the water over to private appropriators (often aggregated into irrigation districts) in accord with state water law, with the individual appropriators expected to pay back the investment. Not too surprising, one cadre of Reclamation officials worked hard in the early years of the service to help eradicate the riparian doctrine and promote the prior appropriation doctrine in the western states, believing in the need to sever the legal tie between land along a watercourse and rights to water and to establish all private water rights solely on the basis of diversion and actual use for irrigation. This, they believed, would allow all unused water to be free of private legal rights and thus available to be dedicated or reserved for Reclamation and other irrigation projects. It would also allow for the delivery of water to the best lands for irrigation regardless of their location, with private rights established under state law when the water was actually delivered and used. The Service desired to get all of the western states' water law systems rationalized into this same system, urging state legislatures to adopt a model legal code incorporating the prior appropriation system that also just happened to allow the federal government to reserve water in a watershed for Reclamation development.[8]

Once on the scene, the *Winters* reserved rights doctrine could be seen, and was at times seen, as another approach to reserving and allocating water in the West, with some features similar to other approaches and some features peculiar to the doctrine, a doctrine that could transcend its particular Indian water rights context. And as will be shown, the decisions in *Winters* could work to the favor of the Reclamation Service in a number of ways, including in the Milk River valley. Alas, many of the very first Reclamation Service officials, in the central office at least, could not see the link between their interests and the Fort Belknap lawsuit. The *Winters* litigation horrified Reclamation officials not in the valley as much as it did the non-Indian irrigators directly affected. These officials viewed the *Winters* litigation, and especially the arguments of the U.S. attorney on behalf of the Indians, as nothing but an illegitimate and backward attempt to preserve and extend the riparian doctrine—rights to water reserved in perpetuity to a piece of land along a watercourse without regard to use. This was a variant of the riparian doctrine being asserted in the West *by* federal lawyers and imposed *as* federal law by the federal courts, to the hindrance of the federal Reclamation Service's attempts to reshape western water law in a different direction. Reclamation officials thus made an attempt to stifle the government's arguments in the *Winters* case, an effort described below.[9]

MONTANA IN 1905: PRIOR APPROPRIATION AND THE RIPARIAN DOCTRINE

Turning specifically to Montana, where the reserved rights doctrine first appeared out of the context of the local litigation to protect the water supply for the reservation, as of 1905 the prior appropriation system had not swept the field of other legal theories for rights to water. At the time of the *Winters* litigation, lawyers and legal scholars could legitimately and even persuasively label Montana a state that preserved the riparian doctrine in some form and did not just follow the prior appropriation doctrine. Others could view ambiguous and somewhat contradictory statutes and court rulings and argue the other conclusion. No one could dispute that by a combination of federal law and state statute people in Montana could establish a right to the use of water by appropriation on the public domain lands of the United States or on unsold state lands, or that appropriation had some role to play in the use of water on privately held land. But there were sound reasons to argue in 1905 that the law of Montana recognized that the riparian doctrine applied in some form to certain significant categories of lands, including federal and tribal lands that had never been part of the open public domain.

Two decisions of the high court in Montana were particularly important sources for those who believed the riparian doctrine still held some validity in Montana and could logically apply to the Fort Belknap reservation lands, whether those lands were conceived of as federal or tribal lands. The first is *Thorp v. Freed,* an 1872 decision from the justices of the Montana Territorial Supreme Court. In *Thorp* the plaintiffs asserted that they had a prior appropriation right to waters they diverted out of Prickly Pear Creek and asked the territorial district court to enjoin users above them on the creek from taking water during a shortage.[10] The district court refused to issue the injunction, apparently (it is hard to tell from the Supreme Court opinion) at least partly on the basis that the territorial statutes did not completely abrogate, and in fact recognized to a certain degree, the existence of riparian rights in people along a watercourse who had taken private title to public land. If so, all who owned land along the watercourse might have equal rights to the water, including the right to divert water for irrigation, regardless of the dates of first use. Water should be shared equally among these riparian land owners in times of shortage; the plaintiffs did not have a paramount or absolute right to the water of the creek just because of the time of their appropriation. Whatever the lower court reasoning, the Territorial Supreme Court affirmed its ruling rejecting the plaintiffs' claim. Only two justices participated, and they did not agree on the reasoning, so there was no official position of the court. Chief Justice Decius Wade, in a long, clearly stated, and forceful opinion, denied that the common law had been altered significantly in Montana by the territorial statutes and denied that prior appropriation rights as claimed by the plaintiffs existed in Montana, that is, with regard to the relationship between private landowners along a watercourse. Justice Wade is an example of one of the people about whom Pisani had written, who believed that the prior appropriation system was an evil that greedy opportunists were trying to foist on the West. He went to great length—the last twelve pages of his opinion—to explain why he believed a modified riparian system could meet the needs of irrigation in an arid land, producing among other things an "equitable distribution" of the waters for irrigation, and why the prior appropriation system would lead to a disaster of private monopoly, rendering valueless most of the available public lands on which people were depending for settlement and economic development. His final paragraph is most illustrative: "What says the government of the

United States to the doctrine that renders the public domain of Montana utterly of no value? The doctrine of prior appropriation robs the general government of its property, by making the government lands of no value. And all these consequences, so disastrous in any view, are to be visited upon Montana, that a few individuals may have what does not now, and never did, belong to them?"[11]

In contrast, Justice Hiram Knowles, in a not very clear opinion, began by noting that in the federal mining law and the Desert Land Act of 1877, the federal government had recognized or authorized appropriations of water on public domain lands when allowed under local law. He then concluded that the territorial statutes had in fact changed the common law significantly to allow for vested rights to appropriations by people on public lands along a watercourse, rights that could be maintained as the person patented the public land into private land. Such appropriations could have legal priority over the rights of others with land along the watercourse under certain circumstances, that is, especially when the appropriations occurred before others received their patents to the land. Justice Knowles's view of Montana water law appeared to recognize some common law riparian concepts, especially in the way even appropriation rights were tied to the land along a watercourse and in the way the doctrine might apply when people took title to public land before anyone began using the water. But this was a heavily modified common law. He affirmed the lower court simply because the plaintiffs had not proved that the district court's denial of their claims was in error in the face of arguments from the defendants that even if the law was as assumed by the plaintiffs, the defendants had equivalent appropriation rights and had not interfered with the plaintiffs' appropriation opportunities. Justice Knowles's opinion was sufficiently murky, however, that it was entirely possible in future years to see it as proof that riparian rights still existed in Montana to some degree, especially in the light of Chief Justice Wade's emphatic opinion to that effect. And Justice Knowles himself, in his subsequent career as a federal judge, would recognize that these riparian rights concepts still had particular relevance in Montana law to land retained by the federal government, as discussed below.[12]

Montana retained these territorial statutes after it became a state in 1889, and *Thorp v. Freed* remained a key court discussion of Montana water law until Montana revised its water law statutes in 1895. The Montana Supreme Court interpreted the new statutes in 1900 in *Smith v. Denniff*, the single most important Montana decision on the appropriation and riparian doctrines at the time the government filed the

Winters litigation.[13] The key point here is that the court in *Smith v. Denniff* continued to recognize riparian rights as having a certain validity in Montana state law. The central holding in *Smith* made the other point—that a system of prior appropriation *did* exist in Montana *and* extended to privately held lands carved out of the public domain, noting that the system of water allocation described in the revised Montana statutes put an end to arguments against the existence or reach of the prior appropriation system based on uncertainties or ambiguities in prior statutes and court cases. In discussing the origin and nature of the appropriation right in Montana, however, the state Supreme Court explained that obtaining a water right by appropriation was a method of water allocation based originally in federal statutes governing activities on the federal public domain, statutes that recognized and sanctioned an exception to the traditional common law riparian doctrine by allowing private individuals to make use of water on federal public lands they did not own, as a "grant from the United States government as owner of the land and water." Montana statutes recognized and incorporated this appropriation system and later extended it to unsold state lands that the state had received from the federal government out of the public domain. The state court then noted that when land passed from federal control into private ownership in Montana *before* any rights to water by prior appropriation had affected that land under the method authorized by Congress, the common-law riparian doctrine would normally have applied in full to that land and water *except* for the fact that Montana, in its 1895 statutes, had by implication asserted to *itself* the ownership of unappropriated water in the state and then clearly authorized appropriation of this water by private individuals. The court's explanation indicated that the statutes allowing for appropriation modified the riparian doctrine and yet continued to work with some of the concepts of that doctrine, especially the way in which water rights were part of the rights to land along a watercourse:

> [T]his privilege or right to appropriate the water of a stream can in any and every case be taken advantage of or exercised only by one who has riparian rights, either as owner of riparian land, or through grant of the riparian owner. . . . It may be remarked, *obiter,* that the common-law doctrine of riparian rights assured to each riparian owner the right to the reasonable use, without substantial diminution in quantity or deterioration in quality to the detriment of other riparian proprietors, of the waters of a stream flowing by or over his land. The doctrine of "prior appropriation" confers upon a riparian

owner, or one having title to a water by grant from him, the right to a use of the water of a stream which would be unreasonable at the common-law, and to this extent the doctrine of prior appropriation may be said to have abrogated the common-law rule.[14]

The court also noted that while the state's law code granted the right to appropriate water, "yet it does not pretend to legalize the exercise of such privilege, in violation of the vested rights of other land owners." Whatever the court meant precisely by that statement (and it may have been referring to the fact that a nonriparian landholder could appropriate water under the statutes but not without permission of the riparian landowner where the point of diversion would be), the reference to the "vested rights of other land owners" could later be argued to mean the riparian rights of landowners who took or held title to the land before it could come under an appropriation regime under federal or state law.[15]

Courts other than the state courts of Montana that had reason to pass on the status of Montana water law reviewed the Montana statutes and opinions such as *Smith v. Denniff* and concluded that riparian rights retained some practical validity in Montana, adding their considerable weight to any such assumptions. Two were noted more than others. In *Cruse v. McCauley*, in 1899, the federal district court in Montana—in the person of Judge Knowles, former justice of the Territorial Supreme Court in the *Thorp* case—had before it a generic type of state water dispute that ended up in federal court due to the diversity of the parties, not because of a federal question.[16] Judge Knowles applied his understanding of federal law and the Montana state statutes and case law and concluded that a modified form of the riparian law continued to exist in Montana. In his view, when the United States obtained these lands, it was entitled by the common law doctrines to the water incident to the land. The United States had the power to dispose of the land and water as it chose, and by statute declared that waters flowing over the public domain were subject to appropriation if allowed under local law, which it was. That was as far as the United States had disposed of its rights to the water:

> [I]f the water was not so appropriated when it flowed over the public domain, it was not subject to appropriation when after the land over which it flowed became private property. . . . If a person receives a patent from the United States for land subject only to accrued water rights—that is, existing water rights—and as an incident to, or a part of, this land, there is water flowing over the same or upon the same,

he would have all the rights the United States had at that time. I do
not think any state law or custom can take away such rights, except
for some public purpose. Under this view the plaintiff became a
riparian proprietor of the waters of McDonald Creek.[17]

Judge Knowles added that if a person became entitled to the use of
water in Montana "by virtue of his riparian proprietorship," that right
to use water extended to the person's requirements for "domestic,
agricultural, and irrigating purposes." A riparian right to the use of
water was vested and "superior and paramount" to any actual uses by
appropriation initiated subsequent to when the landowner became a
riparian proprietor.

In the other important example, in 1903, two years before Rasch
filed the *Winters* case, the Wyoming Supreme Court, in a case called
Willey v. Decker, had before it a water dispute on the Wyoming-
Montana border that required the Wyoming court to describe and
understand the implications of Montana water law. The Wyoming
court, in a lengthy opinion that relied in part on *Smith* and the opinions
in *Thorp* and also dipped into a variety of other authorities, understood
Montana to be a "California doctrine" state with regard to water law.
This meant that Montana preserved the riparian doctrine as a kind of
common law baseline for water rights except to the extent specifically
modified by federal and state statutes, and thus preserved the riparian
rights of landowners who held title to land before a water rights
allocation scheme under appropriation statutes affected the land or its
watercourse—exactly as described above in the *Cruse* case.[18]

Based primarily on *Smith* and *Thorp* from the Montana state courts
and opinions such as *Cruse* and *Willey* from other courts, legal scholars
in the early part of this century (mostly from outside Montana) considered Montana to be a state that retained the riparian doctrine in
modified form. For example, both of the standard western water law
treatises of the early twentieth century, by Samuel Wiel and C. S.
Kinney, considered Montana to be a state where riparian law remained
valid and vital, explaining as in *Willey* that Montana fit into the category
of states that followed a variant of the "California doctrine" in which
the riparian system applied to some lands and water uses and prior
appropriation applied to others. The United States originally had common
law riparian rights to the water on the public lands, which passed to
private landholders if the land was patented before an appropriation
scheme applied. The common law riparian system continued to exist,
and might even be partially recognized in state law, but could also be

partially abrogated by prior appropriation concepts, such as allowing a landowner to divert water from a watercourse for irrigation.[19]

The idea that Montana was a state that preserved a significant core of riparian rights did not go uncontested. Others in Montana, among them irrigators, boosters, litigants, and lawyers, countered that the Montana statutes were wholly committed to the doctrine of prior appropriation in all circumstances, the federal law and statutes allowed this and did not interfere, and that those who believed otherwise had misinterpreted the federal and state statutes and the opinions in *Thorp* and *Smith*. It turned out that William Hunt, the Montana federal district judge in whose court the United States filed the *Winters* case, was one of the people who believed that the riparian doctrine had no meaning for the arid-region public lands, presumably including those in Montana, as he would demonstrate in a law review article a few years later.[20] These people would eventually win the day in Montana, but not until 1921. In that year, in *Mettler v. Ames Realty Company,* the Montana Supreme Court ruled that the common law riparian doctrine ceased to prevail in Montana upon the enactment of the first territorial statutes in 1865, statutes that replaced it with the prior appropriation system. After selectively surveying the statutes and language in past opinions (which is what most everyone did), the court concluded:

> It is submitted that the policy established by the measures above is irreconcilable with the application of the doctrine of riparian rights even in the modified form in which that doctrine now prevails in the states adhering to the California rule; that our Constitution and statutes proceed upon the theory that artificial irrigation is absolutely necessary to the successful cultivation of large areas of land within the state; that the doctrine of appropriation was born of the necessities of this state and its people; and that it was intended to be permanent in its character, exclusive in its operation, and to fix the status of water rights in this commonwealth.[21]

It is hard to square the ruling in *Mettler v. Ames* with the prior history of statutes and court decisions. Rather than a clear and consistent legal understanding over time favoring prior appropriation disingenuously assumed in *Mettler,* Montana law up to that time was a confusing and contradictory stew of water law concepts. Perhaps the one constant was that legal experts outside Montana looked at the stew from time to time and concluded that riparian rights appeared still to be one of the ingredients, with real bases for this conclusion. This is one of the reasons why, as will be explained in more detail below, U.S. Attorney

Rasch believed in 1905 and 1906, at both the trial court and appellate court level, that a riparian rights theory was his strongest legal theory in the *Winters* litigation. In his view, if the riparian doctrine and riparian rights still had some validity in Montana, as it appeared they did, they should logically apply with the greatest force to Indian reservation lands that had never been part of the open public domain. These lands had instead been tribal lands from time immemorial, and reserved federal/ tribal land from well before the time the federal government and the territorial and state statutes had authorized or recognized the validity of appropriations from the Milk River and patented claims to public land. Federal lands that never became part of the public domain were, in this view, unaffected by the appropriation system; the reservation lands were *never* part of the open public domain. Thus the common law riparian rights incident to this land from the beginning entitled the Fort Belknap reservation to a sufficient share of the water, for domestic and irrigation and other needs, rights that should not be affected or under- mined by upstream appropriations under the basic water law of Montana. This theory, if true, would obviate the need to resort to legal theories more particularly oriented to specific federal law and powers or to a battle of priority under the state law of prior appropriation.

FEDERAL LAW: RIGHTS TO WATER "NECESSARY FOR THE BENEFICIAL USES OF GOVERNMENT PROPERTY"

A state law or common law riparian rights claim was not the only legal tool in the U.S. attorney's hands in 1905 to protect water rights for the Indian lands, and probably not even the most compelling tool. As of 1905, federal and Montana state court decisions (and legal treatises and law review articles) existed stating that federal law protected the federal government's use of water to satisfy needs on the federal lands in the western states. The preeminent statement of this position, cited and quoted often by Rasch and other government lawyers, by the appellate court in the *Winters* and *Conrad* decisions, *and* by the United States Supreme Court in the *Winters* decision, came from the 1899 opinion of the Supreme Court in *United States v. Rio Grande Dam and Irrigation Company.* The *Rio Grande* case concerned whether the federal govern- ment had the authority to block a proposal to build a dam on the Rio Grande River in New Mexico that would be allowed under the prior appropriation statutes of the Territory of New Mexico. In its opinion, the Supreme Court agreed that the western states (and territories) undoubtedly had the power to change the common law rules of water allocation within their respective jurisdictions to permit rights to water by appropriation. Moreover, Congress had recognized and assented, in statutes such as the Mining Laws of 1866 and 1870 and the Desert Land Act of 1877, to the territorial and state systems of appropriation of water on the federal public lands in contravention of the common law riparian doctrine. The federal government's authority to control what the states did with the water was limited at best. But the Court noted two limitations on the power of the states, stemming from federal law, and one was that "in the absence of specific authority from Congress a State cannot by its legislation destroy the right of the United States, as the owner of lands bordering on a stream, to the continued flow of its waters; so far at least as may be necessary for the beneficial uses of the government property."[22] This *Rio Grande* language became a central prop in the government's arguments in *Winters* and in other efforts to control western water allocation. The Supreme Court went out of its way to repeat this statement in a 1903 decision also involving the Rio Grande River, *Gutierres v. Albuquerque Land and Irrigation Company*, a decision also cited by Rasch and the courts in the *Winters* and *Conrad* litigation.[23]

There were problems with the statement from the *Rio Grande* case, however, that made it less than a definitive ruling. First, it was *just* a statement or conclusion, without sufficient analysis. A bigger problem was that it was "dicta," that is, a statement that was not essential to the main issue and ruling in the case, which concerned the federal government's control over navigable waterways. The parties had not litigated the issue of federal control over water for use on federal lands. The Court's statement on this issue was gratuitous, not a resolution of a litigated issue that lower courts would necessarily feel bound to follow. As used in the *Gutierres* decision the statement was also dicta. And in this key statement in the *Rio Grande* and *Gutierres* opinions, the Court did not make clear what was the source of this federal power over water related to federal lands. Was it based on an ownership or proprietary theory, that the federal government retained ownership of land *and* water acquired by the federal government before the formation of the western states? Was it founded on some sort of federal common law of riparian rights? Was the source of authority the Commerce Clause of the federal constitution, which was also the source of the federal government's preeminent authority over navigable waterways? Or was the source the Property Clause of the Constitution instead, which provides that Congress shall "make all needful rules and regulations" for the property of the United States? All of these were legitimate possibilities in 1905. Even as some theories (such as a federal common law theory of riparian rights) would eventually be discredited, others (such as federal authority under the Commerce or Property clauses) would gain in legitimacy over time.[24]

Despite these uncertainties, in 1905 the *Rio Grande* language from just a few years before was seen as a direct and powerful statement from the Supreme Court with obvious implications for protecting the rights to water in the Milk River for uses on the federal Indian reservation. Moreover, I do not want to give the impression that the *Rio Grande* dicta had no basis in law or support among lawyers. For example, the water law treatise writers saw nothing remarkable in the concept of federal power or authority over water in the West to protect and serve intended uses of federal lands.[25] And while I will not itemize the decisions here, there were prior rulings from the Supreme Court, and prior and subsequent rulings from the federal appellate courts (citations to which can be found in the law review treatises and in the *Winters* briefs and decisions as well as elsewhere) that lent definition and justification to the concept embodied in the quotation from the *Rio Grande* case. As of 1905 and 1906, there were no Supreme Court or important lower federal court decisions that effectively countered these notions of federal power over water for use on the reserved federal lands. And while the Supreme Court's *Kansas v. Colorado* decision in 1907 cast doubt on the proposition that the federal government had extensive control over the allocation of water in the West just because of the presence of arid public lands in general, that decision quoted the specific *Rio Grande* language again and did not explicitly undermine either the language or the principle.[26] Thus it turned out to be a plausible application or extension of the *Rio Grande* principle for the United States to make use of the *Rio Grande* language in its *Winters* briefs, for the Court of Appeals in *Winters* to quote and rely on the *Rio Grande* language, and for the Supreme Court to rule in *Winters* that "[t]he power of the Government to reserve the waters and exempt them from appropriation under the state laws is not denied, and could not be," citing *Rio Grande*.[27]

The defendants in the *Winters* case really had only one useful federal court decision to point to, and they rode it hard. This was the 1897 opinion out of the Ninth Circuit in *Krall v. United States,* a decision of a divided appellate court that reversed the lower federal court in Idaho. In Krall the appellate court held that when the federal government established a military reservation along a watercourse on public domain land previously open to public entry, this fact alone did not mean that the United States now had such rights to the water in the stream so as to require the courts to shut down a preexisting upstream appropriator. The private appropriator, a person by the name of Krall, had followed the federal statutes and unequivocal Idaho appropriation statutes and appropriated water for irrigation while his land was part of the public domain. Krall then patented the land. The government subsequently transformed public domain land along the same watercourse into a military installation and sought to use the creek's flow to irrigate its military land—and to do so on the back of Mr. Krall. The federal district court in Idaho allowed this to happen over Krall's objections, but the Court of Appeals reversed, holding that the government's action in creating the military post could not destroy previously vested private rights to water.[28]

The *Winters* defendants had to try to make the most of *Krall,* but *Krall* was an easy target for Rasch and the United States, for a number of reasons: The decision in *Krall* had come before the Supreme Court's decision in *Rio Grande* and thus was of dubious authority for any broad propositions of law when compared to the key statement in *Rio Grande* and the views of other courts and scholars. *Krall* was a divided opinion; Judge William Gilbert had written a strong dissent in *Krall* (and the lower court had ruled for the government, too). Most important, the *Krall* case had extraordinarily favorable facts for the private irrigator that were not present in the *Winters* situation, in which the Indians were on land they had occupied for a long time and which had been reserved for them years before any private appropriations began. How little influence the *Krall* opinion really had can be seen by the fact that *all* of the judges who participated in the Ninth Circuit's decision in *Krall* also participated in the appellate decisions in *Winters* and did not even see the need to discuss *Krall,* let alone find it controlling.

Perhaps just as important for the immediate context of the *Winters* case, the Montana Supreme Court, at the end of 1904 and just before the filing of the *Winters* litigation, stated a view of the legal relationship of federal lands and water similar to the United States Supreme Court's earlier statement in *Rio Grande.* In *Story v. Wolverton,* the Montana courts faced a dispute between private parties arising out of an adjudication of titles to water in Bear Creek. The State of Montana itself intervened in this private litigation so that the Montana attorney general could argue that when the federal government granted to Montana one section of land in this watershed out of a former federal military reservation, it also granted the waters that went with the land. The state court disagreed, noting that the federal government abandoned the military reservation in 1886 (which previously it had irrigated to grow crops for troops) yet did not grant the lands to the state until 1891, in a grant that said nothing about water. Thus the federal land had essentially become open public domain in 1886 and the water allowed to flow in the channel subject to appropriation. No federal water rights went with the subsequent land grant to the state. Of importance for the *Winters* litigation, however, was the state court's understanding of the status of the land and water when it *was* still held and used by the federal government as a military reservation:

> Prior to the time of settlement upon the lands in question, and prior to the appropriation of water of Bear creek by any one, both the land and the water were the property of the [federal] government. When the government established the reservation, it owned both the land included therein, and all the water running in the various near-by streams to which it had not yielded title. It was therefore unnecessary for the government to "appropriate" the water. It owned it already. All it had to do was to take and use it.[29]

The implications for the *Winters* litigation could not have been clearer— although the agreements between the federal government and the tribes whittled away at the Indian reservation, the government and the Indians never yielded title to the reserved lands or the water "running in various near-by streams." Thus the federal government and the Indians had no need to "appropriate" water under state law to use the water on the reservation land; they could just take and use the water they "owned." In response to *Story,* the Montana legislature reformed its water laws in 1905 (just before the first *Winters* ruling, it turned out), to add a provision stating that the United States could make use of water in Montana only "in the same manner and subject to the general conditions applicable to the appropriation of the waters of the state by private individuals."[30]

The aspect of *Story v. Wolverton* important to the *Winters* litigation suffered from some of the same infirmities as the *Rio Grande* language: The discussion in *Story* of the federal government's authority over water while it owned the military reservation was peripheral to the main holding of abandonment of the reservation. More important, the Montana Supreme Court's interpretation of *federal* law had no binding effect on the federal courts. (But then neither, of course, did the state legislature—the federal courts never considered the 1905 state statute as relevant to the *Winters* case.) These technical problems did not lessen the practical effect of *Story v. Wolverton*. The opinion added immediate weight to any analysis by the federal court in Montana of the scope of federal control over water for the public lands. Thus Rasch did not miss an opportunity to cite *Story* in his briefs, and the Ninth Circuit cited and quoted the passage from *Story* in support of its holding for the government and the Indians.[31]

INDIAN TREATIES, WINANS, AND THE POSSIBILITY OF WATER RIGHTS

Further complicating the water law picture at the time of *Winters,* and adding additional possibilities for federal or tribal control of Milk River water for the reservation lands outside of state law, was the issue of treaty rights. As of 1905 there were no Supreme Court, lower federal court, or important state court opinions directly linking Indian treaties and water rights. Thus the possible role of treaty rights for protecting the water supply for the Fort Belknap reservation was less defined by case law. The irony is that it was the treaty rights basis that emerged in both the lower federal courts and in the Supreme Court as most central to the decisions.

This may be because what did exist in 1905 was a well-ingrained judicial approach to interpreting and applying treaties. As the United States Supreme Court explained in detail in its 1899 opinion *Jones v. Meehan* (a case concerning title to land that had been reserved in a treaty with Chippewa bands), while citing from its decisions throughout the nineteenth century:

> In construing any treaty between the United States and an Indian tribe, it must always . . . be borne in mind that the negotiations for the treaty are conducted on the part of the United States, an enlightened and powerful nation, by representatives skilled in diplomacy, masters of a written language, understanding the modes and forms of creating the various technical estates known to their law, and assisted by an interpreter employed by themselves; that the treaty is drawn up by them and in their own language; that the Indians, on the other hand, are a weak and dependent people who have no written language and are wholly unfamiliar with all the forms of legal expression, and whose only knowledge of the terms in which the treaty is framed is that imparted to them by the interpreter employed by the United States; and that the treaty must therefore be construed, not according to the technical meaning of its words to learned

lawyers, but in the sense in which they would naturally be understood by Indians.[32]

Perhaps not a very flattering or accurate view of the ken of Indian
peoples, but just the same a method of analysis that, if faithfully applied,
could shift the usual legal and cultural perspective on agreements and
contracts when reviewing Indian treaties. That is, the courts would not
analyze a treaty or agreement to determine the objective meeting of the
minds of two equal parties but would instead construe the treaties or
agreements "in the sense they would naturally be understood by the
Indians."

Just a month and a half before the government initiated the *Winters*
litigation, the Supreme Court reaffirmed this approach to Indian treaties
in a decision with the most direct implications yet for the *Winters*
litigation, *United States v. Winans*.[33] *Winans* concerned the 1855 treaty
between the United States and the Yakima Indian Nation in which the
Yakima Nation ceded certain lands to the United States, retained other
lands, reserved the exclusive right to take fish in all streams on or
bordering the reservation, and also reserved "*the right of taking fish at all
usual and accustomed places [on the ceded lands], in common with citizens
of the Territory.*" By the turn of the century, non-Indians had obtained
legal title to land encompassing a "usual and accustomed" fishing place
of the Yakimas along the Columbia River and had constructed a fish
wheel at the site. The landowners excluded the Indians from coming on
the land and fishing from this site, just as they excluded any non-
Indians who did not have legal title to this land. The United States sued
on behalf of the Yakimas asserting the Indians' right to fish at this place.
The Ninth Circuit rejected this claim, ruling that the treaty placed the
Indians on equal footing with ("in common with") the non-Indian
citizens of the State of Washington, all of whom could be excluded as
trespassers from this land by the legal owners.

The Supreme Court reversed, in an opinion by Justice Joseph
McKenna (who three years later would write the Supreme Court's
opinion in *Winters*) that applied and did not simply make a rhetorical
bow to the principles of treaty construction noted above. The Court
began by criticizing the Ninth Circuit's approach as inconsistent with
the appropriate principles for applying treaties:

> In other words, it was decided that the Indians acquired no rights but
> what any inhabitant of the Territory or State would have. Indeed,
> acquired no rights but such as they would have had without the
> treaty. This is certainly an impotent outcome to negotiations and a

convention, which seems to promise more and give the word of the Nation for more. And we have said we will construe a treaty with the Indians as "that unlettered people" understood it, and "as justice and reason demand in all cases where power is exerted by the strong over those to whom they owe care and protection," and counterpoise the inequality "by the superior justice which looks only to the substance of the right without regard to technical rules."[34]

The next question for the Court then was how to determine what the treaty meant *to the Indians*. How the Indians understood the treaty at the time of execution "may be gathered from the circumstances." And the circumstances, as explained by Justice McKenna, derived from the Indians' historical occupancy or possession and activities:

> The right to resort to the fishing places in controversy was a part of larger rights possessed by the Indians, upon the exercise of which there was not a shadow of impediment, and which were not much less necessary to the existence of the Indians than the atmosphere they breathed. New conditions came into existence, to which those rights had to be accommodated. Only a limitation of them, however, was necessary and intended, not a taking away. In other words, the treaty was not a grant of rights to the Indians, but a grant of rights from them—a reservation of those not granted. And the form of the instrument and its language were adapted to that purpose. . . . As a mere right, it was not exclusive in the Indians. Citizens might share it, but the Indians were secured in its enjoyment by a special provision of means for its exercise.[35]

The impact of the *Winans* decision for the legal context of the *Winters* case is clear. The Supreme Court released its opinion in *Winans* on May 15, 1905. As will be explained in more detail below, U.S. Attorney Rasch became involved in the water supply problem at the Fort Belknap reservation in late May or early June of 1905 and filed the complaint on June 26, 1905. I do not know for sure that Rasch had a copy of the *Winans* decision when he filed his complaint in the *Winters* case, although the structure and content of the complaint indicates to me that he might have. More important, the federal district judge in Montana, William Hunt, did rely primarily on *Winans* in his memorandum decision on August 7 in favor of reserved treaty rights to water for the Fort Belknap reservation. Rasch made use of *Winans* in his subsequent brief to the Ninth Circuit, although less for the specific facts and holdings of the decision and more to reaffirm the general principles of how to interpret Indian treaties, and the Ninth Circuit and subsequently the Supreme Court cited to *Winans* (with little discussion about the case) in support of their *Winters* opinions affirming the district court.

On the one hand, *Winans* and the treaty rights theory presented obvious opportunities to anyone arguing the position of the federal government and the Indians in the *Winters* litigation, especially in the general treaty construction principles *and* in the concept of a treaty as "not a grant of rights to the Indians, but a grant of rights from them— a reservation of those not granted." On the other hand, *Winans* also presented a few problems for the water rights litigation at Fort Belknap. For one, the 1855 Yakima treaty included the explicit reservation of rights to usual and accustomed fishing places, although that provision was susceptible of different interpretations; the 1888 Fort Belknap treaty did not have such an explicit reference to water or water rights. For another, one aspect of the specific holding in *Winans* was an emphasis on the long-standing practice of the Indians involved, a practice ingrained in and integral to the culture of the Yakima people— fishing from these "usual and accustomed places." Using water for irrigation was *not* a historical practice of the Gros Ventre and Assiniboine people who signed the Fort Belknap treaty. Perhaps it is at least partly for these reasons that Rasch focused on *Winans* more for its general principles than for its specific holding (and continued to believe the other legal theories were stronger even after the district court's ruling squarely based on the treaty rights theory), and that Rasch and Judge Hunt both emphasized not just the 1888 treaty but also the 1896 treaty, with the more specific reference to irrigation, as evidence of intent.

Still, the obvious opportunity for anyone about to litigate the water issue for the Fort Belknap reservation on a treaty rights theory was this: (1) begin with the general principles of treaty interpretation that required trying to understand that treaty as the Indians would have understood it under the circumstances at the time of execution; (2) emphasize the Indians' occupancy and use of the reserved land and the waters on and bordering that land from time immemorial; (3) note that the 1888 treaty described the boundaries of the reservation to include the Milk River; (4) emphasize the explicit reference in the 1888 treaty that the Indians had retained the lands they did "to enable them to become self-supporting, as a pastoral and agricultural people"; (5) emphasize what was the given paradigm of the time—successful agricultural and pastoral activities on land in that area would require irrigation; (6) emphasize the "fair bargain" aspect of the treaty, namely, that the Indians would not have ceded so much land to the United States without assurances that the value of what was retained would be protected; (7) use the more explicit reference to irrigation in the subsequent 1896 treaty as proof of the original understanding; and (8) then conclude that it would be "an impotent outcome to the [treaty] negotiations" (to use the phrase from *Winans*) to interpret the treaty, as the Indians would have understood it, in any way other than as reserving the waters (not granting them away) when they reserved the land. This is how Rasch constructed the treaty rights portion of his complaint and briefs in the *Winters* litigation. For example, to return to the passage quoted above from his brief in the Court of Appeals, Rasch made these arguments and even went beyond the specific point of reserving water for irrigated agriculture:

> Can there be any question as to how these Indians must "naturally" have understood the treaty of 1888? Why, at that time, not a drop of the waters of the stream was or had ever been taken from its channel by a white man for any purpose. The entire stream was then and always had been a part of the Indian country, and a part of the Indian's reservation theretofore occupied by them. They and their fathers, from time immemorial, had seen the waters of the stream flow down past and through their reservation in abundance, and at no time had they known or seen the channel of Milk River other than as a flowing, living stream. When the extent and area of the new reservation was determined and defined by treaty and agreement, one half of the stream was specially, particularly, and carefully reserved as a part and portion of the reservation, and while at that time the Indians may have not made use of much, if any, of the waters for irrigating purposes, they knew that the very object and purpose which actuated them in consenting to a diminution of their territorial domain, to-wit: "to obtain the means to enable them to become self-supporting as a pastoral and agricultural people," required the use of those waters to enable them to accomplish those very objects and purposes. With all of these things before them, it would be preposterous to assume that they understood their bargain with the Government in any other way than that there was secured and reserved to them the flowing, living stream as they had always known and seen it.[36]

How compelling a legal case this could be in 1905 or 1908 as applied to the circumstances at the Fort Belknap reservation can be seen

in Justice McKenna's discussion of the 1888 treaty and the rights to
water flowing from it in his 1908 *Winters* opinion. This part of the
Winters opinion is an obvious echo of his view of such matters in the
Winans decision (although, oddly, McKenna did not cite to *Winans* in
this part of the *Winters* opinion), and includes the most quoted phrase
from all the *Winters* litigation (italicized here):

> The case, as we view it, turns on the agreement of May, 1888,
> resulting in the creation of Fort Belknap Reservation. In the con-
> struction of this agreement there are certain elements to be
> considered that are prominent and significant. The reservation was a
> part of a very much larger tract which the Indians had the right to
> occupy and use and which was adequate for the habits and wants of a
> nomadic and uncivilized people. It was the policy of the Government,
> it was the desire of the Indians, to change those habits and to become
> a pastoral and civilized people. If they should become such the
> original tract was too extensive, but a smaller tract would be inade-
> quate without a change of conditions. The lands were arid and,
> without irrigation, were practically valueless. And yet, it is contended,
> the means of irrigation were deliberately given up by the Indians and
> deliberately accepted by the Government. The lands ceded were, it is
> true, also arid; and some argument may be urged, and is urged, that
> with their cession there was the cession of the waters, without which
> they would be valueless, and "civilized communities could not be
> established thereon." And this, it is further contended, the Indians
> knew, and yet made no reservation of the waters. We realize there is
> a conflict of implications, but that which makes for the retention of
> the waters is of greater force than that which makes for their cession.
> *The Indians had command of the lands and the waters—command of all*
> *their beneficial use, whether kept for hunting, "and grazing roving herds*
> *of stock," or turned to agriculture and the arts of civilization. Did they*
> *give up all this?* Did they reduce the area of their occupation and give
> up the waters which made it valuable or adequate? . . . If it were
> possible to believe affirmative answers, we might also believe that the
> Indians were awed by the power of the Government or deceived by
> its negotiators. Neither view is possible. The Government is asserting
> the rights of the Indians. But extremes need not be taken into
> account. By a rule of interpretation of agreement and treaties with the
> Indians, ambiguities occurring will be resolved from the standpoint
> of the Indians. And the rule should certainly be applied to determine
> between two inferences, one of which would support the purpose of

the agreement and the other impair or defeat it. On account of their relations to the Government, it cannot be supposed that the Indians were alert to exclude by formal words every inference which might militate against or defeat the declared purpose of themselves and the Government.[37]

THREE MUTUALLY REINFORCING LEGAL THEORIES FOR RESERVATION WATER RIGHTS: THE COMPLAINT IN THE *CONRAD* CASE AT THE BLACKFEET INDIAN RESERVATION

Thus when the *Winters* litigation began, the legal context included at least three reinforcing conceptual approaches for understanding why the government and/or the Indians could have rights to water at the Fort Belknap reservation without regard to the state law of prior appropriation: (1) a common law riparian rights theory; (2) a right under federal law to the continued flow of its waters as necessary for the beneficial uses of the government property; and (3) a treaty reserved rights theory. Any competent attorney for the government would have to have been aware of these legal possibilities, and it is clear that Rasch was so aware from the very beginning of the *Winters* litigation. Moreover, it appears that Rasch believed, for logical reasons when viewed from the distance of a hundred years, that these legal theories constituted a far more compelling basis for the establishment of the reservation's water rights than a state law prior appropriation claim, whatever the facts of that claim. Rasch's client—Superintendent Logan and the Department of Interior—had reasons to expect or prefer a prior appropriation claim under state law on behalf of the reservation, and so Rasch acquiesced by including in his complaint an allegation of facts to establish a prior appropriation claim. When the evidence exploded that claim, he was already well prepared to shift the focus because the *Winters* complaint had emphasized the other theories in its presentation of facts, and undoubtedly happy to proceed on a stronger legal basis.

To make the point more clear, it is important to note something that has so far gone unnoticed: the complaint in the *Winters* case, filed on July 26, 1905, was the *second* Indian water rights case filed by Rasch in 1905. The court decisions in *United States v. Conrad Investment Company*, involving water rights on the Blackfeet Indian Reservation in Montana, may have followed and relied on the decisions in *Winters,* but the Blackfeet case began first: Rasch filed the United States' complaint against the Conrad company in January of 1905, nearly six months before he filed the *Winters* case. And while the Blackfeet complaint did allege facts consistent with a prior appropriation claim, that complaint emphasized allegations of fact irrelevant to a prior appropriation claim but relevant to the other theories. Also, the remedy requested from the court in the *Conrad* case—an injunction to require the entire flow of the stream to reach the Blackfeet reservation—was far more extensive than could be justified by a prior appropriation claim for a certain amount in present use.[38]

The Blackfeet case concerned rights to the water in Birch Creek, a tributary of the Marias River forming the southern boundary of the reservation as established in the same 1888 agreement as the Fort Belknap reservation. The complaint first described the reservation of the lands in 1888 by the United States and the Indians for the Indians, noting specifically that the reservation boundary extended to the middle of the Birch Creek channel. Rasch then noted that this land had been the permanent home and residence of these Indians; that ever since the establishment of the reservation the Indians and the United States had been pasturing and grazing large numbers of cattle and horses on the land along Birch Creek; and that this land, though of a "dry and arid character," was "well fitted" for the grazing of cattle and horses and for growing grass, grain, and vegetable crops when made productive by irrigation with large quantities of water. The complaint described the efforts of the United States and the Indians beginning in 1898 (and prior to the acts of the defendant) to construct an irrigation system capable of diverting a flow of 2,000 cubic feet per minute for irrigation and for domestic and other purposes, which had allowed the irrigation of 10,000 acres of grass, grain, and vegetables—with the result that the United States, through "agricultural pursuits" "has been enabled . . . to train, encourage and accustom large numbers of the Indians residing upon the reservation, to habits of industry and to promote their civilization and improvement," language echoing the purposes described in the 1888 agreement.

To this point, the *Conrad* complaint had alleged facts consistent with a water rights claim based on any of the theories described above— riparian rights, a federal right to water to serve the specified needs of federal property, treaty rights, and prior appropriation. The complaint then moved to matters more difficult or even impossible to square with a prior appropriation claim. First, Rasch described what amounted to an in-stream flow right related to grazing, something easy to imagine under a classic riparian system or under the other theories but little

consistent with the diversion concept inherent in the classic prior appropriation system. He alleged that in order to enable the Indians and the
United States to use the lands along Birch Creek for pasturing and
grazing livestock as they did, "it is necessary and essential that the
waters of said Birch Creek should be permitted to flow down the
channel of said creek, to supply and furnish said stock with drinking
water." If the waters of the creek were not permitted to flow, depriving
the livestock of water for drinking purposes, this would "render valueless for grazing, feeding and ranging purposes large tracts of lands
within said reservation, situate along and contiguous to the channel of
said Birch Creek."

Second and more telling, Rasch added a claim to the reservation of
all of the waters of the creek, beyond what was currently used by the
Indians and the United States on the reservation, to meet future needs
consistent with the purposes for which the reservation was established—
precisely what became central to the reserved rights doctrine as
described by the courts in the *Winters* and *Conrad* cases and in modern
times. The allegation in full, crafted by Rasch in January of 1905, reads
as follows:

> That in order to promote the civilization and improvement of the
> tribes of Indians upon said reservation, and to encourage habits of
> industry among them, and in order to make all the lands within said
> reservation, which are adapted and suitable for farming and ranching
> and the pursuits of agriculture, susceptible of cultivation and pro-
> ductive in the raising thereon of crops of grain, grass and vegetables,
> great quantities of additional water flowing in said Birch Creek will
> from time to time be required and necessary for the proper irrigation
> of the said lands within said reservation, and the reclamation of said
> lands. That for the purpose of subserving and accomplishing the ends
> and purposes for which said reservation was created, and in order to
> subserve the best interests of the Indians residing thereon, and the
> best interest of your orator in furthering and advancing their civil-
> ization and improvement, and encouraging habits of industry among
> them, and to induce and enable said Indians to engage in and carry
> on the pursuits of agriculture and stock-raising as aforesaid, it is essen-
> tial and necessary that all of the waters of said Birch Creek should be
> permitted to flow down the channel of said Birch Creek, uninter-
> ruptedly and undiminished in quantity, and undeteriorated in quality.[39]

Rasch followed this with the allegation that despite "the riparian and
other rights" of the United States and the Indians "to the uninterrupted

flow of all of the waters of said Birch Creek, down the natural channel of said creek," the defendant had constructed a dam and reservoir on Birch Creek above the points of use on the reservation and capable of diverting all of the water of the creek, thus depriving the reservation. The United States concluded by asking the court for an injunction preventing the defendant from maintaining the dam and reservoir or "in any manner impeding, obstructing or preventing the waters" of Birch Creek "from flowing down the channel" of the creek.

With the *Conrad* case already conceptualized and filed, Rasch was well oriented to the legal possibilities for water rights for Indian reservation when forced five months later to respond quickly to the worsening water rights situation at the Fort Belknap reservation.

This assessment of the legal tools available to the government to protect the water rights for the reservation comes with two caveats. First, I do not mean to imply that there were no plausible or reasonable legal arguments for the contrary view, only to stress the nature and breadth of legal arguments outside of the state law of prior appropriation to establish water rights for the reservation. The irrigators sued by the government argued that the federal government by statutes and practice had not only recognized the validity of prior appropriation systems but had essentially ceded control over water allocation to the states, that Montana in its constitution, statutes, and case law had completely abrogated the common law riparian doctrine and replaced it with the prior appropriation system exclusively, and that the silence of the 1888 Fort Belknap treaty as to water rights in the context of the times meant that only land was reserved and not rights to water. The defendant irrigators also emphasized that any approach to this issue that stripped these public-land settlers of the water on which they based their efforts at prosperity ran counter to the national policy, expressed in law, supporting settlement and development of the public lands. But in 1905 and 1906 (that is, through the district and appellate court levels of *Winters*) the irrigators could not rely on any prominent Supreme Court decision for substantial support of their position and could appeal to few lower federal court opinions (none that were close), while at every turn the federal and state court decisions contained language favoring some sort of protection for water for the reserved lands. The Supreme Court's *Kansas v. Colorado* decision in 1907 perhaps added the most weight to the *Winters* defendants' arguments before the Supreme Court, although far from the sort of definitive statement that would limit the federal government and the Indians to state law prior appropriation claims for water at Indian reservations. (The impact of the *Kansas v. Colorado* decision is further discussed below, as part of the discussion of the Reclamation Service's response to the lower court ruling in *Winters*.) By any measure, I would argue, the non-Indian irrigators did have the weaker legal position, strictly considered, once the context shifted from competing prior appropriations claims. At the same time, few in Montana outside of those in the legal profession active in water litigation would have been aware of this fact, given that most of the people in Montana whose lives depended in part on the use of water or rights to water were accustomed to thinking primarily in terms of the prior appropriation system. Moreover, the fact that the government apparently had the stronger legal hand did not predetermine precisely how the courts would rule. There were a number of legal theories and approaches that the courts could have used to explain rulings in favor of the government's case. Nothing predetermined that the courts would resolve this case with precisely the form of treaty reserved rights theory that they did.

The second caveat is that the discussion of the doctrine and case law context in 1905 could imply that such a complex and controversial lawsuit could be and was decided wholly within the "law box" (a term coined by Robert Gordon, the legal historian)—that is, by objective appeal to doctrine and case law without regard to the social context of the litigation. This is no more true than the opposite, in which the courts and the law are seen as merely a vehicle for expressing the passions, interests, and prejudices of either judges or the larger society. Instead, I believe that the "social context" in Montana's Milk River valley in the years from 1905 to 1908 has been misunderstood and was by no means completely unfavorable to the claims of the federal government for water on behalf of the Indians and the Fort Belknap reservation lands. This is not to deny that many of the non-Indians in the Milk River valley (and elsewhere in the West) were appalled at a decision that prevented public-land settlers with an early priority date from diverting water so that it could flow instead to an Indian reservation that diverted water for irrigation at a later date, especially when combined with the implication that the future demands of the reservation could increase the reservation's call on the natural flow. Thus the Montana legislature in 1907 denounced the *Winters* decisions with the lament that "water will pass down the stream, unchecked"— that is, unused by farmers. Every water right in the region had been "rendered invalid, or so vague, unreliable and indefinite as to be of no substantial value" to the settlers and others basing the development of the region on that water, with the result that "settlement has been retarded" and the decisions "will seriously and permanently stifle prosperity" in northern Montana.[40] Once the *Winters* decisions became more widely known and were taken out of the specific context into a national arena, denunciations from the dominant western interests grew especially strident. In one of the great statements of this type, which can stand as the archetype for thousands of such statements about the Indian reserved rights doctrine from the time of the first ruling in *Winters* to modern times, Wyoming Rep. Frank Mondell had this to say in 1914 when he was asked on the floor of the House whether he thought the *Winters* decision was "not a proper construction of the law of waters":

> I will say that to me it is funny, not to characterize it otherwise, and I doubt if the Supreme Court would have said just what it did say under any other state of facts than those existing in that particular case, because I can not believe that any court anywhere, in a matter affecting an arid region, would finally say that there is a power existing anywhere that may stay development until the crack of doom because there is somebody too indolent or too indifferent to develop or allow development. That kind of theory is monstrous when you attempt to apply it to a country whose very life depends upon the useful application of water; it is contrary to the natural law of things. There can not be any power of that kind anywhere.[41]

But despite the fact that many in the valley and in the West had these sentiments, other non-Indian people in the Milk River valley—including certain lawyers, judges, irrigators, and developers, as well as newspaper publishers—could favor or find opportunity in a water law decision favoring the reservation, even in the face of a remedy that enjoined public-land settlers from diverting water for irrigation. This was true as well of people in other parts of the West and the nation[42] Their reasons for this varied, many having nothing to do with Indians. The main point here is that the result in the *Winters* case was not an anomaly, either legally or in its relationship to the immediate social context surrounding the litigation.

CHAPTER 3

Commencement of the Winters *Case*

A Federal Court Decision for Fort Belknap and Its Place in the Water Issues of the Milk River Valley

"**R**ain is Greatly Needed" was the page-one headline of the April 29, 1905, edition of the *North Montana Review* in Glasgow, at the east end of the Milk River valley. According to local cattleman M. E. Milner, "[t]he drought of the past two seasons has been so intense and so prolonged that the range is in a bad condition. You can dig down a hundred feet and find absolutely no moisture in many parts of the state. Rivers and streams which have never been known to go dry before have ceased to run."[1] A month later, on June 3, Superintendent Logan first raised the alarm with his superiors in the Indian Office about the lack of water in the Milk River at the Fort Belknap reservation. Logan wrote this to the commissioner of Indian affairs, Francis E. Leupp:

> Owing to the extreme shortage of the water supply in Milk River this year, with prospects of a very dry season ahead of us, it became absolutely necessary for me to look up the water rights on the Milk River and to find out the status of the water rights on this Reservation. . . . So far this Spring we have had no water in our ditch whatever. Our meadows are now rapidly parching up. The Indians have planted large crops and a great deal of grain. All this will be lost unless some radical action is taken at once to make the settlers above the Reservation respect our rights. To the Indians it either means good crops this fall, or starvation this winter.[2]

Logan requested that the government file suit against the settlers to protect those "rights," and the rights he had in mind appear to be those established under the state law prior appropriation doctrine. He informed the commissioner of an 1898 water rights filing by former superintendent Luke Hays for 10,000 miner's inches out of the Milk River for irrigation on the reservation, which Logan was sure "was one of the first appropriations made upon Milk River." Logan recommended suing those upstream irrigators whose use of water and claim to water rights dated after 1898. He felt that if only prior appropriators above the reservation were to take water, even in these drought conditions "there would be plenty of water reach us to give us at least one good irrigation this summer, and from that we could at least raise a crop." Logan also noted that he had spoken to the local U.S. attorney about filing a suit to protect the water rights of the reservation, and that the attorney would be happy to cooperate but could only act after the Department of Justice instructed him to commence the suit.[3]

Charles Larrabee, the acting commissioner of Indian affairs (and one of the negotiators of the 1888 Fort Belknap treaty, now in charge of the office in Leupp's absence), responded to Logan's letter by asking Secretary of the Interior Ethan Hitchcock to request assistance from the Department of Justice. Larrabee thought in terms of the rights as held by the Fort Belknap Indians, asking Attorney General William Moody to take steps to protect "the water rights of the Indians"; Logan had focused more on the rights as related to the land. Secretary Hitchcock did as he was bid, by letter to Moody. On June 13, Moody wired to Rasch: "Take promptly such action as may be necessary to protect interests of Indians against interference by *subsequent appropriators* of waters to Milk River."

Rasch immediately wrote to Logan to tell him that the litigation authorization had arrived. Rasch noted the attorney general's reference to an action against subsequent appropriators, but Rasch then reminded Logan that the law provided greater opportunities for protection, opportunities that Rasch was pursuing on behalf of the Blackfeet reservation in the other case: "I believe I told you that in the action pending against the Conrad Investment Company, relative to the waters of Birch Creek of the Blackfeet Reservation, I should take the position that *neither prior nor subsequent appropriators have the right to divert the waters of the stream because of the fact that the Government, as I shall contend, has a riparian right*." Rasch's subsequent complaint and other statements about the *Winters* case indicate that Rasch used the term "riparian right" to mean something more than the classic common law/state law riparian doctrine. For him it was a shorthand way to refer to the combined, reinforcing implications of riparian rights/federal authority over federal property/treaty rights—that is, the combined impact of the way in which riparian rights were still recognized in Montana law with the *Rio Grande* concept of the federal government's authority to have control over water necessary to serve the specific needs of federal property, with the needs defined here by the specific purposes of the 1888 agreement establishing the Fort Belknap and Blackfeet reservations.[4]

Just three weeks after Logan's letter to the commissioner, on June 26, 1905, Rasch filed his Bill of Complaint for the Fort Belknap reservation water rights in federal court in Helena (a long trip from the Milk River in 1905), which began at the trial court level as *United States v. Mose Anderson.*[5] The complaint named as defendants Mose Anderson, Henry Winters, sixteen other upstream irrigators, and three irrigation companies (most of whom appear to be irrigating as part of cattle operations). As would be usual, the complaint did not specify the underlying legal theories or legal conclusions (except for the most broad conclusions). Instead, Rasch alleged facts in the complaint that, if proven, would support his understanding of the underlying legal theories or conclusions, acting in the name of the United States "for and in its own behalf, and for and in behalf of its wards, the Indians residing upon [the reservation]."

Rasch did allege facts in the complaint to support a prior appropriation claim, expanding that claim slightly from what Logan had outlined. Piecing together allegations in various paragraphs of the complaint, Rasch alleged that the United States, through the actions of the officers and agents of the Fort Belknap agency, first appropriated 1,000 miner's inches from the Milk River in 1889 for the domestic needs of the agency and to irrigate grain, grass, and vegetables to sustain the agency; that the United States and the Indians of the reservation then appropriated 10,000 miner's inches in 1898 for irrigation purposes (the Luke Hays filing); that the United States and the Indians had "constantly and uninterruptedly used and enjoyed" the appropriated waters since the dates of appropriation; and that the defendants' appropriations were junior to those of the reservation and should cease in the present circumstances of scarcity.

But as in the Blackfeet reservation complaint, Rasch did not confine the Fort Belknap complaint to facts and a claim for relief based on a prior appropriation theory. Instead, he alleged facts and requested an injunction that made sense only if based on riparian rights, treaty rights, and other nonappropriation theories. The paragraphs alleging these facts were not buried after the facts of the appropriation claim. The reverse is true—following the organization of the complaint in the

Blackfeet/*Conrad* case, Rasch's complaint in the Fort Belknap/*Winters* case began with and emphasized facts consistent with a riparian/ federal/treaty right to have all the water of the Milk River flow to the Fort Belknap reservation, a coherent set of facts into which Rasch shoehorned the facts of a prior appropriation claim. Thus after identifying the parties, Rasch's complaint began by describing the 1888 reservation of the Fort Belknap lands by the United States and the Gros Ventre and Assiniboine people, with marked emphasis on the facts that the boundary of the reserved lands extended to the middle channel of the Milk River and that the Indians had occupied and resided on these lands as their permanent residence without interruption. The complaint then described how the reservation lands along Milk River were "well fitted and adapted" for cattle raising and for the production of grass, grain, and vegetable crops, and that "ever since the establishment" of the reservation the Indians have held and grazed large herds of cattle and horses on this land.

Next the complaint described how the land along the Milk River, however well fitted for farming and grazing uses, was "of a dry and arid character," and could only be made productive by irrigation with "large quantities of water" from the Milk River. It is at this point that the complaint described the attempts at irrigation on the reservation and alleged that these irrigation efforts began "long prior" to the acts of the defendants disturbing the flow of the river. Again as in the *Conrad* complaint, Rasch's complaint in the Fort Belknap case then abandoned any limitation to a prior appropriation claim by incorporating an instream flow allegation based on the drinking needs of grazing livestock and then a claim to *all the water* naturally flowing in the Milk River so that it would be available as needed to satisfy the purposes of the reservation. This latter claim is so striking in its implications from the very beginning of the *Winters* litigation that it bears full quotation:

> That in order to enable your orator to maintain said agency, and in order to promote the civilization and improvement of the said bands and tribes of Indians upon said reservation and the encouragement of habits of industry and thrift among them, and in order to make all of the said lands within the said reservation which are adapted and suitable for farming and ranching and the pursuits of agriculture susceptible of cultivation and productive for the raising thereon of crops of grain, grass and vegetables, large quantities of water flowing in said Milk River will be required and necessary for the purpose of irrigation of the said lands within said reservation and the reclamation of said

lands. That for the purpose of subserving and accomplishing the ends and purposes for which said reservation was created, and in order to subserve the best interest of your orator and of the Indians residing upon said reservation, and the best interest of your orator in further- ing and advancing the civilization and improvement of said Indians, and to encourage habits of industry and thrift among them, and to induce and enable said Indians to engage in and carry on the pursuits of agriculture and stock-raising as aforesaid, it is essential and necessary that all of the waters of said Milk River should be permitted to flow down the channel of said river, uninterruptedly and undiminished in quantity, and undeteriorated in quality.[6]

Rasch then moved on to describe the actions of the defendants in diverting the waters of the Milk River upstream of the reservation to the irreparable injury of the United States and the Indians, "notwith- standing the riparian and other rights" of the United States and the Indians "to the uninterrupted flow of the all of the waters of said Milk River down the natural channel of said river."

Consistent with the complaint in the *Conrad* case, Rasch then asked the court for a permanent injunction "perpetually and forever" enjoin- ing the defendants "from in any manner constructing, erecting, keeping up, or maintaining any dams or reservoirs of any kind or character in or across the channel of said Milk River or its tributaries and from in any manner impeding, obstructing or preventing the waters of said Milk River or its tributaries from flowing down the channel of said river" to the reservation. He also asked for a temporary restraining order on the same terms, preventing the defendants from diverting water from the Milk River pending a hearing on the request for an injunction. Judge William Hunt immediately issued the temporary restraining order and set July 17 for the first hearing on the injunction request.

The defendants quickly sought modification of the temporary restraining order, asking that it reflect only current needs and uses at the reservation and not prevent the defendants from diverting water above that amount if available in the river. Judge Hunt responded by modifying the wording of the restraining order on July 8, so that it now prevented the defendants from diverting water from the Milk River so as to "deprive the complainant of said waters, upon its said land, up to and not exceeding the number of inches of said waters [11,000] claimed by complainant in the Bill of Complaint in this suit." Rasch explained to Logan by letter that the judge meant by this modification that the defendants could not divert any water needed on the reservation pending

further developments and were to contact and rely on Superintendent
Logan's determination of what was needed on the reservation at any
particular moment. Rasch's July 8 letter to Logan also provided further
clues of Rasch's intentions in the litigation. He outlined for Logan the
evidence that he needed help assembling to establish in court the uses of
water at the Fort Belknap reservation and the dates of the appropriations by the reservation and the defendants. But Rasch also notified
Logan that "[a]s I told you when you were here, I shall rely upon the
appropriations made in 1890 and 1898, and upon the riparian doctrine,
but the principal proposition in the case is the use that was made of the
waters for beneficial purposes upon the reservation," an apparent reference to a *Rio Grande*–reserved treaty rights approach.[7]

It was a good thing for Rasch that he had a preferred approach
other than the prior appropriations claim, as statements and evidence
submitted by the defendants at the July 17 hearing indicated that many
or most of the defendants' appropriations predated the 1898 appropriation claim by the reservation to 10,000 miner's inches. The evidence
also cast doubt on the size of the government's 1890 appropriation,
indicating that it was closer to 100 than 1,000 inches, and on the total
size of the reservation's appropriation and ability to make use of water
(whatever the date), indicating it was closer to 5,000 inches, not 11,000.
The defendants disputed the government's authority to challenge water
rights properly established under the law of Montana or to claim any
rights to water except under that system. And the defendants also
emphasized for the court that they had settled public lands and were
developing communities on the basis of irrigated agriculture, as sanctioned and encouraged by federal and state law and policy. If prevented
from diverting water, their lands would be rendered valueless and the
settlements and communities would fall apart.[8]

The weakness of the government's prior appropriation claim turned
out not to matter, as Rasch could have predicted. On August 8, 1905,
Judge Hunt issued a preliminary injunction in favor of the government,
to be in effect during the pendency of the suit. He explained his reasons
in an oral ruling the day before, a transcript of which he had placed in
the court record as a Memorandum Order. He based his ruling almost
wholly on a treaty rights analysis, with significant reliance on the
Supreme Court's decision in *Winans*:

> I think that an injunction should be granted. Prior to 1888 nearly the
> whole of Northern Montana north of the Missouri River and eastward
> from the main chain of the Rocky Mountains was recognized as

Indian country occupied in part by the tribes of Indians now living upon the Fort Belknap Reservation. By the treaty of May 1, 1888, the Indians "ceded and relinquished to the United States" their title and rights to lands not embraced within the reservation then established as their permanent homes. The purposes of the treaty were that means might be had to enable the Indians to become "self-supporting, as a pastoral and agricultural people, and to educate their children in the paths of civilization."

The consideration for the cession and relinquishment was that the United States should expend annually a large sum of money for the Indians in the purchase of live stock, agricultural implements, and other things, in assisting the Indians to build homes and inclose their farms, and in any other respect to promote their civilization, comfort and improvement. Article III., Treaty of May 1, 1888, 25 Statutes at Large, 114. The "cultivation of the soil" was also specially mentioned by Article V. of the Treaty.

A fair construction of the preamble and provisions of the treaty is that an essential object thereof was to encourage farming among the Indians. This being correct, notice of conditions of climate and soil of Montana tell us that water for irrigation is indispensable in successful farming throughout that portion of Montana wherein the Belknap Reservation lies.

The parties to the agreement evidently appreciated this necessity, and purposely fixed a boundary line of the reservation at a point in the middle of the main channel of Milk River opposite the mouth of Peoples Creek, and thence up Milk River in the middle of the main channel thereof to the place of beginning. I believe the intention was to reserve sufficient of the waters to insure to the Indians the means wherewith to irrigate their farms. This construction of the Treaty seems to me to be in accord with the rules the Supreme Court has repeatedly laid down in arriving at the true sense of treaties with Indians. United States v. Winans, decided May 15, 1905. While in the Treaty of October 8, 1895, reference is made to a scarcity of water which renders the pursuit of agriculture "difficult and uncertain;" yet Article II. of that treaty expressly refers to the irrigation of the farms of the Indians. Irrigation was undoubtedly contemplated and was provided for, although the Treaty of 1895 recognized that probably the main reliance of the Indians for self-support would be found in cattle raising.

In my judgment, when the Indians made the treaty granting rights to the United States, they reserved the right to the use of the waters of Milk River, at least to an extent reasonably necessary to irrigate their lands. The right so reserved continues to exist against the United States and its grantees as well as against the State and its grantees. From this it follows that patents if any issued by the Land Department for lands held by defendants are subject to the treaty, and defendants can acquire no rights to the exclusion of the reasonable needs of the Indians. These needs appear to be five thousand inches. To that extent injunction will issue. U.S. v. Winans, *supra*.[9]

In the equally brief injunction order, Judge Hunt concluded that the evidence submitted at the July 17 hearing established that the government's present water needs at the Fort Belknap reservation were "not less than five thousand inches of the waters of the Milk River." Thus he issued a "general injunction during the pendency of this suit" precluding the defendants "from in any manner interfering with the use of said waters" by the government on the reservation.[10]

The defendants immediately appealed Judge Hunt's ruling to the Circuit Court of Appeals, arguing that the 1888 agreement did not reserve any rights to water, that nothing in the treaty affected the rights of the defendants to appropriate water under state and federal law, and that nothing in the treaty or any other area of federal law assigned water rights to the reservation on any basis other than the law of appropriation in Montana as sanctioned by state and federal statutes and cases or any rights superior to the appropriation rights of the defendants under that law.[11] Issues surrounding the appeal process will be discussed in another section below, but the key point is that this first ruling by Judge Hunt, and its essential basis, would stand through the rest of the litigation—through the appeal of the preliminary injunction and an appellate court affirmance in early 1906, a final decree by the lower court making the injunction permanent and a second appeal to and affirmance by the appellate court in later 1906, and finally the Supreme Court affirmance in April 1908.

One obvious question was why did the critical rulings come in the Fort Belknap case when Rasch filed the Blackfeet reservation case first, six months earlier? Why do we speak of the *Winters* doctrine and not the *Conrad* doctrine? The answer also seems obvious, although it is necessarily speculative. The Conrad Investment Company dam on Birch Creek represented a potential threat, not an immediate problem. Rasch filed that case in January, when no irrigation was taking place to be interfered with, and he did not pursue immediate injunctive relief. Instead the parties moved the *Conrad* case at a regular trial pace. The

Fort Belknap problem was immediate—no water in the river when the time came for irrigation—and so Rasch pursued injunctive relief aggressively, obtaining a restraining order at the time of filing and prompting the key ruling from Judge Hunt little more than a month after filing. And once the *Winters* case got rolling and Judge Hunt ruled, the parties held *Conrad* in at least partial suspension waiting to see what the appellate courts made of Judge Hunt's approach to Indian water rights, with constant references (as will be seen below) to the fact that the decisions in the Fort Belknap case would have obvious implications for the Blackfeet reservation situation, as they did.

Hunt's injunction order alarmed the people in the affected areas upstream of the Fort Belknap reservation, around the communities of Havre and Chinook. Norris Hundley implied that the alarm and indignation spread throughout the valley.[12] But at least as indicated by newspaper accounts and editorials from towns along or below the reservation, people elsewhere in the valley saw the ruling less as something to fear and more as an opportunity to further policy goals already desired, especially the construction of a reclamation project and possibly the further transfer of Fort Belknap lands along the Milk River to non-Indian farmers. To document this point it is necessary to back up and discuss the water story that really did dominate the news and the lives of the people in the Milk River valley in 1905 and after.

At the time the federal government filed the complaint in *Winters,* and as the case made its three-year journey through the courts, the farm and town settlers along the Milk River appear to have reached a rough sort of consensus regarding their situation:[13] Most people felt that large-scale, commercial irrigated agricultural development was the key to a prosperous future for the valley, involving livestock production based in part on irrigated hay production, farming of standard crops such as wheat and oats and certain vegetables, and also the cultivation and possibly processing of more exotic irrigated crops such as sugar beets. The natural flow of the Milk River would never be sufficient for this purpose, they had come to believe, because of the limited and fluctuating amount of the flow and the timing of the flow, and because under the prior appropriation system only some would benefit fully from the limited flows without a more appropriate sharing of the resource for the broadest development of the valley. Most of the people in the valley had thus turned their hopes toward coordinated and comprehensive river development for irrigation, coinciding with or influenced by the passage of the Reclamation Act in 1902. Due to the lobbying of the Milk

River residents and their congressional delegation, one of the first group of projects selected for implementation by the Reclamation Service under the act was the Milk River–Saint Mary River project. By early 1905 the Reclamation Service had set aside approximately one million dollars for the work and had engineers in the field planning and designing the project and ready to begin construction on the first phase. The engineers were poised to begin the first phase of the project, a plan to increase the amount of water at the head of the Milk River by constructing a canal that would divert water from the headwaters of the Saint Mary River into the headwaters of the Milk River. The two rivers began in the same general area on the east side of the Rocky Mountains in Montana, and both flowed from Montana into Canada, but only the Milk River flowed back into Montana (see map 1), so why not take some of the waters from the Saint Mary before they flowed off forever? Storage projects near the head of the Milk River would then store the augmented flows of the Milk, retaining the waters usually "lost to use" in the spring and early summer runoff. The rest of the Milk River project called for a series of diversion dams, primary canals, and laterals that would store and deliver water all along the Milk River valley after the river reentered the United States (the area referred to here as the Milk River valley), making maximum use of the waters of the river. The people of the valley formed the United Milk River Irrigation Association to work with the federal government to realize the project; in 1905 the Reclamation Service also worked with the irrigators and others from two smaller groups, an upper Milk River and a lower Milk River water users association, to help resolve specific, more local problems that stood in the way of the project.

Perhaps the most important obstacle to the Reclamation project concerned water rights. The federal government would be the agent to deliver the managed river to the settlers, but the federal government demanded in turn that the settlers first put their water rights house in order. In an illustration of the disorder that could accompany the prior appropriation system, the river was subject to a huge number of private claims, many not perfected at all or perfected only for a fraction of the claimed amount, apparently making it impossible to know what water was actually in use (vesting rights to it) and what water was available for the project. The government demanded a reduction of the large number of claims to a settled or adjudicated list of who really had put to use what amounts of water, including the establishment of a systematic and consistent way to recognize and record an appropriate water right, the proper duty of water in this region, and so forth. Only then could the Reclamation Service determine who had rights to water and for what land, and what water Reclamation could reserve and dedicate to the project, just as it had already withdrawn and reserved public lands in anticipation of developing the project.[14]

This is why news about the federal court's injunction in the *Winters* case shared page one of the August 9 edition of the *Milk River Valley News* in Harlem with a story about the effort to settle the general water rights situation: "Thousand to be Sued: Action to be begun to secure adjudication." The latter story described a decision by irrigators in the Harlem area and elsewhere in the valley to file in state court at Fort Benton, Montana, a suit to adjudicate the water rights in the Milk River basin in the general region from Havre to Glasgow, naming as defendants up to 1,500 people and entities claiming water rights. The paper indicated that the suit was being filed at the request of officials from the Reclamation Service, "who demand that all water rights in the basin shall be adjudicated before the beginning of work on the great Milk River irrigation system."[15] And the equal treatment of the Indian water rights and Reclamation stories in this edition obscures the fact that by far the greatest amount of newspaper coverage in the valley's communities on water issues in these years concerned continuing reports on the need for and progress on the Reclamation project in general and the more specific question of how to resolve the water rights situation—whether and how to proceed with a basinwide adjudication, objections to such an adjudication, how to resolve the water rights issues without the expense and time of an adjudication, how to influence the political system to get the Reclamation Service to move forward with the project no matter what the valley residents might accomplish, and so forth. Even the possibility of developing a sugar beet industry as part of the commercial irrigated agricultural development of the valley received significantly more newspaper attention than the *Winters* case. The Indian water rights case received merely episodic coverage.

The possible threat to the valley's water supply that caused far more concern than *Winters,* as measured by newspaper coverage and local and government action, came from Canada. Unhappy particularly about the plan to divert the waters of the Saint Mary River (which flowed into and stayed in Canada) into the Milk River (which flowed into Canada briefly and then back to Montana), Canadians threatened to divert large amounts of water from the Milk River for their own development if the United States government and the Montanans tried to develop the comprehensive water project without consulting and sharing water with Canada. Under pressure from the settlers to resolve this uncertainty, by early 1909 the United States negotiated a Saint Mary River–Milk River apportionment agreement as part of the larger Boundary Waters Treaty between the United States and Canada (or more precisely, Great Britain, as the sovereign of the British Dominions), reserving certain amounts to each country for the future development of their respective parts of the region.[16] The sporadic and fruitless efforts of some locals to get the government to undo the *Winters* decision stand in contrast.

Within this context, it is not surprising to discover that while the non-Indian people along the Milk River had little or no regard for the Indians at Fort Belknap, the valley's non-Indian residents as a whole were not as disturbed as has been supposed by the *Winters* decisions. The upriver irrigators in the Chinook and Havre area who were ordered by the courts not to divert water from the Milk but instead to let it flow to the reservation were, of course, outraged, as Norris Hundley has documented. And they found a few allies elsewhere in the valley, most notably a prominent Harlem businessman and politician, Thomas Everett, with an interest in the Harlem Ditch Company, whose intake was also above the reservation's ditch. But most of the valley and its residents were not upstream of the reservation, including others in the Harlem area, and the people who lived even with or downstream of the reservation, from Harlem east, were not adversely affected by the outcome of the litigation. Far more important, they had little sympathy for the affected irrigators in the Chinook and Havre area. These upper-valley irrigators (mostly cattlemen irrigating hay) were a source of vexation to more than just the Fort Belknap Indians, as they were the most resistant in the valley to negotiating a valleywide accord on water rights to pave the way for the Reclamation project. This was primarily because the upstream irrigators had some of the earliest water rights in the valley and the best geographic position for diverting the river's water and thus the least need for coordinated development to secure a water supply. The *Montana Homestead* in Hinsdale, for just one example, pointedly emphasized that the bulk of the water users willing to join the general adjudication suit as plaintiffs were from Harlem and on downstream, while most of the defendants were irrigators from the Chinook area unwillingly dragged into the suit.[17]

The people downstream of Chinook and Havre, from Harlem on east, never treated the *Winters* decision as a problem or considered it to be of great interest. They often ended up listening to denunciations of *Winters* by the Chinook and Havre irrigators at meetings of the valley-wide irrigation association. This was just part of the price of participating in the association, which worked for the adoption of resolutions to the federal government on issues relevant to the Reclamation project. (The association also held numerous meetings and produced endless resolutions in these years that listed various grievances associated with water development in the valley and yet ignored the Indian water rights case,[18] and the association never did adopt a resolution in these years that included a direct denunciation of the water rights decisions.) And some of these people were willing to agree to proposals to dismember the Fort Belknap reservation because it would give them access to reservation land while also helping the Chinook and Havre folks to undo the court decisions. However, too much attention and anguish over the impact of *Winters* could possibly scare off the government Reclamation project and private economic development; one can read between the lines of several news stories and editorials to see the boosters' efforts to emphasize the positive. And at its best, these downstream people believed, *Winters* could be an opportunity for them: It could leave water in the river that might just come past the reservation to them. Far more important, if the Indians were entitled to a large share of the natural flow of the river at irrigation times, this only emphasized the need for a coordinated river development project to store and deliver as much of the river's flood waters as possible for the benefit of the future development and prosperity of the non-Indian people, something these people thought was already required by the physical conditions of the river. That the Chinook and Havre irrigators were stung by the decisions was all the better—this might help bring these people into a more united front with the rest of the valley in the Reclamation effort, since they no longer had a secure water supply.

Thus in stark contrast to the newspapers in Havre and Chinook, the newspapers surveyed in Harlem and the towns further down the valley *never* denounced the government's *Winters* suit or the courts' decisions in all the years of the *Winters* litigation, up to and through the Supreme Court's opinion in 1908. Nearly all of the stories in these newspapers about the filing of the Fort Belknap suit or Judge Hunt's injunction order or the later stages in the litigation were perfunctory news accounts describing the events. These stories usually reported the government's claims or the courts' orders verbatim or at face value without elaboration, comment, denunciation, or any follow-up in subsequent editions—this in newspapers in which elaboration, comment, often denunciation, and countless follow-ups were integral to any story of significance.[19]

The few exceptions to the usual perfunctory news account were even more telling. On occasion the editors of these newspapers would use some event or observation about the Indian water case as a vehicle to comment on the Reclamation project, including comments on the problem people upstream. An example is a quotation, emphasized by Norris Hundley, from the *Milk River Valley News,* the newspaper in Harlem, soon after the Supreme Court's opinion in *Winters* in 1908: "[A]s the winter has been very dry and the Indians awarded all the waters in the Milk river the settlers will stand a very poor show of making a living the coming summer unless something is done at once."[20] Hundley included this as part of his description of the alarm and dismay in the valley at the Supreme Court's decision, otherwise indicated by reports from the Havre and Chinook areas. But the statement in the Harlem paper was included within an editorial not directed against the *Winters* decisions; the *Milk River Valley News* never denounced the Fort Belknap water rights decisions, and in fact, as will be seen, had good things to say about them. Instead, the comment was inserted into the Harlem paper's lament about the federal government's delay in developing the Reclamation project that would solve the valley's water supply and allocation problems, needed to allow full use of the "unlimited flood waters which go to waste." The valley residents were finding themselves increasingly frustrated by their lack of control over the implementation of the project, as it became clear the federal government would develop and deliver the managed river and reserved water only when its attention and the political situation could be oriented in the valley residents' favor. Moreover, the editorial made clear that the ultimate enemy of the "plan of the masses," as the paper referred to the Reclamation project, was not the federal government and certainly not the Indians, but instead the political power of "the amalgamated opposition who appear to be inclined to leave this productive section to the will of the large stock and sheep barons, who reside in gaudy homes in other parts of the country." While such "livestock barons" were spread throughout the valley, the livestock men flourished most obviously in the upper parts of the valley and, as irrigators of hay pastures, had been the target of both the government in the *Winters* case and lower valley residents who had needed a resolution of their water rights problems and other support to allow the Reclamation project to proceed.

Even more indicative of these attitudes are other news stories and an editorial from the same Harlem newspaper and comments in the Malta and Hinsdale papers. The first news story of relevance is from July 26, 1905, soon after the government filed the Fort Belknap suit and the federal court had issued a temporary restraining order against the

upper-valley irrigators. The *Milk River Valley News* in Harlem noted
that "Chinook water users are greatly exercised by the suit," and that
the Indian water rights case "still further complicates the question of
general irrigation of the valley." But the paper also noted that "no matter
how it is decided it will not settle the difference between Chinook and
Harlem water users, nor any of the questions affecting the great
national irrigation project."[21] Approaching the same issue in a different
way, the newspaper in Hinsdale (fifty-five miles downstream of the reservation) later responded to Judge Hunt's injunction with these words only:
"With practically all the running water in Milk river decreed to the
Belknap Indians, it would seem to us that the water right question of
the upper valley is practically settled, rather, adjusted."[22] The Malta paper,
the *Enterprise,* made a similar comment midway through a discussion
not of the Indian water rights case but of the status of the Reclamation
project as reviewed in a recent irrigation association meeting. Noting
the confusion in the valley over who had what rights to water and that
the federal government indicated the confusion had to be settled before
the project could go forward, the paper commented that "[i]t is difficult,
too, to obtain data as to the normal flow of the stream, and with an
allowance of 5,000 inches to the Indians of the Belknap Reservation, *it
would seem that other vested rights carry vastly more wind than water.*" The
story then ended with optimism that the confusion will soon be cleared
up and the "government ditch" constructed, "the only solution for the
future of a country with possibilities under irrigation."[23] Three days
later the *North Montana Review* in Glasgow, at the end of the Milk
valley, printed verbatim the story from the *Enterprise.*[24]

It is necessary to jump ahead in the story to note the most amazing
items of all—the news story and editorial in the January 9, 1908, edition
of Harlem's *Milk River Valley News.* These were the paper's first report
and comment on the Supreme Court's decision to affirm of January 6,
1908. The headline of the news story was "Indians Get Water," with a
subhead that included the statement "Result is Quite Satisfactory to
All" (which really would have been news to the Chinook and Havre
irrigators). The story briefly described the Court's decision in tones that
were neutral or even sympathetic, for example, "The suit is the outcome
of the Indians embarking in farming and as the white settlers were
using all of the waters of Milk river, which was very little, the reds were
deprived of the waters." The story then concluded with this comment:

> The decision was received without any surprise whatever by the
> farmers of this vicinity and regretted only by a few, the majority

express themselves as satisfied, as it will establish a right on this river by which everyone will be governed. While, as a matter of fact, the only time farmers in this valley use, and have used for years, the waters of Milk river is when there is water enough in the river to irrigate the entire state if properly used. All that the people want in this portion of the valley is for the government to begin constructing a few diversion dams and latterals which will divert the flood waters upon the land at the proper time.[25]

The editorial in the same edition continued in the same vein, if even more bluntly:

The daily press of Montana has grossly exaggerated the recent decision by the supreme court of the United States in the water right suit of the Indians of Fort Belknap vs. Henry Winters and others. They evidently are not conversant with affairs in the Milk River valley in the section between Harlem and Malta, or otherwise they would not publish such rot as was sent out from Helena by a string fiend, whose imagination is far greater than his ability. Everybody who has visited this community and made a few inquiries regarding the water resources is well aware of the fact that the farmers here have not used the waters of Milk river for a number of years, always depending upon flood water irrigation, and it was this alone that produced the wonderful crops which this community is blessed with every year. *The decision was received in this city with much joy as we all know that this will have a tendency to hasten construction on diversion dams, latterals and storage reservoirs to hold and divert the unlimited flood waters of which there is enough going to waste every year to irrigate every foot of ground between here and Mondak.*[26]

The attitude of the *Milk River Valley News* struck a chord in at least some members in another community, as the newspaper in Hinsdale prominently reprinted the editorial a week later.[27] If the *Winters* decision could be received with "much joy" (admittedly a bit of booster hyperbole; there is little indication of joyous celebration in the streets), it was because *Winters* could be a catalyst to reserve everyone's place in the water development in the valley, illustrating again the unsatisfactory nature of critical resource decisions made solely on the basis of temporal priority.

Logan's 1905 correspondence about the *Winters* litigation with Rasch and with Cyrus Babb, the Reclamation Service engineer in

charge of the Milk River project, further illustrates this basinwide
dynamic, including the tension between upriver and downriver irrigators and the role of the Reclamation project and Reclamation Service.
Rasch's July 8 letter to Logan discussing the injunction concluded with
a warning:

> Please be careful not to allow the water that is being turned down
> [i.e., sent down river instead of into the upriver diversions] in conse-
> quence of the injunction to be used by the Harlem Ditch Company or
> others. I have been informed that the rumor and report is that this
> suit was brought for the benefit of the Harlem Ditch Company, and
> that since the injunction was issued there has not been any more
> water at the head of the reservation ditch than there was before, and
> that the water is taken by the Harlem Ditch Company.[28]

In a similar vein, Babb wrote to Logan on July 10 to say that he, Babb,
had just been in Chinook, and "your injunction has been served and is
now being strictly enforced." Babb then added: "I do not know how
much of a benefit your injunction will do our Service. I understand
there is a very considerable hard feeling about it around Chinook, *and
that a great many people blame the Reclamation Service for it.* I hope you
will get some water, however, and that the Paradise and Harlem canals
will not take it all."[29] The rumors about the Reclamation's involvement
could only stem from the general knowledge that the injunction, if it
remained valid, would undermine the water rights security of the
Chinook and Havre irrigators, assign much of the natural minimum
flow to the reservation, and create the proper circumstances to force to
resolution the issues about water rights, needs, and availability in the
valley necessary for the Reclamation project to proceed. Also, some
people may have known that Babb helped Logan and Rasch gather and
organize evidence on the water users, uses, and needs in the valley in
preparation for the filing of the suit and the July 17 hearing, although
Babb excused himself from actual attendance at the court hearing when
Logan and Rasch desired his presence.[30]

By return mail, Logan reassured Rasch that "[i]t is not true that the
suit was brought in any way, shape or form in the interest of the
Harlem Ditch Co." Logan noted that the Harlem company had an
appropriation right prior to the reservation's 1898 filing, but even so, the
ditch company "agreed with me that whenever there was a rise in the
Milk River, they would open their gates and allow the water to come
through." Moreover, the river had finally risen a few days ago, and the
reservation ditches now had an abundance of water. "This might have

been caused by melting snow, but I am strongly of the opinion that it was principally caused by making the Empire Cattle Co., the Madison Cattle Co., and others close down their head gates and allow the water to pass down to us."[31] Logan said the same things in his return letter to Babb, and added his opinion of the people of Chinook:

> [N]otwithstanding all the talk of the Chinook people that the Harlem Ditch Co. and the Paradise Valley Ditch Co. would take all the water they turned loose, and that I would not receive any, and that my bringing the injunction was simply for the purpose of helping the Harlem Ditch Co. out of the hole, this talk is simply on a par with a good many other fool statements made by different people from Chinook. "The proof of the pudding is in the eating." At the present time and for four days I have had a ditch full of water—as much as I have had at any time in the canal in previous years.[32]

As for Babb's worries about rumors about the involvement of the Reclamation Service, Logan offered to make it clear to the general public that Reclamation was not to blame and, Logan added with just a hint of criticism, that Reclamation had in fact opposed the filing of the suit:

> In regard to the reclamation service being blamed for my action, I am perfectly willing and only too glad to exonerate you and the reclamation people with having anything to do with the matter whatsoever. In fact I can state truthfully that it is my honest opinion that you did not want me to take out this injunction. I think that you felt at the time that your service would be blamed for my action, and I also think you thought I would not get any water. However, "All is well that ends well." We have got the water, and the reclamation service is entirely blameless.[33]

Babb returned his congratulations on obtaining the water, and he admitted like others that "I expect your proceedings in the end will help out the question of the entire water rights of the Milk River Valley," indicating that he understood the immediate benefits of the reservation's victory to the Reclamation Service, even as the local Reclamation officials had been too afraid of the possible backlash to support the suit.[34]

CHAPTER 4

Winters *in the Federal Court of Appeals*

Reclamation Anxiety, Kansas v. Colorado, *and Affirmation by the Court of Appeals*

If local Reclamation Service personnel were skittish about the Fort Belknap case, certain Reclamation officials in Washington, D.C., were positively hostile, even apoplectic upon learning of the nature of the federal government's arguments in the *Winters* case. The arguments came to their attention as Rasch and Logan reported to their superiors the success (so far) of the litigation and the filing of an appeal by the defendants, elevating the *Winters* case out of the complicated local context and into a broader but simplified context, in which the Reclamation Service was on the hunt for anything in the West that smelled of a riparian right. To the Service and its allies, as will be seen, nothing less than the future of American civilization in the arid West hinged on the outcome. Yet despite intense pressure, the Department of Justice and Department of the Interior held firm and did not interfere with Rasch's approach to the Indian water rights litigation, which led to decisions based on theories other than the basic riparian doctrine, anyway.

I have already mentioned how at the time of the *Winters* litigation, the first set of Reclamation officials were working hard to try to eradicate the riparian doctrine in the western states. They wanted to assert the primacy of the prior appropriation system in order to rationalize the water law system in the West and to do so in a way that severed any legal tie between land along a watercourse and rights to water and made rights to water wholly dependent on diversion and actual use. This was necessary, in their view, so that there would exist no rights to water that

was not in use, meaning that water not in use would be free for dedication to Reclamation and other irrigation projects and applied to the most
appropriate public and private lands regardless of the location of those
lands either on or off a stream. The *Winters* litigation, arguments, and
early decisions horrified these Reclamation personnel as much as anyone.
This was especially true of the Reclamation Service's first legal adviser,
Morris Bien, the developer and primary proponent of what became
known as the "Bien code," a form of the prior appropriation system that
Bien tried to persuade western states to adopt. The Bien code would
have also allowed Reclamation to identify and reserve unappropriated
water in a watershed for future development of a Reclamation project
(which Bien justified primarily on the principles of the *Rio Grande* case
as intertwined with the principles of the prior appropriation doctrine).
Bien and others in the central office of the Reclamation Service viewed
with abhorrence the claims for riparian rights put forward by the U.S.
attorney in the *Winters* case, and apparently considered the lower court's
Winters decisions an unfortunately successful application of riparian
principles—rights to water reserved in perpetuity to a piece of land
along the watercourse, whether the water was used or not. Even worse,
this weird variant of the riparian doctrine was being asserted *by* federal
lawyers and imposed *as* federal law *by* the federal courts, to the hindrance of the federal Reclamation Service's attempts to reshape western
water law in a different direction. These Reclamation officials saw
nothing of value in the *Winters* litigation and decisions. They were not
close enough to the local context, as Babb was, to see the tactical value of
the decision (which might not have been important to them anyway).
Further, they were too wrapped up in the fight against riparian rights to
value the strategic possibilities of the emerging doctrine, to realize that
part of the legal justification underlying the *Winters* decisions—that the
federal government had the power to reserve water to suit federal
purposes for the public lands—could be used to *justify* Reclamation
actions to reserve large amounts of water in a public land watershed for
a Reclamation project. This was riparianism, and thus these Reclamation Service officials attempted to have Rasch forced to withdraw any
riparian rights claims and to kill off this variant before it could spread.[1]

Rasch probably contributed to this dynamic by the way he described
the litigation to his superiors. He reported to Attorney General Moody
on August 28 on the success of the litigation and asked for authorization to respond to the appeal. Rasch noted that the attorney general
had authorized him in a June telegraph to protect the rights of the
Indians against interference by "subsequent appropriators," with the

obvious implication being reliance on the state law doctrine of prior appropriation. As previously discussed, Rasch knew, well before he filed the Fort Belknap complaint, about legal theories other than prior appropriation and even preferred to base his case on these, simply working in the prior appropriation claim as well. But in what could only have been a great act of dissembling for the attorney general, and thus what became the standard story of the litigation, Rasch explained how he sued only those he believed, from his discussions with Logan and Babb, to be subsequent appropriators and that "[o]n the strength of the data furnished me, I expected to be able to dispose of the alleged rights of the various defendants upon the fact of appropriation by showing the priority of the Government appropriation of 1898." He then noted as an aside that "while the bill of complaint was primarily drawn upon this theory" (which was hogwash, as shown above), he was "careful" to "invoke other rights in case the necessity should arise." To his dismay, the evidence presented by the defendants "forced me to take the very grounds I sought to avoid in limiting the action to parties who were reported subsequent appropriators."[2]

Once he had demonstrated his obedience to the attorney general's instructions and his allegiance to the prior appropriation system, and then had been freed from that burden by circumstances out of his control, Rasch could then explain the theories he did pursue, which he broke into four different variations, or "propositions," as he called them. It is not clear if he had distinguished the four propositions at the time he filed the complaint, but the facts in the complaint were sufficient to support all four. These were the four propositions:

1. Because the waters of Milk River, so far as the same are a part and portion of the Ft. Belknap Indian Reservation, and needed upon said reservation for domestic and agricultural purposes, *never were,* and never *became public waters* subject to appropriation by any person under state or federal laws [emphasis in original].
2. Because the plaintiff is now and always has been a riparian proprietor of the waters of Milk River, and as such riparian proprietor it has the absolute right to have the waters of the river flow down the channel of the stream to supply its requirements and necessities for domestic and agricultural purposes upon the Indian Reservation, to carry out the objects and purposes for which said reservation was created.
3. Because to permit the diversion of the waters of the river in question, and prevent their flowing down the channel of the stream

to and upon the reservation, would be violative of the treaties, conventions, and agreements made between the complainants the United
States, and the Indians residing upon the reservation, and would
deprive said Indians of the use and enjoyment of rights and property
accorded and secured to them by the provisions of such treaties,
conventions and agreements.

4. Because no state legislation can destroy the right of the United
States, as the owner of lands bordering upon the stream, to the
continued flow of its waters, so far at least as may be necessary for the
beneficial uses of the government property.[3]

He emphasized the fourth point by noting his citations to the *Rio
Grande* and *Gutierres* cases, the only case citations or other legal sources
mentioned in the letter. He also emphasized that by his reading of both
Montana and federal law, "[i]n my presentation of the matter to the
Court here, I relied most strongly upon the riparian rights of the
Government, and in my humble judgment that is the strongest point in
the case," which was like a red flag to the Reclamation officials when
they became aware of it. Rasch noted almost as a disappointment that
Judge Hunt based his injunction order on the third ground argued, "to-
wit: the treaty rights of the Indians," given that a "ruling of the Court in
this case upon the question of riparian proprietorship would have been
very desirable." Rasch ended by noting that "[a] number of intricate and
important questions are involved" in the appeal, which would "likewise
be decisive of another case of like character" pending about the use of
the waters on the Blackfeet reservation.[4]

Rasch remained loyal to his theories, subsequently arguing all of
these propositions in the brief he filed in the Court of Appeals later in
1905 in response to the irrigators' arguments on appeal challenging
Judge Hunt's decision. Rasch collapsed the first and fourth propositions
into the first argument or section of his brief. In this part he emphasized
that the waters of Milk River that were part of and needed upon the
Indian reservation never became public waters subject to appropriation
by any person under state or federal laws. Nothing could destroy the
right of the United States to the continued flow of these waters as
necessary for the beneficial uses of the government property. In the
second section of the brief Rasch focused on "the rights of the
Government as a riparian proprietor," based largely on a discussion of
Montana state law intertwined with federal and other state sources and
emphasizing particularly why the lands of the United States were
especially likely to retain riparian rights. The third section of Rasch's

appellate brief was the treaty rights argument. Rasch used the rest of his brief to analyze and rebut cases and arguments relied on by the appellants, repeating themes and legal arguments from the first three sections and directing most of his rebuttal efforts at the Ninth Circuit's 1897 decision of *Krall v. United States,* discussed above.[5]

Rasch's news about the Fort Belknap litigation and Judge Hunt's decision reached Washington not long after the United States had intervened in the lawsuit Kansas had filed against Colorado in the Supreme Court over rights to the water in the Arkansas River, which originated in Colorado and flowed into Kansas. Kansas had sued to stop Colorado from allowing its appropriating irrigators to diminish the flow of the Arkansas to the detriment of Kansas farmers. Kansas argued among other things that upstream appropriations could not legally undermine the common law riparian rights of downstream landowners in a different state along this interstate river. Horrified at the idea that the Supreme Court might approve of the application of the riparian doctrine to a critical western interstate water dispute affecting irrigation, Reclamation Service officials saw the *Kansas v. Colorado* case as of the highest importance to the success of the Reclamation Act. A triangle of Reclamation officials, Interior Department solicitors, and Justice Department attorneys who focused on Reclamation affairs urged the United States to intervene in *Kansas v. Colorado* and directed the government's arguments in that case, which included the argument that riparian rights had been extinguished by federal and state law in the West.[6]

Imagine their surprise then when they learned that a Department of Justice subordinate was asserting riparian rights on behalf of the United States and the Indians in Montana, against public-land settlers irrigating under the prior appropriation doctrine, in a basin where the Reclamation Service was attempting to develop a Reclamation project— and winning! That the United States was not winning on the basis of the riparian doctrine they seemed not to notice, or perhaps they did not care. It is not clear in what ways the Reclamation officials became aware of the government's position in the *Winters* case (I do not know how widely Rasch's letter to the attorney general circulated), but one way must have been via a Justice Department memorandum explaining the litigation that circulated among the relevant government bureaus near the end of 1905 and ended up in the legal files of the Reclamation Service. This memorandum followed almost word-for-word Rasch's August 28 letter to the attorney general, including, of course, the comment that "the U.S. Attorney, in his representation of the matter, relied strongly upon the *riparian rights* of the Government, which he considered his strongest ground."[7]

This news, combined with the news that the U.S. attorney in Washington might argue for riparian water rights on behalf of the Yakima reservation, prompted Morris Bien of the Reclamation Service to circulate a scathing, three-paragraph memorandum on December 8, 1905, that he titled "Conflicting attitude [of the] Dept. [of] Justice on Irrigation matters":

> In cases involving the water rights for *Indian reservations* in Montana and Washington the United States attorneys are presenting their cases upon the basis of the doctrine of riparian rights, which is *antagonistic* to the *possibilities* of *irrigation development,* both private and national. The cases relate to the Fort Belknap Indian Reservation, Montana (Winters v. U.S.) and the Yakima Indian Reservation, Washington.
>
> At the same time the United States is intervening in the suit of the State of Kansas against the State of Colorado, claiming that the doctrine of riparian rights does not apply to the Western lands.
>
> While there may be some slight basis for a distinction in the case of the claims made for Indian reservations, the conditions are such that the enforcement of these claims would overturn the foundations on which water rights for hundreds of thousands of acres of lands are based and may possibly react against the Indians by a claim of riparian rights on the part of owners lower down on the stream, which would leave the Indian suit, if won on that basis, a barren victory.[8]

Regarding Bien's reference to the Yakima situation, the water conflict at the Yakima reservation is a long and complex story. For the purposes of understanding Bien's memorandum and the responses here, it is sufficient to know that two irrigation companies filed suit in Washington state court in 1905 against the Yakima reservation superintendent and employees, asking for an injunction to prevent reservation officials from taking water from the Yakima River above the intakes of the two companies. The U.S. attorney in Washington, in consultation with the attorney general's office, was trying to figure out how to respond, and especially how to get the case to federal court. As indicated by communications to and from the attorney general's office, this U.S. attorney also knew by this time that he could not prevail on the facts in what had been until then a prior appropriation contest, at least not against one of the companies. He also knew that the attorney general had instructed him to take "all steps necessary to protect the Government's interests in the matter," and that the state law of Washington had preserved the riparian doctrine to a significant degree, thus making a common law riparian claim on behalf of the reservation a likely approach to take along with or in combination with a treaty rights and a *Rio Grande*–type federal power argument. As of December 1905 the Department of Justice did not know what steps the U.S. attorney had actually taken in the litigation, and in truth he had as yet done little to assert these theories. But Bien obviously knew of the interest in pursuing riparian claims to defend the interests of the Yakima reservation.[9]

Bien's memorandum created a disturbance that quickly reached all the way to the White House, as three days later, on December 11, President Theodore Roosevelt referred a copy of it to Attorney General Moody and asked for an explanation.[10] Moody passed the request on to the solicitor general, Henry Hoyt, for a report, and he in turn asked assistants in the department for responses to Bien's memorandum. An unnamed assistant attorney general (initials D.D.C.) who had some responsibility for Indian cases responded quickly, although hardly persuasively. His memorandum acknowledged that U.S. Attorney Rasch "urged upon the Court" in the Fort Belknap case the doctrine of riparian rights, giving the impression that this was the primary legal issue involved in that case by not even mentioning the treaty rights theories or the nature of the court's decision, except for a brief and general reference to protecting treaty rights at the end of the memorandum. And this attorney admitted that Rasch's approach was "not contemplated by this Department's instructions." Yet he concluded that Rasch's action was "in full accord with the position the Department had taken in dealing with violations of the rights of the Indians of whatever sort" whenever requested to do so by the Indian Office, "which has been to use for the protection of such rights all means properly at the Government's disposal." The memorandum then described the Yakima situation as noted above, and disclaimed any knowledge of the Department's position in the *Kansas v. Colorado* case. This memorandum closed with a sincere but less than solid statement of support for the department's approach to the Indian water cases:

> The fact that the Government in one State bases its claim on riparian rights and in another denies the application of that doctrine does not necessarily convict of inconsistency. It is the laws of the respective States which govern [ignoring of course that the *Kansas v. Colorado* case was in the Supreme Court and the government was arguing for a rule of more general application across the West]; and some of the

western States have gone further in modifying the common law
doctrine of riparian rights than others.

However, it is doubtless true that the doctrine of riparian rights
is antagonistic to the possibilities of irrigation development. If, therefore, everything else is to give way to the great irrigation work in
which the Government is now engaged, further contention on the
basis of riparian rights may well cease. But I believe that wherever
the doctrine of riparian rights can be successfully involved on behalf
of the Indians—especially under their treaties—it should be done.[11]

Compare this to the views of Assistant Attorney General Frank L.
Campbell, assigned to the Interior Department to work on Reclamation
matters and one of the government's principal lawyers in the *Kansas v.
Colorado* case. Campbell also responded to the Solicitor General, with a
far more forceful pitch for the Reclamation view of things. He began by
describing Kansas's arguments for riparian rights in the Arkansas River
litigation (and Colorado's position), and then the federal government's
response, emphasizing the extent of the government's attack on the
riparian rights doctrine:

> The position of the Government mainly is that the doctrine of
> riparian rights is inapplicable to the conditions prevailing in the entire
> arid region of the United States; that such doctrine has been abrogated
> by usage and by custom, by Congressional, State and Territorial legis-
> lation, and by decisions of the Federal, State and Territorial Courts;
> that in the arid region water may be taken from streams state and
> inter-state, and applied to the reclamation and irrigation of arid lands,
> and that he who is prior in time of appropriation has prior rights to
> the waters so appropriated.[12]

After further lengthy discussions of all the parties' positions in the
litigation, Campbell described why he and others of the same mind saw
this as so important, in paradigmatic words that would later be echoed
by many in the West who (well after the death of the riparian rights
menace) contended that the reserved rights doctrine undermined the
prior appropriation system and that life without the prior appropriation
system would be unlivably poor:

> The evidence offered by the Government in the above case, and
> which was given by Senators and Representatives, officers of the
> Reclamation Service and officers of the Agricultural Department,
> which evidence has not been and cannot be disputed to the effect that
> practically all of the wealth now existing in the arid region was

created by and is dependent upon the doctrine of the appropriation of waters of streams and the application of the same to the cultivation of lands; that should the doctrine of riparian rights be now established in said arid region, further development would cease, the Reclamation Act would become inoperative, existing wealth be destroyed and the country practically become depopulated.[13]

Campbell then emphasized how even W. H. Code, the chief engineer for the Indian irrigation efforts in the Indian Office, testified on behalf of the government's position in *Kansas v. Colorado,* describing the government's effort to make western Indians self-supporting on their reservations through irrigated farming. Code supposedly testified that if the riparian doctrine invoked by Kansas were to prevail "a stop would be put to all development and such has been made will become of no value and the West will go back to desert and make the Indians dependent upon the Government for support." Campbell also gratuitously added his opinion that the state statutes and courts of Montana did not recognize riparian rights and that while this was unfortunately not true in Washington, state officials were aware of the threat to development and had legislation pending to "get the laws in shape so that the reclamation act can be enforced in that state." Campbell concluded by re-emphasizing that one of the goals pursued by the United States before the Supreme Court was to have that Court declare that riparian rights did not prevail in any arid region. Any contrary contention or doctrine invoked in any other, lesser lawsuit could not be consistent with this position and should not survive.[14]

It would seem from these two statements by the two assistant attorneys general that Morris Bien was right to identify a conflicting attitude in the Justice Department on water rights issues, although admittedly the lawyers in the central office could mount only a lukewarm defense of their subordinates' positions in the Indian cases, positions that were obvious and appealing at the point of litigation. But Solicitor General Hoyt chose not to see the conflict at the Department of Justice as significant, reconciled the two positions as best he could, and suggested that the conflict, if any, resided in the Interior Department and not the Justice Department. He did this in a December 15 draft of a letter from the attorney general to the president. Hoyt drew from the two memoranda of his subordinates to describe the positions of the government in the Montana and Washington Indian water rights cases and in the *Kansas v. Colorado* litigation, although he downplayed the riparian rights attack in the latter and emphasized instead that "[t]he real contention of the Government in that case is that under the general national reclamation act the law is a composite thing; there must be a fair adjustment and distribution between conflicting claims; the national law must be a factor in the equation, and the Federal Government must be heard." Hoyt reconciled the apparent conflicts in a general way by rephrasing the argument from the first memorandum, that because the "whole law of waters is undergoing modification at present, and the evolution is slow," the fact that the government bases a claim for riparian rights in one forum and not another is not an inconsistency, just an indication of the uneven evolution of the law in the two forums. The solicitor general did agree that "the doctrine of riparian rights is antagonistic to the possibilities of irrigation development," and he repeated the concession that if everything must give way to the government's "great irrigation work . . . further contention on the basis of riparian rights may well cease." And yet he believed that "wherever that doctrine can be successfully invoked in behalf of the Indians, especially under their treaties, this should be done." Solicitor General Hoyt presented his main argument for ignoring the conflict, however, in his discussion of the *Winters* litigation itself, taking words from the assistant's memorandum but beefing up the justification by recognizing the unusual source of the Indians' rights:

> [T]he development of the case has made it necessary to invoke the doctrine of riparian rights in the Indian behalf. This is, we think, justified notwithstanding the Government's position in water controversies in other localities. The Indian case is exceptional and their rights antedate modern evolution in the law of waters. The historical attitude of the Department in dealing with violations of the rights of Indians of whatever sort has been to use for their protection of such rights all means proper at the Government's disposal. We have acted in all such matters in pursuance at the request of the Indian Department, as was the case here. I am of the opinion that it was necessary and proper for the Government, in defending Indian rights within the comparatively narrow field of reservation lands, to invoke the doctrine of riparian rights, although elsewhere the Government is recognizing recent modifications of that doctrine.[15]

Hoyt did include a copy of the assistants' memoranda, drawing attention to the fact that Campbell "suggested that the rule of riparian rights ought not to be applied even to the Indian reservations." And it was at this concluding point in the draft of the letter that Hoyt suggested that if an inconsistency existed, "it seems to rest with the

Interior Department," home to the antagonistic needs of the Indian Office and the Reclamation Service. And Hoyt made it very clear that he at least did not intend to change the approach in the Indian cases, or to abandon the responsibility of pursuing the Indian clients' legal interests to the utmost allowed by the law, no matter what the Reclamation officials threatened, by drafting for the attorney general this closing vow:

> [U]ntil the Secretary of the Interior in his supervision of Indian affairs advises me that from his administrative knowledge and judg-ment he has reached the conclusion that the Indians themselves will be benefitted by the abandonment of the contentions in their behalf based on the doctrine of riparian rights, I shall continue to direct the pending litigation above referred to affecting Indian reservations in accordance with the policy heretofore pursued.[16]

Attorney General Moody had the solicitor general's draft letter retyped as a report to the attorney general and passed it on to the president on December 18 headed by a note indicating this was the Justice Department's response to the president's request for an explana-tion. For an unspecified reason the attorney general chopped off the closing reference to inconsistency in the Interior Department and the vow to continue this approach to the Indian water rights litigation until reigned in by the Interior Department. There is no indication (then or later), however, that the attorney general disagreed with this attitude, and there is a clear indication from subsequent events that the Reclama-tion Service got the message: take the problem to the secretary of the interior.[17]

Reclamation proponents responded in two ways to the December 18 letter from the attorney general to the president. In a frontal attack, within two days Morris Bien produced and circulated a brief but even more impassioned, nasty, and demanding rebuttal, perhaps over-reaching in his description of horribles:

> Referring to the statement of the Attorney-General dated December 18, 1905, it appears that to obtain for the Indians rights greater than could be claimed by any white man, the government has been placed in the position of using every available means to accomplish its immediate ends, ignoring broad general principles of policy necessary for the development of the entire arid region.
>
> The attitude of Assistant-Attorney-General Campbell, that the doctrine of riparian rights involves practically the sacrifice of millions

of acres of improved lands and thousands of homes, indicates the
principle on which the government should proceed in litigation concerning irrigation matters.

The Indian is not debarred from using the same means of
obtaining water that are open to the white man. In both cases an
ample water supply is obtainable at comparatively small expenditure.
To ignore such opportunities and demand the destruction of irrigation in two well developed, fertile valleys in the interests of a small
number of Indians, reversing the policy of general development of
the arid region, seems inconsistent and beneath the dignity of a great
government.

The Government has filed an extensive brief with the Circuit
Court of Appeals in the Montana case (U.S. v. Winters, et al.), endeavoring to sustain the doctrine of riparian rights. If this brief can now
be withdrawn, the irrigation policy established by the Reclamation
Act and by the attitude of the government in the Kansas v. Colorado
case, should be followed and the rights of the Indians based on prior
appropriation.

The President in his message of December, 1901, announced the
broad policy: "In the arid states the only right to water which should
be recognized is that of use," and urged that states still adhering to
the doctrine of riparian rights should adopt the doctrine of use.
Considering all that is at stake in the future development of the
country, the United States should lead toward a broad, wise policy
rather than take a backward step to secure a minor advantage.[18]

In a second front, Reclamation proponents realized what Solicitor
General Hoyt had acknowledged—that the key might lay in the hands
of the secretary of the interior, who could stop the Justice Department
from "destroying" the irrigation work of the government by requesting,
in his supervision of Indian affairs, that the Indian Office personnel and
their Justice Department attorneys cease asserting riparian rights on
behalf of Indian reservations. Reclamation proponents tried but could
not quite convince the president to order the secretary of the interior to
act in a certain way. They did, however, persuade the president, on
December 22, 1905, to turn his attention from the attorney general and
demand an explanation from the secretary of the interior, Ethan
Hitchcock.[19]

Secretary Hitchcock responded to the president on January 5, 1906,
and effectively put an end to the demands to squash Rasch's activities in
the *Winters* litigation. The letter was a subtle masterpiece (and appears

to have been written by lawyers in the Department of the Interior),
describing for ten pages without comment the views of all the previous
writers and the government's positions in the different lawsuits, noting
more prominently than others had the treaty rights basis for the federal
court's ruling in the Fort Belknap case, and then concluding in a way
that agreed with all these efforts and reconciled them in a commonsense
manner: The secretary agreed that the *Kansas v. Colorado* case "involves
all of the vital questions affecting the reclamation and irrigation of the
arid land," and upon its result "depends the successful administration of
the Reclamation Act and the future welfare of the entire arid region."
He also agreed that should the Supreme Court approve of the application of the doctrine of riparian rights in the arid lands, not only would
the policy of the government as established in the Reclamation Act be
defeated, but also "the development of the entire arid West [would] be
materially retarded, if not entirely destroyed." Looking just at Montana
and Washington, if riparian rights continued to exist in some form in
those states "it [would] not be possible to successfully administer the
Reclamation Act in said States." Thus the Interior Department agreed
that the federal government's policy should continue to be to do "all in
its power" to have abrogated the riparian doctrine in the west "and to
have adopted by the proper tribunals a uniform rule applicable alike to
each State and Territory in the arid region . . .—the doctrine of prior
appropriation of waters and the application of the same to beneficial use."

   This did not sound too promising for the U.S. attorneys' positions
in the Fort Belknap and Yakima cases, but the secretary rescued the
Indian water rights position by noting a couple of factors that complicated matters: First, it was not clear that the Supreme Court had the
power, in the *Kansas v. Colorado* case, to establish a general rule for the
use of water for irrigation that would apply in all the western states and
territories, unilaterally preventing any state or territory from using the
riparian doctrine. And second, until something changed either as a
general rule or in each specific state, the law in Montana and
Washington did appear to allow for claims for riparian rights to a
certain extent. That being so, "[u]ntil the doctrine which now seems to
prevail in those States is abrogated or modified, this Department knows
of no good reason why the same should not be invoked therein for the
benefit of Indians as well as for white men." Especially because these
were not claims that presented questions of first impression for the
courts in those states, but instead built on existing decisions, "this Department does not regard it as improper for the Government to invoke for
the protection of the Indians the law as announced by the highest courts

therein. So long as the present doctrine prevails in Montana and Washington, there would seem to be no good reason why the Indians should be excepted from its advantages, if any advantages it has."[20]

Secretary Hitchcock's letter ended the debate, at least for the moment, as the Reclamation proponents had failed at persuading either the attorney general or the secretary of the interior to abandon the course set in the Indian water rights litigation. Without interference Rasch argued the case before the Court of Appeals in San Francisco. And this particular controversy effectively ended with the decision of the Court of Appeals on February 5, 1906, to affirm Judge Hunt's injunction order on the same principles of treaty rights.[21] Written by Thomas Hawley, a federal district judge in Nevada sitting on an appellate panel by designation, and joined by the circuit's two most prominent judges, William Gilbert and Erskine Ross,[22] the appellate court opinion began by stating that the "first, and in our opinion the most important question" to be answered was the "true interpretation" of the "treaty" of May 1, 1888. Hawley used all but the last two pages of the opinion to discuss the treaty and its legal implications for water. This included a lengthy discussion of the treaty, its manifest purposes, the underlying circumstances of trying to establish an agricultural and pastoral life on this reservation land, how the Indians themselves might have understood this treaty, the fact that the reservation is explicitly defined to include part of the channel of the Milk River within its boundaries, and the standard principles for interpreting treaties from *Winans* and *Jones v. Meehan* and other Supreme Court cases. The Court of Appeals concluded with this sense of how explicit the reservation of water was under the terms of the treaty:

> The Indians in their untutored and uneducated minds might not have known the exact meaning of the word "irrigation" had it been used in the treaty, but in their wild, and to some extent uncivilized, condition, they knew the use of forests, of lands, and of water. If they were to graze cattle and cultivate soil, they knew it could not be done successfully without the use of water. They knew, as well as the officers of the government, where the boundaries of the reservation were, and that their rights, under the terms of the treaty, extended to the middle of the channel of Milk river, and believed they had as much right to the water as to the land included in the boundaries for their permanent homes for the uses and purposes of the agreement made with the government. The signing of the treaty was not an idle

ceremony. The absence of the words "to irrigate their lands" did not abrogate and destroy their rights as guaranteed by the terms of the treaty. We are of the opinion that it was the intention of the treaty to reserve sufficient waters of the Milk river, as was said by the court below, "to insure to the Indians the means wherewith to irrigate their farms," and that it was understood by the respective parties to the treaty at the time it was signed.[23]

Weaving in other propositions from Rasch's brief, the Court of Appeals noted that once it determined the proper interpretation of the treaty, this necessarily countered the defendants' argument that the Desert Land Act of 1877 and other federal statutes authorized them, under the state law of Montana, to appropriate the waters of Milk River and secure a vested right to the water. Following a line of reasoning common to treatises and court decisions, and made use of by Rasch, the court noted that the doctrine of appropriation established by these statutes applied only to the open public lands and waters, citing *Smith v. Denniff* and *Cruse v. McCauley* from the state and federal courts in Montana as well as other federal cases and treatises. The reserved lands and waters of the Indians were not open public domain. The rights established by appropriation could not affect these reserved rights, as they were made with notice of and subject to, as specified in the statutes themselves, the "existing rights" reserved by the government and the Indians in the treaties. The Court of Appeals finished this discussion by noting, with quotations from and citations to the *Rio Grande* and *Gutierres* cases, that the state statutes authorizing appropriation rights on the public domain and the federal statutes recognizing those rights could not "destroy the right of the United States, as the owner of lands bordering on a stream, to the continued flow of the waters, so far at least as may be necessary for the beneficial uses of the government property."[24] And finally, as if purposefully desiring to ease the worried mind of Morris Bien, the appellate court stated that the views it expressed were conclusive on the questions presented, and thus it was "unnecessary for us to review the statutes and decisions of the courts of Montana upon the questions pertaining to the rights of appropriation as distinguished from the rules of the common law as to riparian rights."[25]

The Department of Justice quickly notified President Roosevelt (just one day after the decision) of the appellate court victory in the Fort Belknap case and now emphasized (as it had not done before) that the basis for the decision was treaty rights and *not* the riparian doctrine. The secretary of the interior conveyed to the attorney general and, through him, to U.S. Attorney Rasch, "its high appreciation for the able manner in which he has conducted this litigation to success." As the *Winters* defendants carried the case to the Supreme Court, the relationship of Indian treaties to the prior appropriation rights of public-land settlers became the critical issue—"of the greatest importance" anywhere there is a water conflict or possible conflict between non-Indian settlers and Indians, according to the commissioner of Indian affairs and the secretary of interior. The Reclamation Service's worries about riparian rights, and the Service's resultant efforts to stymie the government's pursuit of the *Winters* litigation, disappeared. Nothing illustrates this turnaround more than the statement in early 1907 by the attorney general that Assistant Attorney General Campbell now assured him that because the treaty question was determinative, the *Winters* case at the Supreme Court "does not antagonize our position in Kansas v. Colorado."[26]

What to make of this odd tempest, this temper tantrum on the part of the Reclamation proponents? The controversy, as intense and high-level as it was, was in one sense largely irrelevant, as Reclamation's fears about the effect of the *Winters* litigation on the riparian doctrine turned out to be irrelevant to the course of that litigation. An ironic touch came with the Supreme Court's decision in *Kansas v. Colorado* in 1907, when the Court flatly rejected the federal government's propositions. The *Kansas v. Colorado* case is best known, of course, for being the origin of the Supreme Court's concept of "equitable apportionment" of interstate waters. (Without going into any detail, what this meant was that to resolve the dispute between the two states over the waters of the interstate stream, the Court did not prescribe a particular allocation law or mechanism, or accept the idea that one state could take full control of the waters. Instead, the Court began the practice of working with the factual and legal circumstances of a particular conflict to arrive at an allocation approach that ensured that the states had an essentially equal opportunity to benefit from the waters of the stream.) The Supreme Court rejected the federal government's invitation to declare riparian rights extinguished in the arid West, finding this to be an issue for each individual state to decide but also finding that the existence or nonexistence of riparian rights in a state would not be a determinative factor in the equitable allocation of an interstate stream between states. In another big blow, the Court also dismissed the federal government's assertion that the United States had a type of plenary or general national control over the allocation of waters in interstate streams in the West whenever it felt like exercising that control, which the government argued had to exist to allow the federal government to effectuate fully the Reclamation Act's purpose of reclaiming the arid public lands. This was primarily an attempt by the federal government to stretch the relatively limited *Rio Grande* dicta into a pervasive control structure it could not sustain. Justice Brewer, who also wrote the *Rio Grande* decision, described the *Rio Grande* dicta as narrowly as possible, and he appeared to limit the power of the federal government regarding waters in the West to little beyond preserving navigability and taking limited steps to make rules and regulations regarding the public lands. The decision caused much agony within the Reclamation Service and its allies, who had not realized how good they had it when all they had to worry about was the unlikely specter of the riparian doctrine from the Indian water rights litigation.[27] The *Kansas v. Colorado* decision generated a flood of analyses, letters, law review articles, and the like that continued to preoccupy the water community well after the Supreme Court released its decision in *Winters* in 1908, which may partly explain why the reaction to the *Winters* decision from the general legal, engineering, and policy community concerned about water was so muted.[28]

Because the *Kansas v. Colorado* decision took such a limited view of the *Rio Grande* dicta and of the authority of the federal government over water in the West, the last irony is that the Supreme Court's *Winters* decision a year later essentially salvaged the *Rio Grande* dicta. *Winters* illustrated what more there really could be to federal authority over water in the West, if tied to specific, reserved federal (or Indian) lands and not floated as a general superproposition, as it was in *Kansas v. Colorado*.[29] The water law treatise writers and the very few law review authors that analyzed the *Winters* decision understood how it fit into this larger role, for good or bad, depending on their view of federal intervention in western water issues. Some of them clearly understood how the *Winters* decision could be seen as an important contrast with or response to that aspect of the *Kansas v. Colorado* decision. More interesting, federal lawyers trying to assert or protect federal rights to waters for Reclamation projects in the West eventually did learn to use *Winters* as one of the legal authorities that could justify a federal reservation of waters in watersheds identified for Reclamation projects, work that resulted in a general policy statement about federal uses of water without regard to state law by the attorney general in 1914.[30]

Thus one lesson in this episode is how much in transition water policy and water law was at the time and how quickly what looked to be a seminal issue became an irrelevant issue, even as some of the underlying concerns transmuted into different issues.[31] The episode also illustrates how the rather complicated local context and various interests at play could be abstracted (and misunderstood) into a simple black-and-white story to fit a larger national issue, a fate that would repeatedly obscure the specifics of Indian water rights in the future.

Yet another lesson was repeated in later episodes of the *Winters* doctrine, and it may be the most important lesson for the life of the doctrine. Looked at over the century, there is obvious truth in the contention that the federal government did much to bring about water development for the non-Indian West, mostly in terms of the amount of money made available, and much less to assist the Indians in making use of their reserved water rights. A frequent criticism of the federal government's handling of Indian water rights has been that the two federal agencies most responsible for assisting the tribes in securing, protecting, using, and implementing the *Winters* doctrine—the Departments of Interior and Justice—have been hopelessly in conflict over serving the needs of the Indians and serving the needs of non-Indian settlers and the Reclamation Service. Due to power disparities between non-Indians and Indians in the West, the departments generally resolved direct conflicts in Reclamation's favor and catered to Reclamation interests at the expense of Indians.[32] It did not happen that way in this first instance of conflict over *Winters*. Despite obvious conflicts in approach at the subordinate levels of the two departments, and despite intense efforts from Reclamation and its allies (at a time when Reclamation Service was new and highly favored in policy circles) to have the secretary of interior and attorney general order an end to nonappropriation arguments on behalf of the Indians, the secretary and the attorney general held firm and allowed the lawyers in *Winters* and at the Yakima reservation to pursue their cases as they thought best. This was not an isolated event. Over the following thirty years, Indian Affairs officials and Justice Department attorneys chose frequently (and often successfully) to use the *Winters* doctrine as a tool to establish and protect rights to water for Indians. They received the strong support of the higher-ups in the Justice and Interior Departments when doing so, even when political pressure to back off mounted from whatever source (often the states and local water users and their congressional allies, not Reclamation). Yet it was the ways that the government pursued Indian water rights claims, and especially the ways the money flowed, that prevented these efforts from bearing more fruit. This result is what makes the *Winters* doctrine story so complex.

CHAPTER 5

Back in the Milk River Valley, 1905–1907

Reclamation, Reservation Busting, and Sugar Beet Production

Back in the valley, the Court of Appeals' decision in February 1906 to affirm Judge Hunt's ruling made its way into the same set of dynamic relationships as before. Judge Hunt soon entered his final decree in the case, reconfirming and making perpetual the injunction. Hunt's decree referred only to a fixed amount of water—the defendants were enjoined from interfering with the flow of the Milk River "to the amount of five thousand inches" to be allowed to flow down to the reservation. The decree did not repeat anything of the legal basis underlying the injunction or say or infer anything about the more flexible notion of what a reserved right could mean in terms of a changing amount to match needs as these needs were better defined over time. This distinction probably would have meant little to the people at the time, given the common perception that the amount decreed essentially equaled the average natural flow of the Milk River during the irrigation season. But it set in place an official statement of the reservation's rights that would later lead the Reclamation Service, in control of the irrigation facilities in the valley, to view the Fort Belknap reserved right as quantified and fixed in that amount by adjudication. This is in contrast to what seemed to be understood by Judge Hunt and others in the valley as an interim snapshot of the amount of water that the Indians could put to use at that particular time, given the nature of their irrigation works, the amount of land ready for irrigation, the duty of water understood at the time, and so forth. The reserved rights would be left flexible and elastic, raising the possibility of better defining and increasing the amount of water reserved as more was learned about the size of the practical irrigable acreage of the reservation, what amount of water would be needed to irrigate that acreage, and even perhaps the ways in which the total flow of the Milk River might be managed by storage to increase the natural flow available for irrigation. Flexibility in the reserved rights seems to have been part of Judge Hunt's original decision, and the district and appellate court decisions in the contemporaneous and related *Conrad* case were explicit on this point. This flexibility became one of the defining principles of the reserved rights doctrine in general and one of the most threatening aspects to defenders of the prior appropriation system.

Certainly, William Logan understood the ruling in this way, noting later that the Fort Belknap Indians "have the prior water right to as much of the waters of Milk River as they can put to economical use." In his view the Indians were "not confined to any particular amount," although they would be "confined to its economical use." The Indians might never need more water, "but we still maintain the right to use more if it becomes necessary as our cultivated area along Milk River becomes larger." The valley's papers similarly understood Hunt's injunction in this way, and it was precisely this possibility that was so worrisome to the *Chinook Opinion*. The newspaper stated that in an ordinary year the river would be able to supply 5,000 inches to Fort Belknap and yet serve the upstream irrigators, but that was about it. "The worst feature of the decision is the possibility that an immense increase in that amount will be demanded after a while in the name of the Indians."[1]

The Chinook and Havre area irrigators and their allies in the Chinook and Havre newspapers continued to be angry about the court rulings and predicted the end of settlement in the valley. The irrigation defendants appealed Hunt's final decree back to the appellate court (that court reaffirmed its decision on October 1, 1906, in a one-page opinion), appealed the appellate decisions to the Supreme Court (not argued until October 1907 and not decided until January 1908), published stories and editorials of criticism and outrage, petitioned the Montana congressional delegation to do something to negate the decision, planned a delegation to Washington, and demanded an immediate meeting of the valleywide irrigation association to protest the decision, a meeting at which, according to the *Milk River Valley News* in Harlem, "outside of appointing a few committees nothing else was done except adjourn to meet at a later date."[2]

Their appeals proved to be ineffectual—the Supreme Court eventually ruled against them, and Congress never acted to extinguish the decisions recognizing Indian reserved water rights. But Superintendent Logan was sufficiently worried at the time to warn the commissioner of Indian affairs (in a letter in which he called himself "the most unpopular Indian in the country" and said he was apt to "lose my scalp in the mix-up") and appeal to the commissioner for political protection. He also wrote to Rasch to thank him for his efforts, adding that "1300 Indians wish to express their thanks," too, and to assure Rasch that "as soon as they attain the franchise, any time you come up for office you can depend on their undivided support." What the Indians at Fort Belknap really knew about the decision and how they felt I have not yet been able to discover—certainly no one in the non-Indian community thought it an important point to consider, although I assume there was some sort of communication or dialog on the water rights litigation between Logan and other agency personnel and at least the reservation leaders. Finally, further illustrating the relationship to the Milk River Reclamation project, Logan wrote to the Reclamation field supervisor Babb:

> Telegram this date informing me that the Court of Appeals has affirmed the Milk River case. WE OWN THE WATER. I suppose the next move of my Chinook friends will be to take the case to the Supreme Court. That is, they will do that if they are foolish. If they are wise men, they will sign up with the U.S. Reclamation Service as fast as possible, and acquire water rights that way.[3]

Newspapers elsewhere in the valley reported the appellate decision in a factual and evenhanded or implicitly sympathetic way. All that the *North Montana Review* in Glasgow found interesting enough to comment on was that U.S. Attorney Rasch "was in a particularly happy frame of mind" upon hearing of the appellate court decision. As noted above, when the *Milk River Valley News* in Harlem reported on the meeting called in Chinook to protest the decision, the paper simply noted the fact without comment, stated the names of local Harlem men who attended, and dismissed the effort by emphasizing that the meeting ended without action. These lower valley newspapers focused far more of their attention on the status of the Reclamation project, with relevant and sometimes lengthy stories in virtually every edition, compared to essentially one-time stories or brief comments reporting the appellate decision in the *Winters* case. The Reclamation developments of most interest around the time of the 1906 appellate decisions in the *Winters* case were the cheering news that the Reclamation Service had begun work on one part of the headwaters portion of the project (the canal between the Saint Mary and Milk Rivers), news that served to increase the already relentless boosterism of the valley press as to the agricultural potential of the valley and the golden future ahead. But these optimistic stories were overshadowed by stories of despair and anger and of resolutions and delegations protesting a lack of progress on many projects and issues: the basinwide water rights adjudication suit; Reclamation's delay in beginning the other part of the headwaters portion of the project, the storage reservoir; developing problems with Canada; and the government's unwillingness to commit to or begin the diversion and distribution portions of the project in the valley until the headwaters and Canadian problems were resolved in order to guarantee that there would be a sufficient volume of water to make constructing the distribution system worthwhile.[4]

Thus as the *Winters* litigation wound its way through the courts beyond the original ruling in 1905, through the appellate court decisions in 1906, and then through two years before the Supreme Court to its decision in 1908, the case was enmeshed in a number of related and interwoven developments and incidents that put the litigation into a complicated local and national context. One way to understand this set of relationships is to examine more closely a particular set of related developments in the Milk River valley from late 1905 through 1908, during the time the reserved rights decisions moved from one level of the court to the next, always with the same result:

- Logan's continuing struggle to implement and enforce the court's ruling and force the upstream irrigators to leave water in the river for diversion at the reservation;
- an unsuccessful effort to strip most of the irrigable land along the Milk River from the Fort Belknap reservation and open it to non-Indian settlement, a desire already present in the valley which the upriver irrigators latched onto as a vehicle to undo the Fort Belknap water rights decisions;
- an alternative effort by Logan and others to develop sugar beet production on the reservation by leasing irrigable reservation land for sugar beet cultivation and a sugar refinery, a scheme that could capitalize on the water rights;
- the ongoing developments of the Reclamation project, and the way in which the water rights decisions continued to intersect with that effort; and
- the tortured but ultimately successful effort in Congress to force allotments on the Blackfeet reservation, directly

involving and affecting the reserved right decisions in
Winters and *Conrad*.

These developments are described in this and the next chapter.

IMPLEMENTING THE *WINTERS* RULING

The water problems of 1905 returned in the spring of 1906. The
drought situation was not quite as bad as the year before, but bad
enough. The river levels early in the spring were such that reservation
irrigation personnel believed they needed nearly all what natural flow
there was to implement their water rights and irrigate the available
acreage. By early April Logan was writing to the commissioner of
Indian affairs that he had just learned that "whites are taking the water
out above the Reservation." Logan sent letters to the Chinook area ditch
and cattle companies demanding that they shut their gates until at least
5,000 inches were flowing at the reservation, as decreed by the courts,
and threatening court action if they did not comply. He sent a more
pleasant letter to the Harlem Ditch Company requesting that they also
close their gates. Logan told the commissioner that he had sent reservation employees to check to see if the upstream irrigators would comply
with his demands and, if not successful, that he was heading for Helena
that night to get Rasch to swear out a contempt citation and to ask the
court to send a federal marshal to enforce the orders. Logan's threats
seemed to be successful this time, as reservation employees noted water
beginning to run in the ditch just two days later, on April 7.[5]

False relief—beginning a pattern of difficult enforcement, of constant
defiance and grudging compliance. By April 16, Logan again wrote to
the commissioner that "[f]or several days we have been in a constant
struggle to keep the water flowing down to our ditch." The problem of
enforcing an unwelcome water right so outside of the usual state water
rights framework (which were hard enough to enforce) was obvious: "I
have made trips and sent others up the river to the different ditch companies asking them to close down their headgates and allow the water
to flow down to us. This at the time they would do, but in a very few
hours would open up, and again shut off the water, making it necessary
to make another trip and another request to close down."[6] Thus Logan
asked the commissioner to request of the Justice Department that a
marshal be stationed at the reservation during the irrigation season to
enforce their water rights. Logan also noted that ditch companies that

had not been made defendants in the original litigation, and thus were not under the court's injunction order, were refusing to acknowledge the paramount water rights of the reservation. Thus Logan also requested that the attorney general be asked to authorize the U.S. attorney to bring injunction proceedings against three of these ditch companies, the Belknap and Paradise companies of Chinook *and* the Harlem Ditch Company (so much for the suspicion of some that the lawsuit was really for the benefit of this company). Logan wanted to get all of the ditch companies above the reservation under the injunction "and all prevented from using water until such times as we have finished irrigating."[7]

What is more important is that Logan got out of this problem because of Reclamation intervention in the valley, not further Justice Department and judicial intervention. This is because Cyrus Babb, the resident Reclamation Service official, stepped in to try to mediate this specific conflict, recognizing that it interfered with Reclamation's goal of getting the valley's irrigators to work together in general to resolve water rights issues. Using his reputation for technical expertise, he apparently got Logan and everyone else to agree that the river was too short of water at this time to fulfill all 5,000 inches of the reservation's rights. He thus convinced Logan to accept that for the time being the goal would be to try to get 2,500 inches into the reservation's ditch, and got everyone to agree to rely on Babb and his Reclamation employees to recommend a water diversion schedule that would try to achieve this 2,500-inch goal, then allow upriver irrigators to divert water whenever more was available. Logan hailed Babb's resolution of the conflict "in so harmonious a fashion," noting that "I am sure that with my combative disposition I could not have come within a mile of making as good an agreement." He noted to A. H. Reser of Chinook and Thomas Everett of Harlem his feeling that "everything was arranged satisfactorily." And he adroitly used this in-season management accord and its deference to Babb and Reclamation as an impartial shield he could wield with kind words and a gracious manner rather than his usual combativeness. Thus when Reser of Chinook wrote toward the end of April 1906 to ask Logan to allow water-short Chinook irrigators to have more water, Logan responded that while he personally would be disposed to help out,

> I am at present in a most awkward position. We have all practically agreed to leave our troubles for the summer in the hands of Mr. Babb of the Reclamation Service. He [is] to be our guide, friend and philosopher, moreover the target that we can all cuss at. At the

present time we have very little water in our ditch and need more badly, therefore while my heart inclines to you, and I have every desire to grant your wish to divert a part of the water that belong to us I cannot see how I can do it. In the first place, we need the water, in the second, I would be butting in on Mr. Babb's prerogatives and doing away with the melancholy pleasure of cussing at Babb in case the water fails to come down.[8]

Once enough water had come into the ditch for a good flood of the reservation's fields, however, Logan was happy not to wait for Babb to act and instead informed the upstream ranchers directly that they could begin taking water until further notice from him.[9]

Conflict over implementation of the Fort Belknap water rights never did cease in this period, nor did the patterns of that conflict change much. Harmony lasted hardly a month in this instance. By mid-May Logan was in despair that it "doesn't look very much like the agreement, as outlined by Mr. Babb to me as having been made, is going to be lived up to." Yet Logan's unhappiness over continued interference in the flow was more than matched by the uproar in Chinook over the way in which implementing Judge Hunt's ruling had affected their irrigation that year. The Chinook irrigators again demanded a meeting of the valleywide irrigation association to vent their unhappiness, and to the alarm of Babb and many in the valley, made it clear that cooperation over the Reclamation project was in jeopardy. Logan strongly recommended that Babb attend the meeting to protect Reclamation's interests, for "I understand the Chinookers are going to drag the Reclamation Service to a standstill, and furthermore that I am going to come in for a share of the dragging myself. They are claiming now that the we stand in together, and that my suit was brought in the interest of the Reclamation Service to force the people of Chinook into signing up with your Department."[10] Also, the upstream ditch companies made plans to send a committee to Washington to inform officials of their difficulties with the decisions in favor of the Indians and to press for some sort of action to negate or undo those decisions. They hoped at the association meeting to persuade others in the valley to join their cause, especially as they had decided that a promising if indirect vehicle for undoing the court decisions might be a proposal to eliminate the source of the problem— to remove the irrigable lands from the reservation, something that already interested people downstream of Chinook and Havre.[11]

Something unexpected happened, however, between the mid-May problems and plans for the meeting and the June 6 meeting in Chinook—

rain, lots of rain. Heavy rain hit in late May, followed a few days later by what Logan called the worst rainstorm in Montana in thirty years. Writing in mid-June, Logan reported that the river "over whose waters we have been fighting" had been running bank full for nearly three weeks. Logan described for the commissioner of Indian affairs an extensive amount of damage to the reservation's irrigation facilities for which he was going to need funds for repair. And he closed by noting how the rain had resolved that year's in-season conflicts: "I do not think that it will be necessary for us to take any further action against the water users above us on Milk River, for now it is not a question of wanting water, but more a question of how to get rid of water."[12]

The climatic intervention (which continued in 1907—heavy snows and a good early runoff pattern again raised more flood than drought problems[13]) did not change the Chinook irrigators' anger over the Indian water rights decision or their determination to do something about it. But the rain must have taken some of the bite out of their plight. In any event, as usual the rest of the valley's irrigators were politely attentive to this issue at the June 6, 1906, association meeting and then quickly shifted the focus of the meeting to the ongoing problems with the Reclamation project. The association did vote to send a delegation to Washington, but, at least according to the Harlem paper (which was never interested in denouncing the Indian decisions anyway), the only matters officially charged to the delegation by the association and the only matters discussed by the delegation in Washington were (1) the need for a direct appropriation to construct the storage project on the headwaters of the Milk, the Chain Lakes reservoir, and the distribution system in the valley itself (what was called the Dodson Dam and ditches) as the association had become unhappily aware that the Reclamation Service fund had been depleted; (2) a demand that the federal government quit holding up land patent applications, as approving patents and the patent fees could immediately refill the Reclamation fund; and (3) the need to resolve the dispute with Canada or find an alternative way to divert water from the Saint Mary and keep that water and the Milk River water in the United States.[14] Indian water rights were not on the agenda.

AN ATTEMPT TO REMOVE THE IRRIGABLE LAND FROM THE RESERVATION

The Indian water rights dilemma, and the proposal to strip the Fort Belknap reservation of its irrigable lands as the solution to that dilemma, may not have been on that delegation's agenda, but it was still central to the agenda of some. At about the time Judge Hunt first ruled in favor of the water rights at the reservation, in mid-1905, the people in the Harlem area began pushing the Montana congressional delegation to introduce legislation to open up a large portion, at least 40,000-acres, of the Fort Belknap reservation along the Milk River to non-Indian settlement, proposing to compensate the Fort Belknap Indians at a maximum of ten dollars per acre for the land. The news stories discussing this venture—including a festive site visit by Sen. Thomas Carter and Rep. Joseph Dixon arranged by Harlem interests—emphasized that this was irrigable land not currently irrigated or used for agriculture by the Indians and thus would be no loss and a monetary gain to the Indians. According to the Harlem paper Logan supported the proposal. He did at first, at least in concept. And the paper and Logan said the Indians were also largely in favor of the idea at first, although of course one has to take their word for it. There is no indication that anyone of importance asked the Indians directly about the proposal, nor is there any direct statement of approval by the Indians. If the proposal had been implemented, the Fort Belknap Indians would have lost almost all of the river bottom lands and direct contact with the river, leaving them only with the more mountainous lands along Peoples Creek and the other creeks coming out of the Little Rocky Mountains and thus less agricultural and grazing lands and less water. The upland areas were where many of the Fort Belknap residents preferred to live and ranch, but that is not the same as saying they had no use for or interest in retaining the bottom lands. Their subsequent actions indicated disfavor with the proposal; by that time Logan was also opposed to the specific bill, not necessarily because of the idea of removing land from the reservation but for the way the proposal might gut the reservation's water rights. He also began to prefer other schemes for reservation development, especially the sugar beet production idea, over the sale of irrigable lands.

The public discussions of the land proposal never included any specific link to the water rights litigation, and Logan was adamant in correspondence that there was or should be no link to and no effect on the water rights decision. Not everybody agreed that the reservation land proposal was unrelated or should be unrelated to the water rights litigation. What was a landgrab desire in the Harlem area that predated and had nothing specific to do with the water rights litigation became a vehicle for ranching interests in Chinook and Havre to undo the court decisions. By removing most or all of the irrigable land of the

reservation, the Indians' potential reserved rights to water would be significantly reduced, in their view. The water represented by the reserved
rights would return by the state law system of allocation to the early
upstream appropriations, while water for the newly opened reservation
land would come from the Reclamation project and also be allocated
through the state prior appropriations system. As noted in the last
section, the Chinook ditch companies, serving mostly cattle ranches, did
in fact go to Washington and otherwise lobby for the sale of these
bottom lands in order to have the reserved water right leave the reservation with the land.

The elements of this proposal for once allowed Harlem area interests
and the Chinook-Havre irrigators, antagonists in nearly every other
aspect of the water rights and water policy arena, to build a common
interest. The Harlem area people could gain permanent access to land
they coveted (or at least see it added into their local economic base),
while incidentally undoing a water rights decision adversely affecting
the upriver interests. A leader in this particular coalition was Thomas
Everett, a Harlem area rancher and state senator. Everett was able to
maintain good relations with Logan, but he was also a consistent opponent
of the water rights decisions favoring the Indians, given that the intake
of the Harlem Ditch Company (in which he had an interest) was above
the reservation's ditch. He thus approached this issue differently from
the *Milk River Valley News* in Harlem and others downstream, although
Everett also was able to remain favorably viewed in the Harlem paper.
Everett was one of the few people in the lower river willing to be an
active ally of Chinook and Havre's interests in this fight, even spon-
soring a 1907 memorial to Congress from the Montana legislature
deploring the decisions. Everett was also active in efforts to break up the
Fort Belknap and Blackfeet reservations or to otherwise gain non-
Indian access to the reservation lands; and unlike others outside of
Chinook and Havre, he was always willing to tie these activities explicitly
to opposition to the Indian water rights decisions. As illustrated by the
outcome of the valleywide irrigation association meeting in June 1906,
however, this coalition of interests was not ordinarily successful in
making the rest of the valley put a high priority on action intended to
resolve the Indian water rights issue in the way the Chinook irrigators
desired.[15]

In any event, in January 1906, in the first session of Congress after
the lower court decision in *Winters,* Montana Republican Senator
Carter did introduce the bill to survey and open for sale and settlement
all of the reservation along the Milk River except for 5,000 acres to be

selected by the commissioner of Indian affairs. The bill did not specifically mention water rights, but it would have affected them just the
same, as desired by the ranching interests: section 1 called upon the
Department of the Interior to survey precisely the reservation lands
along the Milk River, and section 2 directed Interior to construct irrigation canals in order to irrigate all of this land possible. These lands were
to be "reclaimed under and in conformity with the provisions of" the
1902 Reclamation Act, which was code for, in part, allocating water
from the federally constructed system under state law, as required for
reclamation projects under section 8 of the Reclamation Act. This
provision of Carter's bill did not make a distinction between the lands to
be sold and the lands to be retained by the Indians. Thus while it would
not have extinguished the reserved rights, it would have precluded
them from applying to the Milk River water actually delivered to the
reservation by this irrigation system. It is unclear whether Senator
Carter (or whoever drafted the bill for him) intended this effect.[16]

The irrigation provision led Logan to oppose the bill, just as much
as it was what interested the Chinook cattlemen. Logan worked to
convince the commissioner of Indian affairs of its "detrimental consequences" and to pressure at the least for its amendment. Logan certainly
understood the legislation as extinguishing the Indians' reserved right
to the 5,000 inches ordered by the court, while he felt that his original
understanding of the proposal in Harlem "was not to affect or interfere
with the rights of the Indians" as decreed by the courts. He also argued
that the original premise was that the water to be used for the reclamation of the lands taken from the Indians was to come only from the
diversion of the Saint Mary, with the natural flow of the Milk reserved
for the Indians. The bill language would unfortunately "place the
Indians upon exactly the same level with entrymen and purchasers."
And because Logan so focused on the decreed amount of 5,000 miner's
inches, he criticized the legislation for surrendering a right that was
"certain" in "exchange for one which is, at least as to the amount of
water to which the Indians would be entitled, uncertain," a nice twist
on the usual complaint of the uncertainties presented by the reserved
right compared to the fixed and certain amounts vested under the prior
appropriation system. Logan also recommended that the bill protect
twice the acreage for the reservation, noting that the current reservation
irrigation system could reach 10,000 acres and that with the 5,000 inches
of water decreed by court this land "can be made very valuable in a
short time." He also noted that the Indians "understand" that there
might be a sale of some of the land and that "quite a number of them

have moved in to the irrigated district" along the Milk River, especially Gros Ventres who moved there from the thickly settled area along Peoples Creek, implying an effort by the Indians to preempt the sale of as much of the irrigable land as possible. (The Assiniboines, he noted, had stayed in the mountains and seemed uninterested in the Milk River land.)

More important, Logan began to make arguments that other paths would be better for the reservation, although carefully avoiding open opposition to the reservation land sale proposal. He especially began to emphasize how close he was to bringing to reality the idea of using the reservation's irrigable lands as part of a sugar beet production scheme that would bring irrigated farming work and wages and lease income to the reservation. This would be "the biggest thing that ever happened for the good of these people," and would "solve the labor problem and eliminate forever the necessity of asking Congress for annual appropriations for the maintenance and civilization of these Indians," as they would earn money, gain knowledge as to what could be produced from the soil, and learn business principles. He could report truthfully that the non-Indians in the area of the reservation had also become interested in the sugar production enterprise, seeing direct and indirect economic benefits from the scheme that, in Logan's mind, at least equaled and probably surpassed the benefits to come from the sale of the reservation lands. In contrast, Logan argued, if the land sale went through, this would mean moving back into the diminished reservation and beginning all over again to try to establish a viable irrigated agricultural enterprise, investing the money from the land sale and possibly needing other appropriations as well.[17]

Senator Carter's reservation-busting bill died in the Indian Affairs committees. Nothing in the official documents explains why, although it does appear that one factor was that Logan and then the Indian office became much more interested in the sugar beet development idea as the preferred path to reservation development, which would also benefit non-Indian interests and local economic development. In his book *Command of the Waters,* Daniel McCool stated that the primary reason the measure did not emerge from committee was that Carter's arch political enemy, William Clark, Montana's Democratic senator, blocked consideration of the measure on purely political and personal grounds. I doubt this is the whole story, or at least that the political enmity was more than an incidental factor that could come into play when local and/or Indian Affairs support receded for the legislation. Carter and Clark certainly worked together to advance a contemporaneous bill to break up the Blackfeet reservation, discussed below. However, if McCool's analysis is correct, Clark's undermining of the legislation at least exposes the fallacy in the ideas of western solidarity and monolithic attitudes among the dominant culture in the West toward land and water (and Indians), something already seen in the litigation.

In any event, the proposal died in Congress without anyone making an explicit link between the proposed legislation and the water rights litigation. This was *not* true of the contemporaneous legislation affecting the Blackfeet reservation, explicitly linked to the water rights decisions and to which attention shifted by late 1906, a story to be told in significant detail below. First, however, because of the importance of the sugar production proposal at Fort Belknap, it is necessary to explore that in more detail.[18]

THE SUGAR BEET PROPOSAL

A more intensive and extensive effort to capitalize on the irrigation potential of the Milk River lands of the reservation began officially with a tentative proposal in January 1906 by officers of the Amalgamated Sugar Company of Ogden, Utah. The company proposed to lease at least 5,000 irrigable acres of land on the Fort Belknap reservation along the Milk River for the cultivation of sugar beets and for a sugar production facility employing Indian labor. Logan had been trying for some time to attract the sugar beet industry to the reservation, just as nearly everyone else in the valley was trying to attract the sugar beet refinery to *their* area—the Chinook-Harlem rivalry grew testy on this issue as well. Logan was excited over the proposal, as also seemed to be the Indian Affairs office, the Interior Department, and the congressional delegation. And in this affair, the recently acknowledged preferential water right for the reservation was explicitly a plus factor, as sugar beet cultivation and production was known to depend on a secure and fairly large source of water. Logan stated that the Fort Belknap Indians were enthusiastic, too, and there are indications that at first they were at least interested. Certainly, the reservation's residents were, like Logan, more interested in the sugar beet proposal than they were in the other proposal that would strip lands along the river from the reservation. The people in Harlem, the congressional delegation, and even Superintendent Logan did not see the two proposals as necessarily in conflict, however, at least not at first. It was partly because of the knowledge of the sugar beet proposal that Senator Carter's proposed land removal legislation preserved

5,000 acres of irrigable land for the reservation along the river. And Logan thought the sugar beet development was so important that it should proceed whatever the fate of the land removal legislation, although as noted above, he came to prefer sugar beet production as an alternative to land removal.[19]

The rivalry between Chinook and the reservation/Harlem interests over sugar beet cultivation and the location of the sugar beet refinery again threatened valley solidarity, and again the Indian water rights issues got into the middle of the dispute. This is seen best through a couple of sources. One was a news story in the March 7, 1907, edition of the *Milk River Valley News,* expressing concern that the infighting between Chinook and the reservation people along with interests in Harlem would stymie sugar beet development for that year and longer. In the paper's view the two areas should both begin growing sugar beets (and in fact so should all the valley's farmers from Havre to Glasgow) and should unite in supporting the boosters' efforts to bring the sugar beet industry to the valley. The paper suggested that everyone ignore the issue of the refinery for the time being, and then let the sugar company decide what was the best, most central place for locating the refinery, which the paper implied would likely be in the Harlem area. In echoes of other remarks on the water disputes in the past few years, the Harlem paper blamed the conflict on the fact that "[o]ur neighbors at Chinook, who should be our friends," and were in fact "sensible" farmers, were being "misled by irresponsible newspaper articles" in the Chinook papers and by selfish entrepreneurs who did not have the good of the entire valley in mind.

The Harlem newspaper story was probably sparked by the same reports that sparked a letter three days earlier (March 4, 1907) from Logan to the commissioner of Indian affairs. Logan enclosed a clipping from the *Chinook Opinion* opposing sugar beet development at the Fort Belknap reservation. He asked the commissioner to counter the reports of lobbying efforts in Washington by people in Chinook, who were pressuring the Montana delegation and the administration to prevent the signing of a cultivation and/or refinery lease at Fort Belknap to force the location of the refinery at Chinook. What really bothered Logan was that one of the arguments being made in Chinook was that the sugar beet operation as planned on the reservation would require "a great deal more water than the 5,000 inches allotted by the court," and thus the valley faced a substantial enlargement of the reserved right demand on the water by the Indians. Logan denied that this was so, denied that their dam and ditch could handle much more than 5,000 inches (and said that he did not foresee having the financing to expand the facilities anyway), and reminded the commissioner that the people in Chinook and elsewhere in the valley "knew that the Reclamation people claim that they will have the waters of the St. Mary's lakes turned into Milk River by the spring of 1908 which will give ample water to everyone."

The Indian Office pushed hard for this development. While the proposal to strip land from the reservation died quickly, the sugar beet plan died a slower death, dragging on for the rest of the decade, through the rest of the *Winters* litigation and beyond. As will be seen, the government did execute a contract with the officers of the Amalgamated Sugar Company in 1908, with explicit tribal council approval, leasing for ten years 10,000 acres of land for the cultivation of sugar beets, with an understanding that the Indians would provide the labor to grow the beets and that the sugar people would build the "sugar factory" near the reservation. (One reason for delay was the discovery that congressional action was necessary to authorize the ten-year-lease contract.) Numerous Harlem area businesspeople and farmers got in on the action with smaller contracts to assist in various ways in the project. But getting the lands cultivated turned out to be difficult, the labor force's lack of the necessary skills and lack of real enthusiasm for the work quickly became evident, and the acreage planted and yields from that acreage were never what were hoped. Production, financing, and other problems always prevented construction of anything other than minimal processing facilities near the reservation, never a sugar beet refinery or factory. The Fort Belknap Indians soon lost whatever favorable attitude some of them may have had toward the idea, as much was demanded of them without any apparent gain. The government and the sugar company eventually agreed in 1910 to annul the Amalgamated contract, due mostly, according to anthropologist David Rodnick, to the open antagonism of the Indians, although I could not confirm this. Logan failed in a subsequent attempt to execute a similar lease with a different company, again largely due to objections by the Indians.

Thus sugar beet development turned out to be a short-lived and relatively inconsequential incident in the life of the reservation. This long-term inconsequence masks the importance of the plan at that time—it was in fact much more important to the people of the valley than was the *Winters* litigation. For the purposes here, the point is that in these years the sugar beet scheme became the primary focus of the government's hopes, efforts, and policies for economic development of the reservation—rather than, for example, allotment (which would not happen until 1921) or any sustained effort at stripping irrigable land from the reservation. Harlem residents and the town newspaper realized the possible local economic benefits of having a sugar production factory on the reservation rather than elsewhere in the valley. So the *Milk River Valley News,* for example, tirelessly promoted the idea for the next few years, and Logan could report to the commissioner of Indian affairs that "the Whites on the North boundary of the reservation and along the Milk River have entered into the enterprise." Just as emphatically, others in the valley, especially in the Chinook area, opposed use of the reservation for sugar beet production and processing, hoping to lure the main center of sugar beet production and the sugar refinery to the Chinook area—which eventually did happen after World War I, adding to the upstream-downstream conflict seen in the litigation. The fact that success at sugar depended in part on the water situation—reservation personnel used the government's success at protecting water rights in the *Winters* litigation as an inducement to the sugar company in negotiations—increased the stakes for the government as the *Winters* case carried to the Supreme Court and colored local views of the meaning of that victory. Nothing illustrates this better than Logan's two-sentence letter to the commissioner of Indian affairs upon hearing the news of the Supreme Court's decision in *Winters,* one week before the news about the signing of the sugar beet contract. Logan informed the commissioner of the decision in the first sentence and then concluded, "This is particularly gratifying to me for the reason that it assures us an ample supply of water for our sugar beet operations, as well as for other purposes."

CHAPTER 6

Winters *and Allotment*

*The Blackfeet Reservation Allotment Legislation
and Water Rights*

If any one thing can be said to have happened to the
reserved water rights doctrine immediately after it emerged from the
local context of the dispute over water in the Milk River, it is the way in
which the doctrine and its implications became entangled in and
deflected by the larger issue of allotment. Allotment meant the assignment of reservation land in small tracts to individual Indians and the
sale of the "surplus." The beginning of this process can be seen, even as
Winters was making its way to the Supreme Court, in the relationship
between the water rights litigation for the Blackfeet reservation (the
Conrad Investment Company case) and a legislative effort from 1905 to
1907 to allot the Blackfeet reservation. Before discussing the Blackfeet
situation, it is necessary to describe allotment law and policy in general
and to situate the *Winters* decisions within that framework.

ASSIMILATION, ALLOTMENT, AND
RESERVED WATER RIGHTS

The *Winters* decision appeared in the middle of a particular half-
century campaign on the part of the federal government to induce or
force American Indians to assimilate into the dominant non-Indian
culture. As has been already described above, the western face of
assimilation had much do to with non-Indians' desire for land and
desire to transform western Indians into an idealized type, the small-

tract farmer. By the 1880s non-Indian political and economic leaders
began to see that the demand of non-Indian settlers for land and
resources would soon overwhelm all parts of the West, including the
lands of the Indian peoples. It seemed impossible to the non-Indian
world either to stop non-Indian expansion or to continue pushing the
Indians away from the line of non-Indian settlement in order to maintain a permanent federal buffer or barrier between Indians and non-
Indian society. Reformers of Indian policy believed that if the nation
hoped to avoid an increase in violent conflict, a direct clash of cultures,
and piteously oppressed Indians, the Indians had to adapt to and accept
non-Indian ways of life. Reformers and opportunists also hoped the
process would continue the transfer of "excess" Indian lands to non-
Indian settler control.[1]

The cornerstone of the policy of assimilation in the West was a
deliberate plan to convert the nonsedentary and semisedentary peoples
into stationary, individual, small-tract farmers no different from the
non-Indian settlers—the yeoman-farmer ideal. As I have already noted,
implementing this plan required first that the native peoples be induced
to give up most of the territory they controlled. Land cessions always
had a place in the relationship between non-Indians and Indians, but
these latest cessions were intended to have a transforming effect. Old
patterns of land use and subsistence could not continue on a reservation
significantly reduced in size. Yet such extensive land holdings were not
necessary for a sedentary farming people and would be an actual
deterrent to change. On the reduced reservations the Indians would
learn, with the assistance of the Indian Office, the skills and attitudes
necessary to survive as "civilized" farmers and grazers. The 1888 agreement between the Gros Ventre and Assiniboine peoples and the United
States construed in *Winters* is a classic example of the type of land
cession agreement executed in the late nineteenth century.

The allotment process was the second half of the yeoman-farmer
reform program, first authorized by Congress in the Dawes Severalty
Act of 1887.[2] The act provided for the distribution of plots of land "in
severalty" to individual Indians whenever, in the opinion of the Indian
Office, all or part of a reservation was "advantageous for agricultural
and grazing purposes." Each head of household could select the classic
160 acres; others (such as orphan children) would receive less. The allotments could be larger if suitable only for grazing.[3] After individuals
were settled on allotments, the act then called for the Indian Office to
negotiate an agreement with the Indian group to purchase the "surplus
lands" remaining. Surplus lands purchased by the government that

were suitable for agriculture were to be held for distribution to "actual settlers." The money paid by the United States for the surplus lands was to be held by the United States "for the sole use" of the Indians and would be subject to appropriation by Congress for their "education and civilization."⁴ Upon the completion of the process, the settled Indians were to receive United States citizenship and to "have the benefit of and be subject to the laws, both civil and criminal, of the State or Territory in which they may reside."⁵

In historian Frederick Hoxie's persuasive thesis, the assimilation policy went through two phases, the first somewhat more idealistic and benign than the second. Changing the native peoples' ways of life was always the goal, but at first the non-Indian reformers sought to do so gradually and, it was hoped, with the approval of individual natives as they became aware by experience of the benefits of adaptation. American Indians were not to be thrown free into the individualistic, competitive world of white America until well prepared to take part. Gradual implementation of each phase of the allotment process would be the key to assimilation in the West. A particular reservation would not be broken up until the Indian Office believed the residents were ready, willing, and able to be individual tract farmers; meanwhile, Indian Affairs would work with these residents to teach them how to work the land and sustain a farming operation. Even after allotment (and the government purchase of the surplus lands), the federal government would retain a trust control over the allotments and over the new owners' well-being until these individuals were competently operating their farms and were economically and culturally self-supporting. The goal was gradual and total assimilation, "the incorporation of independent Indian landowners into American society on an equal footing with their fellow citizens."⁶

The gradual assimilation policy exploded in the first decade of the new century. Non-Indian pressures for the native lands increased dramatically. At the same time it became apparent that most of the Indians were not assimilating as hoped. The intended cultural transformation based on an economic transformation was foundering on environmental and economic realities; many of the western reservation lands were very poor places for successful small-tract, commercial, irrigated agriculture, as non-Indian settlers were also discovering. The transformation effort also foundered on cultural realities—the Indian peoples were not plastic to be transformed at the will of the federal government. From their historical experiences in making a living in the area and their various efforts to carve out ways of life for themselves under changed circumstances, almost all of the Indians concluded that they would benefit little from the precise path marked out for them by Congress, the Indian Affairs Office and non-Indian society as a whole.

Non-Indian observers and commentators, including many who were interested in expediting non-Indian development of native lands and resources, then began to argue that gradual assimilation was no assimilation, that the Indians had no reason or incentive to assimilate if "protected" by the federal government. In their view the best plan would be to "free" the Indians from the paternal restrictions of the Indian Office and thrust them into society. Non-Indian society itself would envelop and instruct the Indians in the dominant culture.

The Indian Office and Congress caught the new mood. Congress began passing specific forced allotment acts in the new century. That is, Congress no longer waited for Indian Affairs to decide that the time was right to allot the lands of a particular reservation, nor for Indian Affairs and the Indian residents to reach an agreement to buy and sell the surplus lands. Instead, Congress simply directed the Indian Office to distribute allotments to individual residents of a reservation (or to complete an allotment process already begun) and to sell the surplus lands directly to non-Indian settlers (as the United States no longer agreed to purchase the lands).[7] In pursuit of these aims, Congress even altered past agreements executed by the Indian Office and particular Indian groups concerning allotments and land sales. It was precisely this type of event that resulted in the judicial nadir of the period, the Supreme Court's 1903 decision in *Lone Wolf v. Hitchcock*, which held that Congress could force the individual allotment of tribal land and the sale of unallotted land without the consent of the members of the tribe, unilaterally abrogating a treaty that required such consent.[8] The fact that Congress was willing to force the allotment of the Blackfeet reservation in 1906 and 1907 is a good illustration of the mood and the effects of this decision; remember that the 1896 agreement with the Blackfeet purchasing a tract of land from the reservation included a strong nonallotment provision, based on recognition that the Blackfeet reservation was "unfit" for agriculture and that cattle raising on an unbroken reservation was the means by which the Indians would become self-supporting.[9] As the Blackfeet bill made its way through Congress ten years later, and President Roosevelt even vetoed it once (as described below), no member of Congress or the president mentioned or cared that the legislation was inconsistent with the treaty.

Federal assistance prior to allotment withered, as did federal protection after allotment. The federal government no longer acted as if it had an obligation to protect native lands and lives and made no effort to ensure that the affected individuals could control their lands and resources once thrust into non-Indian society. As Hoxie put it, in essence the federal government became little more than "a real estate agent, acting as the tribe's bursar rather than its benefactor." The inevitable result was that the native peoples lost and non-Indians gained control over native lands and resources.[10]

Winters appeared in the midst of this second, more vicious phase of the assimilation policy. Hoxie dismissed *Winters* as nothing more than another brick in the building of assimilation: "[T]he [Supreme Court's] decision spoke only of water necessary to "change old habits," and said nothing about allottees who refused or were unable to farm. The Court did not recognize a specific tribal share of the river."[11] It is true that the 1888 treaty interpreted by the courts was a true son of the policy of assimilation and forced agrarian transformation, and that in the 1908 decision, the Supreme Court indulged itself in the language of assimilation, speaking of "uncivilized" people who were to become "pastoral and civilized." Yet *Winters'* place in the context of assimilation seems more complicated than this, for at least three reasons.

First, *Winters* is an anomaly within Hoxie's analytical framework. The reserved rights doctrine was at the very least a throwback to what Hoxie describes as the first, more gradual, and (its supporters hoped) consensual phase of assimilation. The doctrine reserved water until the Indians were ready or found a reason to make use of the water on native lands. Even if unable to use the water at present, they would not lose control of the resource to non-Indian settlers (who were inevitably ready to appropriate the waters under state law). *Winters* could be seen as *both* a judicial effort to implement assimilation and an effort to protect the Indians from the ravages of assimilation. In later years (and I do not mean just in modern times—this includes debates in the 1910s, for example), *Winters* and the reserved rights doctrine served as a beacon for those who explicitly rejected the second, savage phase of assimilation.

Second, Hoxie complained that *Winters* did not recognize a "tribal share" of the river. But in a way it did. The injunctions issued in *Winters* and *Conrad* allocated a specific amount of water to the Indians and, more important (at least in theory), assigned an expandable "tribal" right to the river based on what waters would be necessary for life to thrive on the reservation. Of greater significance, *Winters* as well as the treaty fishing case *Winans* before it were rare in the early twentieth century in recognizing that the Indians not only had "command of the land and waters" in the past but also retained some of that command. The reserved rights doctrine may have had little protective impact at the time, but it came into being and did not go away—and it has become perhaps the most potent force at the command of the western tribes in their attempt to protect their lives, resources, and society. And while *Winters* spoke of the need for irrigation water to make the arid lands worthwhile, the *Winters* decisions did not restrict water use on the reservations to irrigation. As the court decisions in *Winters* and *Conrad* emphasized, the United States and the Montana bands involved intended the reservation of land and other resources to be sufficient for the Indians to make a successful life. For this to come true, as explained by the appellate court in *Conrad,* the Indians had a "paramount right" to the use of waters "to the extent reasonably necessary for the purposes of irrigation and stock raising, and domestic and other useful purposes."[12] Perhaps it is fortunate for the Indian peoples that the courts in the years from 1905 to 1908 were not forced to specify exactly what these "other purposes" could be, although as Norris Hundley notes, there were people at the time who believed and commented that the Indians were not restricted to using reserved water for irrigation and should use it in any way that at least tended toward "civilized" life. Remember Carl Rasch's view, expressed to the Ninth Circuit, that what the Indians at Fort Belknap reserved was nothing less than "the flowing, living stream as they had always known and seen it."[13] Later commentators and courts have been able to speculate and even rule that while a reserved right might be *measured* by the amount of irrigable acreage on a reservation, *use* need not be restricted to irrigation, at least not as an automatic restriction. Instead, particular Indian tribes may be able to decide under their circumstances that dedication of reserved waters to some other use, such as fish and wildlife preservation, recreation, mineral development, or municipal development, is a more appropriate use of the water in order for the people to live successful lives on the reservation lands.[14] The reserved rights doctrine could not protect ways of life and cultures that depended on the larger tracts of land lost in the nineteenth century. Nor did the courts in 1905 to 1908 intend it to be other than part of assimilation. But the doctrine has had a life of its own. It has been a tool for preserving some aspects of indigenous life and autonomy that might have been lost, and it may give the native groups significant control over future development.

Third, *Winters* was in direct conflict with what many people saw as the essential tool of farm and town development in the arid West, the prior appropriation system of water allocation sanctioned by state law. Forcing the Indians to adapt to and live by that system would have been the epitome of forced assimilation. As will be seen in some of the congressional debates, many western non-Indians in the years immediately after *Winters* criticized the decision precisely for not allowing this to happen. And some of these people clearly saw the forced allotment of the Blackfeet reservation as a way to begin the undoing of the reserved rights doctrine.

THE BLACKFEET ALLOTMENT LEGISLATION AND WATER RIGHTS

Senator Carter of Montana introduced *two* reservation-busting bills in 1906, both concerning reservations involved in water rights litigation. I described one of them above—the bill to detach the irrigable lands from the Fort Belknap reservation, a little noticed and short-lived effort. The second was far more important to events in the valley and events nationally. This was Carter's proposed amendment to the Indian Affairs appropriations bill in April 1906 to survey and allot the Blackfeet reservation, the site of the *Conrad Investment Company* litigation.

To reiterate from above, Rasch had filed that case in early 1905—before the Fort Belknap litigation—to declare and protect the Blackfeets' rights to water in Birch Creek, the southeastern boundary of the reservation and a tributary of the Marias River. His complaint sought the removal of the Conrad Investment Company's dam on Birch Creek, which was designed to bring water to farming settlers south of the creek and off the reservation. Although filed earlier than the *Winters* case, the *Conrad Investment Company* case had not progressed to the point of court rulings at the time Carter filed his bill. The first formal lower court ruling in *Conrad* did not occur until August 1907. It is possible the court made some informal rulings before that point, although the severely depleted case file does not indicate any, and no one referred to any through 1906 and the first half of 1907. But even with no rulings in the *Conrad* case by 1906, the district and appellate court decisions about Fort Belknap (*Winters*) construing the same treaty clearly indicated what the outcome of the Blackfeet case would be—reserved water rights for the reservation—something Senator Carter and others were well aware of, as will be seen.[15]

The "Conrad" of the Conrad Investment Company was William Conrad, prominent northern Montana land and water developer and a businessman who had been involved in many pursuits, including land speculation, banking, mining, cattle ranching, and direction of a railroad. He was also a Democratic politician, mentioned in a few Montana papers as a possible Senate and even vice-presidential candidate in 1908. Conrad's economic base was in the Marias River valley (note that the town of Conrad is the county seat of Pondera County, bordering the Marias to the south and including a number of tributaries) and in Great Falls, located along the Missouri. He became peripherally involved in Milk River issues primarily through water and land speculation and development in and below the headwaters area of the Milk, Marias, and Saint Mary Rivers. For one thing, Conrad promoted an alternate version of the Reclamation project for the Milk River. Rather than diverting the water of the Saint Mary River into the headwaters of the Milk River and then letting it flow with the Milk into Canada, Conrad promoted diverting water from the Saint Mary into the headwaters of Cut Bank Creek, another tributary of the Marias also on the Blackfeet reservation, letting it run down the Marias almost to the Marias-Missouri confluence. At that point, Conrad proposed, there should be built a dam and canal on the Marias to store and divert water over to Big Sandy Creek, a tributary of the Milk River that joins the Milk about ten miles above Havre. Not only would this have kept the water entirely in the United States, which would not have avoided the Canadian grievance but would have taken away some of the Canadians' leverage, the scheme would have had the added advantage (to Conrad) of bringing more water through lands that Conrad had an interest in and could tap for increased irrigation. Conrad also enthusiastically promoted the breakup of the Blackfeet reservation to add more non-Indian farming settlers to the southern lands along the Cut Bank and Birch Creeks as customers for his water and economic contributors to the development of the area of his dominance.[16]

The complicated history of the Blackfeet allotment bill, spanning two sessions of Congress, illustrates how the Indian reserved water rights issue became understood and bound up in, and ultimately deflected by, the allotment process. As noted above, Congress had passed a number of special allotment acts in 1904, the year before the first *Winters* ruling. Congress passed another allotment act early in 1906, for the Colville reservation in Washington, only slightly after the first *Winters* ruling in December 1905. None of the allotment acts mentioned water rights.[17] Senator Carter's 1906 allotment proposal for the Blackfeet reservation did, however, include a water rights provision. This provision would have authorized the Office of Indian Affairs to survey and allot the lands of the reservation to individual residents and then added the following restriction on water rights, directly intended to stop Rasch's lawsuit *and* subject all water rights on the reservation to Montana state law:

> [A]ll water rights and privileges connected with streams within or adjacent to the [Blackfeet] reservation shall be subject to the laws of the State of Montana; and all proceedings in any pending suit commenced by the United States praying for an injunction to enjoin the use of waters of any such stream shall be suspended, and no like suit shall hereafter be commenced or prosecuted by the United States against any person or company actually using the water of any of the streams aforesaid for a beneficial purpose.[18]

The proposal would have stripped the federal reserved rights from only one reservation, but had it passed, it likely would have been a model for other allotment legislation and reservations and could have killed off the *Winters* doctrine before it even got beyond one ruling.

And it did pass the Senate, at least at first. The presiding officer called Senator Carter's amendment for consideration in the midst of a long series of amendments to the appropriations bill. Carter and many other senators were not present. The few senators present agreed to the amendment without explanation, question, debate, or objection, a measure of the level of awareness and concern about the issue.[19]

What is curious and critical is what happened next—Senator Carter appeared a few minutes later before the Senate, and with Senator Henry Lodge of Massachusetts, one of the Republican leaders of the Senate, *Carter* himself asked that the item be brought back for consideration. He implied that other senators who had not been present when the amendment had passed were going to ask for its reconsideration, so he and Lodge were anticipating that request with their own. Carter then moved to *delete* that portion of his water rights provision that prohibited the government from continuing the Blackfeet lawsuit or from initiating a new one. Carter did *not* ask for the deletion of the other portion of the water rights provision, the language that required that all water rights be subject to the laws of Montana. Several senators asked for an explanation. Carter began by detailing the water problems and other issues at the Blackfeet reservation that led him to propose the provision, including the suit filed by the federal government. He presented a picture of hardy settlers in danger of losing the water they needed to live and of the betrayal of these people by the federal government, a government that had encouraged them to take up the land and had approved their irrigation works.[20]

Before he could explain further, Senator Benjamin Tillman, a Democrat from South Carolina, interrupted and questioned Carter pointedly about the settlers' motives and rights. Tillman inferred that the settlers had intentionally and without authority encroached on the rights of the Indians and were now seeking to insulate themselves from any attempt by the federal government to protect the Indians. Tillman produced a letter from the commissioner of Indian affairs, Francis Leupp, objecting to Carter's provision. Leupp's letter complained about *both* the restriction of water rights to state law and the prohibition on lawsuits. Although the *Winters* decisions were not mentioned in Leupp's letter, Tillman also informed the Senate about the connection between Carter's proposal and the recent federal court ruling concerning the Fort Belknap reservation, that is, the *Winters* case, its first mention in Congress. Carter had not mentioned Judge Hunt's ruling, and once *Winters* was mentioned, Carter clearly hoped to divert the Senate's attention from the news of the ruling, as he quickly brushed aside Tillman's comments about it as "relate[d] to another reservation" and concerning "an entirely different matter." Carter and his fellow Montana senator, William Clark, united on this proposal, responded to Tillman's interference with the characteristic response of western legislators to someone who might question their right to decide for the West. Carter stated that the "Senator from South Carolina should take a trip over that section of the country," and only then would he know the true conditions in Montana and be able to understand the issues. Clark added that the concerns of Tillman and others were the "misapprehensions of Senators who are not familiar with this country."[21]

Yet Carter and Clark then partly conceded the issue to the Indian Office and other opponents by withdrawing their proposal to prohibit government lawsuits against settlers to protect Indian water rights. They explained that they were willing to back away from this provision *because* the allotment process should give them and the settlers the relief they sought. In their view, with the expected passage of the allotment measure, the Blackfeet reservation would be "opened" within three years. Most of the land would be returned to the public domain for non-Indian settlement. The Blackfeet people would own small, individual allotments and would soon be living like non-Indian settlers under state law. The reserved water rights doctrine—and the lawsuit—would be of little relevance. The Montana senators did demand the retention of the provision that required that all water rights be subject to state law. They argued that state law must remain paramount and that Congress should include the express provision to that effect to remain faithful to similar expressions in prior acts, such as in section 8 of the Reclamation Act of 1902. Senator Clark assured the Senate that the Indians' rights would be protected fairly under state law. Debate closed on that point. No senator objected to the measure as revised, and it became part of the Senate version of the appropriations bill.[22]

Unfortunately for the Montana delegation, the version of the appropriation bill that had earlier passed the House did not contain an allotment provision for the Blackfeet reservation. A House-Senate conference committee deleted the Senate's addition, apparently because members of the House thought it inappropriate to attach such important and difficult legislation to the appropriations bill at this stage in the process.[23]

The debate over the water rights provision and its resolution in the first Blackfeet allotment bill provided the first evidence that the reserved rights issue could be submerged and deflected by the allotment process. The guardians of state law and the prior appropriation system might have fought harder and more directly to be rid of the reserved rights doctrine at this very early point if they had not convinced themselves that allotment would be what another congressman later called "the final solution of the Indian question."[24]

The conflict in Congress over this measure appeared to fall into a classic regional pattern—bipartisan western senators supporting state law and the doctrine of prior appropriation being challenged by a meddlesome eastern senator with no connection to or knowledge of the physical conditions of the West. Senator Tillman's explanation for his interest in the Montana issue complicates this picture. Although he had been in touch with Indian Affairs, he said he did not become involved in this matter at their behest. He apologized to Carter and stated that he disliked "meddling" in "local conditions in Montana." Then he added, *"[B]ut this matter was called to my attention by a private letter from a resident of that part of the country,* and it appeared to me that it was queer that Congress should be called to suppress lawsuits begun by the government to protect the wards of the government."[25] Tillman did not identify the letter writer, nor explain why a resident of Montana would write to the senator from South Carolina to press his or her views. Yet the letter meant that some people in Montana had a different view on this subject from that pressed by the Montana delegation, people with different concerns either for the Indians or for different water allocation and land policies (or both). Rather than view Senator Tillman's actions as half of a western-eastern clash, he should be seen as a vehicle instrumental to an intrawestern debate, in which one side was forced to go outside the region for support because the other side controlled the state's political and economic machinery.[26]

Thwarted in his first attempt, in June 1906 Senator Carter tied again. He introduced a separate bill in that session to survey and allot the Blackfeet reservation, apparently including the same water rights provision. The congressional documents do not include a copy of the bill as introduced, but Senator Carter stated on the floor of the Senate that his bill was identical to the measure approved by the Senate as part of the appropriations bill. Because the Senate had already passed the measure in another form in that session, the Senate Committee on Indian Affairs reported the new bill favorably in one day without explanation, and the Senate passed it the next day without debate.[27]

The House substituted for Carter's Senate Bill a separate Blackfeet allotment bill introduced by Rep. Joseph Dixon of Montana. When Dixon's bill emerged from the House Committee on Indian Affairs, it contained an entirely new provision concerning water rights:

> [F]or irrigable lands allotted there is hereby reserved and appropriated out of the waters of the reservation sufficient water to irrigate said irrigable lands, and the United States shall and does hold said appropriation in trust as appurtenant to the land so allotted for the trust period named in the patent to be issued: Provided, That such reservation and trust shall only apply to such waters as may be actually and necessarily appropriated for the irrigable portions of Indian allotments within five years from the date of the approval made by the Commissioner of Indian Affairs of the allotments; And further provided, That subject to the foregoing provisions, that all water rights and privileges on or connected with streams within or adjacent said reservation shall be subject to the laws of the State of Montana.[28]

Stripping away the cloudy language, the new provision proposed to recognize and sanction the concept of the reserved right and then restrict the scope of the right and put a time limit on it. The proposal tried to meld an explicit statement of a form of the federal reserved right with the general attitude toward allotments—the transformation of the Blackfeet to yeoman-farmer and the gradual, but definite, withdrawal of federal oversight and protection. This mixture was repeated more than once over the next decade.

Speaking on the House floor, Representative Dixon said that the Indian Office wrote the water rights provision, except that the office had drafted the provision to allow an individual allottee the entire length of the federal trust period over the allotments (twenty-five years) to make an appropriation from the reserved water. The House committee reduced this to the five years following the allotments, which were scheduled by the bill to be issued three years after the act became law. Dixon argued that eight years was more than enough time to subject the citizens of Montana to the uncertainties inherent in the reservation of water for Indian allottees. Other House members responded to complain that the appropriation period was too short to protect the allottees' rights and to insure that they had made a successful transition to irrigated agriculture. They grumbled that the whole act was intended only to get the land and water in the hands of non-Indian settlers as fast as possible at the expense of the rights of the Indians. Representative Dixon, a Republican, and two prominent Republican supporters, Frank Mondell of Wyoming and Franklin Brooks of Colorado, disagreed with this characterization, although their sympathies clearly lay with the settlers in the dispute over water. Representative Dixon then even played the nationalist card. He claimed that thousands of settlers in northern Montana were moving to Canada because of uncertainties in Montana over the availability of water. At the end of the debate, the House approved the bill on June 14, 1906, by a huge majority, with the water rights language added by the committee.[29]

In this lengthy House debate on water rights for the Blackfeet reservation, no one mentioned the *Winters* case or the reserved rights theory set forth in Judge Hunt's ruling and affirmed by the federal appeals court in that case. Yet the concept and threat of a reserved water right permeated both the water rights provision of the bill and its discussion, and the provision sanctioned the use of a version of the reserved water right as the basis for allocating water in the first instance to the allotments. Representative Dixon and other western members of Congress (of both parties) proved amenable to this modified form of the reserved rights doctrine despite the fact that it was inconsistent with full adherence to the state law system of prior appropriation. This again indicated their feeling that the allotment process would soon reduce all conflict over the control of water to the confines of state water law and the appropriation system.

The water rights provision became even more focused in this regard in the next stage of the bill's progress through Congress. The Senate refused to yield to the House's version of the bill, reiterating its preference at this time for its own water rights provision that subordinated all water rights to state law, sending the bill to conference. This time the House-Senate conference, dominated by western congressmen from both houses, came to a quick agreement on the final version of the bill. Both houses then agreed to the conference report with almost no debate. The conference version of the water rights measure closely resembled the House version, with a few significant changes that confirmed the limited reserved nature of the waters. The provision still reserved waters for the allotments "out of the waters of the reservation." Even more, the provision now stated explicitly that waters that were reserved but not yet used by the allottees would be available for use by settlers, but that *such use by the settlers would not create a right adverse to any Indian allottee who eventually appropriated the water in accord with the provision*. By agreeing to language in direct conflict with the concepts of the prior appropriation doctrine, western congressmen demonstrated that they understood the essential difference between the reserved right and the prior appropriation system, and that they were willing to sanction a version of the reserved right in express language. One reason they were so willing to do so was that new language added by the conference also reduced from five years to *two* the time allottees had to exercise or lose their reserved right after receiving their allotments. A few members of Congress grumbled again on the floor of the two houses that despite the nice-sounding language of reservation, the two-year period for exercising the reserved right was far too short and made a mockery of the allotment process. But the grumblers did not mount a serious campaign to derail the conference report.[30]

They did not have to. Surprising everybody, President Roosevelt vetoed the Blackfeet allotment bill at the end of June 1906 *solely* because of the water rights provision. The possibility of a veto was never mentioned in the congressional debate. Roosevelt's veto message stated that he vetoed the bill based on a report from the Office of Indian Affairs. The Indian Affairs report, attached to the veto measure, objected because the bill did not include an appropriation for the construction of an irrigation system, which the office saw as essential if the Blackfeet were to be able to divert their water and put it to use within the short time allowed. While the bill provided that money from the sale of the surplus lands of the allotted reservation would be used for an irrigation project, the Indian Office concluded that the sale of the lands would take too many years to be of assistance before the two-year water deadline. The Indian Office report argued that settlers would immediately appropriate the reserved waters, and the practical difficulties of ever recapturing the water when it came time to exercise the paper reserved right were "too obvious to require extended discussion."[31]

Roosevelt concluded his veto message by stating that he was anxious to favor in every way the "bona fide homesteaders," provided that such a measure would "explicitly and unequivocally guarantee to the Indians their water rights—that is, the right of each Indian to a sufficiency of water to make his allotment of real use to him."[32] Roosevelt's last statement captures the meaning of the entire course of this bill. (It also further illustrates that the proponents of a special Indian water policy were not totally at the mercy of the Reclamation adherents.) All who spoke about the issue seemed willing to accept the reserved water rights concept in some form, but only because it was connected to the allotment of the reservation and limited in time. They disputed only the mechanics and time limits. Ironically, President Roosevelt vetoed the only legislation (that I can find) ever passed by Congress explicitly stating (rather than implying) that individual appropriators in a western state were barred by federal law from acquiring a vested right by use to unappropriated water.

The Montana delegation finally obtained passage of a Blackfeet allotment act in 1907, but not without a lot more trouble and the development of yet a different version of a water rights provision, one that made little sense by the end. The delegation had the help of a memorial from the Montana state legislature, a memorial introduced by Thomas Everett, a state senator from Harlem, that directly linked the Blackfeet allotment bill to a strong denunciation of the Indian water rights decisions. It was precisely the kind of statement that the Chinook and Havre irrigators and their allies, such as Everett, could never quite produce out of the Milk River valley irrigation association.

The developments leading to the state legislature's memorial are instructive: The constellation of water issues in the Milk River valley continued to ferment in the winter of 1906–07, coming to a head at a meeting of the Milk River Irrigation Association in Harlem on December 12, 1906. The meeting attracted not only one hundred "representative men from every hamlet of the Milk River valley," but also Congressman-elect Charles Pray, Cyrus Babb of the Reclamation Service, and apparently Superintendent Logan, while Senator Carter sent a letter. Three topics dominated the discussion. Two had to do directly with the Reclamation project and were the subjects of resolutions adopted at the meeting. The first concerned the headwaters part of the project. The association pressed the government to have Reclamation move faster in constructing the Saint Mary canal and, especially, to begin work on the storage reservoir at the Chain Lakes. The resolution also stated that the valley irrigators were in favor of investigating "the Marias project," that is, diverting water further into the Marias River and bringing it to the valley that way, avoiding Canada. Second, the association again pressed Reclamation to begin the lower part of the project, the diversion and irrigation structures. The waters of the river were being "allowed to run to waste," and "if work is not hastened on the project settlers will be literally starved out"—many, they said, were already leaving for Canada.

The third topic of discussion was the desirability of "opening" all the remaining Indian reservations in northern Montana, including the Fort Belknap and Blackfeet reservations. But the association could not come to agreement on a specific resolution on this issue. The *Milk River Valley News* noted that because this issue involved the "delicate question of Indian water rights," which was "a vital matter with the settlers in the whole of Northern Montana," the association decided to refer it to "carefully selected committee" to draft a memorial. The committee was composed of one man from Havre, one from Hinsdale, and Everett of Harlem. The committee was told to draft "a strong memorial," but what that memorial would say could "not be determined." The association did agree on two key points—they expressed formally their support for opening up the reservations *and* they informally agreed that in allotting the reservations and developing irrigation facilities "whatever provision shall be adopted for the disposition of water rights in streams included in Indian reservations shall preserve the intent of laws now prevailing in other portions of Montana, which operate to protect the settler in his water right after a minimum period of time has elapsed in which Indians shall be permitted to exercise their right of selection." This was the same sort of formula that Congress was working with in the proposed Blackfeet legislation, a limited reserved right that somewhat mimicked a conditional appropriation, giving the Indians a certain amount of time after declaration of the reservation to perfect the use of water. The fact that a resolution containing these points was not crafted and adopted *at* the association meeting indicates perhaps that the Chinook and Havre irrigators were after more.[33]

The association's committee *never* did produce a resolution for the irrigation association. What emerged instead two months later was Everett's own proposed memorial for the state legislature. Everett's version combined a strong denunciation of the water rights decisions with support for the Blackfeet allotment bill. Meanwhile, the Blackfeet allotment bill was now back in Congress and at the critical moment for legislative adoption. Shortly after the association meeting in mid-December, Senator Clark had introduced the new version of the

Blackfeet reservation allotment bill. This bill contained a water rights provision that the Montana senators assured the Senate "covered the objectionable features" President Roosevelt found in the bill he vetoed in 1906. Although Clark did not mention the *Winters* litigation by name, his new version of the water rights provision *explicitly* extinguished any implied water rights that had been recognized or might be recognized by the courts. It then created a reserved right to an amount of water necessary to irrigate the irrigable lands of any allotment that lasted through the full twenty-five-year federal trust period. The allottee could acquire a vested right to the amount of water actually put to beneficial use in that period. All other waters could be used only according to the laws of Montana. Thus Senator Clark had proposed a longer-term if still limited reserved right for the Blackfeet allottees, one that did not relate to the 1888 reservation agreement.[34]

Although the Senate Indian Affairs Committee approved Senator Clark's allotment bill, it rejected his water rights provision even though he was a member of the committee, gutting any of the reserved nature of the right or other protections. The committee took one path suggested by President Roosevelt's veto message of the year before by adding an appropriation for an irrigation project, to be repaid out of the sale of the surplus lands of the reservation. But the revised bill then provided that the irrigation system would be constructed and operated and all water appropriated *under the laws of the State of Montana* by the United States in trust for the Indians. The bill passed the Senate in January 1907 with little debate. The senators were told by the bill's sponsors—including Senator Clark—that the new bill was essentially the same as the one they had passed the year before, except that it now satisfied the president's objections. They were not told that the water provision was significantly different from what was in last year's bill and significantly different from what was in this year's bill when first proposed.[35]

It was at this point that the Montana state legislature weighed in by adopting Everett's proposed memorial focused directly on the Blackfeet bill (although the Montana congressional delegation did not enter it into the *Congressional Record* until the beginning of the next Congress, in 1908), but using that issue to make a statement on the Indian water rights litigation that was far more extreme than anything ever produced by the valley irrigation association.[36] The legislature's memorial began by noting that the Blackfeet reservation contained thousands of acres of desirable agricultural lands that were "far in excess of what the Indians needed, of no benefit to the Indians and not a source of revenue to the federal or state government. But then the memorial switched gears, to inform Congress that the federal courts in the *Winters* case had issued a permanent injunction reserving 5,000 inches of water for the Indians of the Fort Belknap reservation, based upon an implied reservation of water in the 1888 treaty. The memorial lamented that the amount reserved exceeded the normal low-water flow of the Milk River, leaving none for the settlers, and that the waters were not being used by the Indians "nor being diverted for any useful purposes." The memorial made no connection between this lamentable fact and the Blackfeet allotment bill other than to point out that a similar suit was pending to enjoin the diversion of water by settlers from Birch Creek along the Blackfeet reservation (that is, the *Conrad* case). The water the government sought to reserve for the Blackfeet would not be put to beneficial use, "but, on the contrary, water will flow undiverted downstream." At the same time,

> by virtue of the water rights being impliedly reserved for the Indians by the agreements aforesaid, without limit as to time or place of use, every water right in the entire community from the Missouri and Marias rivers north to the Canadian boundary line and from the summit of the Rocky Mountains to the boundary of Dakota is either rendered invalid or so vague, unreliable, and indefinite as to be of no substantial value to the settlers and others dependent upon such streams for a water supply.[37]

In the absence of a solution from Congress, the "indefinite and unreliable" conditions with regard to water rights was retarding settlement. Worse, many of the region's citizens were moving to Canada, according to the memorial, motivated "by the fear that the clouded and precarious water rights in northern Montana will seriously and permanently stifle prosperity." The memorial concluded by requesting that Congress (1) adopt legislation limiting the Indians' rights to the quantity of water actually used by for irrigation and domestic purposes and "subject to diversion and used according to the laws of Montana", and (2) pass the Blackfeet allotment bill.[38]

The memorial was far from clear as to why and how these two subjects went together. It seems obvious that the people who wanted to undo the Fort Belknap water rights decision simply used the general desire for a Blackfeet allotment bill as a vehicle for their particular concern. That those opposed to the Indian water rights decisions chose the state legislature as the vehicle for this statement indicates, again, that the particular dynamics within the valley itself were never favorable to the Chinook-Havre point of view on these issues. I am assuming—without any specific discussion in the documents—that the state legislators, only a few of whom came from the Milk River area (only Everett in the Senate), were much less affected by or less informed about the local dynamics in the valley. When viewed in the abstract the Indian water rights decisions almost always appalled the dominant settlers and associated economic interests in the West and were an easy target for complaint.

Logan quickly wrote to the commissioner of Indian affairs to warn him of the state legislature's memorial, noting that the memorial ostensibly about the Blackfeet bill "incidentally touches upon the Belknap reservation." Logan wanted the commissioner to know, and for the commissioner to inform others, that as to the water rights situation at Fort Belknap, "the Hon. Senator has not confined himself to the strict lines of veracity." This was because, according to Logan, 5,000 inches was *not* all of the normal flow; because the normal flow was sufficient, as shown in 1906 (even before the rains) to irrigate the reservation's land and then to allow the upstream irrigators to begin diverting; and because 5,000 inches was *not* more water than the Indians can use. "[L]ast year, the first time in the history of the reservation that our rights were asserted and maintained, every drop of water that came down to our land was turned into our ditch and utilized upon the Indian farms, not a drop being allowed to waste." Logan wanted the commissioner to know the "actual conditions" so that he could take steps to prevent any attempt by the Montana delegation "to secure a part of the water belonging to this reservation."[39]

Presumably in part because of objections by Logan and the Indian Office, and partly because of the way the Milk River valley as a whole did not actively support the upstream irrigators crusade, Congress did nothing to pass special legislation undoing the *Winters* decisions or allot or sell off the irrigable parts of the Fort Belknap reservation. Congress did polish off the Blackfeet allotment bill, however. While the separate Blackfeet allotment bill did not survive, its provisions were incorporated into that session's Indian Affairs appropriations bill (along with the minor legislative revision necessary to allow for the sugar beet leases at Fort Belknap). Senator Carter brought this measure to the floor of the Senate, stressing that it had been passed before and was urgently needed and wanted "both by Indians and by settlers." He argued that "it is of very great moment to the northern part of the State of Montana that this vast region, the headwaters of the chief streams of that country, should be open to settlement." Despite his pleas to leave it alone, senators began meddling with the water rights provision. Senator Lodge of Massachusetts offered an amendment without explanation that created a one-year preference right for the Indians to the water from the irrigation system.

Senator Clark followed with an amendment that made the water right appurtenant to the land of the allottee and measured by beneficial use, again with no explanation. The Senate agreed to both amendments without significant debate and then agreed to the bill. The House eventually agreed to the Blackfeet allotment measure at conference without debate or discussion of the water issues. It is not clear what the Indian Office thought about the legislation, but President Roosevelt signed the bill on March 1, 1907—five months before the federal court in Montana officially ruled in favor of the reserved rights of the Blackfeet reservation in the *Conrad* case.[40]

The final result? Congress spent two years constructing, in the water rights provision, a tortured monstrosity of legislative drafting. The act appropriated $300,000 for the construction of an irrigation system to irrigate the allotted lands, to be repaid by the sale of the surplus lands. Congress then added the following complex proviso:

> Provided, That the Indians, and the settlers on the surplus lands, in the order named, shall have a preference right for one year from the date of the President's proclamation opening the reservation to settlement, to appropriate the waters of the reservation which shall be filed on and appropriated under the laws of the State of Montana, by the Commissioner of Indian Affairs on behalf of the Indians taking irrigable allotments and by settlers under the same law. At the expiration of the one year aforesaid the irrigation system constructed and to be constructed shall be operated under the laws of the State of Montana, and the title to such systems as may be constructed under the Act shall be in the Secretary of the Interior in trust for said Indians, . . . [and] Provided, That the right to the use of water acquired under the provisions of the Act shall be appurtenant to the land irrigated, and beneficial use shall be the basis, the measure and limit of the right.[41]

For two years Congress discussed water rights and various water provisions in the context of the Blackfeet allotments. Yet the provision finally approved had appeared only in the last stage in that process. No committee examined or analyzed the full provision, and no report or statement on the floor of either house explained its meaning. The House never even debated the provision, and the debate in the Senate amounted to little. Thus the official documents do not tell what various members of Congress understood by the provision, if they did understand it. The final provision contained inconsistent elements of a very limited reserved rights theory and of complete deference to the state appropriation system.

It imposed a number of contrary or unworkable requirements, and these defects must have been obvious to some at the time. The only message that the provision really carried was Congress's belief (and the belief of others affected—other than the Indians, of course) that the allotment process and large irrigation and storage projects were the answer to the reserved rights dilemma, that soon all the Indians would be working under the same principles as the non-Indian settlers and all would be accommodated with water from irrigation projects. Thus despite whatever attitude people had toward the reserved rights doctrine, they had little reason to push for its formal extinction or for its sanction or to fight language that was less than perfect. Under the circumstances, the doctrine posed no real threat of widespread change in the ways of land use, development, and water allocation.

Congress did not deflect the reserved rights issue into the allotment process in a vacuum. The Montana legislature had pictured an emergency, directly caused by the reserved water right decisions at the Fort Belknap reservation. Precisely what this had to do with breaking up the Blackfeet reservation was never stated explicitly, but the link was made nonetheless. Congress responded to this situation by doing what it was predisposed to do anyway, given the national Indian and water policies— allotment bills and appropriations for irrigation projects. The peculiar local dynamics as they entered into the national legislation simply added the particularly incoherent water rights provision to the Blackfeet allotment bill.

It is not surprising to find that during the first session of the Sixtieth Congress (covering the first half of 1908), Congress replayed its Blackfeet allotment struggle in a bill to allot the Fort Peck Indian Reservation, also in northern Montana. The bill began with the same water rights provision as ended up in the Blackfeet allotment measure. Senator Henry Teller of Colorado immediately objected to the last section of the long, complicated water rights provision. Apparently referring to the requirement that the new water right be appurtenant to the land, he argued that "[t]hat is not a question that we have anything to do with in Congress. It is purely a question of State regulation, and that clause must go out." Why he singled out this provision is unclear, since other portions similarly usurped state water law. Nonetheless the Senate agreed to his amendment without debate, passed the bill with almost no debate, and sent it to the House.[42]

The House then made its contribution to irrational legislative drafting, replacing the Senate's odd but already accepted water rights provision with completely new, odd language. The new provision was even more internally inconsistent than the old. The bill authorized a survey and allotment of the Fort Peck reservation and appropriated $200,000 to begin construction of an irrigation system for the benefit of the allotted lands. In language that clearly stated that Congress was reserving water for the Indians, the bill then provided that "[t]he land irrigable under the systems herein provided, which has been allotted to the Indians in severalty, shall be deemed to have a right to so much water as may be required to irrigate such land without cost to the Indians for the construction of such irrigation systems."[43] Yet at the same time, the provision included a flat statement that "[a]ll appropriations of the water of the reservation shall be made under the provisions of the laws of the State of Montana." The House left unexplained how the federal government could guarantee each allottee the right to so much water as was required to irrigate the land if the appropriation was wholly subject to state law. Nonetheless the revised bill passed the House without debate, and the Senate concurred without debate. Congress did not spend any time discussing, debating, or explaining the water rights language, at least not in the official documents. President Roosevelt signed the Fort Peck allotment bill on May 30, 1908, five months after the Supreme Court's decision in *Winters* and five days after the Ninth Circuit decision in *Conrad*.[44]

The Fort Peck allotment act was further proof that Congress, in order to pass a Montana allotment bill, would approve any water rights language pliable enough to suit a variety of viewpoints, no matter how strange. A few congressmen had an interest in the conflict between the non-Indian settlers and the Montana reservations over water, and they knew that the courts were resolving that conflict in the Indians' favor with the reserved rights doctrine. They also had to be aware that some of the settlers and their allies were worried about this development and were looking to Congress to do something to counter the trend. But they also probably knew that as a whole the people of the Milk River valley were not as outraged and aggrieved about the Indian water rights decisions as the few who were up in arms conveyed, viewing it more as a means to help them secure government investments in storage and irrigation facilities. Others, mostly outside of Congress, saw the developing reserved rights doctrine as a useful tool to help the Indians and wanted congressional support. The attitude in Congress quickly became that Congress had nothing to gain by forcing a direct resolution of the reserved rights issue when the allotments and irrigation projects would make the issue meaningless. And so in the first few years following the *Winters* ruling, as the *Winters* and *Conrad* cases moved through the judicial system, Congress deflected any conflict generated by the reserved rights rulings into the allotment process.[45]

Two documents a few years after the *Winters* litigation illustrate these attitudes and dynamics as well as any explanation here. In 1909 the chief inspector for the Reclamation Service recommended to the secretary of the interior that Reclamation take control of Indian irrigation from the Office of Indian Affairs. It was not just that the irrigation work on Indian projects and non-Indian Reclamation projects was practically the same, duplicating engineering bureaucracies. It was also that "the time is not far distant when the reservations will be part of the State, and the Indian irrigation will be a part of the national irrigation scheme"—the Indians, it was predicted, would be individual property owning, small-tract farmers subject to state laws and provided water through federal Reclamation projects, indistinguishable from their non-Indian farming counterparts.[46] Two years later, and from a completely different perspective, E. B. Meritt, who would be an important Indian Affairs official for decades, pointed to the Blackfeet and Fort Peck legislation and similar laws affecting other reservations and complained:

> I find that the principle laid down in the very favorable decision of the Supreme Court regarding water rights of Indians in the Winters case has been practically nullified by various acts of Congress and as the result of such legislation the water rights of Indians are now dependent on beneficial use in a large number of reservations where the Government is spending millions of dollars on reimbursable funds and are subject to the laws of the several States wherein these projects are located.[47]

It was time, Meritt said, "to evolve a plan whereby these water rights might be better protected." Meritt's plan was a proposed bill for Congress that restated the reserved water rights doctrine and explicitly applied it to every Indian reservation. Meritt's bill never made it to Congress, for reasons discussed in another chapter; and given the inevitable compromises that would have had to occur, it was probably just as well for the future of the doctrine. But Meritt's attitude resembled that of Logan's and Rasch's, and of those in the Interior and Justice Departments that protected Rasch's efforts from Reclamation's attempts to undo them in the legal arena. In just a few years after Meritt made this comment, others in and out of the federal government, especially the attorneys in the Denver field office of the Justice Department, would do their best, within this cultural milieu, to make something more meaningful and complicated out of the *Winters* doctrine.[48]

CHAPTER 7

The Supreme Court's Decision
in Winters

Anticlimax in the Milk River Valley, 1907–1908

Returning to the Milk River valley in the summer of 1907, with the Blackfeet reservation legislation distractions out of the way, matters settled back into the alternating flights of boosterism and anxiety about the Milk River Reclamation project, with almost nary a word about the Fort Belknap water rights case pending in the Supreme Court. The big news for the summer of 1907 was that Secretary of the Interior James Garfield was coming to the valley to inspect the progress on the Reclamation project and tour the reservations, giving the irrigation association a chance to bring its concerns directly to him in a July 1 gathering planned for Harlem. An executive committee composed of Everett and two others prepared a resolution of the association to present to Garfield. It mentioned all the usual issues—especially concern over the slow progress on the headwaters portion of the project and the absence of progress on the other end. The delay was a problem not only in terms of water and facilities available but also because the Interior Department was holding up any land patents in the valley until the completion of the project, which meant that public-land settlers within the project area were having to wait a long time to get title to their lands. (This resolution said the land problem was driving settlers to Canada.) The association's resolution said *nothing* about Indian water rights, the reservations, or the court decisions.

Garfield's visit appeared to be a great success, as he said all the right things to encourage the valley residents without appearing to commit to anything. As part of a series of presentations, Walter B. Sands, an attorney from Chinook, "argued direct from the Indian treaty" to show "that there was nothing in [the treaty] that gave to them priority to the water rights." But nobody else seemed interested in the topic. Everett, for example, spoke instead on the international question—the Canadian threat to an augmented Milk River. The secretary politely responded with platitudes about helping to improve the lives of the Indians through irrigated agriculture (and remarked what a great job Logan seemed to be doing at that) while not interfering unduly with the development of the country occupied by the settlers. These were comments not even worth reporting in the papers; Logan noted them in a letter. Garfield did, however, tour the Fort Belknap reservation to learn more about the sugar beet potential.[1]

The excitement generated by the Garfield visit soon died down, and by December the irrigation association was again meeting, anxious and upset that the Reclamation project had stalled. Representative Pray attributed the continued delay primarily to the fact that the Reclamation Service could not justify proceeding with the project without settling the Canadian question, which was also the view of the editor of the *Milk River Valley News*. But Senator Carter, to the contrary and quite oddly, implied in a letter to the association that the project had been delayed while Reclamation waited for the Supreme Court's decision in the *Winters* case, and that "[i]f the decision is reversed by the supreme court, progress will be made with the opening of Spring." There is no clue to where he got this idea, as no one before had suggested that the Fort Belknap case was a hindrance to the Reclamation project. Senator Carter's letter must have been like a red flag to the Chinook and Havre irrigators, but nothing came of it. Meanwhile Logan was trying to get prepared to be able to break ground during the 1908 irrigation and growing season for sugar beets, as the contract with the Amalgamated Sugar Company was about to be signed.[2]

The next event of importance? The Supreme Court's decision in *Winters,* on January 6, 1908, followed a week later by the news about the signing of the sugar beet contract, followed a week later by bad news about the Reclamation project in a letter from Secretary of the Interior Garfield. January 1908 was a busy month for the Milk River.

THE SUPREME COURT'S DECISION: IN THE MILK RIVER VALLEY

In most discussions of *Winters* the central focus of the discussion, indeed the only focus of discussion, is the Supreme Court's opinion. In this story it is an anticlimax in all ways possible. The record filed by the parties in the Supreme Court from the lower courts had nothing in it but the basic pleadings—complaint, answer, statement of assignments of errors, and nothing more of substance. The briefs in the Supreme Court were unremarkable, especially in the sense that they did not present new ways of looking at the issues in the case, and are not worth reviewing here. The defendants were represented by the same attorneys as in the lower courts, primarily Edward Day of Helena, and they raised refined versions of arguments they made to Judge Hunt and to the appellate court. Carl Rasch was no longer representing the United States, as the Department of Justice had taken over the case at this level. But the briefs filed by the solicitor general, Henry Hoyt, the assistant attorney generals, J. A. Van Orsdel and Edward T. Sanford, and "special attorney" A. C. Campbell (an expert in western water issues hired on special contract by the Justice Department) argued the same basic mix of federal power regarding water for purposes on public land (*Rio Grande*) and treaty reserved rights (*Winans*) that Rasch argued. The only surprise is that in one of the government's briefs, at the end of a very short section, the United States continued to argue that water rights for the reservation were also justified under a common law riparian rights theory recognized by Montana law! I have not found any record of the oral arguments before the Court, which were of little importance by this time, anyway. I did not find any indication that the case got any particular attention in Washington, D.C., or nationally when argued or decided. I did not find any documents or inferences indicating how any of the Court members thought of the case or the way it was decided.[3]

Finally, the Court's opinion itself is unremarkable, in this sense: The opinion by Justice McKenna, author of the *Winans* opinion three years before, not only affirmed the rulings of the lower courts below but did so based on the same legal theories. McKenna focused most on the meaning of the 1888 treaty as a reservation of water but also mixed in the federal power over federal property proposition, with a *Rio Grande* case citation and a statement that the "[t]he power of the Government to reserve the waters and exempt them from appropriation under the state laws" for purposes on federal lands "is not denied, and could not be." (McKenna also stated, just as did Judge Hawley in the Ninth Circuit's appellate decision, that because of the way the Court had approached the issues, "we have not discussed the doctrine of riparian rights urged by the Government.") The Court's *Winters* opinion is very short—the discussion on the merits covered but two pages—and quite conclusory rather than analytical or explanatory, especially on every topic other than the provisions of the 1888 treaty and its general meaning. In fact, as will be examined in more detail below, the opinion said so little that people later had much confusion trying to figure out what its implications were outside of this particular set of facts. Also, McKenna made no attempt to explain how this opinion fit with the Court's view of the very limited federal role in water allocation expressed just the year before in the *Kansas v. Colorado* case. Justice Brewer, the author of the *Kansas v. Colorado* opinion, dissented in the *Winters* case (the lone dissent) but did not write an opinion.[4]

Just as important for this story, the Supreme Court's opinion did nothing to alter the dynamics in the Milk River valley. The Court's opinion was, of course, front-page news in the valley, as already discussed in part above, but the substance was not new and neither were the reactions.[5] If the Court had reversed the lower courts' rulings, or perhaps even if it had relied upon a different legal theory or did more to explain the basis for the rulings, that would have been a change and might have had an effect on the Milk River situation. But as it was the Court's opinion changed nothing, except to extinguish any hope in the opponents that relief would come through the judicial system. The valley had been living with this decision, on these premises, for two and a half years. All the Court did was add another layer of affirmation. The Chinook and Havre opponents of the decisions had already been trying avenues other than judicial to undo this decision; their efforts would continue. Others in the valley had been trying for some time to integrate the substance of the decision into on-going water and agricultural issues, paying only polite attention to the opponents' efforts, and that would continue, too. And within a week the front-page news was the signing of the sugar beet contract, which was why Logan's immediate response to the Supreme Court's decision was that it assured them an ample water supply for sugar beet operations.[6]

As might be expected, how the water rights decision would affect the prospects for the Reclamation project was the most important consideration to many. One of the papers in Helena reported that the decision would deprive all of the ranchers in the Milk River between Havre and Malta of water and force them "either to give up their farms, to depend on the sparse rainfall, or to wait until the St. Mary's irrigation project is finished." It was primarily this report that sparked the dramatic reaction from the *Milk River Valley News* in Harlem discussed in chapter 3, apparently worried that farmers and prospective farmers would be scared away from the valley rather than understand the opportunity presented. The paper could find "joy" in the decision because of what it could mean for hastening the construction of the "diversion dams, laterals and storage reservoirs" to store and distribute the spring flood waters or runoff, and it was this Reclamation project—not the ability to irrigate with the natural flow—that would vastly increase irrigation potential and bring an economic boom and lasting prosperity to the valley. The paper urged the valley's irrigation association to meet immediately, send representatives to Washington, and "demand that work be started in the spring," as the decision provided the association "with abundant ammunition to press its claims on the Milk River project." In the same mood, and presumably with the same worry about the effect of any negative news, the Hinsdale paper reprinted the Harlem's papers comments and added that the outlook for the Milk River valley is "brightening" and that if the government would only begin work on the promised irrigation system, "this valley would be one of the most prosperous sections of the great northwest."[7]

The irrigation association did not meet right away, but a "mass meeting" did take place in Harlem on January 25, 1908, which attracted farmers and businessmen from the whole valley—from Chinook and Havre to Glasgow. The meeting was called by the Harlem Industrial Association—the town businessmen's association—to bring together all farmers "interested in sugar beet culture" to discuss the planned sugar beet enterprise. That was in fact the main topic at the meeting, but people also used the meeting to discuss the need for action on the Reclamation project, especially to have the government start work on the distribution portion of the project. Chinook farmers (such as A. H. Reser) and their allies (e.g., W. B. Sands, the Chinook attorney) were there, promising cooperation in the sugar beet enterprise. They turned the last fifteen minutes of the meeting to their favorite topic—the impact and injustice of the Indian water rights decision. Just before adjournment they convinced those present to adopt a resolution calling on the irrigation association to meet "for the purpose of sending delegates to Washington D.C." to ask Congress "to set right the wrong that has been done the farmers of the Milk River valley."[8]

It is interesting to see what happened to that resolution once it got to the association meeting a month later, but first something quite demoralizing intervened: Secretary of the Interior Garfield sent a letter (written by the head of the Reclamation Service, Frederick Newell) to the Milk River Irrigation Association to clarify that it was not practical for the United States to begin constructing the project's distribution facilities "before an adequate supply of water has been provided for them." Under the circumstances this could only occur when the Montana courts had resolved the "uncertainty as to titles to water in Milk River valley," a reference to the general water rights adjudication proceeding, not the *Winters* case. Work in the valley would also depend on when the headwaters part of the project had been developed to bring more water to the river, and earlier communications had made clear that the government thought it not worth progressing too quickly on that end until the Canadian situation had been resolved. Garfield recognized that people in the valley had urged the government to go ahead with the distribution system now, anyway, because higher-flow years would allow for water to spread that far, and "even an occasional flood watering through government canals would be highly appreciated and valued." Garfield responded, however, that under the current conditions, including the issues of the "ownership of the ordinary flow and the flood flow of the Milk River," it was just as likely that any new distribution facilities would sit idle in any year. The government could not justify spending the stretched Reclamation fund for that kind of project, especially when Reclamation amounts expended in Montana had already been so high in relation to those in other states. Joseph Dixon, now one of Montana's senators, later sent a letter warning that the Milk River project might even be abandoned if a settlement with Canada were not reached.[9]

Thus when the irrigation association did finally meet in Chinook on February 17, 1908, it was Garfield's letter and associated developments—not the Supreme Court's decision in *Winters* or the sugar beet developments—that set the agenda. Events once again overshadowed the desire of the Chinook and Havre irrigators to get the association to focus on the Indian water rights decision and to see it as an outrage demanding priority action. The association produced a resolution on the issue—their first and only—but not of the type they wanted and not without opposition. The association president began the meeting by reading Secretary Garfield's letter and describing the current crisis. He noted that work had been suspended on the upper portions of the project due to difficulties in the ongoing negotiations with Canada over allocation of the Saint Mary and Milk Rivers, to "adverse reports" from the engineers about the proposed Chain Lakes storage reservoir, and to "the fact that the water rights in the upper valley had not been adjudicated." But in his view, and despite the Garfield letter, it was his opinion—which seemed to be shared by those in attendance—that no such obstacles "confronted the lower portion of the project." The association should concentrate on that issue and demand the beginning of the work on the Dodson diversion dam and irrigation canals this spring; "the delegation should go to Washington with that sole object." Reading between the lines, apparently delegates from the upper part of the valley, especially Chinook, were not happy with the sole focus being on the distribution facilities at Dodson and on down (even leaving aside Indian water rights for a moment). They did not want the association to give up demanding action on the headwaters portion of the project. The association eventually approved instructions to their delegation to urge upon the Department of the Interior that work be resumed on the headwaters part of the project and started "somewhere along the proposed canal," and to request information on the Canadian negotiations from the secretary of state.

In his introduction to the meeting, the association president did not even mention the Indian water rights decision as an issue for the meeting. W. B. Sands and the other Chinook delegates and affected people from the Harlem area did raise it, however, and demanded that something be said by the meeting and by the Washington delegation concerning their hardships. Not without a fight—delegates from Glasgow and elsewhere "opposed the committee taking up anything but the work on the Dodson dam." The Chinook interests finally prevailed, but not with a resolution denouncing the *Winters* decision or demanding unilateral action to "set right the wrong that has been done the farmers of the Milk River valley," as they had proposed at the previous mass meeting. Recognizing instead that the valleywide delegates to the irrigation association simply were not with them on the need for a resolution, the Chinook delegates proposed, and the association eventually accepted, an instruction to the delegation to call on Congress "to make an appropriation for the purpose of buying water for the Indians on the Fort Belknap reservation and restore the water of Milk River to the rightful owners, the white settlers." Little victory for the "Chinookers"—who could resist agreeing to a suggestion that Congress buy their way out of the problem, with no sacrifice by anyone?[10]

Given how gloomy things looked in February, surprisingly work *did* begin by July on the diversion dam and what was known as the Dodson-Malta-Glasgow Canal. The people in the lower valley realized they needed to give the Reclamation Service more of a reason to begin that part of the project, and so with the aid of the congressional delegation, they got Reclamation to agree to a "cooperative" venture, to begin work *if* the people to be benefited would subscribe to pay half the cost.

They did subscribe, and the valley celebrated at the site of the diversion dam construction in October. Even with the cooperative arrangement, the Reclamation Service might not have been interested, but the State Department also began giving assurances that negotiations with the Canadians were progressing. By 1909 the Boundary Waters Treaty had worked out an allocation formula that did allow the Americans to tap the Saint Mary River for some water into the Milk and reserved for the Canadians a share of the augmented flow of the Milk if and when the Canadians were ready to use it. Work resumed on the Saint Mary canal and the rest of the headwaters portion of the project.

As for the Indian water rights decreed by Judge Hunt, direct efforts to undo that decision faded. The proposal to strip the irrigable land from the reservation in order to extinguish the water rights fizzled. (This did not, of course, mean the end of the preexisting and quite distinct desire for the land for its own sake, and for the policy of transforming the Indians into individual property-owning, small-tract farmers. Allotments were eventually forced on the Fort Belknap reservation in 1921, with the associated sale of "surplus" irrigable land to non-Indians—events outside the scope of this study). The proposal for a congressiónal appropriation to buy out these reserved rights went nowhere. Finally, even the Chinook people gave in and realized that their best path was not to fight but to be subsidized—to pressure the federal government to finish as quickly as possible the headwaters part of the Reclamation project, bringing more water into the river at irrigation time for their use, and also to get the government in essence to buy from *them* and improve for their use their distribution facilities. As discussed above, allotment and/or storage and irrigation facilities became the non-Indian society's preferred method of dealing with Indian reserved water rights. This is not the whole story of the *Winters* doctrine in the years following the formative litigation, as other parts of this study will describe. But it is a significant part of the story, and central to the experience at Fort Belknap. Congressional appropriations funded irrigation facilities for the reservation, although these facilities were poorly integrated into the valley's Reclamation project. Ultimately, however, the reserved rights at Fort Belknap were "undone" by the realities of capital flows: of what value were the reservation's legal rights (especially as fixed) if the people in the valley and in government made sure that the really significant investments for water development went to the non-Indian farmers and not to the Indians?[11]

THE SUPREME COURT'S DECISION AS
A LEGAL ARTIFACT

The Supreme Court's opinion in *Winters* was unremarkable in terms of the particular context of the Fort Belknap case and the Milk River valley, but that is not the only context to consider. Broadening the focus again, with that opinion was born what would become known in the larger context as the Indian reserved water rights doctrine or "*Winters* doctrine" (among other things immortalizing the misspelled name of Henry Winter, the Chinook area cattleman who was the first-named appellant and apparently an international fugitive at the time of all the appellate opinions bearing his name[12]). Justice McKenna's opinion had some serious shortcomings for a ruling that was to play, eventually, such an important role. Yet what people outside the immediate litigation knew (and know now) of *Winters* came almost entirely from the Supreme Court's opinion. Thus it is worth pursuing here a more penetrating examination of the Supreme Court's *Winters* opinion, to illustrate turn-of-the-century currents in Indian policy, attitudes toward Indians in the non-Indian society, federal Indian law, the federal role in water allocation and, especially, issues and problems raised by the opinion itself, which subsequently influenced how it was received and understood.

For purposes of analysis, the Court's *Winters* opinion can be broken into three parts or steps in the reasoning, none explained in any depth and at times seemingly inconsistent. First, the Court began by describing and trying to understand the meaning, in terms of water, of the 1888 agreement by which the Gros Ventres and Assiniboines ceded and reserved the Fort Belknap lands. The Court noted that the large tract of land originally controlled by the Gros Ventres and Assiniboines was "adequate for the habits and wants of a nomadic and uncivilized people." But it was the "policy of the Government" and the "desire of the Indians," as expressed in the agreement, to "change those habits," for the Indians to change their way of life and become a "pastoral and civilized" people. The original tract of land was "too extensive" for this purpose, but the "smaller tract would be inadequate without a change of conditions" because the lands were arid and "practically valueless" without irrigation. Thus although the parties did not explicitly specify a reservation of water as they did a reservation of land, the agreement made no sense and could not be implemented unless it were interpreted—in what the Court called a "conflict of implications"—as intending to reserve water to fulfill the reservation purposes. The Court seemed to reach this conclusion

THE SUPREME COURT'S DECISION

simply on the logic of the situation, but then buttressed that conclusion by referring, without any case citations, to the "rule of interpretation" that ambiguities in agreements with Indians should be resolved "from the standpoint of the Indians."[13]

The way the Court understood the purposes of the treaty was, of course, in line with the nation's policy to transform the Indians into the American ideal of settled farmers participating in a market economy, whose land, if in the West, would need irrigation. If this was how the Gros Ventres and Assiniboines understood the 1888 treaty, it was only because they understood that this was the transformation being demanded of them, not that this was an attempt to reserve water *for* a way of life integrated into their society (which makes this such a different situation than the *Winans* fishing rights case). Rasch had recognized this, in noting to the Ninth Circuit that at the time of the 1888 treaty "not a drop of the waters of the stream was or had ever been taken from its channel by a white man for any purpose." The Indians who were party to the agreement were accustomed to having "the waters flow down past and through the reservation in abundance, and at no time had they known or seen the channel of Milk River other than as a flowing, living stream." He did not say what "uses" they had made of it, but we know (and he probably knew) that they drank from it, that it was important for ceremonial and spiritual purposes, that it sustained the life of the land and wild and domesticated animals they depended on, and more. Then Rasch also wove in the transformative intention of the land cession agreement—"while at that time the Indians may not have made use of much, if any, of the waters for irrigating purposes," they "knew that the very object and purpose" of the land cession agreement was that they become "self supporting as a pastoral and agricultural people," and they knew this "required the use of these waters to enable them to accomplish those very objects and purposes."

Rasch was able to take this complicated situation and make it work within the legal structures available. The Supreme Court merely affirmed the concept without going to the trouble of dealing with the complications. This was fine for people like Rasch, who already knew what it meant. But it caused no end of problems when applied outside of this very specific context. Thus politicians and legal analysts later felt the Court ignored complications that could have undone the conclusions, including the fact that the 1888 agreement expressly reserved land but not water in a territory and a region where the prevailing view (at least among non-Indians), even in 1888, was that water for irrigation was obtained under the local law of appropriation. In a

number of acts prior to 1888, Congress had expressed a desire to defer
to the local structures of prior appropriation in the allocation of water
in the West.[14] More important, in its work with Indians and irrigation,
the Indian Office had generally followed the territorial and state laws
of appropriation (if not too well), before and after 1888. In this legal
and policy environment, an agreement intended by the parties to
convert Indians to the non-Indian settlers' way of life and yet silent as
to water might just as likely indicate an intent, on the part of the
government at least, that water for the Indians be obtained under the
local water right system common to all irrigation farmers. Given that
the Court and others understood the Indians' intent in signing the
agreement as in accord with the federal government's plan that they
be transformed to the settled life of farmers in the West, then con-
ceivably it would have followed that the Indians understood the water
situation in the same way. The government would have assumed, and
the Indians might have been understood to have assumed, that the
Indian Office would assist the Indians in pursuing the requirements
of state water law. According to Dan Tarlock, a scholar of water law,
"[r]ecent historical evidence suggests that [*Winters*] is wrong because
both the Indian Office and the Indians expected state law to govern
the nascent Indian irrigation program," citing Hoxie's book on assimilation.[15] I do not agree that the historical evidence is as Tarlock concluded (and he is wrong about Hoxie, who did not make so specific a
point about the intent or practice of the Indians or the Indian Office in
the late 1880s, when the parties executed the Fort Belknap agreement).
What is more important, however, is the fact that some people then
and now have not been able to understand why the silence about
water in the 1888 Fort Belknap agreement did not mean that the Gros
Ventres and Assiniboines were to follow local water law to obtain
water rights.

This is not to say that the Court's opinion was wrong, especially
given the way the Court emphasized the function of interpreting the
treaty in the way the Indians would have understood it, and given the
way the government's attorneys and then the district court, with more
knowledge of the particular context and working with Rasch's better
articulation, described what likely was these Indians' understanding.
The problem is less the "correctness" of the Court on this point as its
failure to explore the issue in more depth and explicitly grapple with
and dispatch alternative approaches to interpretation. This became one
of the grounds on which the decision was attacked or dismissed as
people tried to understand its implications in other contexts.

In any event, in the first analytical step of the *Winters* opinion, the Supreme Court ruled that the 1888 agreement reflected an implied intent on the part of both parties to reserve water. Yet that intent was meaningless unless one or both of the parties had the power and authority to reserve the water free of the control of state law. Thus a second basis for or step in the Court's ruling was that "[t]he Indians had command of the land and the waters" before signing the agreement, followed by the rhetorical question "Did they give up all this?", followed by a brief and rather muddy response that concluded no.[16] The implication then was that Indians *had* the authority to "reserve" water necessary for the purposes of the reservation simply by not ceding the water to the United States. But the opinion left too much implied or unexplained. This would have been an eminently logical spot for McKenna to cite to, and better yet, discuss, the *Winans* decision and the concept from *Winans* that such a treaty did not involve a grant by the federal government to the Indians but instead constituted a grant of rights from the Indians to the United States, with all rights not specifically granted reserved to the Indians. McKenna did not do so (the citation to *Winans* comes later, at a different part of the *Winters* opinion). Some of the early court decisions that followed or interpreted *Winters* understood *Winters,* in the light of *Winans,* primarily as a decision whereby Indians, with the acquiescence of the federal government, simply retained control over resources they had controlled prior to the agreement with the United States.[17] But the weakness in the explanation in *Winters* allowed others over the years either to be confused about or actively to deny that *Winters* is about Indians possessing rights and their authority to reserve those rights. These people understood *Winters* instead as simply a flawed and under-explained conclusion about the power and authority of Congress and the rest of the federal government to reserve the water. The Court's discussion of the treaty and the Indians' understanding was intended, in this view, only to help decide what had been the implied intent of Congress when it passed the law adopting the 1888 agreement into law.

Even accepting that the opinion had something to do with authority on the part of the Indians, the skimpiness of the analysis left many critical questions unanswered, some of which could have been or were anticipated by the parties and could have been addressed by the Court. For example, the Court's reasoning presented obvious issues of logic and implementation with regard to watercourses that did not originate on the reservation at the time of the agreement, which was true of the Milk River at the Fort Belknap reservation and would be true at many of the reservations in the West. Could the Gros Ventre and Assiniboine peoples (or others in a similar situation) reserve water in a river that they only partially commanded at the time of agreement? If so, how to measure the amount at their command and the geographic scope of their control? And did this mean that Indian reservations created by executive order or some other method that did not involve an agreement in which the native peoples participated did not have reserved rights? These questions were among those that bedeviled people after the Court's decision, and people who did not like the *Winters* decision would use these questions to try to undermine the legitimacy of the opinion.

To add to the confusion, the Court's second point in *Winters*—that the Indians reserved the water—appeared to some to clash with its third point, which implied that it was the federal government, not the Indians, that had the authority to and reserved the water. The defendants had argued that the admission of Montana into the union in 1889 made the waters in the state absolutely subject to the laws of the State of Montana. (On this premise the Montana legislature had passed the law in 1905, just before the first *Winters* ruling, that stated the United States could make use of water in Montana only "in the same manner and subject to the general conditions applicable to the appropriation of the waters of the state by private individuals."[18]) The Court rejected this argument, but it did so with just the one line that "the power of the Government to reserve the waters and exempt them from appropriation under the state laws is not denied, and could not be." The Court offered no further explanation, and did not identify or analyze any constitutional, property, or water rights theory to explain this ruling. Instead, to support this point the Court simply made two unexplained citations, to *Rio Grande* and *Winans*.[19]

To reiterate from above, *United States v. Rio Grande Dam and Irrigation Company* involved a suit by the federal government to block an irrigation dam on the Rio Grande that the government believed would interfere with downstream navigation. The Supreme Court's main line of reasoning in the *Rio Grande* decision and its holding for the government had little to do with rights to water. Rather, the Court confirmed that while various congressional acts had recognized and deferred to state control over water allocation, that state control had to yield to federal power under the Commerce Clause of the United States Constitution to protect navigational capacity, as expressed in the 1890 Rivers and Harbors Act. But the *Rio Grande* opinion also contained the unexplained and essentially irrelevant (to that decision) passage that "[i]n the absence of specific authority from Congress, a state cannot by its legislation destroy the right of the United States, as owner of the land bordering a stream, to the continued flow of its waters; so far at least as may be necessary for the beneficial uses of the government property," which was either an unclear statement of a federal riparian theory, an equally unclear statement of a property ownership theory applied to water, or a strikingly modern if unexplained statement of federal power and supremacy in an early form of the reserved rights theory. By citing the *Rio Grande* opinion without further explanation, the Court in *Winters* simply injected the questions surrounding this passage and the entire *Rio Grande* opinion into the *Winters* opinion. Even more confusing, McKenna's citation to *Rio Grande* in the *Winters* opinion was to the *wrong page* of the *Rio Grande* opinion! The cited page contained a description of the navigation issue and nothing more.[20]

The citation at this point in the *Winters* opinion to *United States v. Winans* was equally in need of further explanation. At the end of the *Winans* opinion McKenna had rejected a similar argument about the effect of the admission of Washington into the union. McKenna acknowledged that control over the banks of navigable rivers transferred from the United States to the State of Washington when Washington entered into the union. But he also concluded that the federal government had the power before the time of statehood and transfer to "create rights [to the shore lands] which would be binding on the State" after the transfer. This the United States had done by "secur[ing] to the Indians such a remnant of the great rights they possessed" providing for access to the river banks for fishing.[21]

McKenna's use of *Winans* means that while most people then and now understood the relationship between *Winters* and *Winans* as involving the nature and power of treaty rights, McKenna connected the two cases on a completely different point—the power of the federal government vis-à-vis the states to reserve rights to land and water. McKenna obviously and probably consciously avoided linking the treaty rights approaches of *Winans* and *Winters*. This is probably because of the disparities between the two sets of facts. As attractive as the *Winans* opinion was to some (such as Judge Hunt) as an aid to resolving the *Winters* case, *Winans* involved the meaning of an unusual but express reservation of an interest in access to land (access points to fishing spots) for an activity and at a location already central to the existence of the Indians who made the agreement. *Winters,* in contrast, concerned the possibility of an ambiguous or implied reservation of waters for what was *not* an existing, historical activity of the tribes involved—irrigated agriculture. The difference did not have to mean that the *Winans* decision was an inappropriate guide to resolving the *Winters* case, but it would have helped if the Court had explained why the differences did not matter.

Thus what could be said, and was said, about this third part of the *Winters* opinion, was that it held that the United States, not necessarily the Gros Ventres and Assiniboines, had the authority to and did reserve the waters, and that Congress did so implicitly as part of some general and unexplained control over waters in the West to benefit federal lands. Thus some courts and commentators writing shortly after *Winters* understood *Winters* to mean that Congress was the active (if fairly silent) party reserving the water right, and ignored the Indians' role.[22] But then many people questioned how an implied reserved right by Congress for irrigation purposes in this instance squared with what appeared to be decades of congressional deference to the local system of water rights by appropriation. The Court simply did not do enough to make this clear.

All this confusion does not mean that the *Winters* decision was legally unsound, for reasons I have described above. I would agree with others that in many ways the decision was unexceptional if not well explained, that the apparent complications could be overcome, and that it was far from a contradiction to say that both the Gros Ventres and Assiniboines *and* the United States had the authority to and did reserve the water. Moreover, the lower court opinions in *Winters,* particularly the first of the two Ninth Circuit opinions on appeal, were more complete and compelling in their explanations. The two contemporaneous opinions in the *Conrad* case concerning the Blackfeet reservation were also better than the Supreme Court opinion in *Winters* in explaining the rationale for the reserved right. The Ninth Circuit's appellate opinion in *Conrad* was particularly important in this regard. The Court of Appeals issued it a few months after the Supreme Court's decision in *Winters.* The panel of three judges issuing the decision included two judges who had been part of both panels that had issued the Ninth Circuit decisions in *Winters.* The new opinion reaffirmed, explained at some detail, and applied the ruling in *Winters.* The Court of Appeals made crystal clear one of the most controversial points—that the reserved right was not limited to present needs or uses of the reservation. The water had been reserved for the as-yet-unquantified future requirements of the people on the reservation.[23]

Yet the Supreme Court opinion was the only opinion read or known about by those who became familiar with the case. The ambiguities of that opinion and the issues left unanswered created opportunities for misunderstanding and misinterpretation and for arguments that the Supreme Court had ignored contrary law and had no real authority for its ruling. The guardians of the prior appropriation system exploited these problems and questioned the legitimacy of the opinion for decades in debates and litigation over the meaning, validity, and portability of the *Winters* decision.[24]

CHAPTER 8

The People of Winters and the Natural Law of the West

Wyoming Representative Mondell would call it a "monstrous" doctrine, "contrary to the natural law of things" in an arid land, terms and ideas first heard from the Chinook defendants and echoed ever since in the West to refer to *Winters*. Western politicians, western economic interests, and scholars of various types often contended that the systems of water allocation developed in the arid West were products of the physical conditions of the land, a truly natural law, as necessary to human society in the West as water itself. And as can be seen in the exchange between the Montana senators and South Carolina Senator Tillman, a typical response to those who disagree with these arrangements has always been that they do so because they are outsiders, primarily easterners who are ignorant of the true conditions of the West. This attitude was paramount in the arguments of those who fought the reserved rights doctrine in the decade after *Winters*.

Yet this ignores the fact that people in the West produced the *Winters* decision and its rationale. To explain the birth and history of the *Winters* doctrine, one must account for a diversity of attitudes in the West concerning appropriate approaches toward water allocation. The lawyers and judges involved in shaping the *Winters* decisions are a good example, beginning with the United States attorney who filed and diligently pursued the *Winters* and *Conrad* cases. Carl Rasch was responsible for formulating the reserved rights argument in *Winters* and pressing for its adoption by the courts, in the face of opposition not only from the settler defendants and their political allies in the Montana state government and congressional delegation but also from the Reclamation Service and its attorneys within the Department of Justice. Rasch was born in Germany and educated in the Midwest, not in Montana, having moved to Helena in 1891. He pursued a successful private law practice until named United States attorney by President Roosevelt in 1902. Rasch was the United States attorney until 1908 and a federal judge from 1910 to 1911, resigning both posts to return to private practice. His private clients before and after public service appear to have been businesses in general and insurance companies in particular.[1]

While neither a settler nor entrepreneur, Rasch's background indicates a person well acquainted with life, business, and prosperity in settler-era Montana, a person who could identify with the concerns of those living and working in that region. To say that Rasch acted contrary to the proper "western" or "Montana" attitude because he was not a Montana native would be foolish. Many if not most living in Montana in 1905 had been born elsewhere, including farming settlers and other staunch guardians of the appropriation system. Yet in the *Winters* case, Rasch's duties to his clients overshadowed any supposed philosophical or natural disposition to believe that there was only one way to allocate water for a successful, prosperous arid Milk River valley and Montana.

The Montana federal judge who issued the injunction preventing the Chinook irrigators from diverting water, reserved it for the Indians, and chose the reserved treaty rights theory to support it was another Montana resident, albeit an unusual one. William Hunt had also been born and educated outside of Montana, part of a wealthy family prominent in Republican politics. Hunt's extended family apparently was from the New York area—they had a family estate on the Hudson—but Hunt was born in New Orleans and his father was a Republican lawyer and state attorney general there. Hunt's father left in 1876 when it was no longer lucrative or even safe to be a Republican lawyer in Louisiana and went to Washington, where he was a judge on the United States Court of Claims and eventually secretary of the navy and then ambassador to Russia. Hunt was educated at boarding schools in the East and at Yale University, but left Yale for health reasons and eventually studied law at Tulane University. He left New Orleans when his father did, but did not take the position in the Department of the Navy that his father recommended. Instead he decided to strike north and west to see how he could prosper in the new settlements, going first to North Dakota and by 1881 to Montana. Hunt was a lawyer in private practice and the United States collector of customs at Fort Benton from 1881 to 1884. He was sent to Helena in 1884 as a member of the territory's first constitutional

convention, liked it there, and stayed, becoming involved in the Helena
legal community and local Republican politics. Hunt had a successful
private practice for a few years, was the territory's attorney general
(1884–86), a member of the territorial legislature (1888–89), named the
new state's first trial judge (1889), and then a justice on the state supreme
court (1894–1901). His friends and professional allies were the notables
of Montana politics of both parties, including United States Senator
Carter (apparently a close friend); Thomas Walsh, a prominent attorney
and future Democratic congressman and senator (and one of the attorneys for the defendants in the *Winters* case and the primary defense
attorney in the *Conrad* case); and prominent Republicans outside of
Montana, most notably Theodore Roosevelt. By the turn of the century,
Hunt was interested in doing something else, especially in obtaining a
position as a circuit judge. He did not get that, but he did get a more
unusual post—in 1901 President William McKinley appointed Hunt
secretary and then governor of Puerto Rico to help establish the new
colonial government. Hunt's friend Roosevelt reaffirmed the appointment shortly after. Hunt stayed in Puerto Rico until 1904, then decided
to leave and either go to New York and practice law (to "make a pile of
money" as he put it in his memoirs) or get an appointment to a circuit
judgeship in Washington, D.C., or New York. Roosevelt had other
ideas, appointing and persuading Hunt to accept the federal district
court position back in Montana, where he would hear the *Winters* case.

Hunt's life after *Winters* was equally interesting, as he seemed to
make the transition, with the rest of the Republican party, from progressive Roosevelt Republican to more conservative Taft Republican. Hunt
served as a federal district judge until 1911, not unhappily but always
interested in a higher judicial post. In 1909 another personal friend (and
fellow freshman at Yale), President William Howard Taft, named Hunt
to the new Court of Customs Appeals in Washington—boring work, as
he called it, but now at the level of a circuit judge. Then came a bruising
experience. In 1910, Taft nominated him to the new and politically
charged Commerce Court, with jurisdiction to review Interstate Commerce Commission (ICC) rulings. The court was unpopular with
Democrats and some progressive Republicans because the ICC had
become a popular institution, especially with farmers and shippers. The
Senate delayed Hunt's confirmation as Hunt was attacked as another
conservative Republican judge who favored big business interests over
the people. According to Hunt, the main problem was the "objections
from representatives of some farmers in Montana who were displeased
by a decision I had rendered wherein I refused to enjoin the Anaconda

Mining Co. from allowing poisonous fumes from the smelter chimneys to spread over certain lands in the Deer Lodge valley." (I never saw any indication that the *Winters* ruling affected Hunt's career or reputation; he never mentioned it in his memoirs.) Hunt claimed he owed his eventual confirmation in 1911 to the vigorous support of Senator Carter. It did not matter—the Democrats abolished the court as soon as they had the White House in 1912. But they could not get rid of the judges, as much as they might have liked to, given the nature of federal appointments to the bench. So Hunt became an unattached circuit judge at the disposal of Chief Justice Edward White. Hunt wanted White to appoint him to the bench of the Second Circuit, in New York, or the Fourth Circuit, in Richmond, Virginia—close to Washington. But these opportunities fell through. Not until 1916 was a permanent home found for Hunt with an assignment to the Ninth Circuit in San Francisco, reviewing decisions from Montana and elsewhere in the West. Hunt stayed with the court until he turned seventy in 1927, then "retired" to a successful private practice in San Francisco until he died in 1949 at 92.[2]

Hunt brought all of these experiences, identities, and understandings to his work, including a number of years as a prominent actor in the critical early years of developing a settled Montana. And he was clearly no radical, never antithetical to mainstream economic interests wherever he was. Yet Hunt as well did not believe that a reserved water rights ruling was so monstrous as to be incompatible with life in this arid western state. Norris Hundley notes that "[a]s a westerner familiar with the critical importance of water in the region," Hunt quickly agreed to modify the size of his first injunction order (from 11,000 inches to 5,000) "when he realized [the order] provided the Indians with water in excess of their needs."[3] Hunt had no need, given the information before him, to keep the larger injunction when asked to modify it; and the conventional wisdom was that he had awarded the natural flow of the river to the Indians at this lesser amount, anyway. But as Hundley also recognized, Hunt never wavered from the injunction or the reserved rights basis for the decision. More important, Hunt's own rulings remained open-ended in ultimate scope, theoretically reserving additional water for use whenever the Indians could prove a need and willingness to put it to use, whether or not non-Indian settlers had made use of it in the meantime. (As noted above and by Hundley, it was the Reclamation Service with the acquiescence of the Indian Office in later years, not the courts at the time, that wrongly interpreted Hunt's 5,000-inches injunction as a ceiling on the amount of water that the people on the Fort Belknap reservation had a right to.)[4]

Lest it be thought that Judge Hunt was one of those easterners who simply did not understand the critical importance of water to the development of the region or the importance of the prior appropriation system in allocating water, remember that Hunt wrote a short law review article for the *Yale Law Journal* three years after his rulings in the *Winters* case in which he made both those points, denying the validity of claims by public-land grantees to common law riparian rights.[5] Yet Hunt never wavered from his commitment to the reserved rights doctrine. In 1921, when a Ninth Circuit judge, Hunt was a member of the panel for the opinion in *Skeem v. United States,* the first reported appellate decision after *Conrad* to apply *Winters* to an Indian water rights conflict. In *Skeem,* the court liberally construed a provision in an 1898 agreement with the Shoshone-Bannock Tribes of the Fort Hall reservation in Idaho as an open-ended reservation of water for use on Indian allotments. The language of the provision was also susceptible to a construction that protected only water actually appropriated and put to beneficial use by the Indians as of 1898. But the court looked to other provisions in that and earlier agreements, the purposes of these treaties, and explicitly to the concept that native peoples could reserve certain rights while granting others (citing *Winters* and *Winans*) and concluded that the provision reserved whatever water would be needed to irrigate the allotments, no matter when the owners first began to use the water.[6]

Like Hunt, the other judges in the Ninth Circuit who ruled consistently and without dissent for the reserved rights doctrine in the various opinions of *Winters* and *Conrad* were all turn-of-the-century westerners, if not in origin then at least at the time of the rulings and for a number of years prior. This includes Judges William Gilbert and Charles Wolverton of Oregon; Thomas Hawley of Nevada; and William Morrow, Erskine Ross, and John DeHaven of California. Much is known about Gilbert, Ross, and Morrow; less has been written about the others. For this study, the most important point is that these were all men from the dominant economic and political circles of their states who approached judicial issues comfortably within that framework. After a review of a set of cases involving natural resources, David Frederick, author of a study on the Ninth Circuit, concluded, for example, that Gilbert and Ross "strongly believed in the importance of capitalizing on the West's natural resources for development." And Frederick notes that in these cases Gilbert and Ross differed somewhat on the importance of the government's interests, with Ross less inclined than Gilbert to favor the government's interests and more inclined to favor property and business interests, and that in many of the critical cases (such as the smelter pollution and timber depredation cases) Ross's views prevailed far more often by attracting Morrow or Hunt (or even Gilbert) to his position. Yet the reserved water rights decisions in *Winters* and *Conrad* from these men consistently and without complication favored the federal government and the Indians, despite arguments from the defendants as to how these intrusions by the federal government and federal judiciary into vested water rights under state law were threatening their lives and property and the development of northern Montana. Perhaps an important point is that except for DeHaven, these men all came from California or Oregon, two coastal states that had been states for a comparatively long time and had developed more sophisticated economies and societies than were found in Montana—*and,* most important, where the "California Doctrine" of water law held the field, that complicated mix of prior appropriation rights and riparian rights. It did not appear to be a troubling concept to any of them to further mix in the concept of Indian reserved rights.[7]

The same can said of the author of the Supreme Court opinion in *Winters* (and in *Winans*), Joseph McKenna. McKenna came to California in 1854 at age twelve and was a lawyer in northern California by 1865. Besides his private practice, McKenna served as a county attorney and one term in the state legislature in the 1870s. He served in the United States House of Representatives from 1885 to 1892, when he resigned to accept an appointment from President Benjamin Harrison to be a Ninth Circuit judge. He was with that court for five years, leaving in 1897 to be McKinley's attorney general, then was appointed to the Supreme Court within a year. From early in his career forward McKenna had close ties to railroad magnate Leland Stanford and other railroad interests, which of course had a significant stake in the settlement of the West. McKenna was what could be called the Court's "customary westerner," who wrote many of the Court's western public lands opinions.[8]

Although the motivations and resource philosophies of these men are not known, their actions confirm what much of this study has been about—that people in the West brought a complex set of objectives and experiences to their understanding of western water allocation issues, in general and in particular instances. The development interests and the state law appropriation systems were linked as the dominant economic and political force and the dominant water allocation philosophy; yet a diversity of viewpoints on water (and everything else) always existed in the West, even within the dominant mainstream culture, which is why the wholesale dedication of water resources in the West to individual private appropriators for economic purposes is far from the only thing that happened in the West with regard to water—and why something like *Winters* fit right in.

PART II

The Work of Winters, 1905–1930s

A Case Study from the Uintah Reservation

In the last few decades the *Winters* doctrine and Indian reserved water rights have become a prominent factor in water allocation efforts in the West and in assertions of Indian sovereignty. Almost nothing has been written about the specific impact of *Winters* before the 1960s. Did the *Winters* decision and doctrine lie essentially dormant, even squashed, until resurrected by the Supreme Court in the 1963 decision in *Arizona v. California,* as the literature on *Winters* suggests? Or did the doctrine have an active life in earlier years that not only shaped the doctrine for its role in later years, but also worked in the first part of the century in a way that illustrates complex attitudes and actions concerning water in the West in this time? I contend the latter. What follows is a case study examining that contention—an analysis of the application of the *Winters* doctrine to the water allocation dynamics at the Uintah reservation section of the Uintah and Ouray Indian Reservation in Utah from 1905 into the 1930s, set in the broader context of the other uses and impressions of the *Winters* decisions in these years.

The first part of the book explored how and why lawyers, judges, reservation personnel, and others from the mainstream western economic and legal culture developed the Indian reserved water rights doctrine in the *Winters* litigation from 1905 to 1908. Some of the conclusions bear repeating: For one, the prior appropriation system itself was not nearly as dominant, or universally supported, or as productive of desired outcomes, as has been supposed. Legal theories supporting water rights for Indian reservations outside of the realm of the state law of prior appropriation were well within the western legal mainstream in 1905. Non-Indian settlers and water users in the Milk River valley circa 1905, who might have been thought to be the type of western farming settlers to be beholden to the prior appropriation system, were finding the system to be as much an obstacle as an aid to their plans or dreams for economic development. They found that they could use the *Winters* decision and the ways it interfered with strict application of the prior appropriation system to serve their own interests, especially their efforts to obtain a valleywide Reclamation project. Perhaps just as important was the prevailing attitude in the valley of relative indifference; the Reclamation project and other water allocation issues were far more important than the Indian water rights litigation to all but the affected upstream irrigators. Efforts by the latter to undo the *Winters* decisions could make no headway in this calm. And when the issues did find their way to the national level, where the issues could be abstracted out of the complex local context, concerns over the role and impact of the *Winters* reserved water rights decisions were deflected into allotment efforts expected to neutralize the impact of the doctrine and thus ease the conflict.

The related issue explored in this part of the book is how the reserved rights doctrine survived its early decades despite being at odds with the elements of western state water law and the supposed social, economic, and ideological underpinnings of the law—an antagonism indicated by the number and the vehemence of attacks launched against the reserved rights doctrine by western interests. The answers lie at least partly in a different version of the same dynamic—in the ways that federal and state officials, lawyers, judges, western development interests, and others learned to use the doctrine or to live with it, *and* how they deflected and transformed the conflict over the doctrine into a broad vision of what could be called "Indian reclamation" based in the allotment policy, which corresponded to a more general reclamation vision in the West. In the records for every western Indian reservation I consulted there is a story to tell of the work of *Winters* in these years. This is mostly the work of reservation superintendents and agents, the field staff of the Indian Irrigation Service (a division of the Office of Indian Affairs created around this time to bring together irrigation activities at various reservations), upper-level officials in the Office of Indian Affairs, attorneys in the Department of Justice and Department of the Interior, and non-Indian citizens interested in Indian issues. As noted in the introduction, western American Indians were the least active participants in the work of *Winters* in the years studied here, despite the obvious fact that *Winters* was about Indian water rights and despite the courts' view of Indians in the original *Winters* decisions as active participants in controlling and deciding about their uses of water. The uses of and debates over *Winters* in these years should be viewed as of primary importance for what they reveal about the non-Indian culture's complex relationship to water and rights to water and to people defined as not within the dominant culture.

This does not mean, however, that the work of *Winters* in these early years did not have implications for Indian water rights, favorable implications buried among the problems. In the years following the *Winters* decisions, Indian Affairs and Justice Department officials *were* willing to use *Winters* as part of their efforts to assert and protect water rights for Indian reservations, especially insofar as *Winters* could be used to work with and even mimic the Reclamation Act. That is, the federal government used *Winters* along with other tools to reserve from immediate appropriation a watershed or a volume of water that could be dedicated to an irrigation project, whose water would be used by farmers on individually owned, relatively small-tract farms (carved out of the reservations by allotments) and participating in commercial irrigated agriculture. This is not significantly different from the vision the Reclamation Service and others had for the whole of the West, except for the fact that some of the people on these farms would be of Indian origin, and some of the legal tools in the Indian context (such as *Winters*) were a bit different than those otherwise used by the Reclamation Service. Moreover, if the government could coordinate non-Indian reclamation and Indian reclamation, all the better, even if this meant limiting the reach of *Winters*. Likewise, Justice Department attorneys also began to learn how to use *Winters* to buttress the federal government's claims to reserve water for non-Indian water projects. Yet the end result could be, as will be shown here, the use of *Winters* in a way that did assert and protect reserved water rights, at least for certain Indian lands immediately threatened by non-Indian water use under state water law. In the process, these efforts preserved and developed the doctrine for service at a later date.

Prelude to the Water Rights Litigation at the Uintah Indian Reservation, Late 1800s to 1914

Allotment, Irrigation, State Water Law, and Water Problems

An examination of water rights litigation concerning the Uintah reservation in eastern Utah perfectly illustrates the work of *Winters*. The water rights litigation was an outgrowth of the federal government's troubled effort to transform the Ute Indian peoples of the Uintah reservation into a model of American commercial agriculture. David Rich Lewis's excellent recent study of the government's failed efforts at agrarian change in Indian communities, *Neither Wolf nor Dog: American Indians, Environment, and Agrarian Change,* focused on the Uintah reservation as one of three case studies of how the agrarian transformation envisioned for the Indians by non-Indian society did not succeed. The intended transformation foundered on the environmental and economic realities, that is, the Uintah reservation was a lousy place for successful small-tract, commercial, irrigated agriculture at the turn of the century. The transformation effort also foundered on cultural realities: the Indian peoples of the Uintah reservation had no interest in letting the federal government impose this transformation. The Ute Indians' historical experiences in making a living in the area and their various efforts to carve out ways of life for themselves under the new circumstances made it clear, to them, that they would benefit little from following the path marked out for them by Congress, the Indian Affairs Office, and non-Indian society as a whole.[1]

According to Lewis, one of the many obstacles faced by the government was its posture on water rights for the reservation. He portrayed this as another classical example of how the government failed to capitalize on the potential of *Winters:*

> As irrigation officials moved forward with the [irrigation] project, they met Ute opposition to the costs of further dividing their lands into an agrarian system. Many Utes refused to work on the ditches or prepare their allotments for water, while those who took the wage labor jobs had little time to farm. *But perhaps more serious, officials realized that the reservation had been opened under state law, thereby forfeiting federal protection of Indian water rights affirmed in Winters v. U.S. (1908).* Utah required the filer of primary water rights to show "beneficial use" within fourteen years or else forfeit those rights. In effect, all allotments not cleared, leveled, planted, and using one second-foot of water per 80 acres before 1919 would lose their primary water rights to white homesteaders with secondary or tertiary rights. With those primary rights would go the productive capability and resale value of Ute allotments and any hope of the people becoming self-sufficient farmers.[2]

In fact, however, the federal government made the *Winters* doctrine the central theory of litigation it filed in 1916 to protect the water rights of the Uintah reservation. The government obtained a continuing injunction in its favor, more than a decade of federal court–supervised allocation of water, and then a settlement-based final decree of water rights that would not have had the content it had without the government's use of *Winters* as a sword and shield. The government also used the litigation to gain time to work within the framework of state water law, to make present water needs protected by *Winters* also protected under state law. The government limited the *Winters* claim in the litigation to match its vision of allotment and Indian reclamation and the way Indian water rights should coordinate with non-Indian reclamation. Yet the government refused to agree to language in the final decree that would have limited the future scope of *Winters* rights at the reservation to this particular vision and need.

A series of treaties and executive orders over the last half of the nineteenth century carved the Uintah reservation in eastern Utah out of the much larger historic territory of the various groupings of the Ute peoples. By the turn of the century the reservation covered approximately two million acres and was the home of approximately 1,500 people. Included within the boundaries of the reservation were all or part of a number of creeks and rivers, including the Strawberry River,

Duchesne River, Rock Creek, Lake Fork River (also known as Lake Fork Creek), Uinta River, Whiterocks River, and more. These flow east, southeast, and south out of the Uinta Mountains and merge in various places in the hills and on the arid valley floor, eventually form- ing a single river called the Duchesne River (but at the time occasionally called the Uinta), which shortly thereafter flows into the Green River, the east boundary of the reservation (see map 2).[3]

Prior to these developments, the Utes followed a "subsistence round" of hunting, fishing, and gathering in the arid and semi-arid Great Basin and mountain lands of Utah, Colorado, and New Mexico. They stayed close to rivers and springs, where they could "obtain food from the fish that lived in, the plant life that grew beside, and the game which congregated around the water." The especially well-watered areas along major rivers such as the Green, White, and lower Sevier in what would become Utah were the location of their more permanent, year-after-year habitations. Having the "right" to make use of water, to the extent the concept has meaning when applied to this society, depended mostly on historical identity and occupancy, that is, on the fact that people used the water because they and their ancestors had lived in that area and used that water for a long time. According to Joanna Endter, author of a study on the Northern Utes and their water use, the Utes conceived of water in terms more fundamental than simple physical and subsistence characteristics. Water was one of the two dominant symbols in the Ute spiritual universe, the other being the sun or fire. Nature was a "repository and source" of spiritual force or power, and the "dominant dichotomy of forms in which power appears" was dry/hot and wet/cool. Water had the power to provide and sustain all life, a power both physical and supernatural. Water played an important role in ceremonies, especially in the Sun Dance and sweats. To summarize Endter's conclusions:

> The way Utes conceived of and treated water corresponded to their spiritual beliefs and view of the world. Utes considered water as something which was animate, hence imbued with spirit. It was very sacred to them inasmuch as they believed that water was a source of supernatural power that could heal and cleanse. The special purpose of water was to provide life for all things. Certain springs or lakes which were thought have special healing power or were used for ceremonial purposes were especially sacred to Utes. Utes taught that water was to be respected, preserved, and left free flowing so that it could continue to sustain all living things along its path. There were

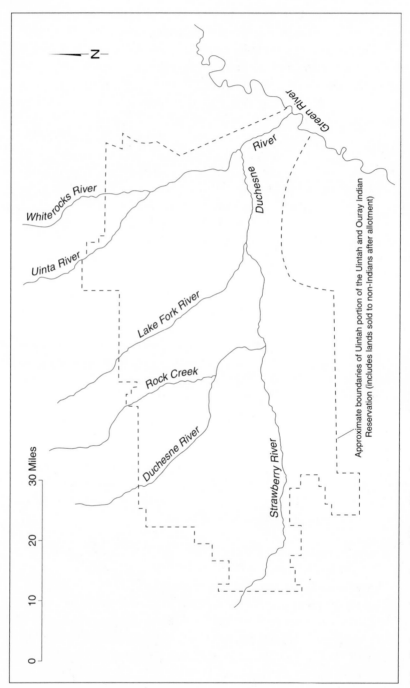

Map 2. Approximate boundaries of Uintah section of Uintah and Ouray Indian Reservation and associated rivers, Utah

strong cultural ethics to share water with other people and with all other forms of life, to treat it carefully when using it, and to take only as much as one needed. Special customs and traditions were observed in the way in which water was used.[4]

Like the 1888 agreement that created the Fort Belknap Indian Reservation in Montana, each step in the reduction of the larger Ute lands to the Uintah reservation was accompanied by the explicitly stated or clearly implicit policy of the United States government that the Ute people should transform themselves or be transformed from the life described above into the agrarian society ideal that non-Indians brought to the West in the nineteenth century. This type of society could be summed up, by the turn of the century, in the integrated concepts of commercial agriculture, allotment of individually owned small-tract farms, and irrigation. The federal and state governments and non-Indian society in general had essentially the same vision for the non-Indian people who were coming to eastern Utah, to be pursued not only on the lands surrounding the Uintah reservation but also on reservation lands themselves, as allotment would make "surplus" reservation lands available for non-Indian settlement.[5]

A vision of intertwined agricultural development in the basin thus justified a provision in the 1899 appropriations bill for Indian affairs that authorized the secretary of the interior to grant rights-of-way to *non-Indians* "for the construction and maintenance of dams, ditches, and canals, on or through the Uintah Indian Reservation in Utah, for the purpose of diverting and appropriating the waters of the streams in said reservation for useful purposes." Congress coupled the authorization with, ironically, one of the clearest, most explicit statements of a pre-*Winters* Indian reserved water right it ever produced— tailored and limited, however, to the present and future needs for water to sustain an agricultural future for the Indian people on the reservation:

> *Provided,* That all such grants shall be subject at all times to the paramount rights of the Indians on such reservation to so much of said waters as may have been appropriated, or may hereafter be appropriated or needed by them for agricultural and domestic purposes; and it shall be the duty of the Secretary of the Interior to prescribe such rules and regulations as he may deem necessary to secure to the Indians the quantity of water needed for their present and prospective wants, and to otherwise protect the rights and interests of the Indians and the Indian service.[6]

Non-Indians did move to the area, and allotment did occur at the reservation, one of the examples of forced allotment by Congress discussed in the previous part of the book. After less coercive efforts failed to produce more than a handful of allotments, Congress forced the total allotment of the Uintah reservation in 1905, approximately 1,400 allotments covering slightly more than 100,000 acres. Most of these allotments were in the eastern parts of the reservation, in the valleys, benchlands, and hills along and above the Duchesne River, Rock Creek, Lake Fork River, Uinta River, and Whiterocks River. The Utes also retained in tribal ownership a 250,000-acre grazing reserve in a strip running along the foothills of the Uinta Mountains north above the areas in which the Utes' allotments predominated.

Out of what remained of the Uintah reservation lands, the government reserved to itself the higher, forested areas to the north and northwest as national forest lands. The government also reserved to itself much of the Strawberry River valley to the west so as to reserve reservoir sites that could be used "to conserve and protect the water supply for the Indians" while also storing water for the "general agricultural development" of the reserved valley lands and other lands. This would become the Strawberry Valley Reclamation project.

The government opened the rest of the reservation land to non-Indian settlement. Settlers moved in, primarily planning a life of irrigated agriculture. While at least some in the government (especially in the Reclamation Service) hoped to manage the allotment process so that all of the non-Indians would be in certain drainages and all of the Indians in others, this did not happen. The result in every watershed (except the Strawberry River basin) was a mix of allotted Ute lands for which the government was trying to develop an irrigation system and non-Indian farmers with their ditch companies. This situation meant, among other things, that the federal government and the non-Indian settlers had to cooperate in the development of a somewhat integrated irrigation system (as envisioned by the Act of 1899), which at one and the same time led to and dampened conflict between non-Indian farmers and the government at the reservation.[7]

To further its allotment policy at the reservation, the government turned its attention to developing an irrigation system for the allotted lands. Indian Office personnel had been investigating irrigation possibilities, planning for irrigation development, and constructing minor irrigation works since at least the 1890s. But until 1905 irrigation efforts affected only small amounts of land. Beginning in 1905 the government sought to develop a system to deliver water to every acre of allotted land possible. For the purposes of this study, two events in these years are particularly notable. First, in mid-1905, just before the government opened the unallotted lands for non-Indian settlement, the Indian agent at the reservation filed water rights claims under Utah state law with the Utah state engineer to irrigate all of the irrigable allotted lands out of the various streams of the reservation. The claims for water totaled more than 1,200 cubic feet per second of water for the purpose of irrigating more than 85,000 acres. The government understood, based on its stream measurements, that these appropriations would utilize a significant portion of the spring and early summer runoff available for irrigation and would "take the entire average flow of the streams during the months of August and September, and in some instances take all of the water during the month of July."

Almost none of the water had been put to beneficial use when the government filed its claims. Like most western states, Utah state law allowed a claimant to file a prospective claim to water rights, one of the various ways in which states moderated the pure prior appropriation system to allow for a limited type of reservation of water. Prospective claims would, when "perfected" (i.e., actually developed and put to use), relate in priority to the date of filing *if* the appropriator initiated the work on the appropriation within six months of filing, used due diligence to perfect the appropriation, and in fact perfected the appropriation within five years. This meant, when the government filed its water rights claims in mid-1905, that by 1911 government officials had to develop the entire irrigation system for the allotted Uintah reservation in at least a rudimentary fashion and see that the water was actually put to beneficial use on the allotted lands. This was a daunting task for an understaffed and underfunded agency serving a populace that had so far proven uninterested in the allotment and irrigation program. Non-Indian farmers were about to take up land, associate into or contract with irrigation companies, and file and pursue their own claims to water, which they were far more likely than the Indian office to perfect under state law within the specified time period.[8]

The second notable event was a financing provision in the 1906 appropriations bill for the Indian Office. Congress authorized development of the irrigation system for the allotted Uintah lands at a total cost of $600,000. The appropriation carried a number of provisos that indicate the interplay of Indian policy and general reclamation: The amount appropriated was to be reimbursed to the Department of the Treasury out of the sale of the unallotted lands of the reservation; the Secretary of the Interior would hold title to the system in trust for the

Indians; and the ditches and canals could be extended to serve non-Indians, too, who would have to pay an equitably apportioned cost of the system. Most important here, Congress provided that *"such irrigation systems shall be constructed and completed and held and operated, and water therefor appropriated under the laws of the State of Utah."*[9] Thus the appropriation arranged for significant financial assistance for the irrigation system for the allotted lands, while at the same time apparently locked the irrigation efforts into state water law, admittedly the path already chosen by the Indian Office.

Given these circumstances, many people were understandably pessimistic about the chances of successful development and protection of the water rights for the reservation in a water-short Uintah basin. That non-Indians were far more likely to perfect rights to water at the expense of the Indians was one of the main reasons the Reclamation Service believed the reservation should be allotted, so that non-Indians and Indians were separated into different watersheds. A 1904 analysis by someone in the Reclamation Service—probably the director, Frederick Newell—succinctly described the problem faced by the Indian Office in 1906:

> Under the laws of the State of Utah, the Whites, when they take up the land will make filings, presumably claiming in the aggregate, the entire flow; they will proceed at once to construction, and may complete their ditches before the Department has finished its works. When scarcity of water occurs, as it will through complete development of the area, the controversy in the local courts will inevitably tend to confirm to the whites the use of the water on the ground that they have made their filings, have completed their ditches, and put the water to beneficial use, while the Indians may not have done so. In short, proceeding with the best of intentions, it is easy to predict that the same course of events may follow here as has occurred on other Indian reservations, where, starting with an ample supply of water and great extent of good lands, the Indians are now practically derived of means of support, although the Government has spent large sums, and has had a more or less direct oversight of the matter.[10]

The Office of Indian Affairs also noted that what had already become established as the standard western solution to water scarcity situations of this type—"more" water, in the form of reservoir storage—was not available at the Uintah reservation for the allotted lands, as "the most important storage site has been preempted under a reclamation project as a reservoir for a foreign watershed." This was a muted complaint about the Reclamation Service's plan to store the waters of the Strawberry River and divert most of that water over the mountains to benefit non-Indian settlers in the Provo area, not Indian and non-Indian irrigators in the Uintah basin.

Thus even before the efforts to perfect the water rights for the allotted lands had really begun, the Indian Office noted that "very grave difficulties are to be overcome for the proper protection of the Indians, possibly demanding some amendment of existing law or an entrance upon tedious and expensive litigation."[11] Yet this seemingly hopeless situation did not affect Indian Affairs' official vision for the region, a vision of mixed and general reclamation in which the farmers, both Indians and non-Indians, would work in the same way in the same area. Thus the commissioner of Indian affairs, Francis Leupp, reported to President Roosevelt in 1906 concerning the Uintah lands that "this Office is anxious, for the sake of the Indians, to have the surrounding country settled up by a good and thrifty class of white farmers," and that the Indian Office "stands ready, as it has stood ready from the start, to see that every drop of water not needed by the Indians for the development of their farms shall be allowed to go to the white settlers."[12]

All the less rosy scenarios predicted came to pass, according to records from the Indian Office over the next decade: The non-Indian farmers and irrigation companies completed their irrigation systems and put water on the land, thus perfecting their water rights (although grand crops, good market access, and commercial success were not their reward). The irrigation companies often constructed their canals and ditches "across Indian allotments and reserved lands without authority of law and in utter disregard of the rights and interests of the Indians," leading to conflicts with the Indian Office and site-specific litigation over rights-of-way. The irrigation companies were also taking advantage of government construction by linking to the government canals and ditches for the Indian lands, while (at least according to the Indian Office) refusing to pay their equitable share of the costs of the system. Most important, the Indian Office and the U.S. attorney's office were trying, without success, to get the non-Indian irrigators who used the government system to agree to subordinate their water rights to the Indian water rights whenever perfected.

Meanwhile, the Indian Office was having some difficulty completing all the parts of the irrigation system needed to bring water to the allotments, and far, far greater difficulty in getting the water on the allotted land to be used for the irrigation of crops, due to the lack of agency farming personnel and to the indifference of the Indian allottees.

The Indian Office soon realized (if it did not always know) that it was not going to perfect the rights on more than a relatively few acres by 1911, the end of the period allowed by state law.[13]

The Indian Office responded to this situation in two ways. First, the federal government decided to try to persuade the Utah state government to extend the time allowed for the perfection of claimed water rights. The federal government was relatively successful in this effort— by 1911 the state had extended the allowable time for construction and beneficial use to fourteen years from the date of filing, giving the Indian Office until 1919 to perfect the rights for which it filed.[14]

Second, the Indian Office sought in some fashion to initiate irrigation on the allotted lands simply to perfect the water rights. The government first tried to use appropriation money to pay hired laborers to irrigate allotments for one year in order to be able to claim perfection of the water rights under state law, even though the lands were unlikely to be farmed in the near future. Not having much success at that effort, the government turned its efforts to selling a few allotments and, especially, to leasing allotments to non-Indian farmers at favorable terms— free for five years if the lessee would develop and improve the farm and put water on it—for the express purpose of having the lessees irrigate the land and thus perfect the water rights. The leasing of allotments began fairly soon after allotment, but the government did not begin an aggressive advertising campaign to find lessees until 1915. The government had trouble finding interested parties, as prospective lessees soon became aware that the Uintah basin was not yet proving to be a success for commercial irrigated agriculture. The government eventually found a number of lessees, as the subsequent litigation will illustrate, but the government was much less successful than it had hoped in perfecting water rights through this strategy.[15]

The federal government's water right and water development problems at the reservation were not just prospective *problems,* in the sense of the possibility of harm that might occur in the future if rights were not perfected within the time allowed under state law. Beginning in 1912 dry streams and dry government canals began to be a problem for the allotments, as non-Indian farmers and irrigation companies in the upper parts of the watersheds claimed and used all the water in water-short times, especially in summers. The irrigators on non-Indians lands also, on occasion, intimidated or forcibly prevented Indian Affairs officials, Indian allottees, or allotment lessees from having access to water.[16]

Reliance on the *Winters* doctrine or some other form of federal water control outside of state law could have saved the Indian Office a great deal of effort and anxiety about perfecting water rights under state law, and likely would have given the government leverage in the fight against the non-Indian farmers who were claiming and reducing stream flows. And not everyone in the federal government was comfortable with the continued adherence to state law. In 1911, for example, someone in the Interior Department briefly questioned the policy of following state law to establish and protect the water rights at the Uintah reservation as not consistent with "the Department's policy as to federal control of waters in other aspects (Reclamation Service, Water Power, etc.)," indicating the degree to which some people could see links between Indian water rights and federal efforts to reserve and control water for other purposes.[17]

However, most of those who thought or wrote about the Uintah situation at that time concluded that Congress had abrogated the use of the *Winters* doctrine and deferred to state law in the initial 1906 appropriation for the irrigation system at the reservation (quoted above). This was, for example, the conclusion of E. B. Meritt, an influential Indian Affairs official who later became assistant commissioner and who was one of the proponents at the time of more aggressive use of the reserved rights doctrine in other contexts. Meritt was asked in 1912 by the secretary of the interior for an assessment of the water rights situation at the Uintah reservation. He quoted from *Winters* the statement that the "power of the government to reserve waters and exempt them from appropriation under State laws is not denied," but he also quoted the state water law provision for the Uintah system in the Act of June 21, 1906; and then he quoted from the 1903 *Lone Wolf v. Hitchcock* decision, in which the United States Supreme Court had held that Congress had the power to abrogate treaty rights. Meritt concluded:

> It is apparent, therefore, that in view of the decision of the Supreme Court in the Lone Wolf case and the Act of Congress of June 21, 1906, requiring the waters on this reservation to be appropriated under the laws of the State of Utah, that the favorable decision in the Winters case has been practically nullified by the Act of Congress in question in so far as the principles announced in that decision would apply to the Uintah Irrigation Project.[18]

Meritt's views prevailed without opposition in the Indian Irrigation Service.

William Reed, chief engineer with the Indian Irrigation Service, thus summed up the situation at the Uintah reservation at the beginning of 1913 in dire terms that are representative of the views of those involved in irrigation efforts over the preceding decade: By 1913, the Indian Irrigation Service had been successful in constructing irrigation canals and ditches theoretically able to irrigate 98,000 acres at a cost of $725,000. Unfortunately, little more than 10,000 acres were actually in cultivation under the project, and much of that was leased to non-Indians. Moreover, Indian Office personnel did not expect to see a significant increase in the near future in the rate at which allotted land became irrigated land. This meant they had a severe water rights problem, because state law governed the water rights, as the federal government had "practically released its rights to waters on this reservation to the State of Utah . . . through an act which now seems to have been a mistake." The State of Utah had, in theory, extended the time to perfect the claimed rights to water to 1919, but only under the assumption that the acreage actually irrigated would steadily increase across that time period, which was not happening. The "present rate of progress does not meet the demands made by the state authorities," and given the realities of Indian interest and expertise in irrigated farming, "it is unreasonable to think that under the existing circumstances the requirements of the law could have been met." Leasing Indian allotments to non-Indian farmers had been only marginally more successful, in part because of the active efforts of the irrigators on non-Indian lands to control the available water. Thus, Reed concluded, there was "grave danger" that title to water under state laws will not be perfected, and the Indians "will lose heavily as a result," especially because the "authorities of the state of Utah seem to have a covetous eye turned toward this property," seeing in this situation "an opportunity to locate and make prosperous a large number of farmers, who will add to the number of taxpayers and otherwise become of advantage to the organization." Yet feeling hemmed in by state law, Reed could only prescribe a redoubled effort to interest the Indians in irrigated farming and greater authority and efforts to sell or lease allotments.[19]

CHAPTER 10

National Context of the Uintah Litigation

Growing Interest in the Potential of Winters, *1909–1915*

Something changed in 1914—federal government officials quit believing that *Winters* had no role to play in Uintah water rights. It is not completely clear why this particular shift occurred. The shift in strategy took place, however, in the context of growing interest within the Office of Indian Affairs, the Department of Justice (especially in the Denver, Colorado, office), and Congress in the potential of *Winters;* a concern in the Indian Office and in Congress that this potential was being squandered; and a developing program in the Indian Office and the Justice Department to pursue reserved rights for the reservations, including water rights litigation based at least in part on *Winters*. A description of this broader context will be of use in understanding the particular developments at the Uintah reservation.

I have already described how the *Winters* and *Conrad* litigation and decisions influenced the Blackfeet and Fort Peck allotment legislation in Congress. Yet by 1909, just a year after the Supreme Court's decision in *Winters,* the reserved rights issue disappeared from Congress, at least at the surface level of legislation. Members of Congress continued to introduce allotment measures over the next few years—new bills to authorize the allotment of as yet untouched reservations, amendments to the appropriation bills to allot or sell surplus reservation lands, and amendments to existing allotment acts to authorize the sale of surplus lands after allotment. Most of the bills died in committee. There is no indication that any of these bills contained water rights provisions or that they stalled because of a water rights controversy. The bills that did make it to the floor and the few that became law did not contain water rights provisions and did not spark any controversies over water rights. The *Winters* decisions involved reservation lands in Montana, while many of the bills in this period concerned reservations outside of Montana, especially in North and South Dakota, Wyoming, Washington, and Oregon. But even assuming those few who knew of the *Winters* decisions thought of it only in terms of Montana (which seems unlikely), bills were introduced in this period to allot the Crow and even the Fort Belknap reservations and to amend the allotment act for the Flathead reservation, all in Montana. Yet not even the Montana bills contained water rights provisions or sparked water rights debates. Except for occasional appropriations for irrigation works, the bills and acts did not contain any provisions that concerned water. Congress no longer seemed interested in or concerned by the Indian water rights issues.

One possible explanation for what amounts at the congressional level to even greater deflection into the allotment process is a curious provision intended to protect Indian treaty rights that did begin to appear in the allotment measures adopted by Congress in these years. Among other purposes, this provision may have served to continue the status quo with regard to reserved water rights, freeing Congress from any fights over the issue while the allotment process took effect that might eventually render the issue meaningless. The provision first appeared in an act passed in 1908, in the Sixtieth Congress, at the same time Congress wrestled with the Fort Peck allotment bill. This new act authorized the sale of surplus lands at the Standing Rock and Cheyenne River Indian reservations in the Dakotas, where allotments were already in process under the general allotment act. A provision at the end of the act stated, "[N]othing in this Act shall be construed to deprive the said Indians of the Cheyenne or Standing Rock Indian reservations, in South Dakota and North Dakota, of any benefits to which they are entitled under existing treaties or agreements not inconsistent with the provisions of this Act."[1] This provision entered the bill in the Senate Committee on Indian Affairs. Neither the committee's written report nor the chairman's oral report on the Senate floor explained the purpose or meaning of the added language. Congressional documents do not indicate that this provision had anything to do with the reserved water rights issue, and members of Congress may have had other issues in mind when they approved the clause. Yet the provision seemed well designed to continue the status quo with regard to treaty rights and to avoid having to confront any complex or controversial issues. Few treaty issues were more complex and potentially controversial than reserved water rights.[2]

This treaty rights clause appeared without explanation in each of the allotment measures that Congress adopted in the next five years. This includes acts to conclude the allotment process and sell surplus lands at the Fort Berthold reservation in North Dakota and the Pine Ridge and Rosebud reservations in South Dakota and a new act to allot and sell another portion of the Standing Rock reservation. All of these acts were completely silent about water.[3] During the 1913 debate over the new bill for the Standing Rock reservation, Rep. Scott Ferris, a Democrat from Oklahoma, spoke the sense of Congress with regard to allotment and assimilation: "The final solution of the Indian question is bound to be the intermingling of the white people and gradually swallowing up the Indian, and the only way you can do it is to have the land allotted to the individual Indians and let the white settler come in and buy the surplus lands."[4] The final solution to the Indian question would also be the final solution to the reserved water rights question. Congress put all its energy into the allotment process and, it appears, now saw only a waste of effort in bothering with troublesome water rights provisions. The treaty rights provision was a measure that any person could interpret to suit his or her position on water rights, although the provision did not resolve the issue directly or even obliquely.

The absence of follow-up lawsuits based on the *Winters* decisions in the first few years after *Winters* also surely contributed to the disappearance of Indian water rights issues from the national policy fights in Congress. A host of lawsuits around the West in 1909 or 1910 to establish *Winters* rights might have not only fleshed out the doctrine but also created so much controversy on a wide scale that Congress and others would have had a more difficult time deflecting or ignoring the issue. In Donald Pisani's view, in the dozen years after the Supreme Court's decision in *Winters,* the Indian Office deferred to the demands and the practice of the Reclamation Service and filed for reservation water rights under state law based only on actual present use. According to Pisani, attorneys in the Department of Justice and a few native groups pushed for a more aggressive policy. (For example, the Yakima Indian Nation in Washington threatened in a 1913 petition to Congress to file its own lawsuit in federal court "to settle our water rights," but no Indian nation or other group on behalf of Indian peoples did file a water rights suit independent of the government in these years, if indeed it would have been possible to do so.) But the Reclamation Service strongly opposed the reserved rights concept, and the Indian Office decided not to antagonize the more powerful service.[5]

Pisani may not be completely correct in this explanation, as part of the purpose of this study is to illustrate how Indian Affairs and the Justice Department became more active from 1913 to 1916 in using *Winters* to protect Indian water rights, even through litigation and without at least overt interference from the Reclamation Service. Beginning with the experience of the *Winters* litigation itself, it seems to me that the Reclamation Service never had quite the level of influence over the Indian water rights policy of the Indian Office and the Justice Department as Pisani (and others) have contended. It is true that the Indian Office doggedly pursued water rights for the Uintah reservation under Utah state law, as outlined above. But as also indicated above, Indian Affairs personnel felt constrained to this course of action because of *congressional* action deferring to state law, not because of pressure from Reclamation. The same dynamic affected the actions of the Indian Office at a number of other western reservations. Beginning in late 1911 the Indian Office consciously identified such congressional statutes as the main obstacle to effective use of the *Winters* doctrine and began trying to figure out ways around them, direct and indirect.

Thus where there was no act of Congress requiring adherence to state water law, the Indian Office may not have been so concerned about following state water law. At least this is what some people suspected. Remarks by Representative Mondell of Wyoming once again provide an example. He said on the House floor in 1913 and 1914 that in his experience the Indian Office chose just as often (and mistakenly, he believed) *not* to file for water rights under state law when Indians put water to use on the reservations. According to Mondell, the reservation personnel acted in this way because they believed that the federal courts would protect the Indians' use of the water under the reserved rights doctrine against anyone who might attempt to appropriate the water in the future under state law. For similar reasons, he believed, the Indian Office personnel decided not to file general lawsuits to establish reserved rights or to challenge settler appropriations that might someday interfere with the implementation of a reserved right. Indians would be able to obtain that water under the reserved right doctrine when the time came to put it to use, while to litigate a reserved rights claim when not absolutely necessary might upset the status quo with *Winters.*[6]

Research in various reservation records throughout the West indicates that Mondell was at least partly correct. Mondell's comments appear to have been triggered by the Indian Office having taken this approach to water rights at the Wind River reservation in Wyoming, an effort discussed below. Another example concerns the actions of Indian Office personnel at the Klamath reservation in southern Oregon, as work began on an Indian irrigation project there. By late 1913, the Indian Office and its irrigation personnel began advising Reclamation and Indian Office employees that the Klamath Indians' treaty reserved water rights had precedence over private water rights established under state law, whether the latter were developed as part of the federal Klamath Reclamation project or not. E. B. Meritt, assistant commissioner of Indian Affairs, with the approval of the assistant secretary of the interior, instructed reservation personnel and Indian Irrigation Service engineers not to file for Indian water rights under state law but instead just to post notices of the existence of the paramount reserved rights, file a copy of the notices with the county clerk, and send letters to non-Indians who filed for water rights under state law to notify them that their use of the water was subject to the reservation's paramount reserved rights to the water, even if those paramount rights were at the present not exercised or under development. Reservation personnel followed these instructions.[7]

Thus for these and presumably other reasons, the federal government did not assert *Winters* rights in a series of lawsuits around the West in the five years between the Supreme Court's decision in *Winters* and 1913. This contributed to low awareness of the doctrine, and even more limited concern over it. To the extent that an aggressive litigation policy might have led to a backlash and an express repudiation of the doctrine by Congress, the inaction may have had some unintended value in protecting the reserved rights doctrine for future use. But the inaction also contributed to the fact that the reserved rights theory remained a misunderstood novelty for a number of years instead of an accepted part of the American law of water allocation.

While the issues surrounding Indian water rights, water needs, the *Winters* decisions, and the reserved rights doctrine deserted the main floor of Congress up to 1914 (with one minor exception noted below), the issues did not really disappear from public affairs and public discourse or even from the attention of important members of Congress. With regard to water issues at specific reservations, Indian Office personnel, Justice Department lawyers, and others were at least aware of the *Winters* decision to some degree and were trying to figure out its implications—even if the answer in this period at some reservations was that Congress had given away the rights, as seemed true at the Uintah reservation.[8] What I am going to relate here, however, are seven interrelated episodes or developments in the life of *Winters* in these years that illustrate the manner in which these issues were alive even at the national level as well as the reservation level. These episodes underscored the developing possibilities and problems associated with reserved rights, and they set the stage for the return of Indian water rights and *Winters* issues to the floor of Congress in a spirited if somewhat misguided set of debates in 1914 and 1915. All of these events help explain why the government began preparing in 1913 and 1914 for *Winters*-based litigation to protect the Uintah water rights, litigation filed in 1916.

DEVELOPMENTS IN THE WORK OF WINTERS TO 1914: MONTANA IRRIGATION

The first episode concerns water uses in Montana. Congress continued to appropriate money for the Montana irrigation projects created in connection with the allotments for the Blackfeet and Fort Peck (and Flathead) reservations in Montana. During a debate in 1913 over this appropriation, Democratic Representative John Stephens of Texas argued that it was beginning to appear that the non-Indian settlers taking up the surplus lands were the ones who were reaping the benefit of the projects, not the Indians. This is the first mention in Congress of a major concern that grew in the following years and that would involve new considerations of the role of reserved rights in Montana.[9]

Also, non-Indians in the Milk River valley and the Montana delegation continued to request that Congress open up the Fort Belknap reservation to non-Indian settlement. In 1910, the Senate adopted a resolution directing the secretary of the interior to report on the conditions under which at least part of the reservation could be made available for settlement. Indian Secretary Richard Ballinger's report, submitted February 1, 1911, noted that the 1896 agreement with the residents of the reservation provided that allotments could not be made without the consent of the people of the reservation. Ballinger stated that the Indians were not interested at this time in relinquishing any part of the reservation. Despite the secretary's report, Senator Carter of Montana introduced another bill in 1911 to survey and allot the Fort Belknap reservation. The bill never made it out of committee.[10] Of more interest here, the secretary of the interior's report had attached to it a report from an inspector in the Indian Office who had traveled to the reservation and met with at least some of the Assiniboine residents. The inspector's report indicates that reservation residents were aware of the *Winters* rights but also were aware that the rights had not resulted in the water they needed. The report quotes Hawk Feather, one of the residents of the reservation:

> As you say, you have traveled all over this Milk River Valley and you
> ought to know and see that you can't find anything that we make our
> living on. There was a man here once and he told us that this water
> right belonged to us. He said we would use the water first and raise a
> crop and make a living on that, but we do not get enough water yet.[11]

And from Eyes in the Water, also a reservation resident:

> There are only two things I am living on—the land here and the
> water—and if the white people want it for that I can't spare it. . . .
> The water right belongs to the Indians, but we don't get enough
> water. This year all these ditches are dry, and we will not raise
> anything, and I think we will starve off this winter.[12]

The inspector's report did not try to explain why the Assiniboines were
not receiving enough water—whether the Indian Office or the Indians
had failed to take advantage of the opportunities made available by the
Winters decree, or whether, as the inspector implied, a severe drought
had caused general misfortune throughout the region. Debates in
Congress in later years indicated that Congress and the Indian Office in
large part created the problem by failing to provide the money, expertise,
and implements necessary to make something real out of the right
recognized by the courts.

WATER RIGHTS CONFLICTS AT THE YAKIMA
AND GILA RIVER (PIMA) RESERVATIONS

In the next two developments the *Winters* decisions came to the
attention of national policymakers in the context of what were probably
the two most prominent Indian water disputes outside of the State of
Montana, one at the Yakima reservation in Washington, the other at the
Gila River reservation in the new state of Arizona. As explained at the
national level at least, these disputes also involved the possibility that
these Indians had what could be characterized as prior appropriation
claims that predated settlers' claims. This last fact made the analysis
more complex, but also made the Indians' plight seem more legitimate
to many in Congress, resulting eventually in direct attention by Congress
to their problems.[13]

The Yakima dispute focused around a 1906 decision by Secretary of
the Interior Ethan Hitchcock that allocated a certain portion of the
Yakima River to the Yakima Nation and the rest to non-Indian settlers.

The Yakimas claimed that the secretary had assigned them far less water than they were entitled to. While the Yakimas had been objecting to the secretary's decision since first made in 1906, they were particularly concerned about a bill introduced in 1912 by Senator Wesley Jones of Washington to appropriate money for an irrigation project to irrigate both Yakima and settler lands. The Yakima people believed that the bill would establish in law the secretary's inequitable allocation of water. Petitions from the Yakimas and letters from Samuel Brosius of the Indian Rights Association in Washington, D.C., a non-Indian group formed in 1882 to support the reforms that became the assimilation policy, brought the matter to the attention of Representative Stephens. Stephens arranged for the secretary of the interior to report on the situation and then had that report and the petitions and letters from the Yakimas and their allies printed as a House Document and submitted to the House Committee on Indian Affairs.[14]

According to the petitions and letters, the Yakimas legitimately claimed, for a variety of reasons, a right to at least half the flow of the Yakima River and to all of the flow of certain creeks in the area. But in resolving the 1906 dispute between the settlers and the Yakimas, Secretary Hitchcock had arbitrarily assigned the Yakimas an amount of water far below what they were entitled to. The state and federal governments and the settlers had been relying on that ruling ever since, and the settlers had taken much of the flow of the river and creeks. In claiming rights to that water, the petition from the Yakimas and the letters and the writings by Brosius argued a jumbled mush of riparian, appropriation, and reserved rights theories. For example, the writings expressly mentioned and quoted *Winters* and *Conrad,* asserting a reserved right to land and waters based on the 1855 treaty creating the Yakima reservation treaty. They also argued that the Yakimas had "riparian" rights that predated the coming of the white man. And they argued that the Yakimas had constructed irrigation works, diverted water, and irrigated crops in the late 1890s and early 1900s, before the settlers had appropriated any water. The secretary's ruling had unlawfully deprived them of even this water, a classic prior appropriation claim. The petitions and letters requested that Congress not pass Senator Jones's bill and that the attorney general be directed to file a lawsuit in federal court to determine the Yakimas' rights to water. "If this is not done," the Yakimas' petition concluded, "we are bringing suit in United States court to settle our water rights."[15]

The other water conflict brought to Congress's attention in this period arose on the Gila River reservation in Arizona, home of one group of the Pima Indians. Texas Representative Stephens was the central figure here as well, as he gathered a series of petitions and letters from the Pimas and their allies and had them printed as a House Document. Stephens also introduced and pushed through Congress a joint resolution authorizing a subcommittee of the House Committee on Expenditures to study and report on the problems on the reservation. When the sub-committee submitted its report, he led a short discussion on it in the House and had the report printed as well. The Pimas had two particular non-Indians allies in this fight who supplied Stephens with much of this information. One was Brosius of the Indian Rights Association. The other was a man named Herbert Marten who lived in Sacaton, Arizona, on the reservation. The material submitted to Stephens by Brosius included two letters from Marten to Brosius. Marten's letters indicate that he had extensive knowledge of the history of the Indians and the reservation, the present water problems on the reservation, the efforts of the local Reclamation Service and Indian Affairs officials to deal with the problems, and the legal rights of the Indians, including rights derived from the *Winters* decisions. Marten may have been another example— recall the person who contacted South Carolina Senator Tillman about the Blackfeet issue—of someone who lived in the West and was as familiar as anyone could be with local conditions, yet whose attitude about Indian water rights issues differed from that of the dominant community of non-Indian farming settlers. Because of the political domi-nance of the settlers and their allies, people like Marten had to present their views through channels other than the local congressional delegation.

These writings and the discussions they provoked on the House floor indicated that the Gila River Pimas had irrigated fields with water from the Gila River for hundreds of years, or "from time immemorial," as stated by Representative Oscar Callaway of Texas. Settlers moving into the area immediately upstream of the Indians were diverting much of the river, leaving the Indians with little water at critical periods. Rather than file lawsuits against the settlers to protect the Pimas' water rights, the Indian Office had unwisely spent a half million dollars to develop water wells in the area. The Indians refused to use the well water for a variety of reasons, including the fact that it was too alkaline. The government had at one time promised to correct the situation by building a dam at that stretch of the Gila River to store water for both the Pimas and the settlers but had then decided instead to build Roose-velt Dam on the Salt River, a project that benefited only settlers.[16]

Like the Yakima correspondence, the letters and petitions from the Pimas and their allies mentioned *Winters* and the water rights guaranteed

THE WORK OF *WINTERS*, 1905–1930s

to Indians by those decisions. Marten was much more clear and direct than Brosius about the *Winters* rights held by the Pimas, as Brosius again tended to mix his legal theories. The writings also indicated that the Reclamation Service was arguing that the reserved rights doctrine did not apply to the Gila River reservation because that reservation had been created by executive order, not by treaty (an issue confronted, as I will show, in the Uintah litigation). For this and other reasons the writings and the few members of Congress who spoke argued much more vigorously that the Pimas had established a right to the water of the Gila River by virtue of their prior appropriation. The government had failed to protect these rights, and the Indians lost their water as a result. Thus the government owed them some assistance.

Representative Mondell of Wyoming, always an ardent opponent of the reserved right, took this opportunity to ridicule the notion of a reserved water right and the Indian Office's reliance on anything like it. He argued that it was precisely the reserved rights concept that had caused the problem for the Pimas. Mondell's remarks contain the only mention of the reserved rights doctrine actually on the floor of Congress during the period from 1909 to 1913:

The water which the Pima Indians originally used, and which their forefathers used for many years, was divested by settlers many years ago. The Indian Office, refusing to make the proper application for Indian rights upon the theory that the Government did not have to bow to a State, allowed the water rights of the Indians to be transferred elsewhere and left them with nothing but the flood waters of the Gila. . . . The Government is in a way responsible. If the Indian Office at the proper time had filed with the territorial officials water rights on behalf of the Indians they would have secured them. . . . I worked with the Indian Office here years ago month after month to get them to take out water rights in our State for the benefit of the Indians, in order that they might be protected. Our people did not want to take their water, but the Indian can not sit beside a stream and use water without regard to the forms of law any more than a white man and preserve his rights against others. The Indian Office finally came down off its high horse and admitted in some respects we had a sovereign State with some reserved powers, and they made application in due form. They would have secured these water rights in Arizona just as well, but the Indian Office refused to do it—took the position that, in some peculiar way, the Indian, as the ward of the Government, has a perpetual right, a proprietary right to the water

that flows past his land without regard to the State laws or institutions governing the use of water. This is an illustration of how the
department failed to do its duty. Settlers came along, as it was natural
for them to do, and the Indians were left without anything but flood
waters, and we are now trying to provide water for their use.[17]

In the next Congress, a number of Congress members would agree with
Mondell that western Indians had not been well served by the reserved
rights theory and the Indian Office. But their proposed solution would
not correspond to Representative Mondell's vision. Rather than subordinate all water claims to state water law, these legislators decided
that the years of congressional inaction should end with express recognition of a form of the reserved right and with legislation to bring water
to the Indians based on that right—an effort that affected both the
Yakima and the Gila River Indians and is described in detail below.

PROPOSALS FOR NATIONAL LEGISLATION
RECOGNIZING RESERVED WATER RIGHTS

A fourth line of development in the national life of *Winters* before
1914 has already been alluded to—the beginnings of an effort by Meritt
and others in the Indian Office to propose legislation explicitly recognizing reserved water rights for Indian reservations. The effort began
in a letter from Meritt to Commissioner of Indian Affairs Valentine in
November 1911, during the last years of the administration of William
Howard Taft. It was in this letter that Meritt first objected that "the
principle laid down in the very favorable decision" of *Winters* "has been
practically nullified by various acts of Congress." As a result of this legislation, the water rights of Indians at "a large number of reservations"
were dependent on proving beneficial use under the laws of the western
states, putting at risk the government's expenditure of millions of dollars
in reimbursable funds (that is, reimbursable out of the sales of reservation lands) for irrigation projects for the Indians. Meritt referred especially
to the situation at the Uintah reservation, the Wind River reservation in
Wyoming (subject to a similar statute indicating that water rights for the
reservation irrigation project be obtained in compliance with Wyoming
state law), and the Blackfeet and Fort Peck reservations (interpreting
the water rights provisions in the recent allotment acts as surrendering
to state law). Because of the "great importance of establishing more
certainly and securely the water rights of the Indians," Meritt had been

trying "to evolve a plan whereby these water rights might be better protected." Meritt's "plan" was a proposal for legislation to recognize a version of the reserved rights doctrine, which stated that Congress "reserved on all Indian reservations" as much of the water within or bordering the reservations as was needed or "may hereafter be so needed" by the Indians "for agricultural and domestic purposes." Existing acts inconsistent with this provision were to be repealed. A proviso protected "any prior valid existing rights heretofore lawfully acquired." Meritt concluded by emphasizing that "[t]here is dependent upon its correct solution property rights not only involving millions of dollars but the success or failure, prosperity or poverty of thousands of Indians."[18]

Meritt and Commissioner Valentine asked for review of this proposal by others in the Interior Department, including Phillip Wells, identified as the "chief law officer" for the Reclamation Service. Wells passed it on to the secretary of the interior, suggesting consideration by the secretary and the Department of Justice and noting that the question concerning whether the federal government was limited to state law for water rights for Indians and other federal purposes had been popping up in a variety of forums. This included discussions over the water rights for the irrigation project at the "Colorado Indian Reservation"; in a request from a subcommittee of the Senate Judiciary Committee "for information as to Federal authority over waters and water power"; as a matter recently considered by the National Waterways Commission; and as an issue "pending before the Attorney General upon a submission by the Secretary of Agriculture as to the appropriation of water for forest ranger stations." Wells's list indicated he understood the implications of *Winters* as part of the debate about federal water rights broadly considered, not just for Indian water rights—quite a shift for the Reclamation lawyers from the time of the *Winters* litigation. In another indication, Wells noted that while Meritt was concerned about a host of statutes that subject Indian water uses "to the restrictions, especially restrictions as to the time of beneficial use, imposed by state laws," he (Wells) was "decidedly of the opinion that the Federal Government is not so limited except in cases where Congress has imposed the limitation by express words."[19]

Included in Bureau of Indian Affairs records with another copy of Meritt's proposed legislation is an undated (but apparently written in 1912 or 1913) and unsigned memorandum on "Indian Water Rights," clearly *not* by Meritt because of the way the issues are presented. This memorandum illustrates well the different ways even people familiar with the *Winters* case might have understood the reserved rights concepts and the link to the overarching agrarian policies of the government. More important, this memorandum also indicates that the Indian Office understood by 1912 or 1913 that it was in the beginning stages of what was going to be a significant load of litigation over Indian water rights based on *Winters* theories. The memorandum began by noting that there were two theories as to the nature of the legal title to Indian water rights. One was based upon *"riparian* rights in government ownership and protection from any other user by an implication of law reserving the right for use and benefit of the Indians." As is clear from another reference later in the memorandum, this was how the writer understood the *Winters* and *Conrad* decisions. The writer had no notion of treaty rights or tribal Indian ownership or control of the water and rights—his was a view of the United States as the owner of the water rights protecting the land and water until an Indian allottee received a patent to an allotment, an approach believed to be "of great advantage in affording a reasonable and proper period for preparing an Indian for citizenship." The writer believed on this basis that these rights applied not only to treaty reservations, but also to lands "reserved for allotment purposes" by acts of Congress or Executive Orders, although he recognized that "there appears to be in some Acts of Congress an intention to legislate away the other heretofore well recognized law of prior reservation by the United States"—presumably referring to the Blackfeet and Fort Peck provisions and possibly the Uintah. The writer also recognized that this water rights theory would soon be *"made the basis for several suits pending or to be brought on behalf of the Indians."* This approach was to be preferred to acting under the other possible water rights theory—perfecting rights under the western state law of prior appropriation "under which the Indian, be he ever so backward in his advancement from savagery to civilization, is nevertheless required to display the same ingenuity, industry and perseverance in labor that is necessary for the acquisition and protection of such rights by his white neighbor." The writer concluded by noting, however, that the choice of legal theory to be used to protect the water rights of the Indians was of lesser importance that the "great problem" of federal Indian policy. This was how to "induce the Indians to cultivate and irrigate their allotments and thus make beneficial use" of the water. Perfecting and protecting Indians water rights was a meaningless endeavor without "the education of the Indians to a point where they may be wholly self-supporting."[20]

Meritt carried the campaign into the administration of Woodrow Wilson. An Interior Department review produced a revised version of

Meritt's proposal, which the new secretary of the interior, Franklin Lane, submitted toward the end of 1913 for legislative consideration to Representative Stephens and Senator Robert Gamble, chairs of the House and Senate committees on Indian Affairs.[21] The secretary's transmittal letter, drafted by Meritt, explained that protecting the water rights of the Indians was vital to the successful administration of the Indians' affairs, so that "they may become self-supporting and be raised to a higher standard of civilization." Lane's letter then described the *Winters* decision and commented that the principles of the *Winters* case were "applicable to all Indian reservations where there are no specific Acts of Congress to the contrary." The problem, according to Lane, was that the decision *had* been nullified by acts of Congress at various reservations to the detriment of the Indians and the Indian Office's efforts to protect and promote successful irrigated agriculture at these reservations, with specific reference to the statutes governing the water rights at the Blackfeet, Fort Peck, Wind River, and Uintah reservations. Thus the department recommended to Congress proposed legislation to "better compass the protection of the water rights of Indians," an issue concerning millions of dollars and the "prosperity or poverty of thousands of Indians who are the wards of the Government and whose interests it is the duty of the Indian Bureau and this Department to protect." The first section of the two-section bill established the protection sought:

> There is hereby reserved, on all Indian reservations and Indian allotments held under trust or by other patents containing restrictions on alienation, so much of the waters, either stored or direct flow, within or flowing through or by said Indian reservations and on said Indian lands, or bordering thereon, as may, in the discretion of the Secretary of the Interior, be needed by the Indians for agricultural and domestic purposes and for the purpose of watering stock, or which may hereafter be put to beneficial use by said Indians, so long as said Indian lands shall be held in trust or under restrictions; and the rights reserved shall pass to the Indian allottee when his allotment is no longer held in trust.[22]

Section 2 of the draft then expressly repealed the water rights provisions in the Blackfeet, Fort Peck, Wind River, and Uintah statutes as well as "all other acts or parts of acts, either general or specific, inconsistent with the provisions of this act."[23] Not quite the *Winters* doctrine—especially given that the identification of needed waters would be at the "discretion" of the secretary—but an improvement over a congressional directive to comply with state law, especially when coupled with the recognition that *Winters* rights applied directly at most other reservations. The fate of this proposed legislation in 1914 and 1915 is described below.

INDIAN OFFICE EFFORTS TO ASSERT AND PROTECT INDIAN RESERVATION WATER RIGHTS AROUND THE WEST

The fifth development explored here could be seen as another front opened up by the Indian Office in the same years as part of the same campaign to assert and protect Indian water rights, especially *Winters* rights wherever it was possible to pursue them. The Indian Office began requesting additional staff for the Indian Irrigation Service so that the service could have an in-house legal expert on water rights, critically needed because of a clearly articulated expectation that the federal government would soon be extensively involved in litigation to protect Indian water rights. The Indian Office's proposal and the arguments in support of it are best illustrated in two more unsigned and undated memoranda, one from 1912 and the other probably 1913 or possibly 1914. The first memorandum emphasized that by mid-1912 the federal government had invested eight million dollars in Indian irrigation projects, that the value of this investment "depends almost wholly on the legal rights to use of that water," and even though title to some of that water may be secure under the laws of appropriation and beneficial use, "the only 'good' title to water for irrigation under such laws is a decree of the court." Explicitly mentioning the critical situation with regard to water rights at the Pima, Yakima, Uintah, Crow, and Fort Hall reservations, the memorandum predicted "with reasonable degree of certainty" that the Indian Irrigation Service would soon be heavily involved in litigation at all but a few of the reservations. The service needed a person now with water rights expertise so the agency would "be in a position to act with some degree of assurance when the time comes."[24]

The second Indian Affairs memorandum is more important for providing a lengthy summary of water rights problems and efforts in which the Indian Office was enmeshed by 1913, including the significant extent to which the federal government was already engaged in, had authorized, or was preparing for Indian water rights litigation that included assertions of reserved rights.[25] This long memorandum also included a pointed contrast to the way in which the Reclamation Service had been generously staffed to assert and protect water rights for Reclamation projects. The memorandum began with a direct reference to the *Winters* case and the opportunity it offered to establish water rights for Indian reservations by "implied reservation of water" without the need to prove prior appropriation and beneficial use. The writer then provided detailed examples of water rights issues and activities by 1913 at a host of reservations across the West, which I have summarized as follows:

- *Uintah (Utah).* An example of where Congress had shown a tendency "to legislate away the law of implied reservation of water." The 1906 statute might mean that water rights for the allotments are restricted to state law claims, but the problems inherent in unperfected water rights and the dwindling available supply were becoming acute. Thus it was "only a question of time until the claims for water will have to be adjudicated in the courts" where it will become known "[w]hether the Indians' water rights be finally found to rest on the law of implied reservation or upon the laws of the State."
- *Wind River Shoshone (Wyoming).* Allotted (in part) in 1905 with a provision apparently deferring to state water law for perfecting appropriations. Facilities had been constructed and the requirements of the state law had been complied with, "except, as in the case of the Uintah water rights, beneficial use has been made upon only a small part of the area under ditch." The state denied water to allottees for alleged failure to perfect rights under state law. The federal government had *already filed suit* against Wyoming state officials in a complaint based both on prior appropriation claims and on *Winters* theories (a case filed in 1913 and known as *United States v. Albert Hampleman,* discussed in more detail below).
- *Crow (Montana).* The 1904 legislation allotting this reservation recognized that any water appropriated on the diminished reservation was "subject to the prior rights of the Indians." The Indian Office needed to be better prepared to assert, perfect, and hold these rights under reservation and state law theories.
- *Colorado River (Arizona).* A 1910 appropriation for irrigation facilities at the Colorado River reservation required similar water rights work to protect.
- *Pima (Arizona).* The memorandum briefly described the water rights problem at the Gila River reservation, as outlined

above. It noted that a special assistant to the attorney general was working with Indian Office to obtain the necessary information and "be prepared when the time comes to meet the issue in court."

- *Northern Cheyenne (Montana)*. The state was about to begin a general adjudication of the Tongue River. The Indian Office had asked the attorney general to authorize Justice Department lawyers to appear on behalf of the United States and Indians to assert claims under the theories of implied reservation and prior appropriation. This reservation presented special problems because it was "of comparatively recent establishment" and irrigation by others in the valley began before the establishment of the reservation.
- *Yakima (Washington)*. The memorandum described the 1906 water allocation issue and noted that "conditions indicate that water rights for this fertile land" may have to "conform to State laws" unless Congress acted or something else happened.
- *Owens Valley Paiute (California)*. The Indian Office was experiencing "considerable difficulty" providing water for the allotments in the valley because of conflict with the supply claimed by Los Angeles and non-Indians in the valley. The special assistant to the attorney general had been directed to investigate; water rights for these allotments distributed under the 1887 general allotment act might have to conform to local laws.
- *Southern Ute (Colorado)*. The attorney general, in response to a request from the Indian Office, had authorized the U.S. attorney to file suit to "assert the treaty rights" to sufficient water to irrigate 15,500 acres in the Pine River and other valleys in southwestern Colorado. The suit had not yet been filed because the U.S. attorney "had not had time to work up the mass of data necessary for a proper presentation of the complaint of the government."
- *Umatilla (Oregon)*. Water rights for the Umatilla reservation were in litigation in Oregon state court, which "for the present" the Interior Department had decided was a proper forum. "This case is of interest in that it is the first time the law of implied reservation of water has been presented to a State tribunal." (The Oregon Supreme Court decided this case in 1917, rejecting the *Winters* claims of the federal government, in *Byers v. Wa-wa-ne,* discussed briefly below.)

- *Papago (Arizona)*. The "activities" of the Tucson Farms Company had called into question the water rights for the Papago Reservation, which "may be in litigation within a short time." The Indian Irrigation Service needed to get prepared to assert or defend the water rights of the Indians.
- *Fort Hall Shoshone-Bannock (Idaho)*. State law might control the Fort Hall water rights; if so, 1916 was the end of the period allowed for proving beneficial use. "Undoubtedly there will be an adjudication of the waters and here again the government should be ready when the time comes." (The Ninth Circuit eventually ruled in favor of reserved water rights for allotment at Fort Hall, in the 1921 decision *Skeem v. United States*, discussed elsewhere in the book.)[26]

After this survey, the memorandum concluded by stressing that "[o]ne great difficulty" common to all these matters was the fact that the non-Indian claimants were represented by the best, well prepared counsel while the government was "frequently if not always caught unprepared." The U.S. attorneys lacked the necessary time, assistance, and "a proper knowledge of conditions." The situation was serious. Water rights allow for "whatever possibilities [the Indian lands] have for providing a living by cultivation," and they should not be left "without the protection which a carefully compiled record of local conditions and knowledge of surrounding circumstances would provide." Private irrigation enterprises protected themselves in this way. The contrast with the Reclamation Service was even more telling of the government's priorities. "[Reclamation's] force engaged in work looking to protection against loss of water rights and kindred matters consists of eight or nine Examiners, one for the office of each Supervising Engineer in charge of a district, with a general office division of seven under the Chief Law Officer with a Supervising Engineer in direct charge." The Indian Office in contrast was looking for its first such person to take charge of this work under the direction of the chief engineer.[27]

WINTERS-BASED LITIGATION: SAN CARLOS APACHE, UMATILLA, AND WIND RIVER RESERVATIONS

The sixth development was the beginning of litigation itself at various reservations around the West, an effort already referred to above. Reported decisions did not start appearing until 1916 and after, but suits were filed or prepared or contemplated well before then. As early as 1910 the attorney general, in his annual report, noted that litigation had been authorized (although not yet filed) to protect the water rights of the Gila River reservation as well as reservation rights in Oregon and Colorado. He noted more generally that the "excessive" appropriation of water by non-Indians around various reservations in the West might be "in violation of Indian treaties and subject to be enjoined at the suit of the United States." Beginning a theme of concern for balanced and corresponding Indian and non-Indian irrigation that would play a large role in the policy strategy for the Uintah litigation, the attorney general stated that a way had to be found to be able to protect the Indians and the government's Indian policy "without inflicting needless hardship upon their white neighbors who have diverted the water and are using it in good faith to irrigate their farms."[28] By 1914 the attorney general reported that "substantial progress" had been made in "protecting the water rights reserved to the Indians." He cited as examples litigation in progress involving the water rights of the Indians of the Pyramid Lake Indian Reservation in Nevada (part of broader litigation concerning federal and other rights to Lake Tahoe and the Truckee and Carson Rivers to facilitate the Truckee-Carson Reclamation project) and of the Gila River reservation in Arizona (a suit in state court that actually did not involve the rights of the Indians at that time).[29]

The attorney general's 1914 report did not mention three Indian water rights cases that the United States filed or became involved in in 1913, involving rights to water at the San Carlos Indian Reservation in Arizona, the Umatilla Indian Reservation in Oregon, and (of the most significance by far for the Uintah situation) the Wind River Indian Reservation in Wyoming. These are described in turn.

SAN CARLOS APACHE INDIAN RESERVATION

The attorney general ignored what was an apparent setback for reserved water rights in progress in federal court in Arizona. In what turned out to be an ill-advised first attempt to extend *Winters* to another context, in 1913 the U.S. attorney in Arizona filed suit against a non-Indian irrigator to assert rights for the San Carlos Apache Indian Reservation to the water in what was known as Goodwin Springs. The springs were on reservation lands, but the facts (at least as the court reported them) were not otherwise favorable to the United States, which had knowingly transferred these waters to obvious non-Indian use twenty years before. The lands containing the springs had been made a part of the Indian reservation in 1872 after the abandonment of a military post, Camp Goodwin. However, the waters from the springs had been used since well before that time for domestic and irrigation purposes on Fort Thomas military lands and other lands adjacent to the Goodwin parcel, off the reservation. The government abandoned Fort Thomas in the 1880s and sold the lands to non-Indian settlers soon after, at a price clearly representing the land's value as irrigated. Non-Indians had irrigated the Fort Thomas lands from these springs ever since—Rollo Wightman being the latest owner of the property. Wightman had invested in a number of improvements to the irrigation system in the years he had owned the lands. In 1911 and then again in 1913 the San Carlos reservation superintendent had assigned land on the reservation that could be irrigated from these springs to Indian residents and had tried to force Wightman to stop using the waters from the springs. Wightman refused. Finally the reservation personnel persuaded the Justice Department to authorize the U.S. attorney to sue Wightman in federal district court.

It is not clear what was the status of the *Wightman* litigation in mid-1914, but the case never seemed to go well for the government. The federal court issued a formal written ruling against the United States in January 1916, *United States v. Wightman,* the first reported court decision after *Winters* and *Conrad* in which the government had asserted a *Winters* reserved rights theory for Indian water rights.[30] Reading between the lines of the opinion, it seems relatively clear that the federal judge, William Sawtelle, ruled against the United States simply because on these facts he believed it would have been an "inequitable" result to strip the water from the defendant, whatever the technical validity of the legal claim. But because the United States had argued a *Winters* theory for the rights, and only that theory, the judge was forced to support his decision by explaining why *Winters* did not apply. So he distinguished *Winters* on the grounds that the Fort Belknap treaty clearly (if by implication) contemplated not only irrigated agriculture as critical to the purposes of the reservation but also the use of the actual waters in question for that irrigation, without which the purpose of the reservation would fail and upon which the government had begun to act soon after. In the *Wightman* case, the spring waters in question were sufficient to irrigate the lands of only one or two people and had always been dedicated to the use of the lands off the reservation, with no indication that these waters were integral or necessary to the purposes of the reservation of land and no indication until well after the use of the waters was abandoned to the non-Indians that the waters were desired for use on the reservation. In the court's view, "[m]anifestly, then, the use of these waters is in no just sense necessary to the objects for which the reservation was created, and their use on lands outside the reservation neither defeats nor impedes the fulfillment of the purposes which actuated the creation of the reservation here involved," taking the case out of the orbit of *Winters* in the judge's view. Clouding later discussions, however, the court went on to add (unnecessarily it seems) that *Winters* "turned solely on the agreement with the Indians," which was the "sole basis out of which the equities in favor of the Indians arise." Because the San Carlos reservation lands did not involve a treaty, "there are no equities growing out of such treaty or agreement in this case." Thus *Wightman* came to stand for a ruling that *Winters* rights cannot apply to any reservation not created by a treaty, which was not really what *Wightman* was about. Fortunately for the government's position in the Uintah situation (which also did not involve a treaty, at least not in the final creation of the reservation), the *Wightman* decision did not turn out to be too persuasive an opinion, presumably because everyone could see how that case was really determined by the equities of the facts of use.

UMATILLA INDIAN RESERVATION

The government ended up with another setback for the reserved rights strategy in the second Indian water rights case begun in 1913, concerning rights to water for the Umatilla reservation in eastern Oregon. But again this was a setback that could be explained away in later efforts because of the different environmental context, which resulted in a different understanding of the "purpose" of the reservation treaty; and especially because this was a decision by a state court, not a federal court, and states and state courts were not known to be protectors of the rights of Indians. This case began in Umatilla County Circuit Court in Oregon, as an adjudication of water rights in the Umatilla River, in which the federal government decided it had to participate to protect what rights the Indians had to use Umatilla River water for irrigation. I am not going to explain the Umatilla situation in detail—that would take another case study. Suffice to say that while a lower state court had issued a ruling at least partially favorable to the federal government, the

Oregon Supreme Court ruled on appeal that the 1855 treaty creating the Umatilla reservation did not contemplate that irrigated agriculture would be necessary to the purposes of the reservation, and thus the treaty did not reserve water for this purpose. The court reasoned thus from the fact that the only explicit mention of water in the treaty involved fishing rights; that information given to the court indicated that crops sufficient for the Indians' maintenance could be grown *without* irrigation on most reservation lands; that agriculture on the portion of the reservation that could not be farmed without irrigation was not essential to successful reservation life and could not be farmed without an expensive irrigation project; that efforts at irrigated agriculture did not begin at the reservation for decades after the treaty and well after the surrounding non-Indians began irrigating; and that the circumstances surrounding the treaty and subsequent life on the reservation indicated that the only water uses essential to life on the reservation and thus implicitly reserved in the treaty were for domestic use and stock watering. On this basis, the court concluded, "We cannot find, in the circumstances and conditions attending the negotiations of the Indian treaty of 1855, any suggestion that the waters of the Umatilla river were impliedly appropriated for the use of the Indians whenever they should see fit to avail themselves of these waters. . . . The right claimed is not essential to the maintenance of the Indians or their progress in the arts of the civilized life."[31]

WIND RIVER INDIAN RESERVATION

The third Indian water rights lawsuit filed in 1913, involving the Wind River reservation in Wyoming, *was* successful. This case most closely paralleled the *Winters* case, involving an 1868 reservation treaty with Shoshone and Arapaho tribes in an arid region. The treaty included a description of the reservation as extending into the channel of the Wind River and tributary creeks, and it stated that the purpose of the reservation was to promote the development and civilization of the Indians by inducing them to engage in agriculture and stock raising. As already noted, however, in the eyes of the Indian Office the Wind River situation also paralleled the situation at the Uintah and other reservations in that Congress had agreed to the allotment of the Wind River reservation in 1905 (the 1868 treaty had contemplated the selection of individual tracts of lands for farming as particular Indians desired; Congress and the administration pressured the Wind River Indians into an agreement ratified by Congress in 1905 to allot part of the reservation) and in doing so appeared to have recognized or required that water for irrigating the allotments be obtained under the laws of the State of Wyoming. More precisely, the Wind River allotment Act of March 3, 1905, specified that some of the money earned by the sale of surplus lands "shall be devoted to . . . the performance of such acts as are required by the statutes of the State of Wyoming in securing water rights from said State for the irrigation of such lands as shall remain the property of said Indians, whether located within the territory intended to be ceded by this agreement or within the diminished reservation."[32]

Indian allottees began irrigating allotments out of a number of the reservation creeks without necessarily following the requirements of state law (this appears to have been the practice in Wyoming that bothered Representative Mondell). More important, many of the Indian irrigation uses were junior in time to non-Indian irrigators downstream, at least in the eyes of the state. Shoshone tribal member Annie Duncan and her family were irrigating allotment lands she had selected for herself and her children along Muddy and Red Creeks. Muddy Creek and Red Creek were on the reservation, eventually flowing into Owl Creek, one of the boundaries of the reservation. In 1911 and 1912, Albert Hampleman, the state-appointed water commissioner for this area, went onto the allotments and closed the Duncans' headgates on Muddy and Red Creeks, so that the water would flow downstream to what Hampleman considered the land of senior appropriators, who happened to be non-Indians living off the reservation. State officials ignored demands by the reservation superintendent that the state stop interfering with the irrigation of the Indian allotments. Thus on September 5, 1913, the U.S. attorney in Cheyenne filed suit in federal district court on behalf of the United States and the Indians against Hampleman, alleging unlawful interference by the state with "lands, ditches and water rights of the Indian allottees" that were "within the absolute and exclusive jurisdiction of" the United States.

In a decree signed in June 1916 (never reported in the official case reports) the federal court granted the United States the injunctive relief it sought, agreeing that these water rights were within the "absolute and exclusive" control of the United States and the Indians, perpetually enjoining Hampleman and other state officials from interfering in the allottees' irrigation out of Muddy and Red Creeks. Judge John Riner's decree did not explain the legal theories underlying the decree, but the *only* theory the federal government argued was a *Winters*-based reserved rights theory—that the 1868 treaty had reserved sufficient water to fulfill the purposes of the reservation, one of which was to move the Indians toward irrigated agriculture on individually owned small-tract farms. Thus the Indians' reserved water rights were paramount to any other rights on the river; the rights transferred to the Indian allotments at least as long as the Indian allottees owned and irrigated the lands, and these rights were a matter of federal law, not subject to the jurisdiction or control of state water law. The state tried to argue that the *Winters* decisions were hopelessly predicated on the peculiarities of Montana law, where the riparian doctrine had not been abrogated, and could not apply to a state like Wyoming that had abrogated the riparian doctrine when first a territory and determined all rights by priority appropriation and beneficial use, a system recognized and acquiesced in by the federal government from the time Wyoming became a state. More important, the state argued, the allotment agreement ratified by Congress in the 1905 Wind River allotment act explicitly recognized and deferred to the state water laws of Wyoming for control over water rights for the irrigation of the allotments—the key issue also in the Uintah case. The United States responded that Congress could not by implication give away the treaty rights agreed to by the United States and the Wind River Indians. Given the court's eventual ruling, the federal government's arguments in its March 1915 brief must have been persuasive:

> [Defendant seeks] to show that Congress, by said Act, recognized the ownership of the waters on the reservation by the State of Wyoming, and further that the state had full control and supervision over the waters on the reservation. It is the contention of the plaintiff [the United States] that Congress could not, by implication, thus take away any water rights belonging to the said Indians. If, as contended by plaintiff, the Indians were given water rights by the Fort Bridger Treaty, and if they were not taken away by the act of admission of Wyoming as a state then they certainly were not taken away by any implication however strong in the aforesaid agreement [meaning the allotment agreement ratified in the 1905 Act]. Moreover, Article 10 of the said agreement is as follows:—"It is further understood that nothing in this agreement shall be construed to deprive said Indians . . . of any benefit to which they are entitled under the existing treaties or agreements not inconsistent with the provisions of this agreement." Certainly it cannot be contended in the face of a direct provision of this kind that Congress took away the water rights of the Indians on said reservation.[33]

The Wind River litigation set the stage well for the Uintah litigation—this is precisely the type of argument the federal attorneys used to explain away the impact of Congress's 1906 water provision deferring to state law for the irrigation of the Uintah allotments. But the differences between the Wind River and Uintah situations should be noted, too: the Uintah reservation was not created by a treaty; the water rights provision in the Uintah allotment act was a more definitive directive to follow state law, *and* the Uintah act did not contain a treaty rights reservation provision similar to article 10 quoted above. In the end, the differences did not matter.

WORKING OUT THE IMPLICATIONS OF *WINTERS* BEYOND INDIAN WATER RIGHTS

The seventh and last line of development in the life of *Winters* is one I noted earlier—in the years 1910 to 1914 Justice Department attorneys, especially Ethelbert Ward and John Truesdell, worked out the broader implications of *Winters* for federal water rights outside the Indian water rights context, primarily to buttress claims to water for Reclamation projects and federal purposes. Truesdell and Ward would also be the lead attorneys for the United States in the Uintah Indian water rights litigation, and were central to much of the Indian and non-Indian federal water rights litigation in the West in these years. Truesdell, for example, was the lead attorney for years in the Pima and Pyramid Lake cases. At this stage Ward involved himself more in Reclamation cases. His 1913 brief for the Reclamation Service in water rights adjudication proceedings for the Uncompahgre Valley Reclamation project in state court in Colorado is an example of how Ward could weave *Winters* into the legal arguments for a Reclamation Service claim to reserve unappropriated waters in a watershed while the service developed a specific project.[34] But Ward also advised on the Indian water rights cases, including the *Hampleman* litigation. Ward's and Truesdell's work culminated in this policy statement by the attorney general, in his annual report for 1914:

> The department takes the position that in the arid and semiarid regions, where the legality of diverting and appropriating water for beneficial uses on nonriparian lands is generally established, the original right of the Government to appropriate surplus water for its own uses, particularly for reclamation of its enormous holdings of

arid lands, has not been surrendered by any act of Congress or divested by the mere creation of the States into which those regions have now become incorporated. This position has been sustained by one of the district courts of the State of Colorado [an apparent reference to the Uncompahgre valley work by Ward]. Its soundness has been challenged by certain claimants who would have the Federal user dependent on the permission of State laws. The question, never passed on, I am advised, by the Supreme Court, seems very important theoretically, but in practice it has hitherto been obviated by the general identity of interests, and the disposition of the Government to follow the State administrative procedure wherever practicable.[35]

The same type of argument—combining an insistence upon federal supremacy never surrendered by Congress with close cooperation and compliance with state requirements where practical—would underlie Truesdell's and Ward's approach to the Uintah dilemma. Nothing illustrates this better than the fact that their 1917 legal brief in the Uintah Indian water rights litigation *began* with this quote from the attorney general's report.

WINTERS AND RESERVED WATER RIGHTS IN CONGRESS, 1914–1915

One place where these paths in the life of *Winters* converged was in Congress in 1914 and 1915, in a two-year, highly public flare-up of interest in Indian water rights that occurred just at the time the Indian Office, the Uintah reservation personnel, and the Justice Department attorneys were putting together the Uintah case. The debate began because a few members of Congress, primarily in the Senate, had become convinced (by the Indian Office and others) that non-Indian settlers were gaining control over water that should have gone to the Indian peoples. This loss of control was occurring despite the protection that should have been afforded by the reserved rights doctrine and despite congressional appropriations for irrigation projects intended at least in part to benefit the Indians. These members decided to push for legislation based on an express recognition of Indian water rights, including versions of the reserved rights doctrine, as well as irrigation appropriations directly intended to match water to the rights. They were relatively successful in obtaining more money for irrigation projects. They were not successful in obtaining express recognition of reserved rights.

These proponents of Indian water rights chose the Indian appropriations bill as their vehicle, and they proceeded on three fronts. First, they successfully pushed through a measure for the Yakimas that generally recognized the Yakimas' rights to water and appropriated money to in essence purchase a water supply to satisfy those rights. Second, they obtained assistance for the Gila River Pimas on much the same basis. Their success in these first two measures did not necessarily mean success for the reserved water rights doctrine. The appropriations were seen by many as necessary because of a supposed failure on the part of the federal government to protect the prior appropriation rights of the Yakimas and Pimas. The provisions eventually approved by Congress could be interpreted either to support reserved rights or water rights under the state appropriation systems. Third, and most significant for the reserved rights doctrine, the proponents sought but failed to obtain an express provision in the continuing appropriations for the irrigation projects in Montana and elsewhere that would have recognized the reserved right basis for the water to be provided to the Indians.

Plain old party politics appeared to play at least some role in the nature and timing of these efforts. Woodrow Wilson became president in 1913, breaking the Republican party's sixteen-year hold on the presidency, and the Democrats now also controlled both houses of Congress. Most, though not all, of the senators acting in support of Indian water rights were Democrats, as was their chief ally in the House, Texas Congressman Stephens. The actions and policies they attacked—the 1906 Yakima allocation decision by Secretary Hitchcock, the failure on the part of the Indian Office to assert and protect Indian water rights—were the actions and policies of the past Republican administrations. Party politics does not explain all of the effort, however. The fight in Congress was not overtly partisan in content or tone, and a few of the strongest proponents of the reserved right, notably Senator Carroll Page of Vermont, were Republicans. Further, most of the western Democrats supported the state appropriation system and refused to follow the lead of western Democratic Senators Harry Lane of Oregon and Henry Ashurst of Arizona in support of a reserved rights concept. Thus while party politics may explain some of the effort, the absence of party unity on the specific point of express use of reserved rights theory helps to explain the congressional stalemate on this point—that and the continuing inclination to understand and deflect the issue in the context of the allotment policy.

The proponents of an express recognition of reserved rights first came forward in the consideration of the Yakima appropriation. In late

December 1913, Senator Joseph Robinson, a Democrat from Arkansas, submitted a report from a joint congressional committee that had traveled to the state of Washington to study the Yakima problem. Like the earlier writings on the Yakima dispute, the committee report mixed themes of prior appropriation and reserved rights, although it emphasized factors relevant to a *Winters*-based reserved water rights theory. For example, the committee report noted that the purpose of the 1855 treaty creating the Yakima reservation was to make possible the permanent settlement of the Yakima Indians and their transformation into an agricultural people. Water was needed for this purpose. Echoing *Winans* (although not quoting or citing the decision), the report stated that the 1855 treaty was not a grant of various rights to the Yakimas but a grant of certain rights from them with a reservation of all rights not granted, including those to water. The report also noted that irrigation was little known to the Yakimas in 1855, implying that any reservation of water rights based on the treaty did not stem from water in use at the time the Yakimas entered into the treaty. The report did note that the Yakimas began irrigating in 1859, well before any settlers began irrigating, and that Secretary Hitchcock's 1906 ruling allocating the Yakima River deprived the Yakimas of much of the water they were already using. However, the report also stressed that the Hitchcock ruling was in error because it "totally failed to make provision for future needs," a recognition that the Yakimas' rights to water went beyond present appropriation uses.[36]

The committee report recommended that Congress provide free to the Yakimas water from government storage projects "equal to the amount to which said reservation was equitably entitled when the finding of Secretary Hitchcock was made," a statement that could be interpreted to mean rights based on whichever legal theory one happened to believe in. The report then stated that it was "difficult to determine what the amount should be," but that it should not be less than one-half of the flow of the river and should be sufficient to irrigate one-half of each allotment. The report does not explain exactly why the committee chose this amount, nor the theory under which it was calculated. When Senator Robinson introduced the report on the floor of the Senate, however, he stated explicitly that he thought the Yakima situation was analogous to the *Winters* case. He also stated that the recommendation in the report was based on the fact that the Yakimas had a reserved right to the water of the Yakima River, due to the reservation of land by the Yakimas and by the government for the purpose of transforming the Yakimas into a settled, pastoral people.[37]

On the basis of this report, the Senate Committee on Indian Affairs added a section to the Indian appropriations bill, later approved by the Senate, that appropriated $200,000 to purchase a water supply and irrigation facilities for the Yakima reservation. The Senate's provision said nothing specific about water rights. Members of the House were not satisfied with the Senate's bare provision. The Indian Office was not satisfied with the Senate's measure because it wanted more money. By the time the Indian appropriations bill emerged from the House and then two House-Senate conferences, the provision for the Yakimas appropriated $635,000 to pay for water and facilities. The legislation itself also explained the reason for the appropriation:

> It appearing . . . that the Indians of the Yakima Reservation have been unjustly deprived of the portion of the natural flow of the Yakima River to which they are equitably entitled for the purposes of irrigation, having only been allowed one hundred and forty-seven cubic feet per second, the Secretary of the Interior is hereby authorized and directed to furnish at the northern boundary of said Yakima Indian Reservation, in perpetuity, enough water, in addition to the one hundred and forty-seven cubic feet per second heretofore allotted to said Indians, so that there shall be, during the low-water irrigation season, at least seven hundred and twenty cubic feet per second of water available when needed for irrigation, this quantity being considered as equivalent to and in satisfaction of the rights of the Indians in the low-water flow of the Yakima River and adequate for the irrigation of forty acres on each Indian allotment.[38]

The Yakima appropriation became law in this form. Congress did not openly debate or discuss the meaning of this provision.[39]

The Yakima episode and the resulting provision illustrate two points with regard to the *Winters* doctrine. First, despite the committee report's emphasis on the factors relating to reserved rights, and despite Senator Robinson's clearly stated preference for the reserved rights doctrine as the basis for an appropriation for the Yakimas, the provision that became law did *not* state clearly that Congress's action was intended to help implement the reserved water rights of the Yakimas. Many members of Congress had argued that the Yakimas were prior appropriators who were the victims of government interference, and thus congressional action was needed to make amends for that interference. The explanation eventually written into the Yakima appropriation may be interpreted as supporting whichever theory—prior appropriation or reserved rights—that a member believed appropriate. The fact that the prior appropriation elements were mixed into this debate freed Congress to fund the construction of facilities to satisfy whatever were the water rights of the Yakimas without having to appear to sanction (or deny) the reserved rights theory.

Second, up to 1914, Congress had been able to deflect the reserved rights issue by allotting the reservations and by appropriating money for big irrigation projects capable in theory of satisfying the water needs of Indians and settlers together. By the time of the Yakima debate in 1914 many members (and others outside of Congress) had begun to question whether these projects provided water for Indians or benefited only the settlers. Congress settled the Yakima dispute by appropriating money expressly for a large water supply for the Yakimas only, the only time Congress acted in this manner in the period analyzed here. Congress acted as it did in part because certain members defined the situation as one in which the government had actively violated a treaty reserved right held by the Yakimas. Thus the Yakima provision, even though it fell short of explicit recognition of the reserved right, may be the most prominent victory for the reserved right in terms of legislation directly intended to transform the right into water.[40]

An irrigation appropriation for the Gila River Pimas went through much the same process, although the eventual appropriation was for a study only and then, in a later Congress, for a classic irrigation reservoir intended for settlers and Indians alike. As with the Yakimas, the provision for the Pimas made mention of their water rights, but left unclear whether this meant prior appropriation or reserved rights. The possibility that the Pimas had prior appropriation rights and that the government had failed to protect them played a major role in the consideration of the proposed remedy. The debates indicated that many voted for the Pimas on this basis; but the debates also indicated that some in this Congress supported the Pimas' cause because of a conviction that the government had failed in its trust duty to protect the Pimas' reserved water rights as outlined in *Winters*. These members of Congress introduced reports from the Indian Office and made statements on the floor to the effect that the Pimas had, as one report stated, "a right to take as much of the flow of the stream as may ever be required for the proper use of the Indians." This was a clear statement of the reserved rights doctrine, and these legislators acted on this basis. They were not successful in forcing Congress to acknowledge this point explicitly. Congress once again found a way to act on a particular problem while deflecting the confrontation over the reserved rights doctrine itself.[41]

The third, and most important and divisive, of the congressional proponents' attempts to sanction reserved water rights concerned reservations in Montana and elsewhere that had little or no history of prior appropriation claims. These reservations were also the site of irrigation projects in various stages of planning, construction, or operation that were intended to supply water for both Indians and settlers. Congressional appropriations to build these projects were to be repaid largely from the sale of surplus reservation lands after allotment. Water appropriations from the federal projects were being based on the state law of prior appropriation, either because of an explicit congressional directive or because this was the practice of the Indian Affairs and Reclamation Service officials. Critics in Congress, the Indian Office and elsewhere who had analyzed the implementation of this policy argued that the Indian peoples did not have the training, experience, or materials necessary to put water immediately to use when available, as would be required under the state law of prior appropriation. Non-Indian settlers were able to put water to beneficial use, and consequently they were obtaining rights to all available water from these irrigation projects. Even when Congress had established a preference right to water for the Indians, as it had with the Blackfeet project, the grace period was seen as too short for the Indians to establish their rights. As a consequence, Indians were not benefiting from projects intended for them and paid for out of the sales of their lands.

To the Indian Office and to these members of Congress, the adoption of some form of the reserved rights doctrine seemed part of a possible solution to this problem. Thus in response to a request from the Indian Office, the House Committee on Indian Affairs proposed to add the following provision to the 1914 irrigation appropriations for the Flathead, Blackfeet, Fort Peck, and Fort Belknap reservations in Montana, Uintah and Southern Ute reservations in Utah and Colorado, Wind River reservation in Wyoming, and Fort Hall reservation in Idaho:

> Provided, That the use of so much water as may be necessary to supply for domestic, stock-watering, and irrigation purposes on land allotted or to be allotted to Indians on the . . . Reservation or set aside for administrative purposes within said reservation is hereby reserved, and the failure of any Indian or Indians to make beneficial use of such water shall not operate in any manner to defeat his or her right thereto while said land is held in trust by the United States.[42]

The House committee thus proposed an explicit congressional reservation of water for these Indians. As before, the proposal differed from the *Winters* doctrine as developed by the courts in that it did not recognize reservations of water dating from treaties and executive orders creating the reservations. Moreover, the reserved water rights acknowledged in this proposal would have applied only to land allotted or to be allotted, and it would last only for the trust period of the allotment, or twenty-five years. Even congressional proponents of reserved rights continued to reflect the attitude that allotments were part of a proper policy intended to transform the Indians into individual small-tract farmers like the settlers. The proponents chose the reserved water rights doctrine as a tool to assist in the transformation. Yet even as modified and limited, their proposal did represent a direct attempt to establish a federal system of water allocation in the West, a reserved right that conflicted directly with the western state "use-it-or-lose-it" policy.[43]

Representative Mondell immediately objected on the floor of the House to the committee's reserved water rights proposal. Representative Stephens, head of the House Committee on Indian Affairs, explained that years of training and assistance were necessary before the Indians were ready to use the water effectively for irrigation. Non-Indian settlers were better prepared to make use of the water from the federal projects, so they would establish rights to the water under the state laws of prior appropriation. Indians would not secure rights to any of it. If so, "all the money spent on building the big projects and the effort made in the allotments will be to no avail, and we must do something, because they are our wards; we must protect their water rights in the trust period." Mondell countered that Indians could be protected under state law if only the Indian Office would assist them properly in making their appropriations. He again raised the specter of reserved waters "running unused to the sea" rather than being available for irrigation. Mondell also raised a point of order against the provision as improper legislation attached to an appropriation bill. The presiding officer was forced to delete the provision without a vote on its merits.[44]

The Senate Committee on Indian Affairs then made a similar attempt in the Senate in mid-1914, facing the same dilemma and failing for the same reason. The attempt, however, sparked a debate on the floor of the Senate over the meaning, validity, and wisdom of the reserved rights doctrine that lasted for days and even carried over into the next session. It is not clear how the proponents of the reserved right hoped to succeed with the original provision, needing unanimous support to attach it to the appropriations bill. The obstacles in their path were highlighted when Senator John Shafroth of Colorado (also a Democrat, but no friend of the reserved rights effort) opened the Senate debate—

before the reserved rights provision even came up for consideration—by submitting a memorial from the Colorado General Assembly opposed to federal control of natural resources, especially including water:

> We assert that the States are vested with the right to control the waters within their respective borders—subject only to the right of the Federal Government to protect navigation on those streams that are navigable—to dispose of them to those who will use them for beneficial purposes. . . . Reclamation of arid lands, when under taken by the United States Government, should in all cases recognize the rights of the States to control the waters within their borders.[45]

Colorado's views left the federal government only the navigation servitude, denying even the *Rio Grande/Winters* principle of federal rights to water as necessary for the beneficial uses of federal property. Nonetheless, the proponents of the reserved rights doctrine, led by Democratic Senators Robinson, Lane, and Ashurst (chairman of the Senate Committee on Indian Affairs), along with Republican Senator Page, argued the need for expressly stated reserved water rights for Indians. They invoked and quoted from *Winters* and *Conrad* and argued that Congress had to take explicit steps to sanction and protect these rights or the Indians would never have any water.[46]

The Senate proponents did not end their efforts when the original proposal died on a point of order. Senator Robinson introduced a provision that could not be removed on a point of order because it was not "legislation" as the Senate defined the term, only a restriction directly related to the Montana appropriation. Robinson's proposed language stated that the federal government could not release the money appropriated for irrigation projects in Montana until the state adopted legislation to protect Indian water rights. The state enactment had to ensure that water rights would be held incontestable during the allotment trust period and that beneficial use of water by an allottee at any time during the trust period would perfect a water right with a priority date back to the date of the completion of the project. Robinson was trying to force the states to establish at least a bastardized form of the reserved rights. Opponents argued that the Montana legislature could not pass such a law, as it would contradict the provision in the Montana constitution establishing the appropriation system as the water allocation system in Montana. The Senate rejected this proposal overwhelmingly in the only voice vote on a measure in the decade under study here.[47]

The proponents of the reserved rights doctrine kept hammering at the issue for days. Perhaps simply by wearing their colleagues down,

Senator Robinson and his associates, particularly Senator Page at this point, finally convinced the Senate to agree to a complicated and ambiguous water rights provision attached to the Flathead appropriation only. This provision required that the attorney general affirmatively certify that Indian water rights were "protected and confirmed" by state or federal law before the government could release the appropriated money. But Senator Robinson's new provision did not survive a conference with the House. Many in both houses decided upon reflection and upon pressure from the Montana delegation that this provision established a cumbersome process unfairly attached to only one project in one state. After all the efforts of the proponents of the reserved rights doctrine, the final Indian appropriations act for 1914 did not attach to the irrigation appropriations water rights provisions of any kind that would ensure that the water went to the Indians. Almost as an afterthought to placate the proponents, the Indian appropriations legislation did separately direct the Indian Office to report to Congress on the status of the water rights on several reservations and include recommendations for protecting the rights.[48]

Thus the effort in 1914 to have Congress explicitly recognize or establish reserved water rights for Indians dissolved into authorization for a study. A study seemed appropriate to many of the members in part because of the way in which the guardians of the state law prior appropriation system attacked the Supreme Court's decision in *Winters,* creating doubt as to its meaning, implications, and validity. In a bewildering multifaceted attack, these people argued, among other things, that *Winters* obviously was bad law and the Supreme Court was bound to reverse or confine it in the near future; that no matter what *Winters* appeared to say, the federal government had no authority to reserve waters and no control over water allocation whatsoever; that the Fort Belknap situation was peculiar (or that Montana water law was peculiar) and thus the holding in *Winters* could never be repeated; that despite what some of the language of the opinion implied, the *Winters* case was really a dispute between two parties arguing over who was the earlier appropriator and thus *Winters* did not authorize or recognize a reserved right (the most argued point); that the federal government and the Indians had the authority to create reserved rights only while an area was a territory and not a state and then only for the amount actually in use at that time; that *Winters* really meant only that the Indians would not lose water actually appropriated just because they failed to follow the procedures of state law; that *Winters* simply recognized that the federal government could assist any particular group or individual in appropriating water under state law and thus the settlers participating in Reclamation projects also held *Winters* rights (one of the more bizarre arguments, courtesy of Senator Smith of Arizona); that reserved rights applied only to waters that arose wholly on a reservation and not to waters that began off the reservation; that in all areas that the United States acquired from Spain, the "nomadic" Indians had no rights in land under Spanish law and thus had no rights under American law to reserve; and that *Winters* rights applied only to treaty reservations, not to executive order reservations. Another favorite response, and one that proved difficult to counter, was that if *Winters* created reserved rights (as its proponents believed), there was no need for confirming legislation. Spoken with apparent sincerity, the opponents raised many arguments against the decision that were not accurate or that assumed with certainty issues not addressed by the Supreme Court. Yet few in Congress had read or understood the Supreme Court's brief and ambiguous decision, and presumably few if any had read the lower court opinions in *Winters* or the opinions in *Conrad.* Under these circumstances, members of Congress could believe they faced a complicated and disputed issue of water law that required further study before Congress could act.[49]

In response to the congressional request for a study, the Indian Office filed a water rights status report (actually a series of three reports) early in the following session, in December 1914. The Indian Office stated more than once in these reports that it could not guarantee the safety of Indian water rights unless it relied at least in part on a reserved rights theory. But the Indian Office missed an opportunity to clear up issues raised in the previous year's debate, as the reports did not attempt to explain the legal validity and scope of the right. With the office's bare recommendation, Congress had no more stomach in the 1915 session than in the previous one to acknowledge the reserved water rights doctrine. The proponents of the reserved rights doctrine offered three more provisions that would have added explicit reserved rights language to the new (1915) Indian appropriations bill. The guardians of the prior appropriation system fought off each one on a point of order, ending the debate without a vote. The opponents of the reserved rights doctrine were forced to yield to just one ambiguous provision on water rights simply to move the overall bill in the face of a potential filibuster by the proponents of the reserved right. This provision, attached only to the portion of the bill containing the irrigation appropriations for Montana, again could be interpreted to support whichever water rights theory a person believed appropriate: "Provided That the rights of the United

States, heretofore acquired, to water for Indian lands referred to in this amendment, viz., the Blackfeet, Fort Peck, and Flathead reservation lands, shall be continued in full force and effect until the Indian title is extinguished."[50] Not even this provision made it into law, as a filibuster related to another topic prevented Congress from passing any Indian appropriations bill that session. The Sixty-third Congress ended, and the proponents of the reserved right had failed in their great effort to force Congress to acknowledge, establish, and implement the reserved water rights doctrine.[51]

The congressional defenders of the state law prior appropriation system had all been westerners, a gallery of western senators and representatives from both parties including Representative Frank Mondell of Wyoming and Senators Reed Smoot and George Sutherland of Utah, William Borah of Idaho, Albert Fall of New Mexico, Marcus Smith of Arizona, and John Shafroth and Charles Thomas of Colorado. Most were Republicans, but Smith, Shafroth, and Thomas were Democrats. They steadfastly refused to yield when the proponents made any attempt to have Congress acknowledge the reserved rights doctrine in clear language. The opponents of the reserved right did not care about the legal ambiguities of *Winters,* however much they focused their efforts in that direction to defuse or confuse the issue. They were fighting to preserve a concept they thought of as tantamount to natural law. Senator Borah of Idaho spoke for them all: "[The prior appropriation system is] one of the wisest laws that was ever enacted, and it grew out of the necessity which the pioneer found when he entered the great arid regions of the West."[52] Borah added the standard lament about uninformed easterners that so often accompanied the paean. Senator Sutherland of Utah (named to the Supreme Court in the 1920s) joined the chorus and sang it even better:

> Senators who represent the Western States ought to be given credit for understanding the various problems that are peculiar and local to those States. . . . Whenever a question comes up with reference to the public lands of the West we are met with the opposition of Senators from the East who do not understand the problems by actual contact with them as do we. Our hands are tied.[53]

Curiously, the members of the Montana congressional delegation were *not* among the ardent opponents of the reserved rights doctrine. Their stance epitomized the fate of the doctrine in Congress. The doctrine arose out of water conflicts in Montana, and the Montana settler interests had been vehement in asking Congress to extinguish the reserved right. Yet after their attempts to do just that failed back in 1906 and 1907, the members of the Montana delegation—for the first years, Senators William Clark and Thomas Carter, Representative then Senator Joseph Dixon, and Representative Charles Pray—gradually adopted a less confrontational approach. They saw that they could take advantage of the controversy to obtain large irrigation appropriations for the state, so long as the divisive issue existed but stayed off center stage. They sponsored and supported the allotment and water measures discussed earlier. The Montana members in 1914 and 1915—Senators Henry Myers and Thomas Walsh and Representatives John Evans and Tom Stout—continued this approach. All Democrats, they seemed unwilling to buck the efforts of the Democratic leadership to favor Indians more than past Republican administrations had. Still, the Montana contingent did not actively support the leadership's efforts. The Montana members seemed particularly willing to acknowledge the existence of the court decisions and the reserved rights doctrine as a fact of life. While they did not join in the efforts to establish the reserved right in law, neither did they join the vehement opposition or ever work to overturn the court decisions. They worked instead to draw congressional attention away from the issue of water rights and focus it on allotment and irrigation appropriations. They may have believed that too much effort to resolve the abstract water law issue threatened their continuing appropriations. Others accused them of caring about the irrigation projects only because of the benefits they might bring to the settlers, not the Indians, in Montana. In one particularly heated moment, Republican Representative William Stafford of Wisconsin called this the "rapacity of western people." Statements from the Montana Congress members often unconsciously confirmed the accusations, as they usually focused on the harm to the *settlers* that might occur if the fight over the water rights issue stalled project appropriations. Nonetheless, the allegiance of the Montana Congress members to the prior appropriation system was never at the high level demanded by many of the other western members; they were quite willing to accept the continued existence of the contrary reserved rights doctrine—which was, after all, already functioning in their own state.[54]

At the same time, the proponents of the reserved water right were not all easterners. Whether Congress would have followed the guardians of the appropriation system wherever they led if western members of Congress had presented a united front on the issue cannot be known. But the existence of westerners with a different point of view made the issue something other than the type of local or regional matter that commonly produced automatic congressional deference to local wishes. It is true that the most strenuous supporters of the reserved right, especially after the debate became most heated, were Senator Page of Vermont and Senator Robinson from the transitional state of Arkansas. But, for example, Democratic Senator Ashurst of Arizona supported all the reserved water rights provisions in committee and reported the appropriations bills to the Senate with these provisions. He spoke briefly for the provisions on the Senate floor and voted for the only one to go to a recorded vote. He retired early in the fight, apparently because he saw that it was a futile effort, not because he was a supporter of the appropriation system.[55] Senator Lane of Oregon was the most radical of the supporters of native peoples and the reserved water rights doctrine in particular, and he is discussed further below. Representative Stephens was the primary supporter of the reserved rights provisions in the House. He came from Vernon, Texas, near the Oklahoma border and well into the arid portion of his state.[56]

More important, the proponents of the reserved right, including the eastern senators, stated that they spoke on behalf of a number of people who lived in the West or had intimate knowledge of the conditions of the West, including western Indians, western residents who were not Indians, Indian Office personnel, or "friends" of the Indians who lived in Washington or elsewhere in the East but had obvious contacts throughout the West, such as Brosius of the Indian Rights Association, and others. For one example, Senator Robinson referred during the debate to a person who lived on the Blackfeet reservation (although apparently not an Indian) who testified before a congressional committee that he had seen Montana officials turn Blackfeet people away when they tried to file for water rights under state law. The state officials were telling the Blackfeet people that they could get their rights only from the federal government, which prompted Robinson to want to act to ensure that protection.[57] Again, the members of Congress were in some measure caught up in an intrawestern debate on Indian policy and water rights.

Divided as they were over the legitimacy of the reserved right as a viable water allocation method, the congressional proponents *and* opponents of the reserved right were still united by a common vision of the allotment process and what could be called Indian reclamation. American Indians would be allotted individual plots and become farmers like the non-Indian settlers, irrigating arid lands with water supplied by a federal storage and delivery project paid for out of the sales of their lands—a Reclamation project in all but name, which might even be managed by the Reclamation Service and also provide water to the non-Indian public-land settlers. Even most of those who favored the reserved rights doctrine did not conceive of a different method for using land and water in the West. They sought only to ameliorate the harshest aspects of the allotment policy and appropriation system, acting consistently with (and often in long alliance with) like-minded reformers in and out of the Indian Office. In this view, the Indians should be given a grace period for cultural adaptation before they would be fully subjected to the competitive struggle inherent in the individual privatization of water for gain.

Thus in this period, all members of Congress (except perhaps Harry Lane, who is discussed more fully below) shared the view that eventually all people trying to make productive use of all land in the arid region would share the same system. If that meant using the reserved rights doctrine during the transition to the dominant system (whatever that was), some were for it. Members of Congress with this attitude toward the *Winters* doctrine could not force all of Congress to provide official recognition of the reserved rights doctrine, although they could stymie any attempt to do away with the doctrine. And these people could find common ground with those who had the same long-term vision but no desire to recognize any water allocation system except prior appropriation—common ground in allotments and large-scale irrigation projects, and fuzzy water rights language that satisfied both camps.

It should be noted that toward the end of this first decade after *Winters,* a few voices in Congress and the administration began to suggest that not all Indian peoples should or would become like the non-Indian settlers (just as others recognized that the small-tract irrigated farmer ideal was hardly appropriate even for non-Indians in may areas of the arid West). These people argued that Indians had fundamentally different but equally successful approaches to life in the arid West that they may have "reserved" along with the land and water. Irrigated agriculture might or might not be a part of that life, and not necessarily under the same rules as governed the settlers. One example is the 1911 report on the Fort Belknap reservation from Interior Secretary Ballinger. His report noted that irrigated allotments might not be successful on the reservation due to a shortage of water. More important, the residents resisted allotment and the sale of surplus lands because the land and people were better suited to communal grazing over the whole reservation—officially recognizing what had been apparent to many people on and around the reservation all along. The Assiniboine people actually quoted in the same report were less specific in their views. They did not argue that they wanted to be or did not want to be like the settlers, or that they wanted to maintain or break up the reservation. Instead they focused on the fact that water was no longer available for whatever use they desired to make of the land, whether for grazing animals or for growing crops.[58]

In 1914, the Indian Office stated more explicitly that small-plot, individual, irrigated agriculture was not for all Indians, and the office found a momentary ally in Senator Walsh of Montana. In the report requested by Congress on the status of Indian water rights in Montana, the Indian Office admitted that the policy of allotments for irrigated agriculture on the Blackfeet reservation made little sense. Echoing what had been explicitly stated in the 1896 land purchase agreement with the Blackfeet but then utterly ignored in the haste to force the allotment of the reservation in 1905 and 1906, the Indian Office noted:

> These Indians live almost entirely on their grazing lands and along the streams and lakes. They are natural herdsmen, and some of them are now owners of many horses and cattle. Nature has endowed their environment for stock purposes with an abundance of water, grass, and natural protection against winters, as the reservation is broken and affords good winter range for stock.[59]

The Indian Office then recommended passage of a bill introduced by Senator Walsh to amend the Blackfeet allotment act. Walsh's bill would have prohibited the sale of the surplus lands after allotment. Sale of the surplus lands, according to the Indian Office report, "would destroy the opportunity for grazing tribal herds." This portion of the office's report said nothing about water, yet the report implied that whatever water was necessary to keep the reservation land in good condition for grazing and to water stock had to be protected as a reserved water right.[60]

One more example, if minor, of the slow development of a more complex view of the Indians and their use of resources comes from the House debate in 1914 on the Indian appropriations bill. Representative James Mann of Illinois asked how the people used the land on the unallotted Fort Belknap reservation. Representative Clarence Miller of Minnesota responded that they used "tribal methods of cultivating the soil under tribal customs, rules, and regulations." These customs, rules, and regulations were "obeyed and carefully observed, the same as the white man observes the law of his country."[61]

These may be very minor examples, true, but they stand out from the overwhelming dominance of the assimilation–allotment–irrigated farmer objective. Senator Lane of Oregon especially stood apart from all his peers during the debates of 1914 and 1915. Lane was a physician, former mayor of Portland, and the grandson of Joseph Lane, who had participated in the Oregon Indian wars of the 1850s and had also been a territorial governor and delegate, a senator after statehood, and a vice-presidential candidate in 1860. Hoxie portrays Harry Lane as another of the Senate's twentieth-century critics of the slow assimilation policy, quoting Lane as arguing that the Indians should be "given their freedom" from the control of the Indian Office.[62] Lane may, however, have meant something different by "freedom" than did the other "second-phase" assimilationists Hoxie describes, who simply wanted to thrust the Indians into non-Indian society and force them to transform, perish, or live at the bottom.

Lane first waded into the water rights debate with the conventional criticism of the mainstream allotment and irrigation process, although this argument was not so conventional coming in 1914 from a western senator. He pointed out that even if the Indians were inclined to become yeoman-farmers, they were not benefiting from the large irrigation projects that Congress intended for their use. This was because the Indian Office did not provide sufficient equipment or training, while the Indians had no money to buy the necessary farm implements, all the money from the sale of the surplus lands having gone to pay part of the cost of the irrigation projects, and the Indians' own lands pledged for the rest of the cost. The prior appropriation system allowed them no time to overcome these obstacles and acquire rights by putting water to beneficial use.[63]

Lane advanced to more unusual arguments in his later statements concerning the failure of the allotment process in Montana and in the Southwest. Lane began arguing later in 1914 that a policy of allowing Indians to select individual allotments did not and would not result in the American small farmer ideal. Most Indians, he said, ordinarily selected their allotments from the benchlands above the watercourses, lands that in their experience and knowledge were the best places to reside as part of what had been a communal village, grazing, hunting, and relatively minimal crop-reliant life. Unfortunately, these lands were hard to irrigate and did not have the best soil even when irrigated; so it was not surprising that the Indians had little success at individual irrigated farming. Most Indians shied away from the bottomlands that were the most appropriate for irrigated farming because they were the worst in their natural state, being cold and damp in the winter and mosquito ridden in the summer. Indians could not later turn to the bottomlands if and when they discovered their value for farming, as by then the lands would have been sold as surplus to the settlers.[64]

In the debate over the Arizona appropriations in the last session of
the Sixty-third Congress, in March 1915, Lane fully broke with his
colleagues. He began to question the entire allotment and irrigation
policy and launched into a speech unlike any other given by a member
of Congress in this period:

> The Indian is a communist—you cannot make an individual farmer
> out of him and the result is just to make life easier for whites to take
> Indian water. These have not been his projects; they are never for
> him, except incidentally. . . . This is simply an entering wedge to
> starve the Indian and get his land. If you allot lands to the Indian, you
> should give him a fair opportunity to make use of the land. You are
> undertaking to individualize the Indian. The Indian is a communist.
> They hold their property in common. It is really with many members
> of their tribe a part of their religion not to part with land to
> individuals. They think the curse of God rests on the head of a man
> who divides and parcels out the earth, the mother of mankind. They
> think it is sacrilegious to do so. You are trying to do it. Our attempt to
> individualize the Indian, with the traditions and the religion which
> they have held thousands of years, for aught we know, and to separate
> the Indians into entities does not succeed so far as we have done so. . . .
> The Indians of Arizona and New Mexico live in an arid region and
> should have a general right to water, yet the only Indians in the
> United States today who have the smallest percentage of trachoma
> and tuberculosis and are the most prosperous are the Navajo Indians,
> who are out from under the hands of the Government, off in the
> desert range in the mountains of Arizona and New Mexico with their
> herds and flocks of sheep.[65]

Lane became so incensed that he blocked the appropriation for the Gila
River irrigation project, intended for Pimas and settlers alike, on the
ground that it simply continued a failed policy. He did so even though
both sides to the water rights debate backed the appropriation as the
remedy for the government's failure to protect the rights of the Pimas.[66]

Senator Lane may not have been wholly accurate in his descriptions
of the life of the various Indian peoples, but he seemed much closer to
reality than the rest of Congress and more willing to allow these peoples
relative autonomy in their choices as to how to live. The passage of time
had further exposed that not everyone was wedded to the rhetoric or
reality of individual irrigated farming and the prior appropriation system
as the basis for life in the arid West, whether in the Indian or the non-
Indian communities.

CHAPTER 11

Back at the Uintah Reservation

The Switch to a Winters-*Based Approach and Litigation*

It was in the context of these developments in the life of *Winters* that federal officials recognized that *Winters* might have a role to play in Uintah water rights. The idea may have begun in the Indian Office. For example, an Indian Irrigation Service memorandum written in mid-1913 acknowledged that litigation over the Uintah water rights "appears to be inevitable" and "will probably be one of the hardest fought cases to come on account of the known fact of the scarcity of water and the attitude of the State officials who require of Indians the same diligence as would ordinarily be required of white citizens."[1] More likely it began with the attorneys in the Justice Department's Denver office, who analyzed the water supply problems at the Uintah allotments in the context of all the policy and litigation efforts swirling around them, disagreed that the *Winters* doctrine had no meaning for the reservation, and began contemplating a *Winters*-based lawsuit. Whatever the source, the nature of the change can be seen in a January 1914 letter to Chief Engineer William Reed from Henry Dietz, the superintendent of irrigation for District 2 of the Indian Irrigation Service. Dietz recounted the usual dire situation with regard to water and water rights at the Uintah lands, but he also noted that the U.S. attorney's office was contemplating a lawsuit against an irrigation company "to determine the priority of rights" to the Uinta River. Dietz was not clear about the details of the proposed suit, but he was aware "the case would involve the question of the Indian rights regardless of State Law, i.e., the jurisdiction of the State in the matter

will be questioned." He predicted a "great legal struggle over the water
rights of the Uintah Indians."²

It did not take long from this start for the Indian Office as a whole
to favor use of the *Winters* doctrine at the Uintah reservation. There
remained, however, the troubling provision in the 1906 appropriations
act deferring to state water law in the operation of the Uintah irrigation
system, which some saw as a nearly insurmountable obstacle to a viable
Winters claim. The Indian Office decided to address this issue by taking
advantage of the opportunity presented by Congress, which in its 1914
flurry of interest in these issues had asked the Indian Office to report on
the status of Indian water rights at several reservations, including the
Uintah, and to submit recommendations for protecting those rights.
The report to Congress took the form of a letter from Secretary of the
Interior Franklin Lane to the Speaker of the House of Representatives
in December 1914, in which Lane laid out for Congress the history and
present status of irrigation and water rights at the Uintah reservation.
He painted with similar facts and tone a picture every bit as dismal as
had Chief Engineer Reed in his report nearly two years before, concluding
that the federal government would not be able to protect the Indians'
rights to water under the requirements of state law. This time, however,
Lane emphasized that *if* Congress repealed or modified the water rights
provision in the 1906 act, water rights for the Indians could be protected
and enforced in federal court "following the principles of *Winters*" and
the specific provision in the 1899 Indian appropriations act recognizing
that non-Indian uses of water at the reservation were subject to the
"paramount rights of the Indians." Lane noted that the Justice Department was reviewing the situation at the reservation, but because "the
State controls this matter under the Act of June 21, 1906, it is not
expected that any improvements in the conditions will be had in these
matters without further remedial legislation by Congress."³

Congress did not repeal the water rights provision in the 1906 appropriations act, essentially ignoring Secretary Lane's letter. The Indian
Office forged ahead anyway; but recognizing the uncertain legal situation,
which the office itself had inflamed in its attempt to gain repeal of the
water rights provision, the Indian Office adopted the official position
that the water rights of the non-Indian irrigators at the Uintah reservation were "subordinate to those of the United States for the Indians,
both under the doctrine of reservation by treaty and that of prior appropriation in conformity with state law."⁴ The Indian Office was proceeding with a new confidence. When the office received notice from the
Utah state engineer of a new application for a water right out of a creek

on the reservation, it responded with a letter stating that the Indian Office "does not recognize any but federal jurisdiction governing this appropriation," and that any approval by the state should include a statement that the water right is subject to "all prior rights of the Federal Government and Indians."[5] In a short time the Indian Office had come a long way from a helpless position of total subjection to state water law at the reservation to an assertion that only "federal jurisdiction" governed appropriations there—words that echoed the federal government's approach to the Wind River–*Hampleman* litigation.

Meanwhile, the Department of Justice, working with the Indian Irrigation Service, began preparing a lawsuit to assert and protect the reservation's water rights. The person most responsible for the work was John Truesdell, the special assistant to the attorney general based in Denver to handle federal Indian and non-Indian water issues. The government's position, according to Truesdell, "should be that [the Act of June 21, 1906] does not divest the government or the Indians of any rights they had before the statute was passed, under the doctrine of the *Winters* case," again an echo of the federal arguments in the Wind River case. Any complaint filed should "state the facts which would show what rights the Government and the Indians were entitled to under [*Winters*], which is the doctrine of Government ownership and reservation," and also facts showing what rights are held "under state law irrespective of these other doctrines on account of actual diversion and beneficial use of water." The suit would not name as defendants all those irrigating non-Indian lands. Instead, it would target only those irrigation companies and water users who directly threatened the government's efforts to complete and operate the irrigation project for the allotments by depriving or having the capability of depriving the government's ditches of water. According to Truesdell, this situation prevailed on only two of the streams, Lake Fork River and its tributaries and the Uinta River and its tributaries, including the Whiterocks River. Truesdell concluded by noting that while "[t]his case does not seem to me to be ideal for presenting the question of Government reserved rights to the courts," "in some respects it is a fairly good case for that purpose." And, he warned, "[w]e ought to realize that if we bring a suit of this sort it will have rather serious consequences, and so we ought to be pretty sure that it is a wise thing to do."[6]

In July of 1916 the United States filed two complaints in federal district court in Salt Lake City, precisely as Truesdell outlined. In the two cases, *United States v. Dry Gulch Irrigation Company* and *United States v. Cedarview Irrigation Company,* the United States sued sixteen irrigation companies and 105 individuals over the water rights in the two different watersheds, the upper part of the Uinta River and the Lake Fork River.[7] The substance of a *Winters* claim a decade after *Winters* can be seen in a careful examination of these two complaints. What can also be seen is the way government attorneys and officials could weave such a claim into a general reclamation vision *and* make it at least partially compatible with state law.

One important way in which the situation at the Uintah reservation differed from the facts of the *Winters* case was the absence of a single well-defined treaty or agreement establishing the reservation and stating its purposes. The legal action most directly establishing the Uintah reservation had been an executive order of the president, and one of the primary questions or uncertainties associated with the *Winters* doctrine from its inception was whether and how it would apply to an reservation created in this way. Truesdell's complaint emphasized a set of factors intended to show that the absence of one definitive treaty was unimportant. These factors included the Utes' historical occupancy, use, and claim to the land, including the relevant streams; the series of treaties, other agreements, and actions over many years by which the Utes ceded lands and occupied a reduced part of their former lands; the stated or clearly implied policies and purposes that underlie land cessions/reservations, that is, to transform the Indians living on the reserved land into an agricultural and pastoral people; the fact that the land reserved combined the qualities of being arid and yet possessing several streams, the use of which would thus be necessary to fulfill the purposes of the Ute peoples and the United States in establishing this reservation; the Indians' and the government's continuous control of and title to the reservation lands and streams; and the fact that the Indians gave up lands of great value (in monetary terms) only in expectation that they were retaining and receiving protection for lands also of great value, and the reservation lands were of great value only if they included control over the waters needed to make them livable. The complaints described the 1861 executive order that actually established the reservation as but one step in this long process.

Another legal question that the complaints had to address was the effect of allotment on *Winters* rights, perhaps on somewhat more certain footing after the Wind River litigation. (Although there was no reference to the Wind River litigation in the Uintah records for these years, Truesdell would have been intimately aware of the developments in that case, in part because his partner in the Denver office, Ethelbert Ward, was advising the U.S. attorney's office in Cheyenne, Wyoming, on that case.) Thus the Uintah complaints described a set of facts consistent with a legal theory that *Winters* rights followed the allotment process and attached to the individual allotments held in trust by the government. The allotment process became simply another, further stage in the process of the Indians' cession of land and the retention of other land for an agricultural purpose, an action that carried the unmistakable purpose of a plan to base this life on irrigated agriculture.

ANATOMY OF A *WINTERS* CLAIM, CIRCA 1916: THE COMPLAINTS IN *UNITED STATES V. DRY GULCH IRRIGATION COMPANY* AND *UNITED STATES V. CEDARVIEW IRRIGATION COMPANY*

The anatomy of a *Winters* claim a decade after that litigation can thus be seen in a careful examination of the complaints, woven, as noted above, into a reclamation vision and made as compatible with state law as possible. An extended look at the complaints is useful simply to appreciate the level of sophistication in the attorneys' understanding and application of the *Winters* doctrine to this situation, a level hardly commensurate with a view of the doctrine as moribund in these times.[8]

The complaints began by describing how "from before the time" of the white man, the "Ute or Utah Indians . . . made their homes in, roved over and claimed to own" much of the land between Salt Lake and the Rocky Mountains, land including "many rivers and smaller streams." The land abounded in large and small game and fish and "produced fruits and berries of considerable food value." The Ute Indians, "one great tribe that was in turn made up of numerous sub-tribes, or bands," were a "warlike, nomadic, nonagricultural and nonpastoral people who lived by hunting and fishing and by gathering the natural fruits of the region." The land occupied by them "was Indian country, belonging to said Indians under and by virtue of the so-called Indian title of occupancy and possession" until they ceded parts to the United States. This land was arid, and suitable for crop agriculture and grazing, but only if irrigated.

The complaints then stated that the Ute peoples were "tribal Indians and wards of the United States." It had been and still was the duty and policy of the United States to protect them, "to promote their happiness and their moral and material welfare, and to educate and civilize them." As a means to fulfill this duty, the government had acted "to secure and reserve so much of their land as claimed and occupied by them as might be necessary or useful therefor and to encourage said Indians to farm and cultivate the same," acquiring lands from the Indians for non-Indian settlement only with the Indians' consent. To carry out this "general plan and policy" and to discharge its legal obligations to the tribe, the United States, through "treaties and less formal agreements and by acts of Congress and Executive orders," had reserved to the Ute Indians for their exclusive and perpetual use relatively small areas out of the territory originally occupied. In return the government had received from the Utes the cession of title to the other lands. The motive of the Utes in making these agreements included "their desire for education and civilization" and their "wish to be protected from the intrusions of the whites and the desire to hold the smaller quantities of lands comprised in their reservations by a higher and more indefeasible title." The Utes released their interest in a vast territory "in consideration of" (the legal terminology for a contract or exchange of value) confirmation of their title to the reserved lands and the resources associated with the lands, and in consideration of the "the policy and intent of the United States with regard to their civilization and welfare . . . [and] the setting aside for their benefit of certain sums of money by the United States." The United States had acted to carry out this policy by funding or providing agencies, schools, irrigated farms and gardens, and irrigation systems. The purpose of the government's assistance was "to educate said Indians and civilize them, and make them self-supporting and independent by inducing them to become stock owners and farmers."

According to the complaints, the official establishment of the Uintah reservation by executive order in 1861 was but a product or step of this larger process. The complaints also noted that when established, the reservation extended to the tops of the mountains to the north, so as to encompass "the source of many streams that flow down into the floor of the basin and through the flat lands" of the rest of the reservation. This reservation also contained "great tracts of land suitable for agriculture," but the agricultural lands were arid and "will not produce crops without irrigation and unless irrigated are comparatively valueless." The mountain area, which was not arid, was at "too great an altitude to be susceptible of cultivation." During the "existence of the reservation" (that is, before allotment), these watercourses "were entirely under the control of the United States and of the Indians . . . and available for their use without let or hindrance of others." It is these waters that "have given and they now give the said reservation lands their chief value and they have made and make said lands available for agriculture and for the pasturing of stock." Without these waters the lands could not be used for the intended purposes and would be "comparatively valueless." The government also alleged that the waters had been used for these agricultural purposes ever since the creation of the reservation and that this effort simply continued into the allotment period in an ever-increasing amount "as the Indians grew in civilization and industry." The implication, of course, was that the expressions of intent to reserve lands and water for these purposes *and* the necessary actions to implement this intent had begun prior to the 1906 act of Congress purportedly deferring to state water law.

The complaints continued by noting that prior to and at the creation of the reservation, the Ute Indians lived in part by hunting and fishing, but due to "influence of the United States," and "being induced thereto by their confinement to the comparatively narrow limits of the reservation," the Indians "also became in part a pastoral people and farmers of irrigable land." The allotment process beginning in 1902 and ending in 1905 (again, emphasizing the period before the 1906 act) sought "to further the civilization of the said Indians" and "to induce the Indians, for their own welfare and for the welfare of the United States, to abandon their tribal relations and their ancient habits and to take in severalty and to become the owners of and to work and develop separate tracts of land sufficient for their support and happiness in a civilized and prosperous station in life." The lands allotted were intended to be the "best and most desirable lands" of the reservation, "best adapted to irrigation from the various streams of said reservation along which they lie." The government also reserved forest lands at the headwaters so that "the water supply for said streams and for said Indians would be maintained." And the government reserved tracts of land for agency and school purposes, for reservoir sites, and "for the common use of said Indians for pasture lands."

The complaints to this point—the careful description of the historical process resulting in a reservation of land and streams and the purposes of this reservation—culminated in this description of the meaning of this process for property rights to land and water:

> It has been at all times and is the intention of the United States and of said Indians that only the lands and the water of said reservation that would not and will not be in any way needed for said allotments, pasture lands, Indian school and agency lands for any purpose or need of said Indians or of the United States, should or shall be subject to disposal in any way and that all the remainder of said lands and waters should and shall be reserved to and for said Indians and the United States.[9]

Note that this description of the reserved property rights of the government and the Indians encompassed the allotments and the other Ute land, including the tribally held grazing reserve. But as will be discussed below, the complaint did *not* ultimately conclude with a specific request, in the prayer for relief, for recognition of the water rights for the tribally held grazing land or for any other Ute lands other than irrigable allotments. Truesdell and others later described this as a purposeful decision not to pursue reserved rights to the full logical extent of *Winters* otherwise recognized in the complaints, an episode that will illustrate much about the use of *Winters* in this time.

In the next section of the complaints, the government described the irrigation improvements planned by the government for the allotted lands—emphasizing that they were planned and initiated by 1905, before the allotments were completed and the surplus lands opened for settlement, that is, well before the 1906 act—and then constructed by the government and the Indians. The complaints did refer to the 1906 appropriation act at this point, but only as a source of financing for the construction of the irrigation system, ignoring the water rights provision. The system as planned and constructed, at a cost of $800,000 and largely completed by 1911, was intended to "divert and use the waters of many of the streams of what was the said reservation, and the same are designed to carry water to each Indian allotment lying thereunder, and to the lands reserved for Indian agency and schools and other special purposes." The complaints then described in detail the canals and ditches constructed, the lands that could be supplied with water by each main ditch, and the number of acres actually irrigated so far in the Uinta-Whiterocks and Lake Fork watersheds.

It was at this point in the description of the developing history of irrigation at the reservation (well into the text, at pages 18 and 25) that the complaints described the government's filing of water rights claims in 1905 under Utah state law. The government alleged that it had taken all steps necessary to make these appropriations under state law except apply all of the water to beneficial use, which it had fourteen years from the date of filing (or three more years) to complete. Moreover, the government was taking all necessary steps to put into cultivation the allotted lands and thus apply the waters to beneficial use. The complaints described not just the government's efforts to assist the Indians in becoming irrigation farmers but also the government's allotment leasing program, deemed necessary because the Indians "have as yet become only imperfect farmers" who are "unequal to the task of reducing to cultivation and irrigation more than a small part of said allotments within the time fixed." The government listed the acres of land already irrigated and the total acreage "contemplated" for irrigation, which would be "put under irrigation ultimately and within the time set" by state law (the Lake Fork totals were 8,800 acres irrigated out of 29,920 acres contemplated for irrigation, while the Uinta totals were 14,000 acres irrigated out of 38,380 acres contemplated). The complaints emphasized that because the Indians had not yet been successfully induced to farm their allotments and because the lessees were for the most part "poor men," the success of the effort to apply the waters to beneficial use within the time set by state law "[is] to a large extent dependent upon there being an abundant supply of water" in the rivers at the heads of the government ditches during the irrigation season. "[A] failure of the supply of said water at said points . . . would cause the loss of valuable crops and great and irreparable damage" to the Indians, the lessees, and the United States.

Immediately after this bow to state law, the complaints returned to the *Winters* theme, with a concluding allegation for this section that could satisfy a *Winters* claim and yet not be inconsistent with a state law appropriation *except in terms of the date claimed for priority:*

> The United States, in and by its treaties and agreements with said Indians, as aforesaid, by creating said Uintah Reservation and by all of the acts and things hereinabove set forth, did confirm in said Indians and reserve to them and to itself for the purposes aforesaid, and did appropriate to them and to itself, and did withhold from appropriation by others, of the waters of the said Lake Fork River [or Uinta River], to be taken therefrom by said above described ditches and used by the United States and said Indians and said lessees and grantees thereof for the irrigation of the lands hereinabove described, and for all other proper purposes, *with a priority the first in said river and antedating the establishment of said reservation.*[10]

The complaints stated the amounts of water needed at present (in 1916) for irrigation and the total ultimately needed for all contemplated irrigation—127 cubic feet per second (cfs) and 429 cfs for the Lake Fork watershed and 195 cfs and 553 cfs for the Uinta watershed. These amounts corresponded to the number of acres irrigated or planned for irrigation based on an alleged duty of water of one cfs per seventy acres; the amounts claimed were also greater, although not significantly so, than the amounts claimed in the 1905 filings for these watersheds (383 cfs for the Lake Fork and 520 for the Uinta).

The last portion of the complaints described the defendants' activities, noting that their ditches and diversions were above the "Government and Indian ditches," yet whatever water rights the defendants held were "junior and inferior to all of the water rights" of the United States and the Indians. The government noted that the defendants had all filed their claims after July 1905, with the exception of the Uintah River Irrigation Company. The Uintah company may have filed earlier, "but all rights, if any, gained thereby or by said company or for the ditch or canal of said company are, with the rights of the other defendants and their several ditches, inferior and junior to the rights of the United States and said Indians and their ditches as above described," a dismissing reference clearly not based on a state law appropriation theory.

The government further alleged that the water supply of the Lake Fork and Uinta Rivers was insufficient except at times of high flows to supply the claimed needs of the Indians and the defendants, and that the waters of the streams "will be progressively less able to supply" those increasing needs "unless conserved by storage." Yet the defendants had taken "large quantities" of water from the rivers needed by the Indians and the United States, which should have been allowed to remain in the river to flow to the government ditches. This had caused the United States and the Indians not to be able to irrigate even the lands ready for irrigation and thus to suffer damage to and lose valuable agricultural crops. This also was causing irreparable damage to the United States and Indians "by interfering with the plans of the United States for the putting in cultivation and under irrigation of said allotments for the purpose of carrying out its policy with regard to said Indians." The damage would only escalate as the amount of land ready for and needing irrigation increased.

The allegations in the text of the complaints concluded with two sentences that neatly juxtaposed the impact of the non-Indian irrigation efforts under the reserved rights and state law theories:

> The said Indians, on account of their lack of development in civilization and their dependent condition, are unable to cope with white men in the scramble for water, and are without those resources of self help in the protection of their rights enjoyed by white men generally and by these defendants, and unless their rights in and to the waters of said river are protected from the acts of said defendants as aforesaid by the injunction of this Court, the said Indians will become discouraged in their efforts to become farmers and will desist therefrom and the task of the United States to bring them to habits of industry and thrift and to civilize them will be made more difficult than it otherwise would be. And also, without the relief herein prayed for, the

efforts of the United States, through its agents and by the means adopted as aforesaid to bring the said allotments under cultivation and irrigation and to apply the waters of said river owned by the United States and said Indians and all of it to such beneficial use within the time limited as aforesaid, will fail.[11]

This was followed by the prayer for relief, in which the government described the specific orders and actions it wanted from the federal court. The prayer asked for a decree "establishing and declaring the rights" of the United States and the Indians "to the waters of the Lake Fork [or Uinta] River," to be used through the ditches of the United States "for irrigation and domestic and other proper uses during the irrigation season." The decree should state that these rights were senior to all rights claimed by the defendants, "and that the said rights of the United States and of said Indians *are of first and immemorial priority*" (emphasis added). The government asked the court to perpetually enjoin the defendants from interfering with these rights to water, and to enter an immediate order requiring the defendants to allow the specified amounts of water presently needed for irrigation to pass to the government ditches. This specific injunction was to remain perpetually in force and expand its reach over time as the acreage ready for irrigation increased, requiring that more water be left in the streams for the government ditches, a form of relief that Truesdell and others explicitly derived from the lower courts' decisions in the *Conrad Investment Company* case (the companion to the *Winters* case, involving the Blackfeet reservation). The government's final request was that the court appoint a commissioner to supervise the allocation of water under the injunction and decree. Truesdell's correspondence, as he and others prepared the complaints, indicated that neither the Indian Office nor the Department of Justice trusted state water officials to implement a decree in favor of the reserved rights of the reservation.

The government supported its complaints and request for a temporary restraining order and preliminary injunction with affidavits filed by the reservation superintendent and the irrigation engineer. The affidavits repeated in more detail the facts of the complaint, especially the extent of the irrigation system constructed for the allotments, the number of acres ready for irrigation, the total number of acres contemplated for irrigation, and the ways in which the defendants had deprived the government ditches of water. The government also attached affidavits from farmers on the allotted lands describing their need for water for irrigation and stating that they were not receiving a sufficient supply of water to irrigate their crops that season. All were non-Indian lessees; none was a Ute Indian. As noted above, no individual named or described in the complaints or other court records was a Ute Indian or a member of any other Indian nation.

THE PROCESS OF THE LITIGATION: INJUNCTION, APPOINTMENT OF A COMMISSIONER, IMPLEMENTATION, IRRIGATION, AND SETTLEMENT NEGOTIATIONS, 1916–1920

The defendants responded to the complaints by denying essentially everything in them. In particular, the defendants denied that the Indians or the government had the power to reserve rights to water outside of state law or, if they had that power, that they had taken any legally sufficient action to reserve those rights. Instead the Indian Office and especially Congress, in actions and legislation in 1905 and 1906, had decided that state water law would control the allocation of water to the allotments. For this reason, the defendants denied that the federal courts had any jurisdiction over what the defendants characterized as a water rights dispute under state law between equally situated citizens and property owners. And, they alleged that their claims to water and uses of water were all legal and appropriate under Utah state law and, to the extent that their uses ended up depriving the United States and the Indians of water for their lands, it was only because the defendants had properly perfected rights under state law while the United States and the Indians had not.

On July 26, 1916, after a hearing on the motion for a preliminary injunction, federal Judge Tillman D. Johnson entered exactly the restraining orders and preliminary injunctions requested by the government, including the appointment of the commissioner. Judge Johnson did not explain his order. Subsequent letters from Truesdell and others imply that the whole of the complaints and the underlying legal theories, including the *Winters* claim, found favor with the judge. After this ruling, the parties agreed to delay formal trial on the issues, with the result that the water allocation process on the reservation operated into the mid-1920s under the 1916 injunction orders issued by Judge Johnson, implemented each year in an order reappointing and instructing the commissioner.[12]

Meanwhile, the Indian Office's 1919 deadline for perfecting the appropriations under state law crept closer. In April 1918 Truesdell wrote to Chief Engineer Reed noting that only one year remained and urging the Indian Office to get all of the land under irrigation by then. Indicating the extent to which an uncertain *Winters* claim had been essential to the present federal court injunction, Truesdell worried that "our success in getting practical relief through the Court and the strength of our position as shown in our briefs may lead the men in actual charge of putting the water on the land to rely too much on the law and not to fully appreciate the great importance of getting every acre under water before the permits expire and this making such reliance unnecessary." Truesdell also reminded the Indian Office in other letters that while the litigation involved only rights in the Lake Fork and upper Uinta watersheds, really at stake were the rights to water from all streams for irrigation on all the allotments. Meeting the deadlines for perfecting under state law would "eliminate a cause of legal opposition."

The Indian Office was *not* successful in this endeavor, and so began the trips back to the Utah state engineer, state legislature, and Utah governor for yet another extension of the deadline to perfect the claimed water rights under state law. And again the federal government was successful at least at that, obtaining two more years, to 1921, to perfect its claims. The non-Indian irrigators challenged the extension, arguing that it was not justified by the progress of irrigation on the allotments.[13]

It was also in 1919 that the defendants to the litigation first suggested settlement negotiations. The talks broke off in 1920 without an agreement, in a way that highlights the government's belief in the soundness of its *Winters* position. The federal government's terms for settlement were nothing less than a decree as requested in the prayer for relief in the complaints. In contrast, the defendants offered only that the state engineer be allowed to determine what allotted lands had actually been irrigated by December 1919 and then to assign them the 1905 priority under state law, which the defendants would abide by and not contest. The defendants specifically requested that the federal government abandon its claim that the United States had rights to water independent of appropriations under state water law. The Indian Affairs and Justice Department officials rejected these terms not only because many of the allotments remained to be irrigated as of the end of December (and so they would have lost significant rights to water), but also because the federal officials did not trust the state engineer to make a favorable decision on the government's claims concerning the lands already irrigated, *and* because they were not willing to explicitly disavow the *Winters* doctrine.

The federal government rejected the offered settlement with no apparent internal dispute. This despite the fact that the defendants and their political allies, including the Utah governor and the state's congressional delegation, brought significant pressure to bear on the politically appointed officials at the top, including the commissioner of Indian affairs, the secretary of the interior, and the attorney general, to agree to the defendants' settlement terms. This was a clear attempt by the defendants to bypass what they saw as recalcitrant government attorneys and lower-level Indian Office personnel directing the litigation. In these failed efforts one can see how the government's litigation, especially the uncertain strength of its *Winters* claim, had reversed what had been the relationships of power over the allocation of water at the reservation.[14] As Chief Engineer Reed noted in a late 1919 letter to Truesdell:

> I am very sorry that you could not have been here and heard the wail that these people put up [in Washington, D.C., conferences]. They are entirely a different bunch with a different attitude than when they had the apparent upperhand of use and were handling affairs under State control. I feel quite positive that, should this project revert to State control, the Indian and his land would receive scant consideration; however, they talked very fair about loving the Indian and protecting him, etc.[15]

The only internal dispute that arose out of the settlement talks was whether Truesdell's proposed decree was *too limited* in the water rights it claimed for the reservation under the *Winters* doctrine. As noted above, the text of the complaints had included a reference to all of the reservation's land, including the tribally owned grazing reserve, as land subject to the Indians' and the governments' rights to water. But the relief that the government actually asked for in the complaints concerned water rights only for irrigating the allotments and said nothing about water rights for the 250,000-acre grazing reserve. The injunction matched the relief actually requested by the complaints. So did the government's proposed decree offered in the settlement negotiations; it, too, omitted a claim to water rights for the grazing reserve and apparently provided that the government would claim no more water for the reservation lands. Someone in the Department of the Interior noted this limitation, and it became the subject of an inquiry from the secretary's office.

The response was an out-of-the-ordinary letter to the commissioner of Indian affairs from Truesdell, U.S. Attorney William Ray, and Chief Engineer Reed, seeking to justify the scope of their proposed decree.

Their letter recognized that the government had a potential claim to water for the tribal grazing reserve under the *Winters* doctrine. Their position, in the letter and in the proposed decree, was not, as it could have been, that the litigation was narrowly tailored to prevent non-Indian water users from interfering with the flow of water at the government's irrigation ditches for the allotments, and thus the question of reserved water rights for the grazing reserve was not at issue in the litigation. Truesdell, Reed, and Ray acknowledged that they could have chosen that position but had rejected it. Instead, they had intentionally limited the government's claim for water rights for reservation lands to the amount of water needed to successfully irrigate the allotments. Their reasons were based not in law but in policy—in the reclamation vision of a future community of coexisting Indian and non-Indian small-tract, irrigated agriculture, most viable under well-understood, settled and individual water rights:

> We have thought it sound policy and for the true interest of the Indians themselves and also in strict accord with the best view of the law to conform to these limitations. There is warrant for the contention that under the principle that the United States reserved all the water needed for its purpose in making the reservation it could claim water for all of the land still reserved for Indian purposes when the reservation was thrown open to settlement whether the present plan was to irrigate them all or not and thus could claim water for these grazing lands. . . . Here, however, we have thought, and we believe rightly, that the status of the reservation lands as to allotments, the contemplated irrigation area, the construction of an elaborate and costly system of canals and ditches warrant the Government in saying now what water is claimed for the Indians and in limiting that claim as is proposed. In other words, it is proper not to claim water for the grazing lands.
>
> When development of an Indian reservation has reached the advanced stage that this one has and it is, therefore, possible, as it is here, to see what the needs of the Indians for water will be under the policy of Congress and of this Department as to the extent of irrigable lands necessary, . . . we think it proper for the Government to take a definite stand on the extent of the Indians' water rights. The benefit of this, it may be said, is largely enjoyed by the white settlers, who have secondary rights in the streams, giving them a knowledge of just what the prior rights of the Indians consist of and so allowing them to know what can be counted on as the surplus available to them;

however, we think the Indians, like the whites, are interested in the advancement of the community and so having these matters settled is of value to the Indians themselves. We think these considerations fully warrant doing away with the indefiniteness as to the Indians' rights when that is possible.[16]

Truesdell, Ray, and Reed were not Harry Lane, challenging the wisdom of trying to transform the western Indians. They echoed instead the dominant view of allotment and assimilation and the attorney general's 1910 policy statement seeking to protect the Indians water rights and the government's Indian policy "without inflicting needless hardship upon their white neighbors who have diverted the water and are using it in good faith to irrigate their farms."[17]

The commissioner of Indian affairs, Cato Sells, must have been convinced, as he then wrote to the secretary of the interior to summarize and agree with the views expressed in the letter from Truesdell, Ray, and Reed. Commissioner Sells recognized that the federal government had the legal right to claim *Winters* rights for the grazing reserve, but also that he was "unable to see wherein we could equitably justify a claim of 'reserved' waters for these grazing lands, even though we may have a naked legal right so to do." To press this claim "would not be just to those settlers who have gone into this valley and expended private means in development work, practically under an invitation from the Government so to do."[18]

These policy considerations, which restrained a litigation position for Indian water rights, came not from the policymaking levels of the Interior and Justice Departments, nor from the imposition of Reclamation Service officials hostile to reserved water rights. They came instead from lower-level Indian Affairs and Justice Department officials active in the litigation, and from the commissioner of Indians affairs, who otherwise had been pushing the claims of the Indians to the extent allowed by law. The irony is that Truesdell and Reed, so concerned in this episode with *limiting* their legal claims for the benefit of the non-Indian settlers and comprehensive irrigation development of the basin, were seen by the defendants in the litigation as ruthlessly pursuing paramount rights for the Indians outside of state law to the economic ruin of the settlers and the Uintah basin. This was because Truesdell and company refused to capitulate on at least six issues demanded by the defendants or raised in the process of implementing the injunctions— they refused to disavow reliance on federal reserved water rights outside of state law; refused to agree that reserved rights could not pass to allotments (the opposite position was obviously the key to their case); refused a vigorous demand by the defendants that *Winters* rights not pass to allotted lands sold to non-Indians; refused to agree to allow the State of Utah to administer the decree; rejected the idea that the portion of the allotted lands covered by roads, buildings, and the like should be subtracted from the acreage entitled to water rights under the decree; and sought to make sure that the water rights for the *individual allotments* included the right to irrigate naturally growing pasture grasses for grazing, not just planted crops.[19]

Nothing specific came of these settlement negotiations, but nothing better illustrates the complex contours of the use of the *Winters* doctrine in those times, both the extent to which it was pressed in a sophisticated effort to define and protect Indian reserved water rights and the extent to which the government might limit its use of the doctrine to fit a particular agrarian vision.

IRRIGATION, SETTLEMENT, AND FINAL DECREES, 1921–1923

The Indian Office's fifteen-year effort to irrigate the allotments by inducing Indians to farm, by leasing allotments to non-Indian farmers,[20] and finally "by clearing, plowing, seeding and irrigating with hired labor" finally came to its intended conclusion: In January 1921, the Indian Office filed proof with the state engineer of beneficial use of water on slightly over 60,000 acres of allotted land in the Lake Fork and Uinta drainages, supposedly all of the irrigable allotted land in these basins. The irrigators on non-Indian lands protested the proofs filed by the government. Supervising Engineer Dietz had admitted earlier, in a letter to Chief Engineer Reed, that "[t]here is no question but what Mr. Kneale [the reservation superintendent] has made some very questionable attempts to subdue the land" and had been "very optimistic in his classification," while political pressure from the irrigators of non-Indian lands "will compel the State Engineer to draw a very close line."

The federal court (still Judge Johnson) decided to wait for the decision of the state engineer before deciding what steps to take next, leaving in place the injunction and the commissioner to implement the injunction. It was in this context that settlement negotiations began again, focusing both on the filings with the state engineer and the federal court litigation. The parties worked toward an agreement on the amount of land actually irrigated and the rights to water for that acreage. One issue that had to be addressed stemmed from the fact that while the government filed proof of irrigation on slightly over 60,000 acres in these two watersheds, the government's complaints had claimed water for over 68,000 acres. The Indian Office and Truesdell decided that the 8,000 acres for which proofs were not filed were not irrigable, in either a physical or a practical sense, so they agreed to exclude those acres. The government also acceded, after a lengthy set of negotiations and surveys, to the defendants' objections to the irrigated status of approximately 2,000 of the 60,000 acres for which proofs were filed. The government recognized that it had a colorable legal claim to water for these acres, anyway, despite the lack of irrigation at the time, but decided not to pursue a statement of those rights before the state engineer or in this litigation, as part of the government's effort to settle the litigation. The defendants in turn agreed not to pursue their objections to the irrigated status of the rest of acreage for which proofs were filed. It took two years of negotiations, but finally in 1923 the state engineer agreed to accept the proofs filed by the government as reduced slightly by agreement of the parties. Turning back to the litigation, Judge Johnson then entered final decrees for the two cases in March 1923 as the negotiated settlement of the parties to the litigation.[21]

The final decrees were essentially the same as the government requested in the prayer for relief in the complaints, except for the somewhat reduced acreage. The decrees described the number of acres irrigated from each ditch, the flow of water assigned to this acreage in cfs, and the total amount of water allowed for this acreage in acre feet per irrigation season, all for the purpose of "irrigation" and "for certain domestic, culinary and stock-watering uses." The defendants' rights were declared inferior to the rights of the government and the Indians, and the defendants were perpetually enjoined from interfering with the rights decreed to the government and Indians "or their assigns," which covered allotment lessees and purchasers. The court also retained jurisdiction to oversee the administration of the decrees through the appointment of a water commissioner, which Judge Johnson did for the rest of the 1920s. The decrees also noted that the lands and acreage for which the rights had been decreed had been recognized in final certificates of appropriation issued by the Utah state engineer.

There was nothing in the decrees inconsistent with state law, or that signaled that *Winters* was also a basis for the claims, *except* for the singular description of the priority, which marked them indisputably as based in *Winters:* The rights were held "under a priority that antedates the third day of October, 1861," the date of the executive order establishing the reservation and bearing no relation to the 1905 filings. One other indication of the role of *Winters* in the structure of the decrees comes from the records of the negotiations—alone among the defendants, the Uintah River Irrigation Company resisted for a time joining into the settlement, arguing that its April 1905 water right filings gave it seniority to the reservation's rights even if properly perfected under state law. Government officials refused to concede this point, precisely and primarily because they believed they were fashioning a decree based on *Winters* that happened to coincide, happily in their minds, with much of state law. The company finally decided to yield. Not mentioned in the Uintah documents in this period, but presumably of some influence, was the fact that in mid-1921 the Ninth Circuit Court of Appeals reaffirmed the *Winters* doctrine and applied it to Indian allotments at the Fort Hall Shoshone-Bannock reservation in Idaho, in the *Skeem v. United States* decision mentioned briefly earlier in the book.[22]

Interestingly, the Uintah decrees, originally drafted by Truesdell and finalized after he left government service, did *not* include a statement explicitly limiting the scope of *Winters* rights for the Ute lands to these irrigation rights decreed for the allotments (which would have meant, for example, no reserved rights for the tribally held grazing land or for any allotted land not covered by the final decree). The federal government in fact *rejected* a demand by the defendants to incorporate an explicit provision abandoning any further *Winters* rights. It is not clear why the government refused this demand, given the specifically limiting views expressed by Truesdell, Reed, and Commissioner Sells only two years before. Perhaps the explanation has something to do with the fact that Truesdell and Reed (and Sells) were no longer present; the new people in charge of the litigation, including Truesdell's partner in the Justice Department, Ethelbert Ward, may have taken a different view of this matter. Whatever the reason, or the intent, the result was to effectively preserve the expansive scope of *Winters* for use on the reservation another day. For example, four years later E. B. Meritt, then acting commissioner of Indian affairs, believed that the government might have a hard time claiming the first priority for water to irrigate allotments that were within the scope of the irrigation project but excluded from the decrees in 1923, "as inconsistent with the compromise effected in that litigation." In contrast, he was certain that water rights as of the date of the reservation based on the *Winters* doctrine applied to all other lands of the reservation, allotted or unallotted, although he counseled the local engineer also to file for rights with the state engineer.[23]

THE WORK OF *WINTERS* AT THE UINTAH RESERVATION FOLLOWING THE DECREES, 1923–1931

The decrees did not end this episode of the work of *Winters* at the Uintah reservation, as the 1927 remarks by Meritt quoted just above indicate. Other events into the 1930s carried similar meanings. Administration of the decrees continued through the decade under the commissioner appointed by the federal court. The Indian Office continued to be plagued by conflicts and problems with the settler irrigators, and with the fact that the Utes never did show interest in this type of irrigated farming. For comfort the Indian Affairs personnel involved in the Uintah matters probably looked to the Wind River reservation in Wyoming, home to another favorable *Winters*-based water rights decision in 1926, *United States v. Parkins*. In *Parkins* the United States successfully sued in federal court to enjoin a dam and diversion by a non-Indian irrigator that interfered with the flow of water in Mill Creek to the Wind River reservation irrigation project. The federal government's complaint and legal arguments in *Parkins* included the same *Winters*-based discussion of treaty reserved water rights as in the *Hampleman* case at the same reservation more than a decade before, with a similar result. The court concluded that while the federal government had closely cooperated with the State of Wyoming in the diversion of water for irrigation on Indian allotments, the United States and the Indians had reserved to themselves free of the requirements of state law the waters necessary "for the use and benefit of the lands within that reservation," citing to *Winters*, giving the government the right to use of the waters of Mill Creek for the Indians.[24]

Despite all that had occurred at the Uintah reservation, in federal court and elsewhere in the previous two decades, the non-Indian irrigators and the Utah state engineer continued to posture on occasion that water rights in the Uintah basin really were "subject to the laws of Utah"—as stated by State Engineer George Bacon in 1930—and that the decrees and the continuing federal jurisdiction were illegitimate.[25] Then in 1931, Judge Johnson, still sitting as a federal judge in Utah, notified the parties that he was considering terminating the federal court's supervision of the decree. Justice Department attorney Ward and the Indian Office personnel were uneasy about the prospect, suspicious that the judge's stance must have been at the urging of one of the irrigation companies most covetous of the water decreed to the reservation. The federal officials continued to lack confidence that state officials would fairly and properly administer the decrees to protect the water rights of the reservation. Ward and the others calmed down some after learning that the defendants, too, desired continued federal administration (although they soon got over that desire), and that it was Judge Johnson himself who simply decided that the federal court could not and need not manage the decreed water rights in perpetuity. In the judge's view, the federal courts could instead stand ready to vindicate the rights of the reservation by the appropriate orders should the state not do so. Notwithstanding this measure of security, federal officials still did not trust the state engineer properly to characterize and administer these water rights. The government eventually received a measure of assurance there as well, the final exercise of the power of the *Winters* doctrine in this story.[26]

The parties began discussing the appropriate way to end federal court supervision. Ethelbert Ward continued to worry, for good reason, about the effect of Congress's Uintah water rights provision from the Act of June 21, 1906. The state and the defendants continued to focus on this provision as the source of their belief in total state law control over water rights at the reservation. They did this despite the fact, as Ward noted, that the "priorities awarded to the Government for the Indians" in the 1923 federal court decrees "were not in accordance with the laws of the State of Utah because the Indian ditches were given 'a priority that antedates the 3rd day of October, 1861.'"

Ward's fears were heightened in the ensuing negotiations between the Indian Office, the state engineer's office, and the non-Indian water users. The purpose of the negotiations was to develop an acceptable plan for the state engineer to follow in administering the decreed rights once released from the supervision of the federal courts. The federal government drafted and submitted a proposed agreement that essentially was just another version of the implementation instructions given by the federal court each year to the water commissioner. The defendant irrigators, playing on the known antipathies of the state officials to control over water outside of state law, recommended that the proposed agreement be changed to "eliminate recognition of the prior rights of the Indians" outside of state law. The federal government refused to acquiesce, and the negotiations stalled. The defendants refused to yield *even though* the government obtained from State Engineer Bacon the striking concession that "[t]he rights of the Indians, both under the contention of the legal advisers of the Indian Service and under the laws of Utah, are superior to those of the White settlers," a breakthrough in the state's recognition of the validity of the application of the *Winters* doctrine to the Uintah reservation.

Reed Smoot, Utah Senator, then intervened on behalf of the non-Indian settlers to request of the federal government the basis for its refusal to agree to the terms proposed by these water users. Smoot relied heavily on the 1906 statute to assert that state law governed water rights on the reservation. This gave the federal government one more opportunity to explain how the *Winters* doctrine applied at the Uintah reservation, indicating how the government officials now viewed the nature of *Winters* rights. In a memorandum prepared to advise the secretary on how to respond to Senator Smoot's letter, Acting Commissioner of Indian Affairs B. S. Garber stated flatly that the prior rights of the Indians on the reservation were protected by decrees "which are in accord with the *Winters* case." He also noted the "paramount" water rights provision in the 1899 statute, which complemented the *Winters* doctrine and could not be "lightly disregarded." In Garber's view, Congress did not intend to disregard these paramount rights in the water rights provision of the 1906 appropriations act. Garber explained away the later statute as without effect:

> Legislation is to be construed most favorably to the Indians when dealing with their rights. It is hardly conceivable that Congress intended by the 1906 Act to take away from the Indians something that they already had and give them an inferior right. . . . Furthermore, the decrees in the Federal court, referred to, were entered in 1923, seventeen years after the enactment of that legislation, and those decrees did not recognize the contention that now has been advanced with respect to State jurisdiction, and it may be said that this is not the first instance where this contention has been made.[27]

Garber further noted that the federal district court in Wyoming, in the *Parkins* case, had held that "the United States had exclusive jurisdiction over the waters of the Wind River Reservation" and that the federal court had ruled in this way despite the fact that there existed a similar water rights provision in the 1905 allotment act for the Wind River reservation ostensibly deferring to state water law in the development of an irrigation system for the Indian allotments. Garber also recognized that the Indians at the Uintah reservation were not using the water as the non-Indian farmers did, and thus that under state law these rights to water might be lost by abandonment. To allow this to happen would be "inconsistent with the law governing the water rights of the Indians." Garber relied upon the *Conrad Investment Company* decision, where it was "clearly defined that if an Indian should not use the water to which he is entitled," someone else may make use of it, "but at the time when the Indian needs it the person so using it during the interim must relinquish the water." This would occur "notwithstanding the fact that such person may have expended considerable money in connection with his utilization of the water during the period the Indian was not beneficially applying it to his lands." Garber concluded that under all these circumstances there could be "no valid objection" to the government's proposed agreement recognizing the prior rights of the Indians.[28]

It was up to Secretary of the Interior Ray Lyman Wilbur to respond formally to Senator Smoot's intervention. To convince the Senator that there was nothing wrong with the proposed agreement submitted by the government, Wilbur relied less on the fiery arguments set forth by Garber than on the fact that the government's proposed agreement was consistent with the federal court litigation and decrees and, especially, on the concession made by the state engineer as to the validity of the prior rights of the Indians under both state law and "the contention of the legal advisers of the Indian Service." Wilbur suggested that Senator Smoot address his concerns to the state engineer instead and, especially, to the settler irrigators to ask them to execute the appropriate agreement presented by the government. After this, an uneasy capitulation by the non-Indian irrigators paved the way for the state engineer to begin the state administration of the decreed, paramount water rights of the Indians at the Uintah reservation, the culmination of this episode in the work of *Winters* at the Uintah reservation.[29]

CHAPTER 12

Lessons from the Uintah
Reservation Litigation

In the litigation over the water rights of the Uintah reservation—*United States v. Dry Gulch Irrigation Company* and *United States v. Cedarview Irrigation Company*—the federal court in Utah never produced an opinion analyzing the legal issues presented. As there was never an appeal, no appellate court analyzed the issues. The lower court's decisions were never reported in the official reports and had no value as legal precedent. I have never seen any reference to them in the modern legal literature on the *Winters* doctrine. They are important nonetheless, I would argue, for at least four reasons.

First, contrary to the conventional understanding of what happened to *Winters* in the first decades after the original decision, in this instance Indian Affairs and Justice Department officials aggressively pursued a *Winters* claim, even into litigation, to protect and assert water rights for the reservation against a set of non-Indian settlers irrigating land in the same watersheds. The federal government officials did this despite the obvious uncertainties of the *Winters* claims, including the unknown effect of the allotment process and the very difficult hurdle presented by Congress in the 1906 appropriations act when it explicitly deferred to state water law for the Uintah reservation irrigation system. And these officials pursued this claim without interference or question from the policy-level officials in the Interior and Justice Departments (or from the Reclamation Service). To the contrary, the people directing the litigation had the full support not just of the commissioners of Indian affairs but apparently also of the secretaries of the interior and the attorneys general across several administrations. Moreover, I saw no indication that anyone in the federal government believed that reliance on *Winters* in this instance was extraordinary or a deviation from usual practice or caused problems for other government projects and claims.

The second reason these cases are important is that the federal officials not only pursued the *Winters* claim, their use of the *Winters* doctrine made a real difference in the water allocation decisions for these lands (whether it made a real difference in the long run in the way water was actually used and by whom is a different question). Despite the fact that the federal government made every effort to work also within the framework of state law, for obvious legal and policy reasons, there is no doubt that the federal officials, the state officials, the court, and the defendants understood the *Winters* doctrine as the primary basis and strength of the federal government's position, and understood that the decrees recognized and were built first on that doctrine. The federal government's state law claims were vulnerable from the beginning, vulnerable in 1913 just before the federal government revised its view of the applicability of *Winters* at the reservation, vulnerable at the time the litigation was filed, and still vulnerable when the proofs were filed with the state engineer. If state law and the state administrative machinery had remained the only forum for consideration of the water rights for the Uintah lands, it seems very unlikely the federal government would have obtained a determination of water rights for very many acres. The assertion of the *Winters* theory changed the dynamics of the contest over water rights from one in which the non-Indian irrigators and the state had firm control to one in which they did not, which by itself is the key to the effect of the use of *Winters* here. Moreover, the government obtained these decrees in the end without sacrificing the future scope of *Winters* rights for reservation lands, at least not to any clear or great extent.

Third, these cases are important for the ways in which the litigation process elaborated and gave shape to the *Winters* doctrine. To develop a viable *Winters* claim, the government's attorneys were forced to address and resolve a number of critical uncertainties in the application of the reserved rights doctrine. These included whether the *Winters* doctrine applied to executive order reservations and, if so, how and why; the effect of the allotment process on *Winters* rights; the effect of leases and sales of allotments; whether, why, and how *Winters* rights survived congressional action that purported to defer to state water law in the matter of water rights for the reservation; how the relatively abstract *Winters* rights actually related to state law water rights and the state water allocation and distribution machinery, including how the reserved rights could be measured, quantified, and administered in day-to-day operations; and the effect of litigating, obtaining a decree for, and administering *Winters* rights for certain reservation lands on the future scope of *Winters* rights for the reservation. The simple fact of having to plead a very particular *Winters* claim, and thus of having to decide what were the elements of that claim and what facts satisfied the elements, put flesh on this skeleton of a legal doctrine. The attorneys and others involved in preparing and arguing these *Winters* claims (or defending against them), and who watched the government obtain decrees largely shaped by that effort, had to have gained a level of experience and familiarity with the doctrine that made it part of their legal universe in a fairly developed and sophisticated way, that made it into a tool for understanding and working with water issues. Nothing definitive in the shaping of *Winters* took place in this litigation, but the absence of published opinions should not obscure the impact of the work itself on the practitioners' experience, understanding, and values, and on the development and fortification of the legal reality of the *Winters* doctrine.

These three points emphasize how important and effective was the assertion of the *Winters* doctrine in these cases, important for the doctrine itself and for water rights at the reservation. The progress of this litigation also illustrates the limits of the government's conception of *Winters,* the role it was believed to play, and how much that role as understood actually had in common with other efforts to allocate and use water in the West in those years. This is the fourth point of importance, and it contradicts the other three. While the Uintah litigation embodies the well-defined conflict between the prior appropriation system and the reserved rights doctrine, the conflict masks an underlying shared vision of development held within the dominant culture and illustrated in the way Congress approached Indian water rights issues up to 1915. The development vision of both sides to the Uintah conflict was remarkably the same—a Uintah basin in which society and community would be based on individuals and their immediate families privately owning and working relatively small tracts of land, using as much of the available water of the streams as possible to irrigate those lands to grow food crops or hay for livestock for commercial markets, using irrigation systems largely developed and maintained by aggregate groups. The federal government's version may have included more people of Ute Indian descent in that vision, but only Indians who assimilated and merged into the general populace in cultural and economic outlook; Indians who did not comply would be replaced in the basin by non-Indian farmers. Ute peoples were not participants in the conflict or the shared vision. To reiterate again a singular point about this Ute Indian water rights litigation, which remained active for fifteen years as the federal court supervised the allocation of water into the early 1930s: Ute Indians were entirely absent, except in collective reference.

Building the society envisioned on the natural flow of the area's rivers was not possible, as that flow was not satisfactory in terms of sustained volume, consistency, or timing to irrigate all the irrigable lands for maximum development of the basin. The usual solution by at least the turn of the century to this type of water scarcity all over the West was *not* simply to let the priority system allocate scarce water to the first appropriators. This would not provide the type of efficient, broad-based development that was needed to sustain the society envisioned. The usual solution instead was to develop more water, and deliver it more consistently, by storage of the natural flow. In one part of the Uintah basin, for example, the federal government, the state and the non-Indian settlers worked together to "reserve" the waters of the Strawberry River for storage projects for the purpose of irrigating the settlers' land and (in theory) for the protection of the water supply for the Indian allotments, at least along the lower streams on the reservation. The end result was to be the shared use of the reserved waters of the watershed to suit the needs of both non-Indian and Indian irrigating farmers, whose rights perhaps differed in origin but not in practical application.

Given this development vision, the "real" problem along the reservation's upper rivers and creeks, such as the Lake Fork and the upper Uinta River, was that the engineers had not figured out how to store the waters of these streams to meet the irrigation needs of all the irrigable lands in these watersheds. Other steps had to be taken to spread the water for private land irrigation to the greatest extent possible. At the least this situation required that water be "reserved" for this purpose only, as illustrated by the way the Indian Affairs and Justice Department officials were willing not to pursue claims to water for the tribally owned grazing reserve but were willing to assert water to irrigate individual allotments for grass production for grazing. Also, the government and the settlers agreed without controversy to a provision in the court's instructions to the water commissioner and in the final decrees, applying to *both* the Indian and non-Indian lands, that no water could be diverted for irrigation purposes in any particular irrigation season "except that which is needed for economical and beneficial use in the irrigation of crops."[1] An in-season determination of whether a particular use of water would be economical could be, at least in theory, a way to override the mechanical application of priorities to spread the benefits of water in a water-short year as broadly as possible throughout a watershed. These were two facets of an overall development plan in which, as Commissioner Leupp had stated, "every drop of water not needed by the Indians for the development of their farms shall be allowed to go to the white settlers," in order "to have the surrounding country settled up by a good and thrifty class of white farmers."[2]

These efforts could not completely obscure the fact that there were not enough drops of water to go around, not under this particular vision of land and water use. And so the conflict centered on defining rights to ensure at least an abstract certainty as to which lands would get water at a time of scarcity. Priority by chronology of use had become the accepted western way of defining rights to water in the abstract where scarcity of this type seemed finally unavoidable, even as devices, such as principles of "economic use," were intended to moderate the mechanical application of priorities. The federal government accepted this point—the primary function of *Winters* in the Uintah litigation was as a *priority* device, as a way to manipulate the state's priority rules so as to favor the allotments by extending the concepts of occupancy and intention that had already permeated the workings of priority under state law.

To the non-Indian people directly affected—the settlers in the Uintah basin and, more generally, other groups of settlers irrigating land near Indian lands and their political allies—much mileage could be made out of how radically different *Winters* was from the prior appropriation water allocation system under state law. But the reality of westerners' efforts at water development and allocation in the early twentieth century did not match the mythology of the prior appropriation system; it had more in common with the work of *Winters*.

Conclusion

When Carl Rasch and William Logan squared off against the irrigators of Chinook and Havre in Judge Hunt's Helena courtroom in the summer of 1905 to argue about what rights the Fort Belknap reservation had to the water in the Milk River, no one could have predicted that the outcome would be one of the century's critically important legal and policy pronouncements on not just Indian reserved water rights, but on water policy and law more broadly and on Indian policy and sovereignty in general. No one planned or would have planned for this forum to be the place for this to happen. None of the judges or other immediate participants recognized this fact in the decision. The decision itself, as I have shown, had a logic in the dual context of the law and the local situation of the Milk River in 1905. At the same time it was determined by neither of these and could have had many different outcomes, so that even the decision itself, and not just the impact of the decision, was a contingent, unpredictable event. What happened afterward was more of the same—lawyers and other people finding opportunity (or threat) in this contingent and malleable outcome, understanding and applying the decision in different ways, responding to and being limited by the contexts in which they found themselves and also influencing those contexts.

Understanding the contingent nature of the *Winters* decision is important; understanding the complexity of the legal and social context and how *Winters* fits into that context is critical. The conventional understanding of western water law is still largely the story of the prior appropriation doctrine, often still emphasized as human society's natural adaptation to the physical conditions of aridity in the West. The *Winters* story demonstrates the array of legitimate, if conflicting, ideas and actions about water and water allocation law that were present in the Milk River valley in 1905 and have always been present in the western United States. To think of the *Winters* doctrine as an anomaly or as something imposed from the outside and resisted within is to grossly misunderstand that context. There have always existed in the West compelling alternative legal theories regarding human relationships to land and water, none necessarily more important than the others. Historians, legal scholars, and, especially, working lawyers, have to rethink their mistaken notions about the primacy, rigidity, acceptance, and inevitability of the prior appropriation system in the West at the turn of the century or at any time since.

Once the *Winters* case itself is granted its rightful status in the legal and social context of its time and place, the rest of this story—what I call the subsequent work of *Winters*—should come as no surprise, even if it has undermined another conventional understanding. After the *Winters* decisions, why would people confronted by difficult and complex issues of water use and allocation, especially involving water for Indians but also for public lands or to serve federal land use policies, not make use of this quite comprehensible and appropriate tool? They did use it, often, and to some effect as the Uintah reservation case study demonstrates. At its most basic, understanding the work of *Winters* requires taking a vastly different view of the federal government's interest in using *Winters* to influence water allocation decisions (significant), and of the Reclamation Service's antagonism and supposed strength in opposing its use (minimal). At a broader level, from 1905 on, whenever a water use or allocation issue of this type arose, whether in a local or national setting, the *Winters* doctrine was there, as people tried to make sense of it, apply it, extend or contain it, or contest its use. The outcomes varied widely, due to the opportunities and limitations of the particular social and legal context of the issue and because the *Winters* doctrine was not the only legal or social element at play in these moments. But the shape of western conflicts over water, of the outcomes, and of people's thinking and actions about water in general would not have been what they were without it.

The story of western water law and water use has to be sufficiently complex to make sense of the *Milk River Valley News'* joyous reaction to the *Winters* decision, as well as federal attorneys' tenacious and successful litigation of a difficult *Winters* case in the Uintah basin a decade after *Winters*. This is the real work of *Winters*.

Notes

INTRODUCTION

1. The Supreme Court's decision is *Winters v. United States,* 207 U.S. 564, 28 Sup. Ct. 207 (1908), affirming two appellate decisions by the Circuit Court of Appeals, Ninth Circuit, at 143 F. 740 and 148 F. 684 (1906). These appellate decisions affirmed two rulings by the federal district court in Montana (known at the time as the Circuit Court of the United States for the District of Montana), a preliminary injunction in August 1905 and then a permanent injunction/final decree in April 1906. The district court rulings are not in the official federal court case reports. The district court rulings can be found with other relevant documents from the litigation in National Archive records held at the Federal Archives and Records Center, Seattle (hereafter, Regional Archives, Seattle), in the file *"United States v. Mose Anderson, et al.,"* in Records of the U.S. District Courts, RG 21, U.S. Ninth Circuit, District of Montana, box 6659, folder 747. The federal district court rulings are also discussed in the appellate court opinions and in Hundley, "'Winters' Decision and Indian Water Rights," 25–27; Hundley, "Dark and Bloody Ground of Indian Water Rights," 463; Massie, "Cultural Roots of Indian Water Rights," 21; and McCool, *Command of the Waters,* 41, 43–44. Published court rulings in the Blackfeet reservation case are *United States v. Conrad Investment Company,* 156 F. 123 (D. Montana, 1907), *affirmed* in *Conrad Investment Company v. United States,* 161 F. 829 (9th Cir., 1908). The "pastoral and civilized people" quotation is from the Supreme Court opinion in *Winters v. United States,* 207 U.S. at 576; the other quotation is from the Ninth Circuit's decision in *Conrad Investment Company v. United States,* 161 F. at 832. References in this book to *Winters* or "the *Winters* decisions" usually include the decisions at all levels in the *Winters* litigation, unless the context

indicates otherwise, and may also include the decisions in the *Conrad* case as well where appropriate.

2. With regard to Indian policy in the late nineteenth and early twentieth centuries, the most useful book for this study has been Hoxie, *Final Promise.* Other helpful sources include Hoxie's book about the Crow Indians, *Parading through History;* Prucha, *Great Father,* 2:609–916; McDonnell, *Dispossession of the American Indian;* Berkhofer, *White Man's Indian,* esp. 44–61, 113–14, 153–57, 166–75; Carlson, *Indians, Bureaucrats and the Land;* Lewis, *Neither Wolf nor Dog;* White, *Roots of Dependency;* Wilkinson, *American Indians, Time, and the Law,* 7–31, 54–63, 78–86; Leibhardt, "Law, Environment, and Social Change"; Pisani, "Irrigation, Water Rights, and Betrayal"; and Massie, "Defeat of Assimilation." The *Lone Wolf* case citation is *Lone Wolf v. Hitchcock,* 187 U.S. 553 (1903).

3. For useful accounts of nineteenth-century developments in water law in general and western water law in particular, see Pisani, *To Reclaim a Divided West,* esp. 11–68; Pisani, "Enterprise and Equity"; Dunbar, *Forging New Rights;* Horwitz, *Transformation of American Law,* 32–53; Steinberg, *Nature Incorporated;* Worster, *Rivers of Empire,* esp. 83–96; Wheatley et al., "Study of the Development, Management, and Use of Water Resources," prepared for the Public Land Law Review Commission, 47–58.

4. This situation is best analyzed in McCool's very able book *Command of the Waters.* Also important are Hundley, "'Winters' Decision and Indian Water Rights" and "Dark and Bloody Ground of Indian Water Rights"; two articles by Pisani, "Irrigation, Water Rights, and Betrayal" and "State v. Nation," esp. 277–78; Burton, *American Indian Water Rights,* esp. 2, 6–34, 61–66; and Hoxie, *Final Promise,* 147–87. Dozens of law review articles and legal treatise chapters—all written since the modern resurgence of the reserved rights doctrine began in the 1960s—have commented on the failure of *Winters* rights to translate into real water for American Indians. For just one example, see Shay, "Promises of a Viable Homeland." Additional law review articles and other legal writings are noted below and in the bibliography.

5. For one of the many examples of negotiated agreements that have been completed or are in the works, see the Fort Hall Indian Water Rights Act of 1990, Public Law 101-602, 104 Stat. 3059 (November 16, 1990). For discussions of the recent increase in reserved rights litigation and of various negotiated settlements, see, among many possible works, Burton, *American Indian Water Rights;* Membrino, "Indian Reserved Water Rights"; Blumm, "Reserved Water Rights," sec. 37.05.

6. Hundley, "'Winters' Decision and Indian Water Rights" and "Dark and Bloody Ground of Indian Water Rights"; Pisani, "Irrigation, Water Rights, and Betrayal."

7. Massie, "Cultural Roots of Indian Water Rights," 15–28. While Hundley's articles are well known and frequently cited, and Pisani's is known and occasionally cited, I have not seen any references to Massie's article on the

Winters litigation. Massie's article is based on his master's thesis at the University of Wyoming, a copy of which I have.

8. Historical works that make reference to Indian water rights in the context of other topics will be discussed below at relevant points. Brief articles on Indian water rights were published in the 1970s in the journal *Indian Historian*, e.g., Costo, "Indian Water Rights"; Lamb, "Indian-Government Relations on Water Utilization." Some of these were written by lawyers active in contemporaneous disputes and belong more to the category of the legal literature on the doctrine, noted below (e.g., Veeder, "Water Rights").

9. The legal literature is vast. The best entry into the legal literature on *Winters* is the treatise discussion of reserved water rights, Indian and non-Indian, by Blumm, "Reserved Water Rights." See also Tarlock, "Indian Reserved Water Rights," sec. 9.07 in *Law of Water Rights and Resources;* Cohen, *Handbook of Federal Indian Law,* 575–605. The few books devoted to Indian reserved water rights are mostly collections of essays and most are wholly or in part from the legal community. These usually include some historical context even as they focus on present issues. Examples are McGuire, Lord, and Wallace, *Indian Water in the New West;* Sly, *Reserved Water Rights Settlement Manual;* Folk-Williams, *What Indian Water Means to the West;* and *Indian Water Policy in a Changing Environment.*

Many published writings on Indian reserved water rights are in law reviews. A complete list runs for pages, as can be seen in the bibliography. A short and useful list includes: Abrams, "Big Horn Indian Water Rights Adjudication"; Bloom, "Indian 'Paramount' Rights to Water Use"; Collins, "Future Course of the *Winters* Doctrine" and "Indian Allotment Water Rights"; Dellwo, "Indian Water Rights—The *Winters* Doctrine Updated"; Folk-Williams, "Use of Negotiated Agreements to Resolve Water Disputes"; Getches, "Water Rights on Indian Allotments" and "Management and Marketing of Indian Water"; "Indian Reserved Water Rights: The *Winters* of Our Discontent"; Liu, "American Indian Reserved Water Rights"; Membrino, "Indian Reserved Water Rights"; Pelcyger, "*Winters* Doctrine and the Greening of the Reservations"; Price and Weatherford, "Indian Water Rights in Theory and Practice"; Ranquist, "*Winters* Doctrine and How It Grew"; Shay, "Promises of a Viable Homeland"; Shupe, "Water in Indian Country"; Tarlock, "One River, Three Sovereigns"; Veeder, "Indian Prior and Paramount Rights." Among government documents, see Wheatley et al., "Study of the Development, Management, and Use of Water Resources"; and Trelease, "Federal-State Relations in Water Law."

10. I am indebted to Professor Burton for his suggestion that I think of my analysis of the *Winters* doctrine in the context of "bargaining in the shadow of the law." The term, if not the analytical inquiry, originated with Mnookin and Kornhauser, "Bargaining in the Shadow of the Law." Other articles of note include Cooter and Marks, with Mnookin, "Bargaining in the Shadow of the Law"; Coursey and Stanley, "Pretrial Bargaining Behavior within the Shadow

of the Law"; Jacob, "Elusive Shadow of the Law"; Goldschmidt, "Bargaining in the Shadow of ADR."

CHAPTER 1: PRELUDE TO THE WINTERS LITIGATION

1. The Treaty of Fort Laramie, signed September 17, 1851, can be found in Kappler, *Indian Affairs,* 2:594–96. The Senate ratified the 1855 Blackfeet treaty on April 15, 1856, as 11 Stat. 658 in the United States Statutes at Large; it can be found in Kappler, *Indian Affairs,* 2:736–40. The Senate ratified the 1873 reservation agreement as the Act of April 15, 1874, 43rd Cong., 1st Sess., chap. 96, 18 Stat. 28–29, reprinted in Kappler, *Indian Affairs,* 1:149–50. The *Winters* decisions themselves include references to the treaties, agreements, events, and developments that preceded the 1888 agreement primarily at issue in the litigation; the most complete discussion is in the first decision by the Court of Appeals, *Winters v. United States,* 143 F. at 740–42. Various secondary sources provide either a brief description or a longer account of the events, treaties, agreements, developments, and other details of the relationship between the United States and the Indian peoples of Montana in the second half of the nineteenth century, up to and through the signing and approval of the 1888 agreement. James Welch's novel *Fools Crow* remains for me the best description of the dynamic process of land encroachment, conflict, pressure for land cession, and native action and attitudes in Montana in this period. Other secondary sources relied upon here include Hundley, "'Winters' Decision and Indian Water Rights," 19–21, 26–27; Hundley, "Dark and Bloody Ground of Indian Water Rights," 460–64; Massie, "Cultural Roots of Indian Water Rights," 15–17; Massie, "Defeat of Assimilation," 34–41; Rodnick, *Fort Belknap Assiniboine of Montana,* 1–14; Barry, *Fort Belknap Indian Reservation,* 1–110, 123–27 (Barry's study, first produced as an official reservation history for the Bureau of Indian Affairs, is far from a sophisticated or modern ethnographic analysis of the people of the reservation, but it is a treasure of facts and details of reservation affairs, especially from the perspective of the superintendents and other Indian Office employees on the reservation); Shane, *Brief History of the Fort Belknap Reservation,* 8–9; Prucha, *Great Father,* 1:315–18, 337–53, 402–09, 479–581; and Hoxie, *Final Promise,* 1–53. These sources inform the discussion not just in this paragraph but over the next few pages, until the beginning of the description of the *Winters* litigation.

2. Act of May 1, 1888, 50th Cong., 1st Sess., chap. 213, 25 Stat. 113–33, reprinted in Kappler, *Indian Affairs,* 1:261–66. What Congress approved in this act was a set of general provisions common to all three agreements—a preamble and nine articles—followed by the three separate, different, and specific agreements describing the boundaries of the lands reserved. The first specific agreement established the boundaries of the Fort Peck reservation, agreed to by "the undersigned, chiefs, headmen, and principal men of the several bands of Sioux and Assinnaboine Indians attached to and receiving rations at the Fort Peck Agency," and followed by the marks, seals, and names of 262 Sioux men

NOTES TO PAGES 18–19

and 138 Assiniboine men. The second established the boundaries of the Fort Belknap reservation, agreed to by "the undersigned, chiefs, headmen, and principal men of the Gros Ventres and Assinniboine bands of Indians attached to and receiving rations at the Fort Belknap Agency," and followed by the marks, seals, and names of 94 Gros Ventre men and 130 Assiniboine men. The third agreement established the boundaries of the Blackfeet reservation, agreed to by "the undersigned, chiefs, headmen, and principal men of Piegan, Blood, and Blackfeet Nation, attached to and receiving rations at the Blackfeet Agency," and followed by the marks, seals, and names of 222 "Piegan, Blood, and Blackfeet" men. Congress approved these linked agreements in 1888, and so they will be referred to hereafter as the "1888 agreement"; and because the *Winters* case concerned the Fort Belknap reservation, I will also refer to the "Fort Belknap agreement." The agreement is described in all the *Winters* decisions, such as at 143 F. at 741–44, 746, and 207 U.S. at 565–66, 575–76, and in any number of law review articles and treatises and other writings on *Winters,* including the three historical articles directly about the *Winters* litigation: Hundley, "'Winters' Decision and Indian Water Rights," 19–21, 26–27, 32–33; Hundley, "Dark and Bloody Ground of Indian Water Rights," 460–64; and Massie, "Cultural Roots of Indian Water Rights," 17, 21–22.

The 1888 agreement was not a "treaty," as the United States ceased negotiating and ratifying treaties with American Indians in 1871. There are many reasons for this development; the particular precipitating event appears to have been the frustration of members of the House of Representatives over their exclusion from the policymaking process inherent in treaty negotiations and Senate ratification, which came to a head in 1869 and 1870 as the House balked at appropriating money to fund the Office of Indian Affairs and the federal government's treaty obligations. Despite the end of the formal "treaty" process, the 1888 Fort Belknap agreement has the attributes of a treaty, in that it was negotiated between and executed by the executive branch of the United States and the affected Indians and then "ratified" by being adopted by Congress into law exactly as signed. This and other post-1871 agreements have always been considered the functional equivalent of treaties for the purposes of, for example, the legal concepts of treaty rights. The case law on treaty rights and the reserved water rights doctrine, and the law review and treatise discussions of the topic, do not distinguish rights based in post-1871 agreements from rights based in pre-1871 treaties. More telling, even at the time of the *Winters* litigation, the attorneys for the government, the federal judges, and government officials in the Department of the Interior and the Department of Justice referred to the 1888 Fort Belknap agreement as a "treaty" and spoke of a decision based on "treaty rights," as will be noted in the discussions below. See also Hundley, "'Winters' Decision and Indian Water Rights," 26 n.27; Prucha, *Great Father,* 1:527–33, 598–99.

3. As noted in the introduction, a number of books and articles over the last twenty years have described the failed efforts of the American people and government to induce or force western American Indians to transform their

societies into the dominant culture's ideal of a small-farmer agrarian society, and the consequences of that failure. Two of the most useful here are Hoxie, *Final Promise,* and Lewis, *Neither Wolf nor Dog.* Concepts from Hoxie's book in particular are discussed in detail below.

4. Act of May 1, 1888, 50th Cong., 1st Sess., chap. 213, 25 Stat. 113.

5. Ibid., 25 Stat. 114.

6. John Wright, Jared Daniels, and Charles F. Larrabee to John Atkins, commissioner of Indian affairs, February 11, 1887, Department of the Interior, Records of the Department of the Interior, RG 48, file 6581-1887, "Indian Division, Letters Received," National Archives, quoted in Hundley, "'Winters' Decision and Indian Water Rights," 21.

7. Brief of the Appellee, 45–46 (emphasis added), submitted by Carl Rasch, U.S. attorney (no date; presumably late 1905), *Winters v. United States,* United States Circuit Court of Appeals for the Ninth Circuit, Case No. 1243, in Department of Justice, Records of the Department of Justice, RG 60, box 221, file 58730 (records of the *Winters* case), National Archives.

8. For these reflections I have relied in part on Massie, "Cultural Roots of Indian Water Rights," 15–17, 19–22, 24, as well as on my own consideration of the sources he cited and numerous other writings on the issue of American Indians' relationships to the nonhuman world. For brief comments in the same vein, see Tarlock, "One River, Three Sovereigns," 643–44. Two dissertations providing useful analyses of the cultural and spiritual traditions of two particular peoples—the Yakamas and the Northern Utes—concerning their relationships with water are Leibhardt, "Law, Environment, and Social Change," 222–316; and Endter, "Cultural Ideologies and Political Economy," 89–92, 228–61.

9. Endter, "Cultural Ideologies and Political Economy," 90–92, 232–40. Quotation is at 92.

10. The United States and the Fort Belknap Indians executed this agreement on October 9, 1895. Congress approved it on June 10, 1896, as part of that year's appropriations bill for the Office of Indian Affairs. Act of June 10, 1896, 54th Cong., 1st Sess., chap. 398, 29 Stat. 321, 350–53, reprinted in Kappler, *Indian Affairs,* 2:597, 601–9. Quotation is at 29 Stat. 351. The 1896 act included a similar land purchase agreement with the Blackfeet, including an even stronger nonallotment provision describing how the Blackfeet reservation was "unfit" for agriculture and stating that cattle raising was the means by which the Indians would become self-supporting. The Blackfeet agreement included a specific reservation of the right to hunt and fish on the land and streams of the ceded parcel, as long as the land remained the public land of the United States and in accordance with the game and fish laws of Montana. 29 Stat. 353–57. Few writings on the *Winters* case refer to the 1896 agreement, and then only briefly in describing the events between the 1888 treaty and the 1905 litigation. Only Barry noted that the federal courts made use of the 1896 agreement in their *Winters* decision. See Barry, *Fort Belknap Indian Reservation,* 123–26; see also Massie, "Cultural Roots of Indian Water Rights," 19; Massie,

"Defeat of Assimilation," 40; Shane, *Brief History of the Fort Belknap Reservation*, 8. The government's and the courts' use of the 1896 agreement in the *Winters* litigation is discussed below.

11. The discussion in this paragraph and the next six follows the accounts of Massie and Hundley of the events leading up to the 1905 litigation, discussions central to their articles, Massie, "Cultural Roots of Indian Water Rights," 17–20, and Hundley, "'Winters' Decision and Indian Water Rights," 20–23. I have looked at the documents they relied on, primarily correspondence in the records of the reservation and the Indian Office as well as the Indian Office appropriations bills, and have little quarrel with their accounts. What differences I have are noted in the text. This discussion also relies on Barry, *Fort Belknap Indian Reservation*, 80–109, 111–15, 117–19, 123–27, Rodnick, *Fort Belknap Assiniboine of Montana*, 6–15, 73, and Massie, "Defeat of Assimilation," 36, 39–41; and on the evidence and statements of fact produced in the *Winters* litigation, mostly by U.S. Attorney Carl Rasch, including Bill of Complaint (June 26, 1905) and Testimony (August 15, 1905) in the files of *United States v. Mose Anderson, et al.,* Records of the U.S. District Courts, RG 21, U.S. Ninth Circuit, District of Montana, box 6659, folder 747, Regional Archives, Seattle; Brief of the Appellee (no date; presumably late 1905) in *Winters v. United States,* United States Circuit Court of Appeals for the Ninth Circuit, Case No. 1243, which can be found in Department of Justice, Records of the Department of Justice, RG 60, box 221, file 58730 (records of the *Winters* case), National Archives; and the opinions of the courts in the *Winters* litigation.

12. Massie, "Cultural Roots of Indian Water Rights," 19. My review of the documents indicates that Massie's statement of conditions at the reservation is essentially correct, although there may be little reason to agree with his speculation that financial independence and self-sufficiency based on cattle production were attainable in the first decade of the 1900s absent the interference of the superintendents.

13. The leasing of reservation lands to non-Indians for grazing and for the production of irrigated hay and other crops, including the sugar beet scheme, is discussed in Massie, "Cultural Roots of Indian Water Rights," 19–21, 23; Massie, "Defeat of Assimilation," 36, 38–41, 43–45; Rodnick, *Fort Belknap Assiniboine of Montana,* 10–11, 12, 14–16, 73; Barry, *Fort Belknap Indian Reservation,* 112–13, 117, 129, 130–34. Indian water rights issues intertwine with the sugar beet cultivation and production scheme and with various ongoing efforts by non-Indians to gain access to reservation lands, explained in more detail below. I have tried to find more information on William Logan, superintendent at the Fort Belknap reservation from 1902 to 1910 (who is, as will be seen, a major figure in this story) but have had little success. Barry said that Logan was a "westerner born in Texas and raised on the frontier," who had been "an Army scout, post trader at Missoula and agent for the Blackfeet" before coming to Fort Belknap. Everyone addressed him as Major Logan, but it seems that "Major" was an honorary title bestowed on all Indian agents. Barry, *Fort Belknap Indian Reservation,* iv, 111. There is no record of Logan

having served in the United States Army, see Heitman, *Historical Register and Dictionary of the United States Army.*

14. Massie, "Cultural Roots of Indian Water Rights," 20, 23.

15. These points will become more clear in the discussion below of how the litigation meshed with developments in the Milk River valley. Three letters from Logan to the commissioner of Indian affairs wonderfully illustrate how he integrated these interests—one explaining why it would be better to pursue the sugar beet leasing scheme than to allow for the sale of the irrigable lands to non-Indians and the associated loss of the water rights; the second a defense of his actions upon an accusation of self-dealing and favoritism to non-Indian interests, especially merchants in the Harlem area across the river from the reservation; and a third reporting and reacting to praise of his work from Secretary of Interior James Garfield. See W. R. Logan to commissioner of Indian affairs, April 29 and November 8, 1906, in box 20, "Letters Sent—Commissioner of Indian Affairs, 1902–07," and July 25, 1907, in box 21, "Letters Sent—Commissioner of Indian Affairs, 1907–11," Department of the Interior, Records of the Bureau of Indian Affairs, RG 75, Fort Belknap Indian Agency Papers, Regional Archives, Seattle.

CHAPTER 2: LEGAL CONTEXT
OF THE LITIGATION

1. Hundley, "'Winters' Decision and Indian Water Rights," 22–27; see, e.g., McCool, *Command of the Waters,* 38–40; Tarlock, "One River, Three Sovereigns," 640–41.

2. Trelease, "Federal-State Relations in Water Law," 21.

3. For the conventional discussion of the common law riparian rights doctrine, its rejection in the arid land states, and the development in these states of the prior appropriation system, explained primarily as an adaptation to the physical conditions of the arid lands, see, e.g., Webb, *Great Plains,* 319–33, 348–66, 385–87, 435–52; R. E. Clark, *Water and Water Rights,* 29–34, 60–61, 65–66, 74–87, 235–45, 288–300; Hutchins, completed by Ellis and DeBraal, *Water Rights Laws,* 1–3, 157–75, 254–58, 284–90, 437–44, 488–91; Trelease, "Federal-State Relations in Water Law," 12–35; Dunbar, *Forging New Rights,* 59–72, 85; Dunbar, "Adaptability of Water Law"; McCool, *Command of the Waters,* 39 n.2; Tarlock, *Law of Water Rights and Resources,* chap. 3 ("Riparian Rights"), chap. 5 ("Prior Appropriation Doctrine"). For Kinney's analysis, see Kinney, *Treatise on the Law of Irrigation,* 400–22, 431–34, 632–62, 663–85, 854–59, 870–89, 1005–97. In a long multipart law review article published in 1929, shortly before Webb produced *Great Plains,* Moses Lasky, soon to be regarded as one of the premier water lawyers and scholars in the West, analyzed briefly the history of the prior appropriation system, described the current forms of the doctrine, criticized those who believed the prior appropriation system was perfect or particularly useful in its created or idealized form, and recommended administrative solutions to what he saw as the efficiency and

equity problems posed by strict adherence to the doctrine. Lasky, "From Prior Appropriation to Economic Distribution," quotes are on 169, 248.

4. On eastern developments in riparian law, see Horwitz, *Transformation of American Law*, 32–53; see also Steinberg, *Nature Incorporated*. Karsten, in his recent *Heart versus Head*, contends that Horwitz misread the case law developments in eastern water law in the nineteenth century, one of many ways Horwitz, in Karsten's view, misused state appellate court decisions to construct an inappropriate paradigm of judicial transformation of law to further the needs of industrializing capitalists. Karsten may be right—his use of evidence is persuasive, he is not the first to cast doubt on Horwitz's understanding of doctrinal shifts, and Horwitz's model is far too tidy to be realistic. From my reading of both and of other legal sources, however, it still seems clear that what people living in riparian doctrine states at the end of the nineteenth century were doing with water was very different from what they were doing with it in the eighteenth, that those changes in use were sanctioned by legislative and judicial changes in water law, and that the changes were compatible with other activities taking place in a developing capitalist, market, industrial economy. More to the point here, the work by Pisani and others on parallel developments in western water law stand on their own ground and do not depend on Horwitz's conceptual structure. The most important pieces by Pisani are *To Reclaim a Divided West*, esp. 11–68, "Enterprise and Equity," "Water Law," and "Origins of Western Water Law,"; and by Worster, *Rivers of Empire*, 87–92. McCurdy particularly emphasized the public land aspect of the development of the western water allocation system in "Stephen J. Field and Public Land Law Development." See also Wheatley et al., "Study of the Development, Management, and Use of Water Resources," 47–58, which anticipated some of these themes. Interestingly, the myth of the prior appropriation system as an adaptation to aridity did not fully take root until the 1930s and Webb's analysis. Whatever some boosters and irrigators may have already thought around the turn of the century, and despite Kinney's views noted above, most legal scholars writing at the turn of the century understood, for example, that the prior appropriation system developed out of the particular needs of the nineteenth-century gold mining enterprise and the public land character of the land that held the mining claims. The system was then extended to meet the needs of commercial agriculture for irrigation of lands carved out of the public domain. E.g., Clayberg, "Genesis and Development of the Law of the Waters"; Hess, "Arid-Land Water Rights"; Wiel, *Water Rights in the Western States*, 1:65–172 (Wiel's treatise was the other great western water law treatise at the time, with Kinney's); Lasky, "From Prior Appropriation to Economic Distribution."

5. See, e.g., Meyer, *Water in the Hispanic Southwest;* Glick, *Old World Background of Irrigation System* (Spanish/Mexican water uses and systems); Dobbins, *Spanish Element in Texas Water Law;* Tyler, *Mythical Pueblo Rights Doctrine;* Langum, *Law and Community on Mexican California Frontier* (discussion of nature of Spanish/Mexican law in California); Cutter, *Legal Culture of Northern New Spain* (general study of the nature of Spanish law in Texas and

New Mexico); Wiel, *Water Rights in the Western States,* 1:66–70 (Spanish/ Mexican water law systems); Kinney, *Treatise on the Law of Irrigation,* 117–26, 400–18, 987–1003 (Native American, Spanish, Mexican, and Mormon water uses and allocation systems); Pisani, *To Reclaim a Divided West,* 11–68; Pisani, "Enterprise and Equity," at 16–17, 19–35 (discussing the Spanish, Mexican, Mormon, and formative non-Indian mainstream approaches and attitudes); Dunbar, *Forging New Rights,* 1–17 (brief discussion of Indian, Hispanic, and Mormon approaches to water allocation); Leibhardt, "Law, Environment, and Social Change," esp. 222–316 (Yakama case study); Endter, "Cultural Ideologies and Political Economy," (discussion of Northern Ute and Mormon attitudes toward water, with some historical content); Nabhan, *Desert Smells Like Rain* (discussion of Papago relationship to land and water, with some historical content); Hundley, *Great Thirst,* 1–139 (an able discussion of Paiute, Spanish/Mexican, and early Anglo-American water laws and actions in California; Hundley's descriptions and themes echo Pisani's); Worster, *Rivers of Empire* (various discussions throughout relating to Indians, the Mormon community, John Wesley Powell, William Smythe, and federal reclamation); Powell, *Report on the Lands of the Arid Region;* Smythe, *Conquest of Arid America;* Goetzmann, *New Lands, New Men,* 174 (Emory's attitude toward life in the Southwest); Tarlock, *Law of Water Rights and Resources,* 5-5 (concerning the Mormon and Hispanic communities). Most of the legal works in n. 3 (above) briefly discuss water use in the indigenous, Spanish, and Mormon settlements before focusing on the miners' contribution to the development of the prior appropriation system; they all discuss federal reclamation as well.

6. Pisani, *To Reclaim a Divided West,* esp. 33–68; "Enterprise and Equity," 15–37 (for statement on dominance of prior appropriation system by 1900, see 35–36); "Water Law," 1–6; "Origins of Western Water Law," 24–37. For state constitution provisions that dedicated water to private use and incorporated more or less of the elements of the prior appropriation doctrine, see, e.g., Constitution of the State of Arizona, art. 17, secs. 1–2 (1910); Constitution of the State of Colorado, art. 16, secs. 5–6 (1876); Constitution of the State of Idaho, art. 15, secs. 1, 3–4 (1890); Constitution of the State of Montana, art. 9, sec. 3 (1889); Constitution of the State of New Mexico, art. 16, secs. 1–3 (1911); Constitution of the State of Utah, art. 17, sec. 1 (1895); Constitution of the State of Wyoming, art. 8, secs. 1, 3 (1890). The passion for the prior appropriation system on the part of some western economic interests and their congressional allies is discussed in greater detail below.

7. Looking just at law review articles, the following are examples from the first part of the twentieth century that were critical of the prior appropriation system in its pure form, especially as a relic of frontier days that was now an obstacle to broad and comprehensive economic development, and including citations to state court decisions on the same point: Wiel, "'Priority' in Western Water Law"; Wiel, "Theories of Water Law"; Adams, "Economical Use of Water"; Wiel, "What Is Beneficial Use of Water?"; Hess, "Arid-Land Water Rights," 487–88; Chandler, "Title to Non-navigable Waters," 111, 130; Niles,

"Legal Background of the Colorado River Controversy." The most interesting effort is Lasky, "From Prior Appropriation to Economic Distribution," which is filled with analysis, quotations, citations, and opinions critical of the pure "Colorado doctrine" form of the prior appropriation system. Lasky anticipated by sixty years Charles Wilkinson's pronouncement of the "death" of the prior appropriation doctrine, at 170–72, 216 (in the first part of the article), 269 (second part), 57–58 (third part). See Wilkinson, "Prior Appropriation 1848–1991." Wilkinson is the Moses Lasky Professor of Law at the University of Colorado.

8. A number of books and articles analyze the origins and implementation of the Reclamation Act of 1902. The most useful here have been Pisani, *To Reclaim a Divided West;* Pisani, "State v. Nation"; Pisani "Federal Reclamation" in *Water, Land, and Law in the West,* 159–63; Pisani "Reclamation and Social Engineering in the Progressive West"; Pisani, "Water Law"; Pisani, "Irrigation, Water Rights, and Betrayal"; Worster, *Rivers of Empire* (useful for its description of the implementation of the Reclamation Act, not for its theoretical "hydraulic empire" overlay); and Fereday and Creamer, "Swan Falls in 3-D."

In considering the ways in which westerners systematically worked to get around the prior appropriation system, another point to ponder: In Colorado, the holy land of prior appropriation, what does one call a system in which a city may (1) make a statement of its intent to appropriate and use a huge amount of water some time in the future; (2) manifest that intent and "initiate" the water use with a few signs, surveys, and filings; and (3) slowly pursue the capture of the claimed water over the next few decades—while nonetheless the law says, if and when the water is finally put to use, that the municipality has made a prior appropriation as of the date it first stated and showed its intent? See, e.g., *City and County of Denver v. Colorado River Water Conservation District,* 696 P.2d 730 (Colorado, 1985), one of many western state water law decisions analyzing the "conditional" water rights concept that most western states developed early on as part of the prior appropriation system and that has proved especially useful for long-term urban planning. Many urban areas in the West use water delivered through some type of reserved rights doctrine.

9. See chap. 4. Discussions of the attitudes and actions of the early Reclamation Service officials with regard to western water law, to the riparian doctrine, and to the *Winters* doctrine in particular are in Pisani's "State v. Nation." I have reviewed the primary documents (copies of many on loan from Professor Pisani), and the documents that relate directly to the *Winters* case are discussed and cited below. For an excellent analysis of the relationship over the whole of the century between Bureau of Reclamation water projects and Indian water projects, see McCool, *Command of the Waters;* see also Burton, *American Indian Water Rights.*

10. *Thorp v. Freed,* 1 Mont. 651 (1872), 652–64 (opinion of Justice Knowles), 664–87 (opinion of Chief Justice Wade).

11. *Thorp v. Freed,* 687.

12. *Thorp v. Freed,* 652–64.

13. *Smith v. Denniff,* 60 P. 398, 398–402 (Montana, 1900).

14. *Smith v. Denniff,* 398–99.

15. *Ibid.*

16. *Cruse v. McCauley,* 96 F. 369, 370–74 (D. Montana, 1899).

17. *Cruse v. McCauley,* 374.

18. *Willey v. Decker,* 73 P. 210, 211–27, esp. at 214 (Wyoming, 1903).

19. Wiel, *Water Rights in the Western States,* 1:137–38, 175–80, 277–78, 2:1452; Kinney, *Treatise on the Law of Irrigation,* 648, 657, 870–73, 1088, 3419. I have had access only to the third edition of Wiel (1911; the first was published in 1905 and the second in 1908) and the second edition of Kinney (1912, the first was in 1894), both published a few years after the *Winters* litigation. There is no reason to believe that their views on the nature of Montana water law in 1911 and 1912 were different than they were in 1905. For example, the Montana cases cited by Wiel and Kinney for the proposition that Montana follows or recognizes riparian rights—such as *Thorp, Smith, Cruse,* and *Willey*—were primarily from before 1905. Also, Rasch in his Ninth Circuit brief in the *Winters* case in late 1905 cited to the first edition of Kinney as part of his discussions in favor of the applicability of riparian law in Montana.

20. Hunt, "Law of Water Rights," in which Hunt denied that public land grantees held any common law riparian rights in the West.

21. *Mettler v. Ames Realty Company,* 201 P. 702, 707 (Montana, 1921).

22. *United States v. Rio Grande Dam and Irrigation Company,* 174 U.S. 690, 703 (1899).

23. *Gutierres v. Albuquerque Land and Irrigation Company,* 188 U.S. 545, 554–55 (1903).

24. For discussions of the *Rio Grande* case and its context and implications, see I. G. Clark, "Elephant Butte Controversy"; Pisani, "State v. Nation," 273–77; Dunbar, *Forging New Rights,* 192–94.

25. See Wiel, *Water Rights in the Western States,* 1:147–48, 158, 175–77, 215–17, 236–43, 2:1275; Kinney, *Treatise on the Law of Irrigation,* 657–60, 664–66, 684, 690–93, 813–15, 1091–92, 1098–1105, 1112–24, 1159–61, 2290–92.

26. *Kansas v. Colorado,* 206 U.S. 46, 85–86, 92–93 (1907). This decision and its relationship to the course of the *Winters* litigation is discussed below.

27. *Winters v. United States,* 143 F. at 749 (Court of Appeals), 207 U.S. at 577 (Supreme Court).

28. *Krall v. United States,* 79 F. 241 (9th Cir. 1897), 241–43 (majority opinion by Judge Ross), 243–45 (dissenting opinion by Judge Gilbert), *appeal dismissed for lack of jurisdiction,* 174 U.S. 385 (1899).

29. *Story v. Wolverton,* 31 Mont. 346, 78 P. 589, 589–91 (1904). Quotation is at 78 P. 590.

30. Montana Laws 1905, chap. 44, sec. 1; see *Mettler v. Ames Realty Company,* 201 P. at 707.

31. *Winters v. United States,* 143 F. at 745.

32. *Jones v. Meehan,* 175 U.S. 1, 10–11 (1899), citing *Worcester v. Georgia,* 31 U.S. (6 Pet.) 515, 582 (1832); *The Kansas Indians,* 72 U.S. (5 Wall.) 737, 760 (1866); and *Choctaw Nation v. United States,* 119 U.S. 1, 27–28 (1886). For a still

relevant discussion of treaty interpretation issues, see Wilkinson and Volkman, "Judicial Review of Indian Treaty Abrogation," 601–61.

33. *United States v. Winans*, 198 U.S. 371 (1905). The Supreme Court issued its opinion in *Winans* on May 15, 1905. Rasch filed the complaint beginning the *Winters* case on June 26. Note: The Yakama Indian Nation has changed the spelling of its name; I am following the spelling of "Yakima" used at the time and in the court and government records.

34. *United States v. Winans*, 380–81 (citations omitted).

35. *United States v. Winans*, 381.

36. Brief of the Appellee, 45–46 (emphasis added), submitted by Carl Rasch, U.S. attorney (no date; presumably late 1905), *Winters v. United States*, United States Circuit Court of Appeals for the Ninth Circuit, Case No. 1243, in Department of Justice, Records of the Department of Justice, RG 60, box 221, file 58730 (records of the *Winters* case), National Archives.

37. *Winters v. United States*, 207 U.S. at 575–77.

38. Bill of Complaint (January 1905), in the files of *United States v. Conrad Investment Company*, Records of the U.S. District Courts, RG 21, U.S. Ninth Circuit, District of Montana, box 6659, folder 720, Regional Archives, Seattle. To reiterate, the decisions of the district and appellate courts are reported at *United States v. Conrad Investment Company*, 156 F. 123, 124–132 (D. Montana, 1907), *affirmed*, *Conrad Investment Company v. United States*, 161 F. 829, 830–35 (9th Cir., 1908).

39. Bill of Complaint, 13, *United States v. Conrad Investment Company*, Records of the U.S. District Courts, RG 21, U.S. Ninth Circuit, District of Montana, box 6659, folder 720, Regional Archives, Seattle.

40. Senate Joint Memorial No. 1 (February 26, 1907), Montana Legislative Assembly, 1907 Session, Montana Laws 1907, 590–91, printed at 42 *Cong. Rec.* 712–13 (January 15, 1908). The Montana legislature's reasons for adopting this memorial are discussed below.

41. 51 *Cong. Rec.* 12949 (July 29, 1914).

42. For example, Rep. James Mann of Illinois, a fellow Republican of Representative Mondell's, responded to Mondell's statement quoted in the text with the archetypal statement of the other view: "I do not agree with half of these gentleman about this matter. I think the Government has the right to reserve the water, if it wants to do so, for the benefit of the Indians, just as much a right, or a greater right, as to reserve the land if it wants to do so. Of course I know these States out there operated by the white settlers are endeavoring to put up a different theory of law in order to rob the Indians of their water." 51 *Cong. Rec.* 12950 (July 29, 1914).

CHAPTER 3: COMMENCEMENT OF THE *WINTERS* CASE

1. *North Montana Review* (Glasgow, Mont.), April 29, 1905, 1.

2. W. R. Logan to Francis E. Leupp, June 3, 1905, Department of the Interior, Records of the Bureau of Indian Affairs, RG 75, Fort Belknap Indian

Agency Papers, box 20, "Letters Sent—Commissioner of Indian Affairs, 1902–07," Regional Archives, Seattle, quoted in Massie, "Cultural Roots of Indian Water Rights," 20, and relied upon in Hundley, "'Winters' Decision and Indian Water Rights," 22 (see 21–33 for Hundley's description of the course of the litigation).

3. W. R. Logan to F. E. Leupp, June 3, 1905, Records of the Bureau of Indian Affairs, RG 75, Fort Belknap Indian Agency Papers, box 20, "Letters Sent—Commissioner of Indian Affairs, 1902–07," Regional Archives, Seattle.

4. C. F. Larrabee to Ethan A. Hitchcock, June 9, 1905; E. A. Hitchcock to attorney general (William Moody, who served under Theodore Roosevelt), June 13, 1905; attorney general to C. Rasch, June 13, 1905, all in Department of Justice, Records of the Department of Justice, RG 60, box 221, file 58730 (records of the *Winters* case), National Archives, all cited and quoted in Hundley, "'Winters' Decision and Indian Water Rights," 22–23. C. Rasch to W. R. Logan, June 14, 1905, Department of the Interior, Records of the Bureau of Indian Affairs, RG 75, Fort Belknap Indian Agency Papers, box 52, "Miscellaneous Letters Received, 1902–05," Regional Archives, Seattle. I added the emphasis in the telegram from Moody and the letter from Rasch.

5. Bill of Complaint (June 26, 1905), in the files of *United States v. Mose Anderson, et al.,* Records of the U.S. District Courts, RG 21, U.S. Ninth Circuit, District of Montana, box 6659, folder 747, Regional Archives, Seattle.

6. Bill of Complaint, 7–8, *United States v. Mose Anderson, et al.,* Records of the U.S. District Courts, RG 21, U.S. Ninth Circuit, District of Montana, box 6659, folder 747, Regional Archives, Seattle.

7. Order to Show Cause and Temporary Restraining Order (June 26, 1905) and Order Modifying Temporary Restraining Order (July 8, 1905), *United States v. Mose Anderson, et al.,* Records of the U.S. District Courts, RG 21, U.S. Ninth Circuit, District of Montana, box 6659, folder 747, Regional Archives, Seattle. The court files do not contain the defendants' request for modification of the restraining order. Rasch explained the reasons behind the modification in the letter to Logan on July 8, 1905, Department of the Interior, Records of the Bureau of Indian Affairs, RG 75, Fort Belknap Indian Agency Papers, box 52, "Miscellaneous Letters Received, 1902–05," Regional Archives, Seattle. There are no indications that Rasch as of July 8 knew the weakness of the prior appropriation claim; he focused on the other theories because of their strength and breadth, not because of the weakness of the prior appropriation claim. Logan retained his faith in the strength of the prior appropriation claim, as indicated in a letter to Rasch on July 11 (in response to Rasch's of July 8) and to Cyrus Babb of the Reclamation Service on July 12, Department of the Interior, Records of the Bureau of Indian Affairs, RG 75, Fort Belknap Indian Agency Papers, box 57, "Miscellaneous Letters Sent, 1904–06," Regional Archives, Seattle.

8. The court file does not include a transcript of the July 17 hearing, so I do not know precisely what was presented on that day. But the file does include written statements from the various defendants submitted for the hearing to show cause, as well as a summary of the testimony from witnesses for the

federal government: Affidavit of Cal Shuler, foreman of Empire Cattle Company (July 11, 1905); Affidavit of D. E. Martin (July 11, 1905); Affidavit of J. S. Roberts (July 11, 1905); Affidavit of John Matheson, director, Matheson Ditch Company (July 12, 1905); Affidavit of Thomas Dowen (July 12, 1905); Affidavit of John Prosser (July 12, 1905); Affidavit of John Acher (July 12, 1905); Response of Henry Winter (July 12, 1905); Response of Empire Cattle Company (July 15, 1905); Response of James Cook, president, Cook's Irrigation Company (July 17, 1905); Objection by Cook's Irrigation Company (July 17, 1905); Affidavit of N. A. Sharpless (July 17, 1905); Response by Cook's Irrigation Company (no date; apparently July 17, 1905); Response of Andrew Reser, et al. (no date; apparently July 17, 1905); Summary of Testimony W. R. Logan, C. T. Prall, and Thomas Everett (no date; apparently July 17, 1905), all in the files of *United States v. Mose Anderson, et al.,* Records of the U.S. District Courts, RG 21, U.S. Ninth Circuit, District of Montana, box 6659, folder 747, Regional Archives, Seattle. Another source for understanding the evidence presented, especially regarding the amount of water the government actually required and could use on the reservation, was the injunction order issued by the judge one month later, Order issuing injunction, August 8, 1905, also in the files of *United States v. Mose Anderson, et al.* See also the brief description of the July 17 hearing, with no comment, in *North Montana Review,* July 22, 1905. Most of the defendants were represented by the same attorneys, Edward Day of the Helena firm of Day, Carpenter, Day and Carpenter, joined by Thomas Walsh of Walsh and Newman in Helena.

9. Memorandum Order, August 7, 1905, in the files of *United States v. Mose Anderson, et al.,* Records of the U.S. District Courts, RG 21, U.S. Ninth Circuit, District of Montana, box 6659, folder 747, Regional Archives, Seattle. I have quoted the ruling in full here partly because the lower court ruling in the *Winters* case is not reported in any official court reports.

10. Order issuing injunction, August 8, 1905, in the files of *United States v. Mose Anderson, et al.,* Records of the U.S. District Courts, RG 21, U.S. Ninth Circuit, District of Montana, box 6659, folder 747, Regional Archives, Seattle. One of the ironies of the *Winters* case, and an indication of the problems even the federal government had in implementing the concept of treaty reserved water rights, is the fact that not many years later Department of the Interior officials could be found insisting that the 5,000 miner's inches from the Milk River that Judge Hunt clearly intended to be the *minimum* to which the reservation was entitled was instead the *maximum* that the Indians were entitled to out of the river. See among other sources for this tale, Hundley, "'Winters' Decision and Indian Water Rights," 40–42.

11. Defendants' Assignments of Errors, no date but apparently August 14, 1905, in the files of *United States v. Mose Anderson, et al.,* Records of the U.S. District Courts, RG 21, U.S. Ninth Circuit, District of Montana, box 6659, folder 747, Regional Archives, Seattle; C. Rasch to the attorney general, August 28, 1905, Department of Justice, Records of the Department of Justice, RG 60, box 221, file 58730 (records of the *Winters* case), National Archives.

12. Hundley, "'Winters' Decision and Indian Water Rights," 27; two newspaper editions that Hundley cited for the reaction in the area upstream of the reservation were the *Havre Herald,* August 11, 1905, and the *Havre Plaindealer,* August 19, 1905.

13. The following description of the local context surrounding the *Winters* case is based primarily on a review of newspapers from the communities along the Milk River between the years 1903 to 1910. These papers include, in geographical order as one moves downstream, the *Havre Herald, Havre Plaindealer, Chinook Bulletin, Chinook Opinion* (both Havre and Chinook are above the reservation), *Milk River Valley News* (Harlem—which is just north across the river from the reservation), *Enterprise* (Malta—approximately twenty miles downstream from the eastern edge of the reservation), *Montana Homestead* (Hinsdale—another forty miles downstream), and the *North Montana Review* (Glasgow—thirty more miles downstream, and the last major community on the Milk River before it joins the Missouri River in northeastern Montana). I also looked at one of the Helena papers, the *Helena Independent.* Other primary sources include Montana Senate Joint Memorial No. 2, Montana Legislative Assembly, 1905 Session, Montana Laws 1905, 354, and Senate Joint Memorial No. 1 (February 26, 1907), Montana Legislative Assembly, 1907 Session, Montana Laws 1907, 590–91; the court records for the *Winters* case, that is, the files of *United States v. Mose Anderson, et al.,* Records of the U.S. District Courts, RG 21, U.S. Ninth Circuit, District of Montana, box 6659, folder 747, Regional Archives, Seattle, and the relevant correspondence and agricultural and irrigation records for the reservation, Department of the Interior, Records of the Bureau of Indian Affairs, RG 75, Fort Belknap Indian Agency Papers, boxes 11, 18–22, 52, 57, 59, 359, and 365, Regional Archives, Seattle. I have tried to find relevant letters and other manuscript records from residents along the Milk River, without any success except where the letters ended up in the reservation records.

14. Stories about the Reclamation project, the need and prospects for a water rights adjudication suit, and related issues could be found in most editions of the various newspapers in the valley in all relevant years, from 1904 to 1908 and beyond. A few of the major stories (virtually every edition of some of these newspapers had a reference to the Reclamation project or a closely associated issue) in the time leading up to and through the first part of the *Winters* litigation in 1905 and early 1906 (the lower court and appellate court rulings) include the *North Montana Review,* April 22, 29, May 6, 20, June 3, 10, July 8, August 5, 19, September 9, 30, December 30, 1905, January 20, March 3, 10, 31, May 12, June 16, June 30, 1906; *Milk River Valley News,* June 21, July 5, August 9, 23, September 13, 20, October 11, 1905, January 3, 17, February 21, 28, March 15, 22, April 12, 19, May 3, 10, 24, 31, June 7, 28, 1906; *Enterprise,* August 16, October 18, 1905, January 24, April 4, May 23, 1906; *Montana Homestead,* August 4, September 8, October 13, 1905.

15. *Milk River Valley News,* August 9, 1905.

16. Boundary Waters Treaty, art. 6, 36 Stat. 2448, 2451 (signed January 11, 1909; ratified by Senate March 3, 1909). During irrigation season, understood as between April 1 and October 31, the treaty allocated three-fourths of the Saint Mary's natural flow to Canada and three-fourths of the natural flow of the Milk to the United States. Examples of news stories describing the developing problem with Canada over the Milk River are *North Montana Review,* May 6, 20, 1905, January 20, June 16, 1906, February 22, 1908; *Milk River Valley News,* September 20, December 30, 1905, January 17, 1906, July 4, 20, August 29, 1907, February 20, 27, 1908; *Enterprise,* January 24, July 18, 1906, February 12, June 5, July 3, 1907.

17. *Montana Homestead,* October 13, 1905.

18. See, for example, the June 10, 1907, resolution from the executive committee of the United Milk River Irrigation Association addressed to the Secretary of Interior, printed in *Enterprise,* June 12, 1907, and *Milk River Valley News,* June 13, 1907.

19. See, for example, the news stories on the filing of the *Winters* suit in the *Milk River Valley News,* July 5, 1905; *Montana Homestead,* July 7, 1905; *North Montana Review,* July 8, 1905; and also the *Helena Independent,* July 8, 1905; the very brief mention of the July 17 show-cause hearing on the injunction in the *North Montana Review,* July 8, 1905; and news stories on Judge Hunt's injunction in the *Milk River Valley News,* August 9, 1905; *Enterprise,* August 9, 1905; *Montana Homestead,* August 11, 1905 (a long story simply quoting Judge Hunt's order); *North Montana Review,* August 12, 1905 (a bare mention); and also the *Helena Independent,* August 11, 1905.

20. *Milk River Valley News,* January 23, 1908, quoted in Hundley, "'Winters' Decision and Indian Water Rights," 37.

21. *Milk River Valley News* July 26, 1905.

22. *Montana Homestead* August 18, 1905.

23. *Enterprise,* August 16, 1905 (emphasis added).

24. *North Montana Review,* August 19, 1905.

25. *Milk River Valley News,* January 9, 1908.

26. Ibid. (emphasis added). I did not find Mondak on Montana maps. Mondak, Montana, was a "quiet village" on the Missouri River at the North Dakota border, near Fort Union and "ideally situated" on the Great Northern Railway line. The Post Office operated from 1904 to 1925. It was a planned community and, apparently, an important railroad stop for a short period of time. Mondak was named for its proximity to the Montana–North Dakota border. From Cheney, *Names on the Face of Montana,* 189, from John Harrison, personal communication, December 18, 1996.

27. *Montana Homestead,* January 17, 1908.

28. C. Rasch to W. R. Logan, July 8, 1905, Department of the Interior, Records of the Bureau of Indian Affairs, RG 75, Fort Belknap Indian Agency Papers, box 52, "Miscellaneous Letters Received, 1902–05," Regional Archives, Seattle.

29. C. Babb, Reclamation Service engineer, to W. R. Logan, July 10, 1905 (emphasis added), Department of the Interior, Records of the Bureau of Indian Affairs, RG 75, Fort Belknap Indian Agency Papers, box 52, "Miscellaneous Letters Received, 1902–05," Regional Archives, Seattle.

30. W. R. Logan to C. Babb, July 12, 1905, box 57, "Miscellaneous Letters Sent, 1904–06"; C. Rasch to W. R. Logan, July 13 1905, and C. Babb to W. R. Logan, July 15, 1905, box 52, "Miscellaneous Letters Received, 1902–05," Department of the Interior, Records of the Bureau of Indian Affairs, RG 75, Fort Belknap Indian Agency Papers, Regional Archives, Seattle; C. Rasch to the attorney general, August 28, 1905, Department of Justice, Records of the Department of Justice, RG 60, box 221, file 58730 (records of the *Winters* case), National Archives.

31. W. R. Logan to C. Rasch, July 11, 1905, Department of the Interior, Records of the Bureau of Indian Affairs, RG 75, Fort Belknap Indian Agency Papers, box 57, "Miscellaneous Letters Sent, 1904–06," Regional Archives, Seattle.

32. W. R. Logan to C. Babb, July 12, 1905, Department of the Interior, Records of the Bureau of Indian Affairs, RG 75, Fort Belknap Indian Agency Papers, box 57, "Miscellaneous Letters Sent, 1904–06," Regional Archives, Seattle.

33. Ibid.

34. C. Babb to W. R. Logan, July 15, 1905, Department of the Interior, Records of the Bureau of Indian Affairs, RG 75, Fort Belknap Indian Agency Papers, box 52, "Miscellaneous Letters Received, 1902–05," Regional Archives, Seattle.

CHAPTER 4: *WINTERS* IN THE FEDERAL COURT OF APPEALS

1. Discussions of the attitude of early Reclamation Service officials toward western water law and the riparian doctrine (and toward the *Winters* decisions) can be found in Pisani, "State v. Nation" and "Irrigation, Water Rights, and Betrayal." On the relationship between Bureau of Reclamation water projects and Indian water projects, see McCool, *Command of the Waters;* see also Burton, *American Indian Water Rights.*

2. C. Rasch to the attorney general, August 28, 1905, Department of Justice, Records of the Department of Justice, RG 60, box 221, file 58730 (records of the *Winters* case), National Archives.

3. Ibid.

4. Ibid. Note that Superintendent Logan's annual report for the Fort Belknap reservation, submitted to the commissioner of Indian affairs on September 1, 1905 (just after the court's ruling), implied by omission that the case was not only filed but also won as a prior appropriation claim against subsequent appropriators. It is not clear if Logan was not aware of or did not understand the basis for the ruling or if he was simply ignoring that point to

stress the victory. W. R. Logan to commissioner of Indian affairs, Annual Report, September 1, 1905, Department of the Interior, Records of the Bureau of Indian Affairs, RG 75, Fort Belknap Indian Agency Papers, box 20, "Letters Sent—Commissioner of Indian Affairs, 1902–07," Regional Archives, Seattle; reprinted as an attachment to the 1905 *Annual Report of the Commissioner of Indian Affairs,* H. Doc No. 5, 59th Cong., 1st Sess. (September 30, 1905), 243–44.

5. Brief of the Appellee, submitted by Carl Rasch, U. S. attorney (no date; presumably late 1905), *Winters v. United States,* United States Circuit Court of Appeals for the Ninth Circuit, Case No. 1243, in Department of Justice, Records of the Department of Justice, RG 60, box 221, file 58730 (records of the *Winters* case), National Archives.

6. The best if brief discussion of how the views of the Reclamation Service directed the United States' intervention into the *Kansas v. Colorado* case is Pisani, "State v. Nation." The positions of Kansas, Colorado, and the United States can be seen in the Court's decision, *Kansas v. Colorado,* 206 U.S. 46 (1907), and in the briefs for the parties in the Supreme Court's records, and are discussed in a huge load of Interior and Justice Department documents from the time, such as a memorandum to the solicitor general from the assistant attorney general (assigned to the Department of the Interior at the time), Frank L. Campbell (undated but sometime around December 18, 1905), in the Department of the Interior, Records of the Bureau of Reclamation, RG 115, file 762, "Legal Discussions—General," National Archives. The United States also argued in *Kansas v. Colorado* that the federal government, by virtue of its supreme authority over the public lands and waters and for the purposes expressed in the Reclamation Act, had the right to control—essentially, reserve—sufficient unused water in interstate river basins to reclaim the arid public lands. Reclamation officials focused on the threat of the *Winters* litigation to undermine its position on riparian rights in the *Kansas v. Colorado* litigation, ignoring the possible utility of *Winters* to their argument concerning federal reservations of water to serve identified needs on federal lands.

7. Anonymous and undated memorandum on the *Winters* case in the Department of the Interior, Records of the Bureau of Reclamation, RG 115, file 762, "Legal Discussions—General," National Archives. The copy of the memorandum in the Reclamation files does not state that it came from someone in the Department of Justice, but references in the memorandum to actions of "this Department" indicate its origin. And while the memorandum is undated, references in the memorandum date it somewhere between September 1905 and January 1906, and it was found in the company of documents on this subject from December 1905.

8. "Conflicting attitude Dept. Justice on Irrigation matters," December 8, 1905, Department of the Interior, Records of the Bureau of Reclamation, RG 115, file 762, "Legal Discussions—General," National Archives. Emphasis in the original. A copy of the memorandum can also be found in the Department of Justice files. The name of the author is not on the memorandum, but it is so characteristic of Morris Bien that I have attributed it to him, as did Pisani.

9. I have not yet discussed the Yakima situation and do not propose to do so here at any length because in 1905 it had not yet developed into much and does not appear to have had any influence on the course of the *Winters* case other than Bien's worried linkage. To the contrary, the Yakima water rights story, which became one of the best known of the Indian water rights problems in the West, is a useful case study of the degree of influence of the *Winters* decisions on an existing Indian water rights conflict, and will be discussed elsewhere for that reason. Documents besides Bien's discussing the Yakima situation as part of this late-1905 tempest include the "Memorandum Relative to Cases Involving Water Rights of Indians in Montana and Washington," from an unidentified assistant attorney general and undated but written sometime between December 11 and December 15, 1905, from the Department of Justice, Records of the Department of Justice, RG 60, box 221, file 58730 (records of the *Winters* case), National Archives, and the "Memorandum" to the Solicitor General from Assistant Attorney General Campbell (undated but sometime around December 15, 1905), in the Department of the Interior, Records of the Bureau of Reclamation, RG 115, file 762, "Legal Discussions— General," National Archives. Discussions of the Yakima water issues may be found in Leibhardt, "Law, Environment, and Social Change."

10. I have not found a copy of the president's note or request, but reference is made to it in responding documents, including a letter from the attorney general to the president, December 18, 1905; what appears to be a draft of that letter dated December 15; and the "Memorandum Relative to Cases Involving Water Rights of Indians in Montana and Washington," from an unnamed assistant attorney general and undated but written between December 11 and December 15, 1905, as it became the basis for the attorney general's letter, in the Department of Justice, Records of the Department of Justice, RG 60, box 221, file 58730 (records of the *Winters* case), National Archives.

11. "Memorandum Relative to Cases Involving Water Rights of Indians in Montana and Washington," Department of Justice, Records of the Department of Justice, RG 60, box 221, file 58730 (records of the *Winters* case), National Archives. A copy is also in the Bureau of Reclamation records. In the top left-hand corner of the first page is "D. D. C.", presumably the initials of the author.

12. Campbell, assistant attorney general, memorandum titled "The State of Kansas v. the State of Colorado et al., the United States, Intervenor: Statement of Frank L. Campbell, Assistant Attorney General for the Interior Department, in response to the request from the Solicitor General in regard to the attitude of the Government in the above case," undated but sometime on or shortly before December 15, 1905, in the Department of the Interior, Records of the Bureau of Reclamation, RG 115, file 762, "Legal Discussions—General," National Archives.

13. Ibid.

14. Ibid.

15. Draft letter by H. Hoyt, solicitor general, for attorney general to the president, December 15, 1905, in the Department of Justice, Records of the Department of Justice, RG 60, box 221, file 58730 (records of the *Winters* case), National Archives. Nothing on the letter actually identifies it as a draft or as prepared by the solicitor general, but the subsequent letter from the attorney general, dated December 18, indicates that it was both.

16. Ibid.

17. Attorney general to the president, December 18, 1905, in the Department of Justice, Records of the Department of Justice, RG 60, box 221, file 58730 (records of the *Winters* case), National Archives. Note that Moody was soon to be on the Supreme Court, appointed in 1906, and would join the Court's opinion in *Winters* in 1908.

18. "Conflicting Attitude of the Department of Justice on Irrigation Matters," December 20, 1905, in the Department of the Interior, Records of the Bureau of Reclamation, RG 115, file 762, "Legal Discussions—General," National Archives. Again, there is nothing in the document to establish that it was written by Bien, but it is clearly by the same author as the first unsigned memorandum on the "conflicting attitude" of the Department of Justice, and both seem very characteristic of Bien.

19. I did not find a copy of this request from the president, either, but it is referred to in the response of the secretary of the interior to the president, described below.

20. Secretary of the interior to the president, January 5, 1906, in the Department of Justice, Records of the Department of Justice, RG 60, box 221, file 58730 (records of the *Winters* case), National Archives. Presumably there is also a copy in the Department of the Interior records.

21. *Winters v. United States,* 143 F. 740, 741–49.

22. For descriptions of Judges Gilbert and Ross, see Frederick's history of the Ninth Circuit, *Rugged Justice.*

23. *Winters v. United States,* 143 F. at 745–46.

24. *Winters v. United States,* at 747–49.

25. *Winters v. United States,* at 749.

26. D. D. C., assistant attorney general, to H. Hoyt, solicitor general, February 6, 1906; acting attorney general to the president, February 6, 1906; E. A. Hitchcock, secretary of the interior, to the attorney general, March 6, 1906; F. E. Leupp, commissioner of Indian affairs, to the secretary of the interior, April 3, 1906; and W. J. Hughes, attorney general(?), to H. Hoyt, solicitor general, January 17, 1907, all in the Department of Justice, Records of the Department of Justice, RG 60, box 221, file 58730 (records of the *Winters* case), National Archives.

27. *Kansas v. Colorado,* 206 U.S. 46, 85–95 (1907). Much has been written about the decision, mostly in the legal field. For the best discussion by a historian see Pisani, "State v. Nation," 276–82. The files of the Bureau of Reclamation and of the Interior and Justice Departments are full of documents analyzing, puzzling over, arguing about, anguishing over, or dismissing the *Kansas v. Colorado* opinion.

28. One might expect to find articles in the law reviews and related journals of the time regarding the *Winters* decision, yet the legal periodical indexes for the years 1905 to 1915, which list many articles on water law issues (e.g., a large number of articles on the federal-state relationship with regard to water generated by the *Kansas v. Colorado* litigation and other events) and a few on Indian law, do not include any articles specifically on the *Winters* case or the reserved rights doctrine (in contrast to the dozens that show up in modern times). None of the law journal articles on water law issues even mention *Winters* before 1915, at least not as far as I could find. See *Index to Legal Periodicals,* vols. 1–8 (1908–15); Chipman, *Index to Legal Periodical Literature,* vol. 3 (*1898–1908*); vol. 4 (*1908–22*). Looking well into the 1920s, the only two law review articles I could find (one in 1915, one in 1919) that mentioned the *Winters* case discussed it briefly as part of a series of cases on the federal-state relationship in water law. Bannister, "Question of Federal Disposition of State Waters," 281; Chandler, "Title to Non-navigable Waters," 126. The reasons for the legal writers' neglect of *Winters* are not clear but do reemphasize that the holding was not seen as that exceptional or novel and that the *Winters* case was lost among the main water conflicts and issues of the time—the issues surrounding the implementation of the Reclamation Act; efforts at comprehensive navigable waterway development (discussed in Samuel Hays's book *Conservation and the Gospel of Efficiency*); the interstate stream allocation cases such as *Kansas v. Colorado* and *Wyoming v. Colorado;* 259 U.S. 419 (decided in the 1920s); related efforts at interstate agreements for river allocation (such as eventually resulted in the Colorado River Compact in the mid-1920s); and the fight over control of the hydropower potential and flood waters of the western rivers, culminating in the Federal Power Act of 1920 and federal project authorizations such as for the Boulder Canyon Dam Project (later Hoover Dam) in the 1920s. The answer cannot be that water lawyers were unaware of the *Winters* decisions or their implications. As noted elsewhere, the two prominent western water law treatises from the period—forms of writing intended for practitioners, not academics—do both mention and make use of *Winters,* although neither gives the case an extended discussion. Both writers understood that *Winters* not only had implications for Indian reservations outside Montana, but also that the doctrine could apply to non-Indian federal reserved lands, such as forest reserves. Wiel, *Water Rights in the Western States,* 1:147–48, 158, 175–77, 215–17, 236–43, 2:1275; Kinney, *Treatise on the Law of Irrigation,* 657–60, 664–66, 684, 690–93, 813–15, 1091–92, 1098–1105, 1112–24, 1159–61, and esp. 2290–92. And it cannot be because lawyers and policy people were not using the *Winters* case in litigation and as the basis for policy actions. As I discuss below, the federal government's lawyers and some policymakers were quite well versed in the *Winters* case and made significant use of it, especially after 1912. But discussions of *Winters* that went beyond litigation or practical policy were rare. Certainly, if the doctrine had been at the center of legal debate, people would have been more aware of the specific issues and details related to it. Most in government and in Congress were

markedly ignorant about the meaning and details of the *Winters* decisions, as will be seen.

29. Justice Brewer, who wrote the opinion in *Kansas v. Colorado,* must have thought that *Winters* was a turn away from the correct path—he was the only dissenter to the *Winters* decision, although he did not write a dissenting opinion. Three members of the *Winters* majority had not joined Brewer's *Kansas v. Colorado* opinion the year before: Justice Joseph McKenna, who subsequently wrote the *Winters* opinion, and Justice Edward White had agreed with the result but refused to agree to Brewer's opinion; while Justice Moody, did not take part in that decision. Brewer's opinion in *Kansas v. Colorado* is long and full of a number of, frankly, crazy things, including a rather bizarre reworked version of the late-nineteenth-century "rain-follows-the-plow" theory, a brief but strange digression to talk about the Hudson and Missouri Rivers in the middle of a discussion of the Arkansas (the Hudson must have been a favorite of Brewer's, as there is an even weirder digression about it in the *Rio Grande* case), and other oddities. So it is no surprise that a Court member might have approved of the basic decision in *Kansas v. Colorado* but not joined Brewer's opinion, or might even have joined the opinion but not felt too bound by any of the specific language on any issue, including Brewer's discussion of the idea of federal control over water. It is not hard to agree with Brewer's conclusion in *Kansas v. Colorado* that the federal government did not have the kind of plenary control over water allocation argued by the federal government. Beyond that point the opinion is more murky and inconsistent on what authority the federal government did have than has been supposed. For example, on the one hand, Brewer directly quoted, without challenge, his language from *Rio Grande* about how the state cannot destroy the right of the United States to the continued flow of water as necessary for the beneficial use of government property bordering the stream, at 86; but later, at 92, he seems to be saying that the federal government would be subject to state law for the same purpose. The contradiction is hard to reconcile, unless Brewer was simply trying to make sure that specific authority regarding water for specific public lands bordering a stream could not be converted into a general and full control over water in the West just because public lands existed in the West. It is not surprising then that McKenna, in the *Winters* opinion, completely ignored Brewer's opinion in *Kansas v. Colorado* and returned to *Rio Grande* and *Winans* for the principles he wanted to assert as authority.

30. The judges on the Ninth Circuit Court of Appeals understood right after *Winters* the broader significance of *Winters* for Reclamation projects and other efforts by the federal government to control water. See, e.g., *Burley v. United States,* 179 F. 1, 1–13, esp. 12 (9th Cir., 1910). So did Samuel Wiel and C. S. Kinney, the two prominent water law scholars and treatise writers of the time. Wiel, *Water Rights in the Western States,* 1:147–48, 158, 175–77, 215–17, 236–43, 2:1275; Kinney, *Treatise on the Law of Irrigation,* 657–60, 664–66, 684, 690–93, 813–15, 1091–92, 1098–1105, 1112–24, 1159–61, and esp. 2290–92. For examples of how Department of Justice attorneys, beginning especially with

Ethelbert Ward, John F. Truesdell, and others in the Denver field office who worked on both Indian water rights cases and Reclamation cases, began using *Winters* as part of their justification for Reclamation actions to reserve water in watersheds for Reclamation projects, see "Brief of the United States," June 1913, filed by Ethelbert Ward, Department of Justice attorney in the Denver field office, on behalf of the Reclamation Service in the water rights adjudication proceedings for the Uncompahgre Valley Project in the District Court, Seventh Judicial District, Colorado, Department of the Interior, Records of the Bureau of Reclamation, RG 115, Regional Archives, Seattle; *Annual Report of the Attorney General of the United States for the Year 1914,* printed as H. Doc. 1390, 63rd Cong., 3d Sess., U.S. Serial Set 6810; A. M. Stevenson, attorney, Denver, to Harry M. Daugherty, attorney general, October 10, 1921, in the personnel folder of John F. Truesdell, special assistant to the attorney general, Department of Justice, National Personnel Records Center, St. Louis; "Opening Brief of Plaintiff" and "Corrected Decree" (no date, but apparently 1925 or not long after) in *United States v. Angle,* et al., United States District Court for the Northern District of California, Case No. 30, in Department of the Interior, Bureau of Indian Affairs, Records of the Bureau of Indian Affairs, RG 75, Irrigation Branch, box 779, folder 200, "Irrigation Reports, 1909–42," Regional Archives, Seattle (adjudication of water rights in Stony Creek and tributaries in Northern California; United States brought claims both for the Orland, California, Reclamation project and for Grindstone Creek Indian Rancheria Reservation); and the description of the government's arguments about federal control of water with regard to Reclamation activities in *Mower v. Bond,* 8 F.2d 518, 519–20 (D. Idaho, 1925), and *North Side Canal Company v. Twin Falls Canal Company,* 12 F.2d. 311, 311–14 (D. Idaho, 1926). Law review articles by Bannister and Chandler at the time both explained *Winters* as one of a group of decisions emphasizing federal authority to control water in the West that contrasted with at least the spirit of the *Kansas v. Colorado* decision and with another group of decisions emphasizing state control at the expense of the federal government. Bannister, a Colorado attorney who represented the State of Colorado in water litigation and who supported full state sovereignty over water, thought this a bad thing; Chandler, who represented the federal government in litigation, took the opposite view. Bannister, "Question of Federal Disposition of State Waters"; Chandler, "Title to Non-navigable Waters," 109–10, 126, 129–30.

31. For example, Reclamation officials, once they got over their relief that *Winters* was not about riparian rights, decided for a while to be squeamish about the impact of Indian treaty reserved rights for many of the same reasons, despite the fact that attorneys in the Department of Justice working on behalf of Reclamation soon realized how useful the ruling could be to justify Reclamation's needs. The best, though far from the only, example of this comes from a report in the name of William Taft's secretary of the interior, Walter Fisher, in 1913, apparently written by Reclamation personnel, opposing the application of the reserved rights doctrine at the Yakima Indian Reservation, in Washington:

[Acceptance of the reserved rights theory would mean that the Yakimas] acquired a vested right in the water flowing in the Yakima River, which is undetermined, and must forever remain undeterminable as to quantity; for it is contended that it is to be measured at any given time by what then appears to be the duty of water for that area, of which, from the economic and engineering standpoint, it is then feasible to irrigate; that it must be measured 50 years hence by what then appears the duty of water for the area which it then appears feasible to irrigate, and so for any point of time in the future. This would make it impossible to measure the future water rights of the Indians at any future time; would prevent all irrigation development outside of the Indian reservation; and would amount to a reservation of the total flow of the river, without any obligation on the part of the Indians to utilize the water, which might then flow forever unused to the sea. H. Doc. No. 1299, 63rd Cong, 2d Sess. (January 23, 1913), quoted at 51 *Cong. Rec.* 1264 (December 19, 1913).

Similar words to these have come countless times from western water development interests in the years since the first decision in *Winters,* such as the 1914 remarks from Representative Mondell quoted above. It is interesting to note how many times opponents of the reserved rights doctrine lamented that because of these rights water might flow "unused to the sea," a particularly scary possibility to those who believed in western development based on intensive use of water diverted from the stream.

32. This is a prominent theme in essentially all the writings on the *Winters* doctrine, including the works by McCool, Burton, Hundley, Massie, and Pisani cited in this study.

CHAPTER 5: BACK IN THE MILK RIVER VALLEY, 1905–1907

1. Decree, April 21, 1906, in the files of *United States v. Mose Anderson, et al.,* Records of the U.S. District Courts, RG 21, U.S. Ninth Circuit, District of Montana, box 6659, folder 747, Regional Archives, Seattle; affirmed by the Ninth Circuit Court of Appeals in *Winters v. United States,* 148 F. 684, 685–86; *North Montana Review,* January 11, 1908; Hundley, "'Winters' Decision and Indian Water Rights," 36–37, 40–42, quoting the *Chinook Opinion,* January 9, 1908; and W. R. Logan to C. F. Ellis and Company., October 4, 1908, Department of the Interior, Records of the Bureau of Indian Affairs, RG 75, Fort Belknap Indian Agency Papers, box 59, Regional Archives, Seattle (I could not find the letter to confirm). The irony of the Fort Belknap reservation getting locked into a 5,000-inch yearly maximum, which is inconsistent with the basic principles of the reserved rights doctrine, has been noted in a number of articles in the legal field and also by Hundley.

2. Decree, April 21, 1906, and Defendants' Assignment of Errors, April 28, 1906, in the files of *United States v. Mose Anderson, et al.,* Records of the U.S.

NOTES TO PAGES 104–109

District Courts, RG 21, U.S. Ninth Circuit, District of Montana, box 6659, folder 747, Regional Archives, Seattle; *Winters v. United States,* 148 F. 684, 685–86; *affirmed,* 207 U.S. 564; *Havre Herald,* February 9, 16, 1906; *Havre Plaindealer,* March 3, May 19, 26, 1906; *Chinook Opinion,* February 15, 22, March 1, 1906; *Milk River Valley News,* February 7, 14, 21, 1906; *Montana Homestead,* February 9, 1906; *North Montana Review,* February 17, 1906; see also Hundley, "'Winters' Decision and Indian Water Rights," 31–33.

3. W. R. Logan, Fort Belknap reservation superintendent, to C. Babb, Reclamation Service engineer, February 7, 1906 (emphasis in the original), Department of the Interior, Records of the Bureau of Indian Affairs, RG 75, Fort Belknap Indian Agency Papers, box 57, "Miscellaneous Letters Sent, 1904–06," Regional Archives, Seattle; W. R. Logan to C. Rasch, U.S. attorney, February 7, 1906, box 57, "Miscellaneous Letters Sent, 1904–06"; W. R. Logan to commissioner of Indian affairs, February 17, 1906, box 20, "Letters Sent— Commissioner of Indian Affairs 1902–07," in Department of the Interior, Records of the Bureau of Indian Affairs, RG 75, Fort Belknap Indian Agency Papers, Regional Archives, Seattle.

4. The news stories concerning or mentioning the Ninth Circuit's decision in *Winters* were the *Havre Herald,* February 9, 16, 1906; *Havre Plaindealer,* March 3, May 19, 26, 1906; *Chinook Opinion,* February 15, 22, March 1, 1906; *Milk River Valley News,* February 7, 14, 21, 1906; *Montana Homestead,* February 9, 1906; *North Montana Review,* February 17, 1906; see also Hundley, "'Winters' Decision and Indian Water Rights," 31–33. For an example of some of the news stories around the same time on Reclamation project issues, see *North Montana Review,* December 30, 1905, January 20, March 3, 10, 31, May 12, June 9, June 30, July 7, August 18, November 21, December 8, 15, 1906; *Milk River Valley News,* January 3, 17, February 14, 28, March 15, 22, April 19, May 3, 10, 24, 31, June 7, 28, July 12, December 13, 1906; *Enterprise,* January 24, April 4, May 23, July 18, December 10, 1906.

5. W. R. Logan to commissioner of Indian affairs, April 5, 1906, box 20, "Letters Sent—Commissioner of Indian Affairs 1902–07"; W. R. Logan to Matheson Ditch Company, to Paradise Valley Ditch Company, to Anderson Ditch Company, to Cook Ditch Company, to Empire Cattle Company, to Belknap Ditch Company, and to Harlem Ditch Company, all on April 5, 1906; Russell Ratliff, chief clerk, Fort Belknap reservation, to W. B. Freeman, Chinook, April 7, 1906, all in box 57, "Miscellaneous Letters Sent, 1904–06," Department of the Interior, Records of the Bureau of Indian Affairs, RG 75, Fort Belknap Indian Agency Papers, Regional Archives, Seattle.

6. W. R. Logan to commissioner of Indian affairs, April 16, 1907, Department of the Interior, Records of the Bureau of Indian Affairs, RG 75, Fort Belknap Indian Agency Papers, box 20, "Letters Sent—Commissioner of Indian Affairs 1902–07," Regional Archives, Seattle.

7. Ibid.

8. W. R. Logan to A. H. Reser, Chinook, April 25, 1906, W. R. Logan to Reser, April 18, 1906; W. R. Logan to C. Babb, April 19, 1906, Department of

the Interior, Records of the Bureau of Indian Affairs, RG 75, Fort Belknap Indian Agency Papers, box 57, "Miscellaneous Letters Sent, 1904–06," Regional Archives, Seattle.

9. W. R. Logan to W. B. Freeman, Chinook, May 19, 1906, Department of the Interior, Records of the Bureau of Indian Affairs, RG 75, Fort Belknap Indian Agency Papers, box 57, "Miscellaneous Letters Sent, 1904–06," Regional Archives, Seattle.

10. W. R. Logan to C. Babb, June 4, 1906, Department of the Interior, Records of the Bureau of Indian Affairs, RG 75, Fort Belknap Indian Agency Papers, box 58, "Miscellaneous Letters Sent, 1906–08," Regional Archives, Seattle.

11. W. R. Logan to Thomas M. Evarts, Harlem, May 29, 1906, W. R. Logan to C. Babb, June 4, 1906, Department of the Interior, Records of the Bureau of Indian Affairs, RG 75, Fort Belknap Indian Agency Papers, box 58, "Miscellaneous Letters Sent, 1906–08," Regional Archives, Seattle; *Milk River Valley News,* May 10, 1906.

12. W. R. Logan to commissioner of Indian affairs, June 12, 1906, Department of the Interior, Records of the Bureau of Indian Affairs, RG 75, Fort Belknap Indian Agency Papers, box 20, "Letters Sent—Commissioner of Indian Affairs, 1902–07," Regional Archives, Seattle.

13. *Enterprise,* February 12, April 10, April 17, May 1, 1907. One other indication that 1907 was a good water year was the *absence* in Logan's 1907 correspondence files of letters in which he is trying to implement the decree, threatening to sue, pleading for help, and the like. But before the 1907 season began, Logan was still upset about the way the upstream irrigators treated him and the court's ruling during the 1906 season, as he made known in a letter to the commissioner of Indian affairs: "At no time during the [1906] season, except during the flood time, did we have the full 5000 inches of water in our ditch as the whites above us were constantly 'sniping' a little from time to time, respecting the injunction just enough to keep from being caught." W. R. Logan to commissioner of Indian affairs, February 14, 1907, Department of the Interior, Records of the Bureau of Indian Affairs, RG 75, Fort Belknap Indian Agency Papers, box 20, "Letters Sent—Commissioner of Indian Affairs, 1902–07, Regional Archives, Seattle.

14. *Milk River Valley News,* May 10, June 7, July 12, 1906.

15. Sources relevant to the 1906–07 effort to strip land from the Fort Belknap reservation include S. 3000, 59th Cong., 1st Sess. (January 10, 1906); W. R. Logan to commissioner of Indian affairs, April 5, 7, and 29, 1906, and February 14, 1907, Department of the Interior, Records of the Bureau of Indian Affairs, RG 75, Fort Belknap Indian Agency Papers, box 20, "Letters Sent—commissioner of Indian affairs, 1902–07, Regional Archives, Seattle; *Milk River Valley News,* August 30, September 6, 1905, January 17, February 28, May 10, 1906, February 7, 1907; *Enterprise,* January 17, 24, 1906; Senate Joint Memorial No. 1 (February 26, 1907), Montana Legislative Assembly, 1907 Session, Montana Laws 1907, 590–91; Barry, *Fort Belknap Indian Reservation,* 129; McCool, *Command of the Waters,* 51–52.

16. S. 3000, 59th Cong., 1st Sess. (January 10, 1906); see *Milk River Valley News,* January 17, 1906. While the Fifty-ninth Congress was elected in November 1904, and the Senate met briefly in special session in March 1905 to act on presidential appointments, in the usual practice of the time the true first session of the Fifty-ninth Congress did not begin until December 1905, more than a year after the election. That explains why a bill introduced seemingly as late as January 1906 was in reality early in the first session of that Congress.

17. W. R. Logan to commissioner of Indian affairs, April 5, 7, and 29, 1906, box 20, "Letters Sent—Commissioner of Indian Affairs, 1902–07," W. R. Logan to commissioner of Indian affairs, August 10, 1907, box 21, "Letters Sent—Commissioner of Indian Affairs, 1907–11," Department of the Interior, Records of the Bureau of Indian Affairs, RG 75, Fort Belknap Indian Agency Papers, Regional Archives, Seattle.

18. McCool, *Command of the Waters,* 51–52. McCool also noted that the white farmers enlisted the aid of James J. Hill, the powerful railroad magnate, to press for the reservation land sale bill, to no avail.

19. Sources for the next five paragraphs of text on the sugar beet developments include W. R. Logan to Judge Henry Rolapp, secretary-treasurer, Amalgamated Sugar Company, January 24, 1906, W. R. Logan to commissioner of Indian affairs, March 4, 1907, both in box 57, "Miscellaneous Letters Sent, 1904–06"; W. R. Logan to commissioner of Indian affairs, April 29 and November 8, 1906, March 4, 1907, in box 20, "Letters Sent—Commissioner of Indian Affairs, 1902–07"; secretary of interior to W. R. Logan, August 10, 1907, W. R. Logan to commissioner of Indian affairs, with attached certification of decision of Tribal Council, October 24, 1907, W. R. Logan to F. E. Leupp, commissioner of Indian affairs, December 2 and 27, 1907, W. R. Logan to commissioner of Indian affairs, January 8, 1908, [?] to W. R. Logan, April 24, 1908, all in box 21, "Letters Sent—Commissioner of Indian Affairs, 1907–11"; H. Rolapp to W. R. Logan, April 27, May 14, May 25, August 1, August 28, in box 32, "General Correspondence, 1890–1913, Agency Correspondence, 1906–09"; all the documents in box 365, "Records Relating to the Sugar Beet Program, 1906–09," all in the Department of the Interior, Records of the Bureau of Indian Affairs, RG 75, Fort Belknap Indian Agency Papers, Regional Archives, Seattle; *Milk River Valley News,* April 19, May 3, December 13, 1906, February 28, March 7, July 4, October 24, 1907, January 16, 23, 30, 1908; *North Montana Review,* December 8, 1906. In the existing literature, the sugar beet scheme is best discussed in Barry, *Fort Belknap Indian Reservation,* 129, 130–34; and Rodnick, *Fort Belknap Assiniboine of Montana,* 15–16; see also Massie, "Cultural Roots of Indian Water Rights," 19, 21, 23; and Massie, "Defeat of Assimilation," 39–40, 43–45. I have noticed that the secondary sources differ at times, sometimes markedly, in their description of the details of the contract or contracts, when they were signed, with whom, for what acreage, whether and to what extent a sugar production facility was built and used, how long the sugar beet cultivation and production efforts carried on, and so forth. The differences in detail do not seem to be important.

CHAPTER 6: *WINTERS* AND ALLOTMENT

1. The policies and events of the assimilation period and the allotment process are described in many books and articles. The discussion here is based primarily on Hoxie, *Final Promise,* esp. chap. 5 ("The Emergence of a Colonial Land Policy,") and from ideas, comments, and events gleaned from the primary and secondary sources introduced throughout this book.

2. Act of February 8, 1887, 49th Cong., 2d Sess., chap. 119, 24 Stat. 388 (General Allotment Act, also known as the Dawes Severalty Act; hereafter Dawes Act).

3. Dawes Act, secs. 1–3.

4. Dawes Act, sec. 5.

5. Dawes Act, sec. 6.

6. Hoxie, *Final Promise,* 152.

7. Examples include the Act of April 23, 1904, chap. 1495, 33 Stat. 302 (Flathead reservation, Montana); Act of December 21, 1904, chap. 22, 33 Stat. 595 (Yakima reservation, Washington); Act of March 22, 1906, chap. 1126, 34 Stat. 80 (Colville reservation, Washington); Act of March 1, 1907, chap. 2285, 34 Stat. 1015, 1035–39 (Blackfeet reservation, Montana); Act of May 29, 1908, chap. 218, 35 Stat. 460 (Standing Rock and Cheyenne River reservations, both in South Dakota); Act of May 30, 1908, chap. 237, 35 Stat. 558 (Fort Peck reservation, Montana); Act of May 27, 1910, chap. 257, 36 Stat. 440 (Pine Ridge reservation, South Dakota); Act of May 30, 1910, chap. 260, 36 Stat. 448 (Rosebud reservation, South Dakota); Act of June 1, 1910, chap. 264, 36 Stat. 455 (Fort Berthold reservation, North Dakota); Act of February 14, 1913, chap. 54, 37 Stat. 675 (Standing Rock reservation, South Dakota).

8. E.g., Act of April 23, 1904, chap. 1484, 33 Stat. 254 (Rosebud); Act of April 27, 1904, chap. 1620, 33 Stat. 319 (Devil's Lake reservation, North Dakota); Act of April 27, 1904, chap. 1624, 33 Stat. 352 (Crow reservation, Montana); Act of March 3, 1905, chap. 1452, 33 Stat. 1016 (Wind River reservation, Wyoming); *Lone Wolf v. Hitchcock,* 187 U.S. 553 (1903); see Hoxie, *Final Promise,* 156–58; B. Clark, *Lone Wolf v. Hitchcock.*

9. 29 Stat. 353–57.

10. Hoxie, *Final Promise,* 157. The master of American Indian policy, Francis Paul Prucha, took issue with Hoxie's analysis (when it was still in dissertation form), stating that Hoxie "stresses a radical change in policy after 1900 that does not take account of significant evidence of continuity in policy." *Great Father,* 2:759 n.1. A central theme in Prucha's massive two-volume overview of Indian policy is his argument that the primary impulse in the Indian policy of the federal government (and the nongovernmental actors with the most impact on federal government policy) has always been assimilation, usually conceived of in relatively benevolent if inevitable terms by policymakers who saw themselves as Christian and humane. It seems to me they are both right. A long-term Christian assimilation impulse can be found to underlie almost all policy actions taken at particular times, from wars to removal to

concentration to allotment to neglect to education to termination to the reversal of termination. But as is implied by this list, the preferred policy often shifted. The salient point here is that for whatever reason, forced cessions of land did escalate dramatically in the early twentieth century, during the latter stages of the allotment program. In *Dispossession of the American Indian,* McDonnell documented the land policies and results of the allotment years. Her key point is that the Indian land base shrank from 138 million acres to 52 million acres during the years the Dawes Act was in effect (1887–1934), and most of the loss occurred after the turn of the century. Moreover, much of what was left to the Indians was not good land. It was extremely arid; divided in odd, inefficient checkerboard patterns; overgrazed; eroded; unirrigable or unirrigated; broken into too-small allotments; or clouded by title litigation. These were the real disaster years for the western Indians in terms of losing control over resources and, in turn, losing their economic and cultural autonomy, which depended in large part on control over a sufficient resource base.

11. Hoxie, *Final Promise,* 172.

12. *United States v. Conrad Investment Company,* 161 F. 829, 831.

13. Hundley, "'Winters' Decision and Indian Water Rights," 38 and n.70; Brief of the Appellee, 46, submitted by Carl Rasch, U.S. attorney (no date; presumably late 1905), *Winters v. United States,* United States Circuit Court of Appeals for the Ninth Circuit, Case No. 1243, in Department of Justice, Records of the Department of Justice, RG 60, box 221, file 58730 (records of the *Winters* case), National Archives.

14. See Blumm, "Reserved Water Rights," 252–54, and the cases and articles cited there, including *Arizona v. California,* October Term 1960, No. 8 Orig., Report of Special Master (1960), 265–66; *Arizona v. California,* 439 U.S. 419, 422 (1979; Court approval of stipulation to use of reserved waters for nonagricultural purposes); *Colville Confederated Tribes v. Walton,* 647 F.2d 42, 48 (9th Cir. 1981), 752 F.2d 397, 405 (9th Cir. 1985); but see *In re General Adjudication of the Big Horn River System,* 835 P.2d 273, 275–76, 278–280 (Wyo. 1992). See also Tarlock, *Law of Water Rights and Resources,* 9-46 to 9-46.2 (and cases cited); Ranquist, "Winters Doctrine and How It Grew," 639, 658–59; Trelease, "Federal-State Relations in Water Law," 162–63.

15. *United States v. Conrad Investment Company,* 156 F. 123, 124–32; *Conrad Investment Company v. United States,* 161 F. at 830–35. Judge Hunt did not preside over the Conrad case, at least not at the time of the main hearing and ruling in the district court. He was out of town (apparently sitting by designation on Ninth Circuit appellate cases), and federal judge Charles Wolverton from the federal district in Oregon was sitting in his place by designation. The district court file is in the archives as *United States v. Conrad Investment Company,* Records of the U.S. District Courts, RG 21, U.S. Ninth Circuit, District of Montana, box 6659, folder 720, Regional Archives, Seattle, but little has been left in the file.

16. There are many sources of information about William Conrad. My favorite for seeing the dynamics of the relationships between Conrad and the

Milk River were the fawning stories about Conrad and his schemes in the *North Montana Review,* a Democratically inclined newspaper in Glasgow at the far end of the Milk River, e.g., March 10, May 12, 1906, July 14, 1906, February 22, 1908. Note that Conrad's proposal to divert water from the Marias River, in northwestern Montana, to the Milk via a diversion to Big Sandy Creek has been revived in modern times by Milk River irrigation interests trying to bring additional water into what they see as a chronically water-short river, especially as Canadians have started making plans finally to take the share of the Milk River allotted to them in the 1909 Boundary Waters Treaty. The modern version has been called the Virgelle Canal proposal, as it would take the water from the Virgelle Ferry stretch of the Missouri River just downstream of the confluence of the Marias and then approximately ten miles over the Bear Paw Mountains to Big Sandy Creek. See "Milk River Basin Interviews," completed by Bob Decker, 49th Parallel Institute, Montana State University, December 1989, 47, 51–60, 89–90, 91.

17. E.g., Act of April 23, 1904, chap. 1495, 33 Stat. 302 (Flathead); Act of December 21, 1904, chap. 22, 33 Stat. 595 (Yakima); Act of March 22, 1906, chap. 1126, 34 Stat. 80 (Colville).

18. 40 *Cong. Rec.* 5784–85, 5810–11 (April 24 and 25, 1906; proposed amendment to H.R. 15531, the Indian Office appropriations bill, 59th Cong., 1st Sess.).

19. 40 *Cong. Rec.* 5810 (April 25, 1906). The approval came without a roll call or voice vote. The Senate was operating under a procedure in which provisions of a bill and certain amendments were read and then considered approved without a vote unless someone objected.

20. 40 *Cong. Rec.* 5810–13 (April 25, 1906).

21. 40 *Cong. Rec.* 5811–13. Senator Carter also remarked sarcastically that he was surprised to see Benjamin Tillman "argue the colored man's case so vigorously." 40 *Cong. Rec.* 5813. As governor of South Carolina, Tillman had pushed the bulk of that state's Jim Crow laws through the state legislature. Whether or not prompted by Carter and Clark, Tillman did as they suggested— he went on a speaking tour of Montana later in 1906, including a visit to the Milk River valley, making what looked like campaign speeches at an odd time, just *after* the 1906 congressional elections. *Enterprise,* November 29, 1906.

22. 40 *Cong. Rec.* 5811–13.

23. 40 *Cong. Rec.* 5813 (April 25, 1906), 6463 (May 7, 1906), 7421 (May 25, 1906); H. Rep. [Conf.] 4436, 59th Cong., 1st Sess. (May 25, 1906); see the Reclamation Act of 1902, chap. 1093, sec. 8, 32 Stat. 388, 390 (requiring that state law govern appropriations from federal Reclamation projects).

24. 49 *Cong. Rec.* 1109 (January 6, 1913; remarks of Rep. Scott Ferris of Oklahoma).

25. 40 *Cong. Rec.* 5813 (April 25, 1906; remarks of Senator Tillman; emphasis added).

26. I have not been able to find out who in Montana might have written to Tillman, and why they chose Tillman as their vehicle. But as noted above,

Tillman did make a speaking tour of Montana later in 1906, including a visit to the Milk River valley, for unknown reasons. Perhaps there was a connection.

27. S. 6354, 59th Cong., 1st. Sess.; S. Rep. No. 3976, 59th Cong., 1st Sess. (June 1, 1906; to accompany S. 6354); 40 *Cong. Rec.* 7684, 7716 (June 1 and 2, 1906).

28. H.R. 19681, 59th Cong., 1st Sess.; H. Rep. No. 4723, 59th Cong., 1st Sess. (June 5, 1906; to accompany H.R. 19681); 40 *Cong. Rec.* 7814–15 (June 4, 1906).

29. 40 *Cong. Rec.* 7815–18 (June 14, 1906). This vote was the only roll-call vote on any of the Blackfeet reservation measures studied here. The House approved the measure 154 to 13. The votes of each member were not listed in the *Congressional Record,* only the total. 40 *Cong. Rec.* at 7818.

30. 40 *Cong. Rec.* 7912–13 (June 6, 1906), 8535–36 (June 15, 1906), 8663 (June 16, 1906); H.R. Rep. [Conf.] No. 4942, 59th Cong., 1st Sess. (June 15, 1906).

31. The veto message is printed at 40 *Cong. Rec.* 9740 (June 29, 1906).

32. Ibid.

33. *North Montana Review,* November 21, December 8, 15, 1906; *Milk River Valley News,* December 13, 1906; *Enterprise,* December 10, 1906.

34. S. 7674, 59th Cong., 2d Sess.; see S. Rep. No. 5163, 59th Cong., 2d Sess. (January 21, 1907; to accompany S. 7674); 41 *Cong. Rec.* 1887–88 (January 29, 1907).

35. S. Rep. No. 5163, 59th Cong., 2d Sess. (January 21, 1907; to accompany S. 7674); 41 *Cong. Rec.* 1887–88 (January 29, 1907).

36. Senate Joint Memorial No. 1 (February 26, 1907), Montana Legislative Assembly, 1907 Session, Montana Laws 1907, 590–91, printed at 42 *Cong. Rec.* 712–13 (January 15, 1908).

37. *Ibid.*

38. Ibid.; see also *Milk River Valley News,* February 7, 28, 1907; W. R. Logan to commissioner of Indian affairs, February 14 and March 4, 1907, Department of the Interior, Records of the Bureau of Indian Affairs, RG 75, Fort Belknap Indian Agency Papers, box 20, "Letters Sent—Commissioner of Indian Affairs, 1902–07," Regional Archives, Seattle. The reference to the *Winters* litigation in the memorial from the Montana state legislature was the second of just two explicit references to the *Winters* case in Congress during the two-year debate over the Blackfeet bill and water rights.

39. W. R. Logan to commissioner of Indian affairs, February 14, 1907, Department of the Interior, Records of the Bureau of Indian Affairs, RG 75, Fort Belknap Indian Agency Papers, box 20, "Letters Sent—Commissioner of Indian Affairs, 1902–07," Regional Archives, Seattle.

40. H.R. 22580, 59th Cong., 2d Sess.; S. Rep. No. 5689, 59th Cong., 2d Sess. (January 30, 1907; to accompany H.R. 22580); H. Rep. [Conf.] No. 8069, 59th Cong., 2d Sess. (February 22, 1907); 41 *Cong. Rec.* 2157–59 (February 2, 1907), 2420–22 (February 7, 1907), 2512 (February 8, 1907), 3933 (February 25, 1907); Act of March 1, 1907, chap. 2285, 34 Stat. 1015, 1035–39; *Milk River*

Valley News, February 28, 1907; *United States v. Conrad Investment Company,* 156 F. at 124–32; *affirmed, Conrad Investment Company v. United States,* 161 F. at 830–35. I do not know if the defendant in the *Conrad* case then raised with the federal court the issue of whether and how the new legislation would affect the water rights for the reservation. The new legislation should not have made any difference in trying to understand the nature of the treaty reserved rights based on the 1888 treaty. In any event, neither the lower court nor the appellate court mentioned the new legislation affecting the Blackfeet reservation.

41. 34 Stat. 1035–36.

42. S. 208, 60th Cong., 1st Sess.; S. Rep. No. 202, 60th Cong., 1st Sess. (February 10, 1908; to accompany S. 208); 42 *Cong. Rec.* 1812–16 (February 11, 1908). The remarks of Senator Henry Teller are at 1813.

43. 42 *Cong. Rec.* 7208 (May 29, 1908), reporting H. Rep. No. 1507, 60th Cong., 1st Sess. (April 20, 1908; to accompany S. 208); see Act of May 30, 1908, chap. 237, sec. 2, 35 Stat. 558, 559–60.

44. H. Rep. No. 1507, 60th Cong., 1st Sess. (April 20, 1908; to accompany S. 208); 42 *Cong. Rec.* 7206–14 (May 29, 1908), 7264 (May 30, 1908); Act of May 30, 1908, chap. 237, 35 Stat. 558. The water rights provision is in sec. 2 at 35 Stat. 559–60.

45. In the session that produced the Fort Peck allotment bill, the first of the Sixtieth Congress, members of Congress introduced a number of bills to survey, allot, and sell the surplus lands on various Indian reservations, including the Navajo (Arizona), San Carlos Apache (Arizona), Arapaho (Wyoming), Crow, Fort Berthold, Fort Hall (Idaho), Rosebud, Cheyenne River, and Standing Rock. Some of the bills contained water rights provisions modeled after the provision in the previous session's Blackfeet allotment law. Others were silent about water. Except for one bill to sell surplus lands at the Standing Rock and Cheyenne River reservations in North and South Dakota, which said nothing about water but did contain a curious treaty rights protection discussed elsewhere, none of the bills made it through Congress during that last session before the 1908 presidential election. Nor did any allotment bill pass in the short lame-duck second session of the Sixtieth Congress following that election (December 1908 to March 4, 1909). See H.R. 16737, S. 603, S. 2963, S. 3721, S. 5602, S. 6217, S. 6775, 60th Cong., 1st Sess.; Act of May 29, 1908, chap. 218, sec. 9, 35 Stat. 460, 464. For the only previous analysis that has emphasized the interrelation of the development of the Indian water rights doctrine and the allotment process, see Pisani, "Irrigation, Water Rights, and Betrayal."

46. E. A. Key, Reclamation Service inspector, to secretary of interior, "Memorandum for the Secretary: Irrigation on Indian Reservations," May 21, 1909, Department of the Interior, Records of the Department of the Interior, RG 48, Central Classified Files, 1907–36, box 1436, "Indian Office General, Irrigation, June 25, 1907–August 5, 1909," National Archives.

47. E. B. Meritt, to R. G. Valentine, commissioner of Indian affairs, with attached proposed "Bill to protect and conserve the water rights of Indians," November 17, 1911, Department of the Interior, Records of the Department of

the Interior, RG 48, Central Classified Files, 1907–36, box 1387, "Uintah and Ouray Irrigation, April 9, 1907–April 12, 1912," National Archives.

48. Ibid.; see also Phillip P. Wells, chief law officer, Reclamation Service, to secretary of interior, December 18, 1911, Department of the Interior, Records of the Department of the Interior, RG 48, Central Classified Files, 1907–36, box 1387, "Uintah and Ouray Irrigation, April 9, 1907–April 12, 1912," National Archives.

CHAPTER 7: THE SUPREME COURT'S DECISION IN *WINTERS*

1. *Milk River Valley News,* April 25, June 13, 20, 27, July 4, 20, August 8, 29, 1907; *Enterprise,* June 5, 12, July 3, 1907; *North Montana Review,* June 15, 1907; W. R. Logan to commissioner of Indian affairs, July 23, 1907, Department of the Interior, Records of the Bureau of Indian Affairs, RG 75, Fort Belknap Indian Agency Papers, box 21, "Letters Sent—Commissioner of Indian Affairs, 1907–11," Regional Archives, Seattle.

2. *Milk River Valley News,* December 12, 1907; W. R. Logan to commissioner of Indian affairs, December 27, 1907, Department of the Interior, Records of the Bureau of Indian Affairs, RG 75, Fort Belknap Indian Agency Papers, box 21, "Letters Sent—Commissioner of Indian Affairs, 1907–11," Regional Archives, Seattle.

3. *Winters v. United States,* Case No. 499, October Term 1906, Case No. 158, October Term 1907. I viewed the case file—record index and briefs—on microfilm at the University of Oregon Law Library.

4. *Winters v. United States,* 207 U.S. 564, 575–78.

5. *Chinook Opinion,* January 9, 1908; *Havre Herald* (January 10, 1908); *Milk River Valley News;* January 9, 23, 1908; *North Montana Review,* January 11, 1908; *Montana Homestead,* January 17, 1908; *Helena Independent,* January 7, 1908; W. R. Logan to commissioner of Indian affairs, January 8, 1908; Department of the Interior, Records of the Bureau of Indian Affairs, RG 75, Fort Belknap Indian Agency Papers, box 21, "Letters Sent—Commissioner of Indian Affairs, 1907–11," Regional Archives, Seattle; see also Hundley, "'Winters' Decision and Indian Water Rights," 36–39.

6. *Milk River Valley News,* January 16, 23, 30, February 20, 1908; *North Montana Review,* February 1, 1908; W. R. Logan to commissioner of Indian affairs, January 8, 1908; Department of the Interior, Records of the Bureau of Indian Affairs, RG 75, Fort Belknap Indian Agency Papers, box 21, "Letters Sent—Commissioner of Indian Affairs, 1907–11," Regional Archives, Seattle.

7. *Helena Independent,* January 7, 1908; *Milk River Valley News;* January 9, 23, 1908; *Montana Homestead,* January 17, 1908.

8. *Milk River Valley News;* January 16, 23, 30, 1908; *North Montana Review,* February 1, 1908.

9. *Milk River Valley News,* January 30, 1908; *North Montana Review,* February 8, 22, 1908.

10. *Milk River Valley News,* January 30, February 20, 1908; *North Montana Review,* February 8, 22, 1908. The tension between the Chinook area interests and the focus of the people in the lower river on getting the Dodson-to-Glasgow distribution facilities underway flared up again at an association meeting in April, as reported in the April 11, 1908, edition of Glasgow's *North Montana Review.*

11. *Milk River Valley News;* January 23, February 20, 27, March 12, 26, April 2, 16, May 28, June 11, 1908; *North Montana Review,* February 22, March 28, April 11, 1908; *Enterprise,* March 11, May 6, 20, June 10, July 29, August 25, October 21, 1908; for descriptions of what the future held for the Fort Belknap reservation see McCool, *Command of the Waters,* 51–54, 64–65, 119, 158, 167–68, 256–59; Hundley, "'Winters' Decision and Indian Water Rights," 40–42; Massie, "Cultural Roots of Indian Water Rights," 23, and Massie, "Defeat of Assimilation," 42–43.

12. Hundley discovered from census records that the man's name was in fact "Winter." Hundley, "'Winters' Decision and Indian Water Rights," 17 n.2. A pleading filed in the case in Judge Hunt's court confirms this, "Response of Henry Winter," July 12, 1905, in the files of *United States v. Mose Anderson, et al.,* Records of the U.S. District Courts, RG 21, U.S. Ninth Circuit, District of Montana, box 6659, folder 747, Regional Archives, Seattle. For some reason Rasch put the name "Henry Winters" in the original complaint and it stuck. Winter was known as Winters in some of the valley papers, as indicated by this intriguing item, printed in its entirety, from the January 17, 1906, edition of the *Milk River Valley News:* "Foreclosure proceedings have been instituted in Choteau county to recover about $27,000 from Henry Winters and wife. Winters has left the country, it is said, as a result of disclosures regarding his scheme to kill Stock Inspector Hall and Judge Tattan."

13. *Winters v. United States,* 207 U.S. at 575–77.

14. E.g., Act of July 26, 1866, 39th Cong., 1st Sess., chap. 262, sec. 9, 14 Stat 252, 253; Act of July 9, 1870, 41st Cong., 1st Sess., chap. 235, 16 Stat 217, 218 (Mining Laws of 1866 and 1870); Act of March 3, 1877, 44th Cong., 2d Sess., chap. 107, 19 Stat 377 (Desert Land Act); see also Act of June 17, 1902, Public Law 57-161, chap. 1093, sec. 8, 32 Stat 388, 390 (Reclamation Act).

15. Tarlock, *Law of Water Rights and Resources,* 9-44, citing Hoxie, *Final Promise.* (Tarlock cites pages 162–63 of Hoxie's book; actually the discussion of Indian water rights and irrigation is at 169–72 and 184–85.)

16. *Winters v. United States,* 207 U.S. at 576.

17. E.g., *Skeem v. United States,* 273 F. 93, 94–96; *United States v. Wightman,* 230 F. 277, 282–83; *Pioneer Packing Company v. Winslow,* 294 P. 556, 558–59. *Skeem* involved an agreement between the Fort Hall Indians and the United States that authorized the United States to sell certain reservation lands, protected other Indian lands including certain allotments, and reserved water for the allotments. The court cited *Winters* for the proposition—first derived from the *Winans* decisions—that such an agreement "was not a grant to the Indians, but was a grant from the Indians to the United States, and such being

NOTES TO PAGES 153–157

the case all rights not specifically granted were reserved to the Indians." All three judges on the Ninth Circuit panel in *Skeem* had participated in the *Winters* decisions, including Judge Hunt, who was now on the appellate court. In *Wightman,* the federal district court in Arizona denied the existence of reserved water rights to a particular spring on the San Carlos reservation partly because the San Carlos reservation had been created by executive order and not treaty, viewing *Winters* as turning "solely on the agreement with the Indians," which was the "sole basis out of which the equities in favor of the Indians arise." Because the San Carlos reservation lands did not involve a treaty, "there are no equities growing out of such treaty or agreement in this case." *Pioneer Packing* concerned the Quinaults' treaty right to fish, and relied on both *Winans* and *Winters* for this concept. Among modern legal analysts nobody understands better how the *Winters* decision was grounded in the preceding *Winans* decision than Blumm. Indeed, it may be that he overemphasizes the link. On the one hand, he takes the *Winters* decision and doctrine too much out of their own context, while on the other, he makes some rigid distinctions between "*Winters*" reserved water rights and what he calls "*Winans*" reserved water rights that the cases and history cannot bear. Blumm, "Reserved Water Rights," 218–29, 234–44, 248–54, 257.

18. Montana Laws 1905, chap. 44, sec. 1; see *Mettler v. Ames Realty Company,* 201 P. 702, 707.

19. *Winters v. United States,* 207 U.S. at 577.

20. *United States v. Rio Grande Dam and Irrigation Company,* 174 U.S. 690 (1899). The key passage in the *Rio Grande* opinion is at 703; the citation in the *Winters* decision is to page 702. For a discussion of the *Rio Grande* case and some of the controversy surrounding it see Dunbar, *Forging New Rights,* 192–94; I. G. Clark, "Elephant Butte Controversy."

21. *United States v. Winans,* 198 U.S. 371, 382–84.

22. E.g., *United States v. Conrad Investment Company,* 156 F. at 126–30, 132 (the district court opinion in *Conrad*); *Burley v. United States,* 179 F. 1, 12; *State v. Towessnute,* 154 P. 805, 809; *Mettler v. Ames Realty Company,* 201 P. at 705; Wiel, *Water Rights in the Western States,* 1:147–48, 175–77, 215–17, 236–43, 2:1275; Kinney, *Treatise on the Law of Irrigation,* 657–59, 684, 690–93, 814–15, 1112–24, 1159–61, 2290–92.

23. *Conrad Investment Company v. United States,* 161 F. 829, *affirming* 156 F. 123.

24. Among historical accounts, Norris Hundley and Daniel McCool have examined some of the issues about which legal scholars and others have argued ever since the *Winters* decision. McCool, *Command of the Waters,* 47–49; Hundley, "'Winters' Decision and Indian Water Rights," 17–42. Hundley's primary purpose in writing this 1982 article was to analyze whether the Supreme Court ruled that the Indians or the federal government reserved the waters. He concluded that the Court ruled that *both* acted to reserve the waters and that it made legal and historical sense for the Court to conclude that both did so. Hundley, "'Winters' Decision and Indian Water Rights," 33–35. By more

modern times even legal scholars not necessarily fond of the reserved rights doctrine were no longer questioning the legal validity of the doctrine, usually emphasizing the federal government's power under the property, commerce, and supremacy clauses of the Constitution to use or reserve water for federal purposes outside of state law. E.g., Trelease, "Federal-State Relations in Water Law," x–xi, 8–11, 39–44, 56–80, 104–130, 138–44, 147–147m; Wheatley et al., "Study of the Development, Management, and Use of Water Resources," 80–188, 556–81; see also Tarlock, *Law of Water Rights and Resources,* 9-20 to 9-25, 9-43 to 9-54; Ranquist, *"Winters* Doctrine and How It Grew," 646–56, 687–95. Other authors have analyzed the Indian reserved rights doctrine primarily as an exercise of resource control by the Indians or by both the federal government and the Indians. See, e.g., Blumm, "Reserved Water Rights," 218–29, 234–44, 248–54, 257; Tarlock, *Law of Water Rights and Resources,* 9-44 to 9-45; Ranquist, "Winters Doctrine and How It Grew," 654, 662–64; Veeder, "Indian Prior and Paramount Rights," 631; Bloom, "Indian 'Paramount' Rights to Water Use," 669; Merrill, "Aboriginal Water Rights," 45. The ways in which opponents of the *Winters* decision exploited the ambiguities in the opinion are discussed elsewhere in this book.

CHAPTER 8: THE PEOPLE OF *WINTERS* AND THE NATURAL LAW OF THE WEST

1. *National Cyclopaedia of American Biography,* vol. 48, 346; see also Hundley, "'Winters' Decision and Indian Water Rights," 19–26; McCool, *Command of the Waters,* 38–41. I have not been able to locate any of Rasch's private papers or correspondence or to find out much more about him from Montana papers or other Montana sources.

2. "Memoirs of William H. Hunt" (1941), William H. Hunt Papers, Montana Historical Society; Frederick, *Rugged Justice,* 115, 117, 121, 123–25, 139, 153–54; Hundley, "'Winters' Decision and Indian Water Rights," 26–27, 36; *National Cyclopaedia of American Biography,* vol. 37, 249. Hunt's 125-page typewritten memoirs were written primarily at his children's urgings and for the benefit of his family. They are mostly just a description of the events and changes in his life and a lot of platitudes, with almost no reflection, insights, or substance about his activities. Hunt expressly stated that his judicial life would not be detailed in the memoirs, as he felt that would be of little interest to his children. The quotation about his troubles being confirmed to the United States Commerce Court is about the only time the memoirs flare into something of scholarly interest.

3. Hundley, "'Winters' Decision and Indian Water Rights," 36.

4. Ibid., 36–37, 40–42.

5. Hunt, "Law of Water Rights."

6. *Skeem v. United States,* 273 F. 93, 94–96, construing art. 8 in the 1898 agreement between the United States and the Shoshone-Bannock Indians of the Fort Hall reservation in Idaho. See Act of June 6, 1900, chap. 813, 31 Stat.

672, 674 (ratifying treaty of February 5, 1898). The author of the *Skeem* opinion, William Gilbert, and the other member of the *Skeem* panel, Erskine Ross, had both been members of all the Ninth Circuit panels that ruled in the *Winters* and *Conrad* cases.

7. All of these judges are mentioned in Frederick's *Rugged Justice;* Gilbert, Ross, and Morrow are significant subjects of the book, especially Gilbert and Ross. The discussion of natural resources in the first two decades of the twentieth century is in chap. 5, 98–121; the quotation is at 115. Frederick's book is not a compelling explanation of the place of the Ninth Circuit in the history of the American West, but it is full of useful facts. See also *National Cyclopaedia of American Biography,* vol. 23, 48 (Gilbert), vol. B, 308 (Morrow).

8. There are many sources for bare biographical information about Justice McKenna, but I did not find anything of much depth or relevance. For my purposes, Frederick, *Rugged Justice,* 18–19, 23–26, 37, 56, 62, 68, 70–71, and *National Cyclopaedia of American Biography,* vol. 11, 18, will do.

CHAPTER 9: PRELUDE TO THE WATER RIGHTS LITIGATION AT THE UINTAH INDIAN RESERVATION, LATE 1800S TO 1914

1. Lewis, *Neither Wolf nor Dog,* 3–70, 168–76. To gather from earlier notes, useful studies of Indian policy in the late nineteenth and early twentieth centuries include Hoxie, *Final Promise;* Hoxie, *Parading through History;* Prucha, *Great Father,* 2:609–916; McDonnell, *Dispossession of the American Indian;* Berkhofer, *White Man's Indian,* esp. 44–61, 113–14, 153–57, 166–75; Carlson, *Indians, Bureaucrats and the Land;* White, *Roots of Dependency;* Wilkinson, *American Indians, Time, and the Law,* 7–31, 54–63, 78–86; Leibhardt, "Law, Environment, and Social Change"; Pisani, "Irrigation, Water Rights, and Betrayal"; and Massie, "Defeat of Assimilation."

2. Lewis, *Neither Wolf nor Dog,* 59 (emphasis added).

3. Lewis describes the historic Ute lands and the process by which these lands were reduced to the reservation in *Neither Wolf nor Dog,* 21–30, 34–48. Actually what emerged from this process were two adjoining reservations, known as the Uintah and Ouray Indian Reservation, totaling approximately four million acres, as well as two in Colorado, the Ute Mountain Indian Reservation and the Southern Ute Indian Reservation. The Utah reservation was administered as two separate reservations, to a certain extent, and this study focuses only on the Uintah reservation, primarily because the water rights issues and litigation described concerned only the Uintah reservation. Official acts and executive orders involved in the long process of whittling down the land base of the Utes from their large historic territory in Utah, Colorado, New Mexico, and Wyoming to the Uintah and Ouray reservation in Utah and the Southern Ute and Ute Mountain reservations in southern Colorado include the Treaty of 1848, Act of December 30, 1849, 9 Stat. 984;

Executive Order of December 3, 1861; Treaty of 1863, Act of October 7, 1863, 13 Stat. 673; Executive Order of September 1, 1867; Treaty of 1868, Act of March 2, 1868, 15 Stat. 619; Agreement of 1873, Act of April 29, 1874, 18 Stat. 36; Agreement of 1880, Act of June 15, 1880, 21 Stat. 199. Many of the twentieth-century Indian Office records and litigation documents cited below describe various parts of this process, such as Franklin K. Lane, secretary of the interior, to Speaker of the House of Representatives, December 7, 1914, Department of the Interior, Records of the Bureau of Indian Affairs, RG 75, Irrigation Division, General Correspondence, box 28, "Uintah No. 3," National Archives.

 4. Endter, "Cultural Ideologies and Political Economy," 89–92, 228–61 (indented quotation is from 92, other quotations are from 90–92, 232–40); see also Lewis, *Neither Wolf nor Dog,* 21–30, 34–48.

 5. Lewis, *Neither Wolf nor Dog,* 34–59; see also the documents cited in the preceding notes for official statements of the agrarian purpose or intended effect of the Ute land reductions with regard to Indian people. The governmental policy and the private intentions and actions to develop the area also for non-Indian irrigated agricultural development are highlighted in the pages noted from Lewis and in various documents from the Reclamation Service and other offices. Examples from after 1900 include F. H. Newell to Charles D. Walcott, United States Geological Survey (USGS) director, April 16, 1902; Harold Sawyer Reed, USGS hydrographer, "The Uinta Indian Reservation, Utah, Its Possibilities, Allotment, and Free Lands," December 1903; "Memorandum Concerning Uinta Indian Reservation," June 1904; acting commissioner of the General Land Office to the secretary of the interior, June 9, 1905; President Roosevelt to C. D. Walcott, USGS director, March 28, 1906, and Walcott's response, March 31, 1906, Department of the Interior, Records of the Bureau of Reclamation, RG 115, General Administrative Files, 1902–1919, box 99, file 127, "Uintah Reservation—Utah, thru 1903," and "Uintah Reservation—Utah, 1904 thru ?," National Archives; Department of the Interior, *Annual Report of the Commissioner of Indian Affairs,* September 30, 1905, 145–47, printed as H. Doc. 5, 59th Cong., 1st Sess. See also Kendrick, *Beyond the Wasatch.*

 6. Act of March 1, 1899, 30 Stat. 924, 941.

 7. Lewis ably describes the allotment process in action at the Uintah reservation, *Neither Wolf nor Dog,* 53–59; see also Department of the Interior, *Annual Report of the Commissioner of Indian Affairs,* September 30, 1905, 145–47, printed as H. Doc. 5, 59th Cong., 1st Sess. The commissioner's report is the source of quotations about the purposes of the reservoir site and land withdrawals. Official congressional actions to allot the Uintah reservation include the Act of June 4, 1898, 30 Stat. 337; Act of May 27, 1902, 32 Stat. 263; Act of March 3, 1903, 32 Stat. 998; Act of April 21, 1904, 33 Stat. 207; and Act of March 3, 1905, 33 Stat. 1048, 1069. President Roosevelt issued proclamations in 1905 declaring the allotment process complete, reserving certain of the surplus lands for forestry and water supply purposes, and declaring the rest open for settlement on July 14, 1905, 34 Stat. 3116, 3119; and August 2, 1905, 34 Stat.

3141. For the desires of Reclamation officials to see the reservation allotted so that Indians would be in certain drainage basins and non-Indians in others, which would allow for separate and, they believed, more efficient and less conflicted irrigation developments and make it easier to protect Indian water rights, see F. H. Newell, USGS hydrographer, to C. D. Walcott, USGS director, April 16, 1902; "Memorandum Concerning Uinta Indian Reservation," (author unknown; probably F. H. Newell), June 1904; and H. S. Reed, resident hydrographer, to F. H. Newell, chief engineer, December 1, 1904, Department of the Interior, Records of the Bureau of Reclamation, RG 115, General Administrative Files, 1902–1919, box 99, file 127, "Uintah Indian Reservation—Utah, thru 1903" and "Uintah Indian Reservation—Utah, 1904 thru ?", National Archives.

    8. The 1905 filing of the water rights claims, and the implications of that filing, are described or referred to in many of the documents cited below in this section, as the state law claims are a factor in the subsequent decade-long effort to perfect these rights and, then, to assert and protect *Winters* through litigation. The documents are not consistent in stating the amount of land or water for which claims were filed, although the numbers noted in the text seem to be used most often and in the more authoritative documents. See W. B. Hill, general superintendent of irrigation, Office of Indian Affairs, to Senate Committee on Indian Affairs, March 27, 1906, reprinted in the committee's report on the 1906 Indian Office appropriations bill, S Rep. 2561, 59th Cong., 1st Sess. (April 13, 1906), 131–32; "Uinta Indian Reservation, Utah," undated document discussing the Uintah reservation water situation and the water rights filings (probably late 1905 or early 1906), Department of the Interior, Records of the Bureau of Reclamation, RG 115, General Administrative Files, 1902–1919, box 99, file 127-A, "Reclamation of the Uintah Indian Reservation," National Archives; Department of the Interior, *Annual Report of the Commissioner of Indian Affairs,* September 30, 1905, 145–47, printed as H. Doc. 5, 59th Cong., 1st Sess.; Department of the Interior, *Annual Report of the Commissioner of Indian Affairs,* September 30, 1906, 84, 88–89, 367–70, printed as H. Doc. 5, 59th Cong., 2d Sess.; acting secretary of the interior to Utah state engineer, January 19, 1912, Records of the Department of the Interior, RG 48, Central Classified Files, 1907–1936, box 1387, "Uintah and Ouray Irrigation, April 9, 1907 to April 12, 1912," National Archives; F. K. Lane, secretary of the interior, to Speaker of the House of Representatives, December 7, 1914, Department of the Interior, Records of the Bureau of Indian Affairs, RG 75, Irrigation Division, General Correspondence, box 28, "Uintah No. 3," National Archives; *United States v. Dry Gulch Irrigation Company,* Docket No. 4418, Bill of Complaint, and *United States v. Cedarview Irrigation Company,* Docket No. 4427, Bill of Complaint, Records of the U.S. District Courts, RG 21, District of Utah, Combined Bankruptcy, Civil, and Criminal Case Files, 1880–1931, box 435, folder 4418, and box 436, folder 4427, Rocky Mountain Region of the National Archives, Denver (hereafter, Regional Archives, Denver).

    9. Act of June 21, 1906, 34 Stat. 325, 375–76 (emphasis added). Such a definitive statement deferring to state law so soon after the district court

decision and the first appellate court decision in *Winters* made me wonder if somebody in or connected to Congress drafted this provision in an attempt to prevent a *Winters*-type theory from applying to the irrigation efforts at the Uintah reservation. If so, I could find no hint of such a purpose or connection in the legislative history. It is perhaps more likely that legislators were trying to make this provision comparable to sec. 8 of the Reclamation Act of 1902, which, while more ambiguous, was understood by most as requiring that state water law apply to Reclamation projects and to water appropriations from Reclamation projects.

10. "Memorandum Concerning Uinta Indian Reservation," June 1904, Department of the Interior, Records of the Bureau of Reclamation, RG 115, General Administrative Files, 1902–1919, box 99, file 127, "Uintah Indian Reservation—Utah, 1904 thru ?", National Archives.

11. Department of the Interior, *Annual Report of the Commissioner of Indian Affairs,* September 30, 1906, 88, printed as H. Doc. 5, 59th Cong., 2d Sess.

12. F. E. Leupp, commissioner of Indian affairs, to President Roosevelt, March 27, 1906. The main purpose of Leupp's letter was to get the president's support for the appropriation for the Uintah reservation irrigation system, and to have the president ask the Reclamation Service to delay its proposed plan to divert water out of the Strawberry River system over the mountains, potentially reducing stream flows in that river and then in the lower Duchesne and Uinta Rivers. Leupp wanted the project delayed until "the Indian needs are supplied." The president forwarded the letter to the Reclamation Service. Roosevelt to C. D. Walcott, director, USGS, March 28, 1906. The Reclamation Service responded, in a letter that appears to have been written by Director Newell himself, that it was impossible to delay the Strawberry valley project, as contracts with settlers for the delivery of water had already been signed and the settlers had taken up land and expended money in anticipation of the water arriving soon. Any delay would be a "breach of faith." This letter noted that the Strawberry valley project would not affect the effort to irrigate the Uintah reservation allotments because most allotments were on streams above the rivers where the Strawberry River water would have flowed anyway, and because Indian Affairs had taken the necessary steps to file for water rights to protect the Indian priority, meaning that all the Indian Office had to do was to act to perfect those rights. Director, Reclamation Service, to President Roosevelt, March 31, 1906. These two letters are in Department of the Interior, Records of the Bureau of Reclamation, RG 115, General Administrative Files, 1902–1919, box 99, file 127, "Uintah Indian Reservation—Utah, 1904 thru ?", National Archives.

13. George Woodruff, acting secretary of the interior, to the attorney general, June 13, 1907; acting secretary of the interior to Utah state engineer, January 19, 1912; and George Wickersham, attorney general, to secretary of the interior, August 19, 1912, Department of the Interior, Records of the Department of the Interior, RG 48, Central Classified Files, 1907–1936, box

1387, "Indian Office, Uintah and Ouray Irrigation, Dry Gulch Irrigation
Company, June 13, 1907, to June 2, 1915" and "Uintah and Ouray Irrigation,
April 9, 1907 to April 12, 1912"; W. H. Code, chief engineer, Indian Irrigation
Service, to secretary of the interior, October 9, 1907, and November 9, 1908,
Department of the Interior, Records of the Bureau of Reclamation, RG 115,
General Administrative Files, 1902–1919, box 229, file 757P, "Cooperation with
the Office of Indian Affairs, Utah"; Code to secretary of the interior, May 22,
1908; F. E. Leupp, commissioner of Indian affairs, to secretary of the interior,
December 16, 1908; acting Indian agent, Uintah Reservation, to Code, March
19, 1910; assistant U.S. attorney, Utah District, to John J. Granville, chief
engineer, Indian Irrigation Service, March 25, 1912; F. K. Lane, secretary of the
interior, to Speaker of the House of Representatives, December 7, 1914;
assistant inspector for irrigation to commissioner of Indian affairs, February 2,
1916, all in Department of the Interior, Records of the Bureau of Indian
Affairs, RG 75, Irrigation Division, General Correspondence, box 26, "Uintah,
1908," "Uintah, 1910," and Uintah, 1911–12," box 27, "Uintah, 1916," box 28,
"Uintah No. 3"— all in National Archives.

    14. W. H. Code, chief engineer, Indian Irrigation Service, to secretary of
the interior, November 9, 1908, February 27, 1909, and March 22, 1909, Department of the Interior, Records of the Bureau of Reclamation, RG 115, General
Administrative Files, 1902–1919, box 99, file 127, "Uintah Reservation—Utah,
1904 thru ?", and box 229, file 757P, "Cooperation with the Office of Indian
Affairs, Utah"; Jesse Wilson, assistant interior secretary, to the attorney general,
December 15, 1908; F. E. Leupp, commissioner of Indian affairs, to secretary of
the interior, December 16, 1908; Code to Howard C. Means, superintendent of
irrigation, Uintah Reservation, December 23, 1908; Means to Code, February
18, 1911; Code to secretary of the interior, February 23, 1911, all in Department
of the Interior, Records of the Bureau of Indian Affairs, RG 75, Irrigation
Division, General Correspondence, box 26, "Uintah, 1908" and "Uintah,
1911–12"; acting secretary of the interior to Utah state engineer, January 19,
1912, Department of the Interior, Records of the Department of the Interior,
Central Classified Files, 1907–1936, box 1387, "Uintah and Ouray Irrigation,
April 9, 1907 to April 12, 1912"—all in National Archives.

    15. W. H. Code, chief engineer, Indian Irrigation Service, to secretary of
the interior, November 9, 1908, Department of the Interior, Records of the
Bureau of Reclamation, RG 115, General Administrative Files, 1902–1919, box
229, file 757P, "Cooperation with the Office of Indian Affairs, Utah"; F. E.
Leupp, commissioner of Indian affairs, to secretary of the interior, December
16, 1908; acting Indian agent, Uintah reservation, to Code, March 19, 1910;
Code to secretary of the interior, February 23, 1911, various copies of advertise-
ments for sales and leasing, September 1915 and March 1916, all in Department
of the Interior, Records of the Bureau of Indian Affairs, RG 75, Irrigation
Division, General Correspondence, box 26, "Uintah, 1908," "Uintah, 1910,"
and "Uintah, 1911–12", box 27, "Uintah, 1916"; William M. Reed, chief
engineer and chief inspector of irrigation, Indian Irrigation Service, to

secretary of the interior, January 3, 1913, and Cato Sells, commissioner of Indian affairs, to J. F. Truesdell, special assistant to the attorney general, March 3, 1917, in Department of the Interior, Records of the Department of the Interior, RG 48, Central Classified Files, 1907–1936, box 1387, "Uintah and Ouray Irrigation, 1912–1918"—all in National Archives.

16. See G. Wickersham, attorney general, to secretary of the interior, August 19, 1912, and W. M. Reed, chief engineer and chief inspector of irrigation, Indian Irrigation Service, to secretary of the interior, January 3, 1913, Department of the Interior, Records of the Department of the Interior, RG 48, Central Classified Files, 1907–1936, box 1387, "Uintah and Ouray Irrigation, April 9, 1907 to April 12, 1912" and "Uintah and Ouray Irrigation, 1912–1918"; F. K. Lane, secretary of the interior, to Speaker of the House of Representatives, December 7, 1914, assistant inspector for irrigation to commissioner of Indian affairs, February 2, 1916, Department of the Interior, Records of the Bureau of Indian Affairs, RG 75, Irrigation Division, General Correspondence, box 27, "Uintah, 1916," box 28, "Uintah No. 3"—all in National Archives.

17. "Memo, Indian Irrigation—former Uintah Reservation, Report of Chief Engineer, October 17, 1911," author unknown, November 2, 1911, Bureau of Reclamation copy in the Department of the Interior, Records of the Bureau of Reclamation, RG 115, General Administrative Files, 1902–1919, box 99, file 127, "Uintah Reservation—Utah, 1904 thru ?", National Archives.

18. E. B. Meritt, "Memorandum for Secretary Fisher," January 2, 1913, Department of the Interior, Records of the Department of the Interior, RG 48, Central Classified Files, 1907–1936, box 1387, "Uintah and Ouray Irrigation, 1912–1918," National Archives.

19. W. M. Reed, chief engineer and chief inspector of irrigation, Indian Irrigation Service, to secretary of the interior, January 3, 1913, Department of the Interior, Records of the Department of the Interior, RG 48, Central Classified Files, 1907–1936, box 1387, "Uintah and Ouray Irrigation, 1912–1918," National Archives.

CHAPTER 10: NATIONAL CONTEXT OF THE UINTAH LITIGATION

1. Act of May 29, 1908, chap. 218, sec. 9, 35 Stat. 460, 464.

2. Act of May 29, 1908, chap. 218, sec. 9, 35 Stat. 460, 464; S. Rep. No. 439, 60th Cong., 1st Sess. (April 1, 1908; to accompany S. 1385); 42 *Cong. Rec.* 4753–55 (April 15, 1908).

3. See Act of May 27, 1910, chap. 257, sec. 11, 36 Stat. 440, 443; Act of May 30, 1910, chap. 260, sec. 11, 36 Stat. 448, 452; Act of June 1, 1910, chap. 264, sec. 14, 36 Stat. 455, 459; Act of February 14, 1913, chap. 54, sec. 10, 37 Stat. 675, 678.

4. 49 *Cong. Rec.* 1109 (January 6, 1913; remarks of Rep. Scott Ferris).

5. Pisani, "Irrigation, Water Rights, and Betrayal," 161–63, 164–66. Hoxie, McCool, and McDonnell all generally agreed with Pisani's point, McCool in a significant analysis. See Hoxie, *Final Promise,* 172; McCool, *Command of the*

Waters, 113–19; McDonnell, *Dispossession of the American Indian,* 74–86, esp. 75 and nn. 8–10. For the memorial of the Yakimas see H. Doc. 1304, 62 Cong., 3d Sess., 4 (printed January 25, 1913; memorial of Yakimas dated June 8, 1912).

6. 49 *Cong. Rec.* 1021 (January 4, 1913); 51 *Cong. Rec.* 3661–62 (February 19, 1914). Mondell's comments are discussed further below.

7. E. B. Meritt, assistant commissioner, to H. W. Hincks, assistant engineer, Indian Irrigation Service, March 4, 1914; Hincks to county clerk, Klamath Falls, April 6, 1914; John H. Lewis, Oregon state engineer, to Hincks, June 1, 1914; Hincks to W. M. Reed, chief engineer, June 6, 1914; acting chief engineer to Hincks, June 23, 1914; L. M. Holt, superintendent of irrigation, Indian Irrigation Service, to Hincks, February 3, 1915; E. B. Meritt to Holt, October 22, 1917; Holt to Hincks, October 29, 1917; Hincks to Chewaucan Land and Cattle Company, November 8, 1917, Department of the Interior, Records of the Bureau of Indian Affairs, RG 75, Irrigation Branch, Irrigation Project Case Files, Klamath, box 722 "Water Rights [Klamath] 1914–17," Regional Archives, Seattle; see also supervising engineer to project engineer, Reclamation Service, Klamath Falls, "Effect of Indian Reclamation on Klamath Project," November 17, 1913, Department of the Interior, Records of the Bureau of Reclamation, RG 115, General Administrative Files, 1902–1919, box 229, file 757N, "Cooperation with the Office of Indian Affairs, Oregon," National Archives.

8. This has been my experience as I have dug through reservation records throughout the West. I am providing only examples in this book, chiefly from the Uintah and briefly for the Wind River and Klamath reservations and a few others.

9. 49 *Cong. Rec.* 1040–42 (January 4, 1913).

10. S. Res. 271, 61st Cong., 2d Sess., 45 *Cong. Rec.* 8794 (June 23, 1910); S. Doc. No. 805, 61st Cong., 3d Sess. (February 1, 1911), submitted to Congress at 46 *Cong. Rec.* 1797 (February 1, 1911); S. 9963, 61st Cong., 3d Sess.

11. S. Doc. No. 805, 61st Cong., 3d Sess., 8–9 (February 1, 1911), submitted to Congress at 46 *Cong. Rec.* 1797 (February 1, 1911).

12. Ibid.

13. The conflicts and litigation over water at the Yakima and Gila River reservations are complex stories that deserve their own case studies. I am touching here only on the most minor aspects of these stories, especially the ways in which people at the national level understood the relevance of the *Winters* decisions to these conflicts in years 1909 to 1914. The Gila River water rights situation is the subject of master's thesis by Shelly Dudley, a historian-researcher-archivist for the Salt River Project, "Pima Indians, Water Rights, and the Federal Government." There is no published historical or legal study particularly focused on the water rights issues at the Yakima reservation, but Leibhardt's excellent dissertation, "Law, Environment, and Social Change in the Columbia River Basin," includes water issues among its topics.

14. S. 6693, 62nd Cong., 2d Sess.; H. Doc. No. 1299, 62nd Cong., 3d Sess. (January 23, 1913); H. Doc. No. 1304, 62nd Cong., 3d Sess. (January 25, 1913).

For a discussion of the formation and activities of the Indian Rights Association, see Hoxie, *Final Promise,* 11–12, 76, 79, 159, 162–67, 174, 176–82, 197–98, 227–28. For an example of the approach of Samuel Brosius and the Indian Rights Association to Indian water rights issues, see Brosius's October 23, 1912, speech on "Indian Water-Rights for Irrigation" at that year's session of the annual Conference of Friends of the Indian at Mohonk Lake, New York, which can be found in Department of the Interior, Records of the Department of the Interior, RG 48, Central Classified file, 1907–1936, box 1412, "Yakima, Irrigation, General, October 25, 1912 to March 15, 1913," National Archives. Brosius described at length the problems at the Uintah, Pima, and especially Yakima reservations; argued for a mix of prior appropriation and reserved rights theories to protect the Indians' water rights; and complained about the lack of resources in the Indian Office to address these issues as well as the lack of assistance from (and even active interference of) the Reclamation Service. For Brosius, development and civilization for the Indians depended on the success of the allotment program, while the "shibboleth of the allotment plan of the Government" might be said to be that the government would reserve in trust the land and water for the "untutored allottee" to be able to meet his needs "after he has adopted our civilization at the termination of the twenty-five year trust rather than at its beginning."

15. H. Doc. No. 1304, 62nd Cong., 3d Sess., 3–8 (January 25, 1913). Senator Jones's bill died in committee. How the subsequent Congress tried to resolve the Yakima dispute is described later in this chapter.

16. H. Doc. 521, 62nd Cong., 2d Sess. (February 8, 1912); H.J. Res. 250, 62nd Cong., 2d Sess.; 48 *Cong. Rec.* 770–81 (January 9, 1912); H. Rep. No. 1506, 62nd Cong., 3d Sess. (February 14, 1913); 49 *Cong. Rec.* 1019–21 (January 4, 1913), 3184–92 (February 14, 1913). Representative Callaway's remark is at 49 *Cong. Rec.* 3187 (February 14, 1913).

17. 49 *Cong. Rec.* 1021 (January 4, 1913).

18. E. B. Meritt to R. G. Valentine, commissioner of Indian affairs, with attached proposed "Bill to protect and conserve the water rights of Indians," November 17, 1911, Department of the Interior, Records of the Department of the Interior, RG 48, Central Classified Files, 1907–36, box 1387, "Uintah and Ouray Irrigation, April 9, 1907–April 12, 1912," National Archives.

19. P. P. Wells, chief law officer, Reclamation Service, to secretary of interior, December 18, 1911, Department of the Interior, Records of the Department of the Interior, RG 48, Central Classified Files, 1907–36, box 1387, "Uintah and Ouray Irrigation, April 9, 1907–April 12, 1912," National Archives.

20. "Indian Water Rights," emphasis added (undated and unattributed memorandum, apparently from somebody in the Indian Office; given the attached copy of Meritt's legislation, which I know was altered by late 1913 or early 1914, it appears that this document was probably written in late 1912 or 1913), Department of the Interior, Records of the Bureau of Indian Affairs, RG 75, Irrigation Division, General Correspondence, box 653-3, National Archives.

21. Secretary of the interior to Rep. John Stephens, with attached "Bill to protect and conserve the water rights of Indians" (no date, but appears to be 1913), Department of the Interior, Records of the Bureau of Indian Affairs, RG 75, Central Classified Files, 1907–1939, box 89495, and draft of same letter from secretary of the interior to Sen. Robert Gamble, Department of the Interior, Records of the Department of the Interior, RG 48, Central Classified Files, 1907–1936, box 1387, "Uintah and Ouray Irrigation," National Archives.

22. "Bill to protect and conserve the water rights of Indians" (no date, but appears to be 1913), Department of the Interior, Records of the Bureau of Indian Affairs, RG 75, Central Classified Files, 1907–1939, box 89495, National Archives.

23. "Bill to protect and conserve the water rights of Indians" (no date, but appears to be 1913), Department of the Interior, Records of the Bureau of Indian Affairs, RG 75, Central Classified Files, 1907–1939, box 89495, National Archives..

24. "Superintendent to pass upon water rights" (undated and unattributed memorandum from someone apparently in or connected with the Indian Irrigation Service, almost certainly from mid- to late 1912), Department of the Interior, Records of the Bureau of Indian Affairs, RG 75, Irrigation Division, General Correspondence, box 653-3, National Archives.

25. "Water Rights" (undated and unattributed memorandum, appears to be 1913 or possibly 1914), Department of the Interior, Records of the Bureau of Indian Affairs, RG 75, Irrigation Division, General Correspondence, box 653-3, National Archives. It is possible that this memorandum is also by the same person who wrote the last two unattributed memoranda, but the similarities are less striking.

26. "Water Rights" (undated and unattributed memorandum, appears to be 1913 or possibly 1914), Department of the Interior, Records of the Bureau of Indian Affairs, RG 75, Irrigation Division, General Correspondence, box 653-3, National Archives. I have reservation records that further describe the water rights issues in these years at these reservations (and more) as outlined in the memorandum, but I have not delved into them here.

27. For additional documents describing the need for the Indian Irrigation Service to hire someone experienced in water law, eventually authorized in the Indian appropriations bill for fiscal year 1915 (adopted in mid-1914), see "Memorandum—Necessity for legal assistance," (unattributed—apparently the same person again), March 25, 1913; W. M. Reed, chief engineer, to commissioner of Indian affairs, March 26, 1913; and W. M. Reed, "Memorandum for Commissioner Sells," August 9, 1914, all in Department of the Interior, Records of the Bureau of Indian Affairs, RG 75, Irrigation Division, General Correspondence, box 653-3, National Archives. Three other documents that highlight a variety of issues and problems in Indian irrigation in these years, see W. H. Rosencrans, consulting engineer, to R. G. Valentine, commissioner of Indian affairs, "Report on the Irrigation of United States Indian Lands," October 23, 1913, Department of the Interior, Records of the

Department of the Interior, RG 48, Central Classified Files, 1907–1936, box 1436, "Indian Office, General, Irrigation, 1912 to 1917", National Archives; F. H. Abbott, "Brief on Indian Irrigation, prepared under the direction of the Board of Indian Commissioners" (undated, but early 1914 or possibly late 1913), and C. Sells, commissioner of Indian affairs, to secretary of interior, March 13, 1914 (responding to issues raised in Abbott's brief), both in Department of the Interior, Records of the Bureau of Indian Affairs, RG 75, Irrigation Division, General Correspondence, box 653-3, National Archives.

28. Department of Justice, *Annual Report of the Attorney-General of the United States for the Year Ended June 30, 1910,* printed as H. Doc. 1003, 61st Cong., 3d Sess., U.S. Serial Set 5969, 29–30.

29. Department of Justice, *Annual Report of the Attorney-General of the United States for the Year 1914,* printed as H. Doc. 1390, 63rd Cong., 3d Sess., U.S. Serial Set 6810. The Pyramid Lake, Nevada, litigation and what is known as the Orr Ditch decree is an extensive story in its own right that needs its own case study. The same is true of the Gila River litigation—what became known as the Globe Equity decree. See Dudley, "Pima Indians, Water Rights, and the Federal Government," esp. 39–72, which contains a useful summary of *Winters*-based litigation.

30. *United States v. Wightman,* 230 F. 277, 278–84 (D. Arizona, 1916). There is no indication that the government appealed the district court's ruling.

31. *Byers v. Wa-wa-ne,* 169 P. 121, 122–28 (Oregon, 1917).

32. Act of March 3, 1905, 33 Stat. 1016, 1016–20. Documents relevant to this and the next few paragraphs come from the court records of *United States v. Hampleman,* Docket No. 753, Records of the U.S. District Courts, RG 21, District of Wyoming, Civil Case Files, box 119, folder 753, Regional Archives, Denver, and from records of the Wind River reservation, Department of the Interior, Bureau of Indian Affairs, Records of the Bureau of Indian Affairs, RG 75, Wind River Agency, General Correspondence Files, 1890–1961, boxes 1, 2, 6, 64, and Correspondence and Reports Related to Irrigation, 1905–41, box 1, Regional Archives, Denver. Also relevant are the court records in a subsequent suit filed in 1925 concerning water rights for the reservation, discussed briefly below, *United States v. Parkins,* Docket No. 1555, Records of the U.S. District Courts, RG 21, District of Wyoming, Civil Case Files, 1912–25, box 255, folder 1555, Regional Archives, Denver, with a reported decision at *United States v. Parkins,* 18 F.2d 642, 642–43. Again, I am providing only the highlights of the Wind River situation.

33. Reply Brief on Behalf of Plaintiff (March 31, 1915), 1–2, *United States v. Hampleman,* Docket No. 753, Records of the U.S. District Courts, RG 21, District of Wyoming, Civil Case Files, box 119, folder 753, Regional Archives, Denver,

34. "Brief of the United States," June 1913, Ethelbert Ward on behalf of the Reclamation Service, water rights adjudication proceedings, Uncompahgre Valley Project, Seventh Judicial District, Colorado, Department of the Interior, Records of the Bureau of Reclamation, RG 115, Regional Archives, Seattle.

35. Department of Justice, *Annual Report of the Attorney General of the United States for the Year 1914,* printed as H. Doc. 1390, 63rd Cong., 3d Sess., U.S. Serial Set 6810.

36. H. Doc. No. 505, S. Doc. No. 337, 63rd Cong., 2d Sess. (December 20, 1913); 51 *Cong. Rec.* 1263–83 (December 19, 1913).

37. 51 *Cong. Rec.* 1263–65 (December 19, 1913; remarks of Sen. Joseph Robinson).

38. H. Rep. [Conf.] No. 1031, 63rd Cong., 2d Sess. (July 28, 1914), 155.

39. Act of August 1, 1914, chap. 222, 38 Stat. 582, 604–05; S. Rep. No. 519, 63rd Cong., 2d Sess. (May 15, 1914), 58; H. Rep. [Conf.] No. 1031, 63rd Cong., 2d Sess. (July 28, 1914); 51 *Cong. Rec.* 10851 (June 22, 1914), 11469–70 (July 1, 1914), 12944–51 (July 29, 1914).

40. Unfortunately, as McCool and others have noted, Congress's action in 1914 did not end the conflict between the Yakimas and the settlers over water, nor did it work to the advantage of the Yakimas to the degree that it should have. McCool, *Command of the Waters,* 58.

41. Act of August 1, 1914, chap. 222, 38 Stat. 582, 587, 588–89; H. Doc. No. 791, 63rd Cong., 2d Sess. (February 25, 1914); S. Rep. No. 519, 63rd Cong., 2d Sess. (May 15, 1914), 30; 51 *Cong. Rec.* 3930 (February 25, 1914), 10594 (June 17, 1914), 10918–20 (June 22, 1914); 52 *Cong. Rec.* 994 (January 5, 1915), 4905–07, 5085 (March 1, 1915).

42. H.R. Rep. No. 199, 63rd Cong., 2d Sess. (January 28, 1914; to accompany H.R. 12579), reported at 51 *Cong. Rec.* 3661–62 (February 19, 1914).

43. Ibid.; see also 51 *Cong. Rec.* 3661–62, 3672, 3674–75 (February 19, 1914); S. Rep. No. 519, 63rd Cong., 2d Sess.(May 15, 1914), 33, 40; 51 Cong Rec. 10595–89, 10834–35, 10851 (June 17 and 22, 1914).

44. 51 *Cong. Rec.* 3661–62 (February 19, 1914).

45. 51 *Cong. Rec.* 10544 (June 16, 1914), introducing the Joint Memorial of the Colorado General Assembly (March 8, 1913).

46. 51 *Cong. Rec.* 10595–600, 10653, 10769–89, 10834–35, 10851, 10936–46, 11019–36 (June 17, 18, 20, 22, 23, and 24, 1914), 12604–16 (July 24, 1914), 12877–78 (July 28, 1914), 12941–51 (July 29, 1914); 52 *Cong. Rec.* 999–1002 (January 5, 1915), 1309–21 (January 9, 1915), 4824–29 (February 27, 1915), 4899–4907, 4926–44, 4965–66, 5082–87 (March 1, 1915).

47. 51 *Cong. Rec.* 10936–46 (June 23, 1914).

48. 51 *Cong. Rec.* 11019–36 (June 24, 1914), 11916–17 (July 9, 1914), 12604–16 (July 24, 1914), 12877–78 (July 28, 1914); H. Rep. [Conf.] Nos. 1007 and 1031, 63rd Cong., 2d Sess. (July 22 and 28, 1914); Act of August 1, 1914, chap. 222, 38 Stat. 582, 583.

49. See 51 *Cong. Rec.* 3662 (February 19, 1914; remarks of Representative Mondell), 10771–77, 10780–81, 10783, 10785–87 (June 20, 1914; remarks of Senators George Sutherland, Reed Smoot, Marcus Smith, Francis Warren, Henry Myers, John Shafroth, and William Borah), 10851 (June 22, 1914; remarks of Senator Smoot), 10936, 10938–40, 10942–43 (June 23, 1914; remarks of Senators Sutherland, Shafroth, and Myers), 11020–24 (June 24, 1914;

remarks of Senators Charles Thomas, John Works, and Myers), 12607, 12613 (July 24, 1914; remarks of Senator Sutherland), 12949 (July 29, 1914; remarks of Representative Mondell); 52 *Cong. Rec.* 4824–29 (February 27, 1915; remarks of Senator Albert Fall), 4905–07, 4935–36, 4941–42 (March 1, 1915; remarks of Senators Smith, Fall, and Clarence Clark).

50. 52 *Cong. Rec.* 4942–43 (March 1, 1915).

51. H. Doc. Nos. 1215, 1250, 1274, 63rd Cong., 3d Sess. (December 8 and 9, 1914); H.R. 20150, 63rd Cong., 3d Sess.; H. Rep. Nos. 1228, 1509 [Conf.], S. Rep. No. 1022, 63rd Cong., 3d Sess. (to accompany H.R. 20150); 52 *Cong. Rec.* 994, 1000–02 (January 5, 1915), 1309–21 (January 9, 1915), 4824–29 (February 27, 1915), 4899–4907, 4926–44, 4965–66, 5082–87 (March 1, 1915), 5367, 5407, 5497 (March 3, 1915), 5526–27 (March 4, 1915).

52. 51 *Cong. Rec.* 10597–98 (June 17, 1914; remarks of Senator Borah).

53. 51 *Cong. Rec.* 12613 (July 24, 1914; remarks of Senator Sutherland).

54. See, e.g., 40 *Cong. Rec.* 7814–16 (June 14, 1906; remarks of Rep. Joseph Dixon); 42 *Cong. Rec.* 1813 (February 11, 1908; remarks of Sen. Joseph Dixon); 49 Cong. Rec. 1041 (January 4, 1913; remarks of Rep. Charles Pray); 51 *Cong. Rec.* 3662–63 (February 19, 1914; remarks of Representatives Stout and Stafford), 10774–75 (June 20, 1914; remarks of Senator Myers), 11019–20 (June 20, 1914; remarks of Senator Myers), 11916–17 (July 9, 1914; remarks of Representative Evans); 12604–06, 12607, 12610 (July 24, 1914; remarks of Senators Myers and Walsh), 12877–88 (July 28, 1914; remarks of Senators Walsh and Myers); 52 Cong Rec. 4927–29 (March 1, 1915; remarks of Senator Myers).

55. Hoxie does show that in general Senator Ashurst did not deviate from the mainstream attitude toward assimilation and allotments and in fact was one of assimilation's "policymakers" in the period 1913–20. Hoxie, *Final Promise,* 109, 111, 181, 185–86.

56. Concerning Senator Ashurst's position in this debate in these years, see S. Rep. No. 519, 63rd Cong., 2d Sess. (May 15, 1914; to accompany H.R. 12579); 51 *Cong. Rec.* 10532 (June 16, 1914), 10594 (June 17, 1914), 12611 (July 24, 1914). Representative Stephens's actions on behalf of the Indians and the reserved rights doctrine have been noted elsewhere and in the discussion above concerning actions in the House during the Sixty-third Congress.

57. 51 *Cong. Rec.* 10943 (June 23, 1914; remarks of Senator Robinson).

58. S. Doc. No. 805, 61st Cong., 3d Sess. (February 1, 1911), 2–3, 7–9.

59. H. Doc. No. 1215, 63rd Cong., 3d Sess.(December 8, 1914), 20.

60. Ibid.

61. 51 *Cong. Rec.* 3660 (February 19, 1914).

62. Hoxie, *Final Promise,* 179.

63. 51 *Cong. Rec.* 10596, 10598–99 (June 17, 1914).

64. 51 *Cong. Rec.* 12607 (July 24, 1914); 52 Cong. Rec. 4903 (March 1, 1915).

65. 52 *Cong. Rec.* 4900 (March 1, 1915). Senator Lane's description of Indian religious attitudes toward land closely matched the tenets of the Dreamer religion then prevalent among various indigenous groups in the Pacific Northwest. See Ruby and Brown, *Dreamer-Prophets of the Columbia*

Plateau. My thanks to Professor Richard M. Brown for suggesting the relationship. Senator Lane's observations were echoed unconsciously in remarks from Senator Smith of Arizona, an unabashed supporter of the western establishment. Smith complained about how hard it was to get the Papagos in Arizona to stay in a specified place. He spoke about the "peculiar nature" of the Papagos in that they abandon land "the minute it does not become profitable for them to remain there," something of course that could have also been said of many non-Indians in the West. 51 *Cong. Rec.* 10858 (June 22, 1914).

66. 52 *Cong. Rec.* 4905–07 (March 1, 1915). At the urging of a number of senators, Lane eventually backed off and let the appropriation pass the Senate. 52 *Cong. Rec.* 5085.

CHAPTER 11: BACK AT THE UINTAH RESERVATION

1. "Memorandum—Necessity for legal assistance," March 25, 1913, Department of the Interior, Records of the Bureau of Indian Affairs, RG 75, Irrigation Division, General Correspondence, box 653-3, National Archives.

2. Henry W. Dietz, superintendent of irrigation, Indian Irrigation Service, to W. M. Reed, chief engineer, Indian Irrigation Service, January 29, 1914, and W. M. Reed to Dietz, February 9, 1914, Department of the Interior, Records of the Bureau of Indian Affairs, RG 75, Irrigation Division, General Correspondence, box 26, "Uintah, 1913–14–15," National Archives.

3. F. K. Lane, secretary of the interior, to Speaker of the House of Representatives, December 7, 1914, Department of the Interior, Records of the Bureau of Indian Affairs, RG 75, Irrigation Division, General Correspondence, box 28, "Uintah No. 3," National Archives. Matters of style and the nature of the arguments indicate that Meritt of the Bureau of Indian Affairs was the principal author of the letter. The act requesting the report is the Act of August 1, 1914, 38 Stat. 582, 583.

4. C. Sells, commissioner of Indian affairs, to secretary of the interior, June 2, 1915, Department of the Interior, Records of the Department of the Interior, RG 48, Central Classified Files, 1907–1936, box 1387, "Indian Office, Uintah and Ouray Irrigation, Dry Gulch Irrigation Company, June 13, 1907, to June 2, 1915," National Archives.

5. Joseph Bryant, engineer, Uintah Irrigation Project, to H. W. Dietz, superintendent of irrigation, Indian Irrigation Service, March 21, 1916; Dietz to commissioner of Indian affairs, March 24, 1916; E. B. Meritt, assistant commissioner of Indian affairs, to Dietz, April 5, 1916; Meritt to W. D. Beers, Utah state engineer, April 5, 1916, Department of the Interior, Records of the Bureau of Indian Affairs, RG 75, Portland Area Office, Indian Irrigation Service, Irrigation District No. 2, Project Case Files, 1916–1934, box 809, folder U, W-60, "Water Rights, Miscellaneous, 1916–1922," Regional Archives, Seattle.

6. J. F. Truesdell, special assistant to the attorney general, to H. W. Dietz, superintendent of irrigation, Indian Irrigation Service, October 30, 1915, and Truesdell to William W. Ray, U.S. attorney, District of Utah, November 17,

1915, Department of the Interior, Records of the Bureau of Indian Affairs, RG 75, Irrigation Division, General Correspondence, box 26, "Uintah, 1913–14–15," National Archives. A number of documents over the next half year detail the information-gathering effort, of which these are only examples: assistant inspector for irrigation to commissioner of Indian affairs, February 2, 1916, Department of the Interior, Records of the Bureau of Indian Affairs, RG 75, Irrigation Division, General Correspondence, box 27, "Uintah, 1916," National Archives; Truesdell to Dietz, April 19, 1916; Truesdell to Ray, May 8, 1916; Truesdell to J. Bryant, engineer, Uintah Irrigation Project, May 19, 1916; Truesdell to Ray, July 13, 1916, Department of the Interior, Records of the Bureau of Indian Affairs, RG 75, Portland Area Office, Indian Irrigation Service, Irrigation District No. 2, Project Case Files, 1916–1934, box 809, folder U, W-20, "Water Commissioner and Suits," Regional Archives, Seattle.

7. The complaints and accompanying affidavits are in Bill of Complaint, *United States v. Dry Gulch Irrigation Company,* Docket No. 4418 (July ?, 1916), and Bill of Complaint, *United States v. Cedarview Irrigation Company,* Docket No. 4427 (July 17, 1916), Records of the U.S. District Courts, RG 21, District of Utah, Combined Bankruptcy, Civil, and Criminal Case Files, 1880–1931, box 435, folder 4418, and box 436, folder 4427, Regional Archives, Denver. What many others referred to as Lake Fork Creek, Truesdell always referred to properly as Lake Fork River, which thus became its name in the litigation.

8. Bill of Complaint (July ?, 1916), *United States v. Dry Gulch Irrigation Company,* Docket No. 4418, and Bill of Complaint (July 17, 1916), *United States v. Cedarview Irrigation Company,* Docket No. 4427, Records of the U.S. District Courts, RG 21, District of Utah, Combined Bankruptcy, Civil, and Criminal Case Files, 1880–1931, box 435, folder 4418, and box 436, folder 4427, Regional Archives, Denver.

9. Bill of Complaint, 12–13, *United States v. Dry Gulch Irrigation Company,* Docket No. 4418, and Bill of Complaint, 12–13, *United States v. Cedarview Irrigation Company,* Docket No. 4427, Records of the U.S. District Courts, RG 21, District of Utah, Combined Bankruptcy, Civil, and Criminal Case Files, 1880–1931, box 435, folder 4418, and box 436, folder 4427, Regional Archives, Denver.

10. Bill of Complaint, 23–24 (emphasis added), *United States v. Dry Gulch Irrigation Company,* Docket No. 4418, and Bill of Complaint, 30–31 (emphasis added), *United States v. Cedarview Irrigation Company,* Docket No. 4427, Records of the U.S. District Courts, RG 21, District of Utah, Combined Bankruptcy, Civil, and Criminal Case Files, 1880–1931, box 435, folder 4418, and box 436, folder 4427, Regional Archives, Denver.

11. Bill of Complaint, 27–28, *United States v. Dry Gulch Irrigation Company,* Docket No. 4418, and Bill of Complaint, 35, *United States v. Cedarview Irrigation Company,* Docket No. 4427, Records of the U.S. District Courts, RG 21, District of Utah, Combined Bankruptcy, Civil, and Criminal Case Files, 1880–1931, box 435, folder 4418, and box 436, folder 4427, Regional Archives, Denver.

12. *United States v. Dry Gulch Irrigation Company,* Docket No. 4418, Order issuing temporary restraining order and setting date for a preliminary injunction hearing, July 10, 1916; Order issuing injunction and appointing commissioner, July 26, 1916; Answer, June 30, 1917; Joint Order in Dockets No. 4418 and 4427 reappointing and instructing commissioner, April 12, 1917 (the first of such orders issued yearly; the rest will not be noted here); *United States v. Cedarview Irrigation Company,* Docket No. 4427, Order issuing temporary restraining order and setting date for a preliminary injunction hearing, July 17, 1916; Order issuing injunction and appointing commissioner, July 26, 1916, Answer, June 30, 1917; Joint Order in Dockets No. 4418 and 4427 reappointing and instructing commissioner, April 12, 1917, Records of the U.S. District Courts, RG 21, District of Utah, Combined Bankruptcy, Civil, and Criminal Case Files, 1880–1931, box 435, folder 4418, and box 436, folder 4427, Regional Archives, Denver; J. F. Truesdell, special assistant to the attorney general, to W. W. Ray, U.S. attorney, District of Utah, July 13, 1916, and H. W. Dietz, superintendent of irrigation, Indian Irrigation Service, to W. M. Reed, chief engineer, Indian Irrigation Service, July 26, 1916, Department of the Interior, Records of the Bureau of Indian Affairs, RG 75, Portland Area Office, Indian Irrigation Service, Irrigation District No. 2, Project Case Files, 1916–1934, box 809, folder U, W-20, "Water Commissioner and Suits," Regional Archives, Seattle. The court records for the Uintah cases contain only pleadings (complaint, answer, etc.), orders, and decrees and reports of the water commissioner; the files have been purged of any briefs or other documents containing legal analysis. A copy of one brief filed by Truesdell and Ward in the Uintah cases (on the issue of the "United States' Ownership of Unappropriated Waters of Innavigable Streams in Public Land States") did surface in the 1940s files of the Gila River litigation in the Regional Archives in Los Angeles. My thanks to Shelly Dudley for sending me a copy.

13. J. F. Truesdell, special assistant to the attorney general, to W. M. Reed, chief engineer, Indian Irrigation Service, April 17, 1918; A. Vogelsang, acting secretary of the interior, to the president of the Senate, December 28, 1920; chief engineer to Charles Burke, commissioner of Indian affairs, October 31, 1921, Department of the Interior, Records of the Bureau of Indian Affairs, RG 75, Irrigation Division, General Correspondence, box 27, "Uintah, 1918–19" and "Uintah, 1920–21," box 28, "Uintah No. 3", National Archives; Truesdell to Albert H. Kneale, superintendent, Uintah Indian Reservation, February 7, 1919; Truesdell to Kneale, February 8, 1919; Truesdell to the attorney general, February 8, 1919; H. W. Dietz, district supervising engineer, Indian Irrigation Service, to Truesdell, March 5, 1919; Truesdell to W. M. Reed, October 9, 1919; Truesdell to Dietz, November 13, 1919; Truesdell to Dietz, November 29, 1919; Dietz to Truesdell, December 3, 1919; Truesdell to the commissioner of Indian affairs, April 6, 1920; E. B. Meritt, assistant commissioner of Indian affairs, to Dietz and Kneale, April 19, 1920, Department of the Interior, Records of the Bureau of Indian Affairs, RG 75, Portland Area Office, Indian Irrigation Service, Irrigation District No. 2, Project Case Files, 1916–1934, box

809, folder U, W-20, "Water Commissioner and Suits," Regional Archives, Seattle; F. K. Lane, secretary of the interior, to Utah governor, January 3, 1919, Department of the Interior, Records of the Department of the Interior, RG 48, Central Classified Files, 1907–1936, box 1387, "Uintah and Ouray Irrigation, January 21, 1918, to July 18, 1928," National Archives.

14. Consolidated Irrigation Companies—Defendants in the U.S. Indian Water Suit, to W. W. Ray, U.S. attorney, Utah District, and H. W. Dietz, district engineer, Indian Irrigation Service, June 23, 1919; J. F. Truesdell, special assistant to the attorney general, to W. M. Reed, chief engineer, Indian Irrigation Service, October 9, 1919; Truesdell to Dietz, November 13, 1919; Truesdell to Dietz, November 29, 1919; Dietz to Truesdell, December 3, 1919; Dietz to Truesdell, January 31, 1920 (two letters); Truesdell to the commissioner of Indian affairs, April 6, 1920, Department of the Interior, Records of the Bureau of Indian Affairs, RG 75, Portland Area Office, Indian Irrigation Service, Irrigation District No. 2, Project Case Files, 1916–1934, box 809, folder U, W-20, "Water Commissioner and Suits," Regional Archives, Seattle; Truesdell, Ray, W. M. Reed, and John R. T. Reeves to commissioner of Indian affairs, October 18, 1919; C. Sells, commissioner of Indian affairs, to secretary of the interior, October 20, 1919; W. M. Reed to Truesdell, October 27, 1919, Truesdell to the attorney general, November 29, 1919, Department of the Interior, Records of the Bureau of Indian Affairs, RG 75, Irrigation Division, General Correspondence, box 27, "Uintah, 1918–19," and box 28, "Uintah No. 3," National Archives.

15. W. M. Reed to J. F. Truesdell, October 27, 1919, Department of the Interior, Records of the Bureau of Indian Affairs, RG 75, Irrigation Division, General Correspondence, box 27, "Uintah, 1918–19," National Archives.

16. J. F. Truesdell, special assistant to the attorney general, W. W. Ray, U.S. attorney, Utah District, W. M. Reed, chief engineer, Indian Irrigation Service, and J. R. T. Reeves to commissioner of Indian affairs, October 18, 1919; Department of the Interior, Records of the Bureau of Indian Affairs, RG 75, Irrigation Division, General Correspondence, box 28, "Uintah No. 3," National Archives.

17. Department of Justice, *Annual Report of the Attorney-General of the United States for the Year Ended June 30, 1910,* printed as H. Doc. 1003, 61st Cong., 3d Sess., U.S. Serial Set 5969, 29–30.

18. C. Sells, commissioner of Indian affairs, to secretary of the interior, October 20, 1919; Department of the Interior, Records of the Bureau of Indian Affairs, RG 75, Irrigation Division, General Correspondence, box 28, "Uintah No. 3," National Archives.

19. Consolidated Irrigation Companies—Defendants in the U.S. Indian Water Suit, to W. W. Ray, U.S. attorney, Utah District, and H. W. Dietz, district engineer, Indian Irrigation Service, June 23, 1919; J. F. Truesdell, special assistant to the attorney general, to W. M. Reed, chief engineer, Indian Irrigation Service, October 9, 1919; Truesdell to Dietz, November 13, 1919; Truesdell to Dietz, November 29, 1919; Dietz to Truesdell, December 3, 1919;

Dietz to Truesdell, January 31, 1920 (two letters); Truesdell to the commissioner of Indian affairs, April 6, 1920, Department of the Interior, Records of the Bureau of Indian Affairs, RG 75, Portland Area Office, Indian Irrigation Service, Irrigation District No. 2, Project Case Files, 1916–1934, box 809, folder U, W-20, "Water Commissioner and Suits," Regional Archives, Seattle; W. M. Reed to Truesdell, October 27, 1919, Truesdell to the attorney general, November 29, 1919, Department of the Interior, Records of the Bureau of Indian Affairs, RG 75, Irrigation Division, General Correspondence, box 27, "Uintah, 1918–19," and box 28, "Uintah No. 3," National Archives; *United States v. Dry Gulch Irrigation Company,* Docket No. 4418, and *United States v. Cedarview Irrigation Company,* Docket No. 4427, joint Order reappointing and instructing commissioner, March 29, 1920, Records of the U.S. District Courts, RG 21, District of Utah, Combined Bankruptcy, Civil, and Criminal Case Files, 1880–1931, box 435, folder 4418, and box 436, folder 4427, Regional Archives, Denver.

20. By 1919, more than three dozen lessees had filed damage claims against the federal government, based on allegations that the government had induced them to come to the reservation to farm under false assurances that water was available to irrigate the farms and that markets existed for the crops grown. See A. Vogelsang, acting secretary of the interior, to the president of the Senate, December 28, 1920; chief engineer to C. Burke, commissioner of Indian affairs, October 31, 1921, Department of the Interior, Records of the Bureau of Indian Affairs, RG 75, Irrigation Division, General Correspondence, box 28, "Uintah No. 3," National Archives.

21. A. Vogelsang, acting secretary of the interior, to the president of the Senate, December 28, 1920; chief engineer to C. Burke, commissioner of Indian affairs, October 31, 1921, H. W. Dietz, supervising engineer, Indian Irrigation Service, to J. F. Truesdell, special assistant to the attorney general, January 4, 1922, Department of the Interior, Records of the Bureau of Indian Affairs, RG 75, Irrigation Division, General Correspondence, box 27, "Uintah, 1920–21" and "Uintah, 1922, 1923, 1924," box 28, "Uintah No. 3," National Archives; Dietz to W. M. Reed, chief engineer, Indian Irrigation Service, October 9, 1919; Truesdell, "Memorandum Concerning . . . Uintah Basin Suits, Utah," with proposed decrees attached, March 10, 1922; W. L. Woolf, attorney for defendants, to Alfred A. Charles, engineer, Uintah Irrigation Project, March 25, 1922; A. A. Charles to Dietz, March 29, 1922; F. M. Goodwin, assistant secretary of the interior, to the attorney general, April 1, 1922; W. D. Ritter, assistant attorney general, to Ethelbert Ward, special assistant to the attorney general, April 5, 1922; Ward to Dietz, June 10, 1922, Department of the Interior, Records of the Bureau of Indian Affairs, RG 75, Portland Area Office, Indian Irrigation Service, Irrigation District No. 2, Project Case Files, 1916–1934, box 809, folder U, W-20, "Water Commissioner and Suits," Regional Archives, Seattle; Albert Fall, secretary of the interior, to Utah Sen. William King, November 5, 1921, Department of the Interior, Records of the Department of the Interior, RG 48, Central Classified Files, 1907–1936, box 1387, "Uintah and

Ouray Irrigation, January 21, 1918, to July 18, 1928," National Archives; *United States v. Dry Gulch Irrigation Company,* Docket No. 4418, Decree, March 16, 1923; *United States v. Cedarview Irrigation Company,* Docket No. 4427, Decree, March 16, 1923, Records of the U.S. District Courts, RG 21, District of Utah, Combined Bankruptcy, Civil, and Criminal Case Files, 1880–1931, box 435, folder 4418, and box 436, folder 4427, Regional Archives, Denver; "Indians vs. Whites Suit is Settled," *Salt Lake Tribune,* March 22, 1923. Truesdell left the employ of the Justice Department in 1922, and Ethelbert Ward replaced him as the lead attorney in the Uintah case. Thus it was Ward who finalized the decrees and then supervised the administration of the decrees until the federal court ended its supervision of the decrees in 1931.

22. *United States v. Dry Gulch Irrigation Company,* Docket No. 4418, Decree, March 16, 1923; *United States v. Cedarview Irrigation Company,* Docket No. 4427, Decree, March 16, 1923, Records of the U.S. District Courts, RG 21, District of Utah, Combined Bankruptcy, Civil, and Criminal Case Files, 1880–1931, box 435, folder 4418, and box 436, folder 4427, Regional Archives, Denver; J. F. Truesdell, special assistant to the attorney general, "Memorandum Concerning . . . Uintah Basin Suits, Utah," with proposed decrees attached, March 10, 1922, Department of the Interior, Records of the Bureau of Indian Affairs, RG 75, Portland Area Office, Indian Irrigation Service, Irrigation District No. 2, Project Case Files, 1916–1934, box 809, folder U, W–20, "Water Commissioner and Suits," Regional Archives, Seattle; *Skeem v. United States,* 273 F. 93, 94–96.

23. *United States v. Dry Gulch Irrigation Company,* Docket No. 4418, Decree, March 16, 1923; *United States v. Cedarview Irrigation Company,* Docket No. 4427, Decree, March 16, 1923, Records of the U.S. District Courts, RG 21, District of Utah, Combined Bankruptcy, Civil, and Criminal Case Files, 1880–1931, box 435, folder 4418, and box 436, folder 4427, Regional Archives, Denver; W. L. Woolf, attorney for defendants, to A. A. Charles, engineer, Uintah Irrigation Project, March 25, 1922; Charles to H. W. Dietz, supervising engineer, Indian Irrigation Service, March 29, 1922; E. B. Meritt, acting commissioner of Indian affairs, to W. E. Blomgren, acting supervising engineer, Indian Irrigation Service, August 29, 1927, Department of the Interior, Records of the Bureau of Indian Affairs, RG 75, Portland Area Office, Indian Irrigation Service, Irrigation District No. 2, Project Case Files, 1916–1934, box 809, folder U, W–20, "Water Commissioner and Suits," Regional Archives, Seattle.

24. *United States v. Parkins,* 18 F.2d 642, 642–43; Docket No. 1555, Records of the U.S. District Courts, RG 21, District of Wyoming, Civil Case Files, 1912–25, box 255, folder 1555, Regional Archives, Denver. The federal government filed the case in 1925.

25. George M. Bacon, Utah state engineer, to Paul F. Henderson, engineer, Indian Irrigation Service, September 11, 1930, Henderson to Bacon, September 17, 1930, Department of the Interior, Records of the Bureau of Indian Affairs, RG 75, Portland Area Office, Indian Irrigation Service, Irrigation District No.

2, Project Case Files, 1916–1934, box 809, folder U, W-20, "Water Commissioner and Suits," Regional Archives, Seattle.

26. The information in this paragraph and the subsequent paragraphs describing the ramifications of the judge's decision come from Ethelbert Ward, special assistant to the attorney general, to the attorney general, January 26, 1931, and February 19, 1931; Ward to C. A. Engle, supervising engineer, Indian Irrigation Service, March 6, 1931, B. S. Garber, acting commissioner of Indian affairs, "Memorandum for Mr. Ely," April 23, 1931; Ray Lyman Wilbur, secretary of the interior, to Utah Sen. R. Smoot, April 24, 1931; Engle to the commissioner of Indian affairs, May 1, 1931, Department of the Interior, Records of the Bureau of Indian Affairs, RG 75, Portland Area Office, Indian Irrigation Service, Irrigation District No. 2, Project Case Files, 1916–1934, box 809, folder U, W-20, "Water Commissioner and Suits," Regional Archives, Seattle; *United States v. Dry Gulch Irrigation Company,* Docket No. 4418, and *United States v. Cedarview Irrigation Company,* Docket No. 4427, Order modifying decrees, February 17, 1931, Records of the U.S. District Courts, RG 21, District of Utah, Combined Bankruptcy, Civil, and Criminal Case Files, 1880–1931, box 435, folder 4418, and box 436, folder 4427, Regional Archives, Denver; "Federal Judge Ends Vigil for Water Users," *Salt Lake Tribune,* February 15, 1931; "Distribution of Basin Water Yet Unsettled," *Salt Lake Tribune,* May 10, 1931.

27. B. S. Garber, acting commissioner of Indian affairs, "Memorandum for Mr. Ely," April 23, 1931; Department of the Interior, Records of the Bureau of Indian Affairs, RG 75, Portland Area Office, Indian Irrigation Service, Irrigation District No. 2, Project Case Files, 1916–1934, box 809, folder U, W-20, "Water Commissioner and Suits," Regional Archives, Seattle.

28. Ibid.

29. Ethelbert Ward, special assistant to the attorney general, to the attorney general, January 26, 1931, and February 19, 1931; Ward to C. A. Engle, supervising engineer, Indian Irrigation Service, March 6, 1931; B. S. Garber, acting commissioner of Indian affairs, "Memorandum for Mr. Ely," April 23, 1931; R. L. Wilbur, secretary of the interior, to Utah Sen. R. Smoot, April 24, 1931; Engle to the commissioner of Indian affairs, May 1, 1931, Department of the Interior, Records of the Bureau of Indian Affairs, RG 75, Portland Area Office, Indian Irrigation Service, Irrigation District No. 2, Project Case Files, 1916–1934, box 809, folder U, W-20, "Water Commissioner and Suits," Regional Archives, Seattle; *United States v. Dry Gulch Irrigation Company,* Docket No. 4418, and *United States v. Cedarview Irrigation Company,* Docket No. 4427, joint Order modifying decrees, February 17, 1931, Records of the U.S. District Courts, RG 21, District of Utah, Combined Bankruptcy, Civil, and Criminal Case Files, 1880–1931, box 435, folder 4418, and box 436, folder 4427, Regional Archives, Denver; "Federal Judge Ends Vigil for Water Users," *Salt Lake Tribune,* February 15, 1931; "Distribution of Basin Water Yet Unsettled," *Salt Lake Tribune,* May 10, 1931.

CHAPTER 12: LESSONS FROM THE UINTAH
RESERVATION LITIGATION

1. *United States v. Dry Gulch Irrigation Company,* Docket No. 4418, Decree, March 16, 1923; *United States v. Cedarview Irrigation Company,* Docket No. 4427, Decree, March 16, 1923, Records of the U.S. District Courts, RG 21, District of Utah, Combined Bankruptcy, Civil, and Criminal Case Files, 1880–1931, box 435, folder 4418, and box 436, folder 4427, Regional Archives, Denver. The court's yearly instructions to the water commissioner are in the same files.

2. F. E. Leupp, commissioner of Indian affairs, to President Roosevelt, March 27, 1906, Department of the Interior, Records of the Bureau of Reclamation, RG 115, General Administrative Files, 1902–1919, box 99, file 127, "Uintah Indian Reservation—Utah, 1904 thru ?", National Archives.

Bibliography

FEDERAL AND STATE COURT DECISIONS

Anderson v. Spear-Morgan Livestock Company. 79 P.2d 667 (Montana Supreme Court, 1938).

Arizona v. California. October Term 1960, No. 8 Orig., Report of Special Master (December 5, 1960); 373 U.S. 546 (1963); 439 U.S. 419 (1979), 460 U.S. 605 (1983).

Arizona v. San Carlos Apache Tribe. 463 U.S. 545 (1983).

Burley v. United States. 179 F. 1 (9th Cir. 1910).

Byers v. Wa-wa-ne. 169 P. 121 (Oregon Supreme Court, December 11, 1917).

California Oregon Power Company v. Beaver Portland Cement Company. 295 U.S. 142 (1935).

City and County of Denver v. Colorado River Water Conservation District. 696 P.2d 730 (Colorado Supreme Court, 1985).

Choctaw Nation v. United States. 119 U.S. 1 (1886).

Colorado River Water Conservation District v. United States. 424 U.S. 800 (1976).

Colville Confederated Tribes v. Walton. 460 F. Supp. 1320 (E.D. Wash. 1978); 647 F.2d 42 (9th Cir. 1981); 752 F.2d 397 (9th Cir. 1985).

Cruse v. McCauley. 96 F. 369 (D. Montana, August 30, 1899).

Gutierres v. Albuquerque Land and Irrigation Company. 188 U.S. 545 (1903).

Hough v. Porter. 98 P. 1083 (Oregon Supreme Court, 1909).

In re General Adjudication of All Rights to Use Water in the Big Horn River System. 753 P.2d 76 (Wyoming Supreme Court, 1989), *affirmed by equally divided court without opinion,* 492 U.S. 406 (1989); 835 P.2d 273 (Wyoming Supreme Court, 1992).

Jones v. Meehan. 175 U.S. 1 (1899).

The Kansas Indians. 72 U.S. (5 Wall.) 737 (1866).

Kansas v. Colorado. 206 U.S. 46 (1907).

Krall v. United States. 79 F. 241 (9th Cir. 1897), *appeal dismissed for lack of juris-diction,* 174 U.S. 385 (1899).

Lone Wolf v. Hitchcock. 187 U.S. 553 (1903).

Mettler v. Ames Realty Company. 201 P. 702 (Montana Supreme Court, 1921).

Mower v. Bond. 8 F.2d 518 (D. Idaho 1925).

North Side Canal Company v. Twin Falls Canal Company. 12 F.2d 311 (D. Idaho 1926).

Pioneer Packing Company v. Winslow. 294 P. 556 (Washington Supreme Court, 1930).

Skeem v. United States. 273 F. 93 (9th Cir., May 2, 1921).

Smith v. Denniff. 24 Mont. 20, 60 P. 398 (Montana Supreme Court, March 12, 1900).

Sowards v. Meagher. 108 P. 1112 (Utah Supreme Court, 1910).

State v. Towessnute. 154 P. 805 (Washington Supreme Court, 1916).

Story v. Wolverton. 31 Mont. 346, 78 P. 589 (Montana Supreme Court, December 1, 1904).

Thorp v. Freed. 1 Mont. 651 (Montana Territorial Supreme Court, 1872).

United States v. Conrad Investment Company. 156 F. 123 (D. Montana, August 5, 1907), *affirmed, Conrad Investment Company v. United States,* 161 F. 829 (9th Cir., May 25, 1908).

United States v. McIntire. 101 F.2d 650 (9th Cir. 1939).

United States v. Parkins. 18 F.2d 642 (D. Wyoming, October 11, 1926).

United States v. Powers. 305 U.S. 527 (1939).

United States v. Rio Grande Dam and Irrigation Company. 174 U.S. 690 (1899).

United States v. Walker River Irrigation District. 11 F. Supp. 158 (D. Nevada 1935), 14 F. Supp. 11 (D. Nevada 1936), *reversed* 104 F.2d 335 (9th Cir. 1939).

United States v. Wightman. 230 F. 277 (D. Arizona, January 11, 1916).

United States v. Winans. 198 U.S. 371 (May 15, 1905).

United States ex rel. Ray v. Hibner. 27 F.2d 909 (D. Idaho 1928).

Willey v. Decker. 14 Wyo. 496, 73 P. 210 (Wyoming Supreme Court, August 3, 1903).

Winters v. United States. 207 U.S. 564, 28 Sup. Ct. 207 (January 6, 1908), *affirming* 143 F. 740 (9th Cir., February 5, 1906) and 148 F. 684 (9th Cir., October 1, 1906).

Worcester v. Georgia. 31 U.S. (6 Pet.) 515 (1832).

Wyoming v. Colorado. 259 U.S. 419 (1922).

GOVERNMENT DOCUMENTS—UNITED STATES

Boundary Waters Treaty between the United States and Great Britain. 36 Stat. 2448–2455 (signed January 11, 1909; ratified by Senate March 3, 1909).

Department of the Interior. *Annual Report of the Commissioner of Indian Affairs,* 1890–1932.

————, Bureau of Indian Affairs. Records of the Bureau of Indian Affairs, RG 75, Fort Belknap Indian Agency Papers, Federal Archives and Records Center, Seattle.

————, Bureau of Indian Affairs. Records of the Bureau of Indian Affairs, RG 75, Irrigation Branch, Irrigation Project Case Files, Federal Archives and Records Center, Seattle.

————, Bureau of Indian Affairs. Records of the Bureau of Indian Affairs, RG 75, Irrigation Division, General Correspondence, National Archives.

————, Bureau of Indian Affairs. Records of the Bureau of Indian Affairs, RG 75, Wind River Agency, General Correspondence Files, 1890–1961, and Correspondence and Reports Related to Irrigation, 1905–41, Rocky Mountain Region of the National Archives, Denver.

————, Bureau of Reclamation. Records of the Bureau of Reclamation, RG 115, General Administrative Files, 1902–1919, and Legal Discussions— General, National Archives.

————, Bureau of Reclamation. Records of the Bureau of Reclamation, RG 115, Federal Archives and Records Center, Seattle.

————. Records of the Department of the Interior, RG 48, Central Classified Files, 1907–1936, National Archives.

Department of Justice. *Annual Report of the Attorney-General of the United States*, 1900–1930.

————. Records of the Department of Justice, RG 60, National Archives.

————. Personnel Records of the Department of Justice, National Personnel Records Center, St. Louis.

Fort Hall Indian Water Rights Act of 1990. Public Law No. 101–602, 104 Stat. 3059 (November 16, 1990).

Heitman, Francis B. *Historical Register and Dictionary of the United States Army, from its organization, September 29, 1789, to March 2, 1903*, 2 vols., printed as H. Doc. 446 (March 2, 1903), U.S. Serial Set 4535–36. Washington, D.C.: Government Printing Office, 1903.

Hutchins, Wells A., completed by Harold H. Ellis and J. Peter DeBraal. *Water Rights Laws in the Nineteen Western States*. Vol. 1. Misc. Pub. No. 4206, United States Department of Agriculture, 1971.

Kappler, Charles J., comp. and ed. *Indian Affairs: Laws and Treaties*, 2d ed., 7 vols. Washington, D.C.: Government Printing Office, 1904.

Kendrick, Gregory, ed. *Beyond the Wasatch: The History of Irrigation in the Uinta Basin and Upper Provo River Area of Utah*. Bureau of Reclamation, 1988.

Records of the U.S. District Courts, RG 21, U.S. Ninth Circuit, District of Montana, Federal Archives and Records Center, Seattle.

————, RG 21, District of Utah, Combined Bankruptcy, Civil, and Criminal Case Files, 1880–1931, Rocky Mountain Region of the National Archives, Denver.

————, RG 21, District of Wyoming, Civil Case Files, 1912–25, Rocky Mountain Region of the National Archives, Denver.

Trelease, Frank J. "Federal-State Relations in Water Law." Legal Study no. 5 prepared for the National Water Commission (1971).

United States Congress. *Congressional Record,* 1908–1915.

————, House of Representatives, House Reports and Documents, 1890–1915.

————, Senate, Senate Reports and Documents, 1890–1915.

United States Statutes at Large (Stat.), 1849–1930.

Wheatley, Charles F., Jr., et al. "Study of the Development, Management, and Use of Water Resources on the Public Lands." Summary and Legal Study (vol. 1) prepared for the Public Land Law Review Commission (1969).

GOVERNMENT DOCUMENTS—STATES

Arizona. Constitution of the State of Arizona, 1910.

Colorado. Constitution of the State of Colorado, 1876.

Idaho. Constitution of the State of Idaho, 1890.

Montana. Constitution of the State of Montana, 1889.

Montana. Montana Laws, 1890–1910.

New Mexico. Constitution of the State of New Mexico, 1911.

Utah. Constitution of the State of Utah, 1895.

Wyoming. Constitution of the State of Wyoming, 1890.

NEWSPAPERS

Chinook Bulletin, Chinook, Montana, 1905–1906.

Chinook Opinion, Chinook, Montana, 1902–1910.

Enterprise, Malta, Montana, 1902–1910.

Havre Herald, Havre, Montana, 1902–1910.

Havre Plaindealer, Havre, Montana, 1902–1910.

Helena Independent, Helena, Montana, 1902–1910.

Milk River Valley News, Harlem, Montana, 1902–1910.

Montana Homestead, Hinsdale, Montana, 1902–1910.

North Montana Review, Glasgow, Montana, 1902–1910.

Salt Lake Tribune, Salt Lake City, Utah, 1916–1932.

BOOKS

Barry, Edward E. *The Fort Belknap Indian Reservation: The First One Hundred Years, 1855–1955.* Bozeman: Montana State University, 1974.

Beck, Robert E., ed. *Water and Water Rights.* 4 vols. Charlottesville: Michie Company, 1991, 1996.

Berkhofer, Robert. *The White Man's Indian: Images of the American Indian from Columbus to the Present.* New York: Knopf, 1978.

Burton, Lloyd. *American Indian Water Rights and the Limits of the Law.* Lawrence: University Press of Kansas, 1991.

Carlson, Leonard. *Indians, Bureaucrats and the Land: The Dawes Act and the Decline of Indian Farming.* Westport, Conn.: Greenwood Press, 1981.

Checchio, Elizabeth, and Bonnie G. Colby. *Indian Water Rights: Negotiating the Future.* Tucson: University of Arizona Water Resources Research Center, 1993.

Cheney, Roberta Carkeek. *Names on the Face of Montana: The Story of Montana's Place Names.* Rev. ed. Missoula: Mountain Press Publishing Co., 1984.

Chipman, Frank E. *Index to Legal Periodical Literature.* Vol. 3, *1898–1908.* Boston: Boston Book Company, 1919.

———. *Index to Legal Periodical Literature.* Vol. 4, *1908–22.* Boston: Chipman Law Publishing Company, 1924.

Clark, Blue. *Lone Wolf v. Hitchcock: Treaty Rights and Indian Law at the End of the Nineteenth Century.* Lincoln: University of Nebraska Press, 1994.

Clark, Robert E., ed. *Water and Water Rights: A Treatise in the Law of Waters and Allied Problems.* Vol. 1. Indianapolis: Allen Smith & Company, 1967.

Cohen, Felix S. *Handbook of Federal Indian Law.* Edited by Rennard Strickland. Charlottesville: Michie Company, 1982.

Cutter, Charles C. *The Legal Culture of Northern New Spain, 1700–1810.* Albuquerque: University of New Mexico Press, 1995.

Dobbins, Betty Eakle. *The Spanish Element in Texas Water Law.* Austin: University of Texas Press, 1959.

DuMars, Charles T., Marilyn O'Leary, and Albert Utton. *Pueblo Indian Water Rights.* Tucson: University of Arizona Press, 1984.

Dunbar, Robert G. *Forging New Rights in Western Waters.* Lincoln: University of Nebraska Press, 1983.

Folk-Williams, John A. *What Indian Water Means to the West: A Sourcebook.* Santa Fe: Western Network, 1982.

Foreman, Richard L. *Indian Water Rights: A Public Policy and Administrative Mess.* Danville, Ill.: Interstate Printers and Publishers, 1981.

Frederick, David. *Rugged Justice: The Ninth Circuit Court of Appeals and the American West, 1891–1941.* Berkeley: University of California Press, 1994.

Getches, David, ed. *Water and the American West: Essays in Honor of Raphael J. Moses.* Boulder: University of Colorado Natural Resources Law Center, 1988.

Glick, Thomas F. *The Old World Background of the Irrigation System of San Antonio, Texas.* El Paso: University of Texas at El Paso, 1972.

Goetzmann, William H. *New Lands, New Men: America and the Second Great Age of Discovery.* New York: Viking, 1986.

Hare, Jon C. *Indian Water Rights: An Analysis of Current and Pending Indian Water Rights Settlements.* Washington, D.C.: Bureau of Indian Affairs, and Oakville, Wash.: Confederated Tribes of the Chehalis Reservation, 1996.

Hays, Samuel. *Conservation and the Gospel of Efficiency: The Progressive Conservation Movement, 1890–1920.* Cambridge: Harvard University Press, 1959.

Horwitz, Morton. *The Transformation of American Law, 1780–1860.* Cambridge: Harvard University Press, 1977.

Hoxie, Frederick. *A Final Promise: The Campaign to Assimilate the Indians, 1880–1920.* Lincoln: University of Nebraska Press, 1984.

———. *Parading through History: The Making of the Crow Nation in America, 1805–1935.* New York: Cambridge University Press, 1995.

Hundley, Norris. *The Great Thirst: Californians and Water, 1770s–1990s.* Berkeley and Los Angeles: University of California Press, 1992.

Hurst, James Willard. *Law and the Conditions of Freedom in the Nineteenth-Century United States.* Madison: University of Wisconsin Press, 1956.

———. *Law and Economic Growth: The Legal History of the Lumber Industry in Wisconsin, 1856–1915.* Cambridge: Harvard University Press, Belknap Press, 1964.

Index to Legal Periodicals. Vols. 1–8 (1908–15). New York: American Association of Law Libraries, 1908–15.

Indian Water Policy in a Changing Environment: Perspectives on Indian Water Rights. Oakland: American Indian Lawyer Training Program, 1982.

Karsten, Peter. *Heart versus Head: Judge-Made Law in Nineteenth-Century America.* Chapel Hill: University of North Carolina Press, 1997.

Kinney, Clesson Selwyne. *A Treatise on the Law of Irrigation and Water Rights.* 2d ed., 4 vols. San Francisco: Bender-Moss Company, 1912.

Langum, David J. *Law and Community on the Mexican California Frontier.* Norman: University of Oklahoma Press, 1987.

Lewis, David Rich. *Neither Wolf nor Dog: American Indians, Environment, and Agrarian Change.* New York: Oxford University Press, 1994.

Lord, William B., and Mary G. Wallace, eds. *Symposium Proceedings on Indian Water Rights and Water Resources Management.* Bethesda, Md.: American Water Resources Association, 1989.

McCool, Daniel. *Command of the Waters: Iron Triangles, Federal Water Development, and Indian Water.* Berkeley and Los Angeles: University of California Press, 1987. Reprint, Tucson: University of Arizona Press, 1994.

McDonnell, Janet A. *The Dispossession of the American Indian, 1887–1934.* Bloomington: Indiana University Press, 1991.

McGuire, Thomas R., William B. Lord, and Mary G. Wallace, eds. *Indian Water in the New West.* Tucson: University of Arizona Press, 1993.

Meyer, Michael C. *Water in the Hispanic Southwest.* Tucson: University of Arizona Press, 1984.

Miklas, Christine L., and Steven J. Shupe, eds. *Indian Water 1985: Collected Essays.* Oakland: American Indian Law Training Program, 1986.

Nabhan, Gary Paul. *The Desert Smells Like Rain: A Naturalist in Papago Indian Country.* San Francisco: North Point Press, 1982.

Novak, William J. *The People's Welfare: Law and Regulation in Nineteenth-Century America.* Chapel Hill: University of North Carolina Press, 1996.

Pisani, Donald. *To Reclaim a Divided West: Water, Law, and Public Policy, 1848–1902.* Albuquerque: University of New Mexico Press, 1992.

———. *Water, Land, and Law in the West: The Limits of Public Policy, 1850–1920*. Lawrence: University Press of Kansas, 1996.

Powell, John Wesley. *Report on the Lands of the Arid Region of the United States, United States Geographical and Geologic Survey of the Rocky Mountain Region*. Edited by Wallace Stegner. Cambridge: Harvard University Press, Belknap Press, 1962.

Prucha, Francis Paul. *The Great Father: The United States Government and the American Indians*. 2 vols. Lincoln: University of Nebraska Press, 1984.

Rassier, Phillip. *Indian Water Rights: A Study of the Historical and Legal Factors Affecting the Water Rights of the Indians of the State of Idaho*. Boise: Idaho Department of Water Resources, 1978.

Rodnick, David. *The Fort Belknap Assiniboine of Montana: A Study in Cultural Change*. New Haven: Yale University Press, 1938.

Ruby, Robert H., and John A. Brown. *Dreamer-Prophets of the Columbia Plateau*. Norman: University of Oklahoma Press, 1989.

Smythe, William E. *The Conquest of Arid America*. New York: Macmillan Company, 1905.

Sly, Peter W. *Reserved Water Rights Settlement Manual*. Washington, D.C.: Island Press, 1988.

Sourcebook on Indian Water Settlements. Oakland: American Indian Resources Institute, 1989.

Steinberg, Theodore. *Nature Incorporated: Industrialization and the Waters of New England*. New York: Cambridge University Press, 1991.

Tarlock, A. Dan. *Law of Water Rights and Resources*. New York: Clark Boardman, 1988, 1996.

Tribal Water Management Handbook. Oakland: Indian Lawyer Training Program, 1988.

Tyler, Daniel. *The Mythical Pueblo Rights Doctrine: Water Administration in Hispanic New Mexico*. El Paso: Texas Western Press, 1990.

Webb, Walter Prescott. *The Great Plains*. Boston: Ginn & Company, 1931.

Welch, James. *Fools Crow*. New York: Penguin Books, 1986.

Western States Water Council. *Indian Water Rights in the West: A Study Prepared for the Western Governors Association*. Denver: Western Governors Association, 1984.

White, Richard. *The Roots of Dependency: Subsistence, Environment, and Social Change among the Choctaws, Pawnees, and Navajos*. Lincoln: University of Nebraska Press, 1983.

Wiel, Samuel C. *Water Rights in the Western States*. 3d ed., 2 vols. San Francisco: Bancroft-Whitney, 1911.

Wilkinson, Charles. *American Indians, Time, and the Law: Native Societies in a Modern Constitutional Democracy*. New Haven: Yale University Press, 1987.

Worster, Donald. *Rivers of Empire: Water, Aridity and the Growth of the American West*. New York: Pantheon Books, 1985. Reprint, New York: Oxford University Press, 1992.

318   BIBLIOGRAPHY

ARTICLES AND CHAPTERS

Abrams, Robert H. "Reserved Water Rights, Indian Rights and the Narrowing Scope of Federal Jurisdiction: The *Colorado River* Decision." *Stanford Law Review* 30 (July 1978): 1111–48.

———. "The Big Horn Indian Water Rights Adjudication: A Battle for the Legal Imagination." *Oklahoma Law Review* 43 (Spring 1990): 71–86.

Adams, Frank. "The Economical Use of Water as Affecting the Extent of Rights under the Doctrine of Prior Appropriation." *California Law Review* 2 (July 1914): 367–76.

Back, William D., and Jeffrey S. Taylor. "Navajo Water Rights: Pulling the Plug on the Colorado River?" *Natural Resources Journal* 20 (January 1980): 71–90.

Bannister, L. Ward. "The Question of Federal Disposition of State Waters in the Priority States." *Harvard Law Review* 28 (January 1915): 270–93.

Bell, D. Craig, and Norman K. Johnson. "State Water Laws and Federal Water Uses: The History of Conflict, the Prospects for Accommodation." *Environmental Law* 21 (Fall 1990): 1–88.

Bloom, Paul L. "Indian 'Paramount' Rights to Water Use." *Rocky Mountain Mineral Law Institute* 16 (1971): 669–93.

Blumm, Michael. "Reserved Water Rights." In *Water and Water Rights*. Vol. 4, edited by Robert E. Beck. Charlottesville: Michie Company, 1991, 1996.

———. "Unconventional Waters: The Quiet Revolution in Federal and Tribal Minimum Streamflows." *Ecology Law Quarterly* 19 (August 1992): 445–80.

Bond, Frank M. "Indian Reserved Water Rights Doctrine Expanded." *Natural Resources Journal* 23 (January 1983): 205–12.

Brienza, Susan D. "Wet Water vs. Paper Rights: Indian and Non-Indian Negotiated Settlements and Their Effects." *Stanford Environmental Law Journal* 11 (1992): 151–99.

Burness, H. S. "United States Reclamation Policy and Indian Water Rights." *Natural Resources Journal* 20 (October 1980): 808–26.

———. "The 'New'" *Arizona v. California:* Practically Irrigable Acreage and Economic Feasibility." *Natural Resources Journal* 22 (July 1982): 517–23.

———. "Practically Irrigable Acreage and Economic Feasibility: The Role of Time, Ethics, and Discounting." *Natural Resources Journal* 23 (April 1983): 289–303.

Campbell, Susan Millington. "A Proposal for the Quantification of Reserved Indian Water Rights." *Columbia Law Review* 74 (November 1974): 1299–1321.

Chambers, Reid P. "Indian Water Rights after the *Wyoming* Decision." *Harvard Indian Law Symposium* (1989): 153–63.

Chambers, Reid P., and John E. Echohawk. "Implementing the *Winters* Doctrine of Indian Reserved Water Rights: Producing Indian Water and Economic Development without Injuring Non-Indian Water Users?" *Gonzaga Law Review* 27 (Spring 1992): 447–70.

Chandler, Albert. "Title to Non-navigable Waters in Western States." *St. Louis Law Review* 4 (1919): 109–30.

Clark, Ira G. "The Elephant Butte Controversy: A Chapter in the Emergence of Federal Water Law." *Journal of American History* 61 (1975): 1015–33.

Clayberg, John. "The Genesis and Development of the Law of the Waters in the Far West." *Michigan Law Review* 1 (November 1902): 91–101.

Collins, Richard. "The Future Course of the *Winters* Doctrine." *University of Colorado Law Review* 56 (Spring 1985): 481–94.

———. "Indian Allotment Water Rights." *Land and Water Law Review* 20 (Spring 1985): 421–57.

Cooter, Robert, and Stephen Marks, with Robert H. Mnookin. "Bargaining in the Shadow of the Law: A Testable Model of Strategic Behavior." *Journal of Legal Studies* 11 (June 1982): 225–51.

Costo, Rupert. "Indian Water Rights: A Survival Issue." *Indian Historian* 5 (Fall 1972): 4–6.

Coursey, Don L., and Linda R. Stanley. "Pretrial Bargaining Behavior within the Shadow of the Law: Theory and Experimental Evidence." *International Review of Law and Economics* 8 (December 1988): 161–79.

Dellwo, Robert D. "Indian Water Rights—The *Winters* Doctrine Updated." *Gonzaga Law Review* 6 (Spring 1971): 215–40.

———. "Recent Developments in the Northwest Regarding Indian Water Rights." *Natural Resources Journal* 20 (January 1980): 101–20.

DuMars, Charles, and Helen Ingram. "Congressional Quantification of Indian Water Rights: A Definitive Solution or a Mirage?" *Natural Resources Journal* 20 (January 1980): 17–43.

DuMars, Charles, and A. Dan Tarlock. "New Challenges to State Water Allocation Sovereignty." *Natural Resources Journal* 29 (Spring 1989): 331–46.

Dunbar, Robert G. "The Adaptability of Water Law to the Aridity of the West." *Journal of the West* 24 (1985): 57–65.

Feldman, Stephen M. "The Supreme Court's New Sovereign Immunity Doctrine and the McCarran Amendment: Toward Ending State Adjudication of Indian Water Rights." *Harvard Environmental Law Review* 18 (Summer 1994): 433–88.

Fereday, Jeffrey, and Michael Creamer. "Swan Falls in 3-D: A New Look at the Historical, Legal and Practical Dimensions of Idaho's Biggest Water Rights Controversy." *Idaho Law Review* 28 (Summer 1992): 573–643.

Folk-Williams, John A. "The Use of Negotiated Agreements to Resolve Water Disputes Involving Indian Rights." *Natural Resources Journal* 28 (Winter 1988): 63–93.

Foster, Kenneth. "The *Winters* Doctrine: Historical Perspective and Future Applications of Reserved Water Rights in Arizona." *Groundwater* 16 (May/June 1978): 186–91.

Franks, Martha C. "The Uses of the Practicably Irrigable Acreage Standard in the Quantification of Reserved Water Rights." *Natural Resources Journal* 31 (Summer 1991): 549–85.

Getches, David H. "Water Rights on Indian Allotments." *South Dakota Law Review* 26 (Summer 1981): 405–33.

————. "Management and Marketing of Indian Water: From Conflict to Pragmatism." *University of Colorado Law Review* 58 (Winter 1988): 515–49.

Goldschmidt, Jona. "Bargaining in the Shadow of ADR: Analysis of Judicial and Attorney Attitudes toward Settlement under a Medical Screening Panel System." *Justice System Journal* 16 (Spring 1994): 15–32.

Hess, R. H. "Arid-Land Water Rights in the United States." *Columbia Law Review* 16 (June 1916): 480–95.

Hundley, Norris, Jr. "The Dark and Bloody Ground of Indian Water Rights: Confusion Elevated to Principle." *Western Historical Quarterly* 9 (October 1978): 454–82.

————. "The 'Winters' Decision and Indian Water Rights: A Mystery Reexamined." *Western Historical Quarterly* 13 (January 1982): 17–42.

Hunt, William. "Law of Water Rights." *Yale Law Journal* 17 (1908): 585–88.

"Indian Reserved Water Rights: The *Winters* of Our Discontent." *Yale Law Journal* 88 (July 1979): 1689–1712.

Jacob, Herbert. "The Elusive Shadow of the Law." *Law and Society* 26 (August 1992): 565–90.

Kirk, Peggy Sue. "Cowboys, Indians, and Reserved Water Rights: May a State Court Limit How Indians Use Their Water?" *Land and Water Law Review* 28 (Summer 1993): 467–88.

Lamb, Terrence J. "Indian-Government Relations on Water Utilization in the Salt and Gila River Valleys of Southern Arizona, 1902–1914." *Indian Historian* 10 (Summer 1977): 38–45.

Lasky, Moses. "From Prior Appropriation to Economic Distribution of Water by the State—Via Irrigation Administration." *Rocky Mountain Law Review* 1 (April 1929): 161–216, (June 1929): 248–70, 2 (November 1929): 35–58.

Lawson, Michael. "The Navajo Indian Irrigation Project: Muddied Past, Clouded Future." *Indian Historian* 9 (Winter 1976): 19–29.

Lichtenfels, Christine. "Indian Reserved Water Rights: An Argument for the Right to Export and Sell." *Land and Water Law Review* 24 (Winter 1989): 131–51.

Lieder, Michael. "Adjudication of Indian Water Rights under the McCarran Amendment: Two Courts Are Better than One." *Georgetown Law Journal* 71 (February 1983): 1023–61.

Liu, Sylvia. "American Indian Reserved Water Rights: The Federal Obligation to Protect Tribal Water Resources and Tribal Autonomy." *Environmental Law* 25 (Spring 1995): 425–62.

Martinis, Berrie. "From Quantification to Qualification: A State Court's Distortion of the Law in In re General Adjudication of All Rights to Use Water in the Big Horn River System." *Washington Law Review* 68 (April 1993): 435–55.

Massie, Michael. "The Defeat of Assimilation and the Rise of Colonialism on the Fort Belknap Indian Reservation, 1873–1925." *American Indian Culture and Research Journal* 7, no. 4 (1984): 33–49.

————. "The Cultural Roots of Indian Water Rights." *Annals of Wyoming* 59 (Spring 1987): 15–28.

McCallister, Elizabeth. "Water Rights: The McCarran Amendment and Indian Tribes' Reserved Water Rights." *American Indian Law Review* 4, no. 2 (1976): 303–10.

McCurdy, Charles. "Stephen J. Field and Public Land Law Development in California, 1850–1866: A Case Study in Judicial Resource Allocation in Nineteenth-Century America." *Law and Society Review* 10, no. 2 (1976): 235–66.

McElroy, Scott, and Jeff J. Davis. "Revisiting *Colorado River Water Conservation District v. United States*—There Must Be a Better Way." *Arizona State Law Journal* 27 (Summer 1995): 597–648.

McGovern, Gina. "Settlement and Adjudication: Resolving Indian Reserved Rights." *Arizona Law Review* 36 (Spring 1994): 195–222.

Membrino, Joseph. "Indian Reserved Water Rights, Federalism, and Trust Responsibility." *Land and Water Law Review* 27 (Summer 1992): 1–31.

Merrill, James L. "Aboriginal Water Rights." *Natural Resources Journal* 20 (January 1980): 45–70.

Mnookin, Robert H., and Lewis Kornhauser. "Bargaining in the Shadow of the Law: The Case of Divorce." *Yale Law Journal* 88 (1979): 950–97.

Moore, Michael R. "Native American Water Rights: Efficiency and Fairness." *Natural Resources Journal* 29 (Summer 1989): 763–91.

Morreale, Eve Hanna. "Federal-State Conflicts over Western Waters—A Decade of Attempted 'Clarifying Legislation.'" *Rutgers Law Review* 20 (Spring 1966): 423–526.

Newville, Ed. "Pueblo Indian Water Rights: Overview and Update on the Aamodt Litigation." *Natural Resources Journal* 29 (Winter 1989): 251–78.

Niles, Russell Denison. "Legal Background of the Colorado River Controversy." *Rocky Mountain Law Review* 1 (February 1929): 73–101.

Pacheco, Thomas H. "How Big Is Big? The Scope of Water Rights Suits under the McCarran Amendment." *Ecology Law Quarterly* 15 (November 1988): 627–69.

Palma, Jack D., II. "Considerations and Conclusions Concerning the Transferability of Indian Water Rights." *Natural Resources Journal* 20 (January 1980): 91–100.

Pelcyger, Robert S. "Indian Water Rights: Some Emerging Frontiers." *Rocky Mountain Mineral Law Institute* 21 (1975): 743–75.

————. "The *Winters* Doctrine and the Greening of the Reservations." *Journal of Contemporary Law* 4 (Winter 1977): 19–37.

Peregoy, Robert. "Jurisdictional Aspects of Indian Reserved Water Rights in Montana and on the Flathead Reservation after *Adsit*." *American Indian Culture and Research Journal* 7, no. 1 (1983): 41–86.

Pisani, Donald. "State v. Nation: Federal Reclamation and Water Rights in the Progressive Era." *Pacific Historical Review* 51 (August 1982): 265–82. Reprinted. in Donald Pisani, *Water, Land, and Law in the West: The*

Limits of Public Policy, 1850–1920. Lawrence: University Press of Kansas, 1996.

———. "Reclamation and Social Engineering in the Progressive West." *Agricultural History* 57 (January 1983): 46–63. Reprinted. in Donald Pisani, *Water, Land, and Law in the West: The Limits of Public Policy, 1850–1920*. Lawrence: University Press of Kansas, 1996.

———. "Irrigation, Water Rights, and the Betrayal of Indian Allotment." *Environmental Review* 10 (Fall 1986): 157–76. Reprinted. in Donald Pisani, *Water, Land, and Law in the West: The Limits of Public Policy, 1850–1920*. Lawrence: University Press of Kansas, 1996.

———. "Enterprise and Equity: A Critique of Western Water Law in the Nineteenth Century." *Western Historical Quarterly* 18 (January 1987): 15–37. Reprinted in Donald Pisani, *Water, Land, and Law in the West: The Limits of Public Policy, 1850–1920*. Lawrence: University Press of Kansas, 1996.

———. "The Origins of Western Water Law: Case Studies from Two California Mining Districts. *California History* 70 (Fall 1991): 242–57. Reprinted in Donald Pisani, *Water, Land, and Law in the West: The Limits of Public Policy, 1850–1920*. Lawrence: University Press of Kansas, 1996.

———. "Federal Reclamation." In Donald Pisani, *Water, Land, and Law in the West: The Limits of Public Policy, 1850–1920*. Lawrence: University Press of Kansas, 1996.

———. "Water Law." In Donald Pisani, *Water, Land, and Law in the West: The Limits of Public Policy, 1850–1920*. Lawrence: University Press of Kansas, 1996.

Price, Monroe E., and Gary D. Weatherford. "Indian Water Rights in Theory and Practice: Navajo Experience in the Colorado River Basin." *Law and Contemporary Problems* 40 (Winter 1976): 97–131.

Ranquist, Harold A. "The *Winters* Doctrine and How It Grew." *Brigham Young University Law Review* (1975): 639–724.

Royster, Judith V. "A Primer on Indian Water Rights: More Questions than Answers." *Tulsa Law Journal* 30 (Fall 1994): 61–104.

Rusinek, Walter. "A Preview of Coming Attractions? *Wyoming v. United States* and the Reserved Rights Doctrine." *Ecology Law Quarterly* 17 (May 1990): 355–412.

Shay, Monique. "Promises of a Viable Homeland, Reality of Selective Reclamation: A Study of the Relationship between the *Winters* Doctrine and Federal Water Development in the United States." *Ecology Law Quarterly* 19, no. 3 (1992): 547–90.

Shimizui, Eileen. "Indian Water Rights: An Examination of the Current Status of the Department of Interior's Guidelines and the Opposition to Them." *Federal Bar News and Journal* 38 (March 1991): 88–91.

Shrago, Alvin H. "Emerging Indian Water Rights: An Analysis of Recent Judicial and Legislative Developments." *Rocky Mountain Mineral Law Institute* 26 (1980): 1105–56.

Shupe, Steven J. "Water in Indian Country: From Paper Rights to a Managed Resource." *University of Colorado Law Review* 57 (Spring 1986): 561–92.

———. "Indian Tribes in the Water Marketing Area." *American Indian Law Review* 15 (Spring 1990): 185–205.

Sly, Peter W., and Cheryl A. Maier. "Indian Water Settlements and EPA." *Natural Resources and the Environment* 5 (Spring 1991): 23.

Sondheim, Harry B., and John R. Alexander. "Federal Indian Water Rights: A Retrogression to Quasi-Riparianism?" *Southern California Law Review* 34 (Fall 1960): 1–25.

Stanton, David M. "Is There a Reserved Water Right for Wildlife on the Wind River Indian Reservation? A Critical Analysis of the Big Horn River General Adjudication." *South Dakota Law Review* 35 (Summer 1990): 326–40.

Storey, Lee H. "Leasing Indian Water off the Reservation: A Use Consistent with the Reservation's Purpose." *California Law Review* 76 (January 1988): 179–220.

Tarlock, A. Dan. "One River, Three Sovereigns: Indian and Interstate Water Rights." *Land and Water Law Review* 22 (Spring 1987): 631–71.

———. "Indian Reserved Water Rights." In A Dan Tarlock, *Law of Water Rights and Resources,* sec. 9.07. New York: Clark Boardman, 1988, 1996.

Thorson, John E. "Proceedings of the Symposium on Settlement of Indian Water Rights Claims." *Environmental Law* 22 (Spring 1992): 1009–26.

Toren, Peter. "The Adjudication of Indian Water Rights in State Courts." *University of San Francisco Law Review* 19 (Fall 1984): 27–51.

Trelease, Frank J. "Federal Reserved Water Rights since PLLRC." *Denver Law Journal* 54 (1977): 473–92.

———. "Uneasy Federalism—State Water Laws and National Water Uses." *Washington Law Review* 55 (November 1980): 751–75.

Upite, Daina. "Resolving Indian Reserved Water Rights in the Wake of *San Carlos Apache Tribe.*" *Environmental Law* 15 (Fall 1984): 181–200.

Veeder, William H. "Indian Prior and Paramount Rights to the Use of Water." *Rocky Mountain Mineral Law Institute* 16 (1971): 631–68.

———. "Water Rights: Life or Death for the American Indian." *Indian Historian* 5 (Summer 1972): 4–9.

———. "Confiscation of Indian Water Rights in the Upper Missouri River Basin." *South Dakota Law Review* 21 (Spring 1976): 282–309.

———. "Water Rights in the Coal Fields of the Yellowstone River Basin." *Law and Contemporary Problems* 40 (Winter 1976): 77–96.

Walker, Jana L., and Susan M. Williams. "Indian Reserved Water Rights." *Natural Resources and the Environment* 5 (Spring 1991): 6.

Wallace, Mary B. "The Supreme Court and Indian Water Rights." In *American Indian Policy in the Twentieth Century,* edited by Vine Deloria, Jr., 197–220. Norman: University of Oklahoma Press, 1985.

Wardlaw, Rebecca E. "The Irrigable Acres Doctrine." *Natural Resources Journal* 15 (April 1975): 375–84.

White, Michael D. "McCarran Amendment Adjudications—Problems, Solutions, Alternatives." *Land and Water Law Review* 22 (Spring 1987): 619–29.
Wiel, Samuel C. "'Priority' in Western Water Law." *Yale Law Journal* 18 (January 1909): 189–98.
———. "Theories of Water Law." *Harvard Law Review* 27 (April 1914): 530–44.
———. "What Is Beneficial Use of Water?" *California Law Review* 3 (September 1915): 460–75.
Wilkinson, Charles. "Prior Appropriation 1848–1991." *Environmental Law* 21 (Spring 1991), v–xviii.
Wilkinson, Charles, and John Volkman. "Judicial Review of Indian Treaty Abrogation: 'As Long as Water Flows, or Grass Grows Upon the Earth'— How Long a Time Is That?" *California Law Review* 63 (1975): 601–61.
Williams, Wes, Jr. "Changing Water Use for Federally Reserved Water Rights: Wind River Indian Reservation." *University of California at Davis Law Review* 27 (Winter 1994): 501–32.

DISSERTATIONS, THESES, AND OTHER UNPUBLISHED MATERIAL

Dudley, Shelly. "Pima Indians, Water Rights, and the Federal Government: *U.S. v. Gila Valley Irrigation District.*" Master's thesis, Arizona State University, 1996.
Endter, Joanna Lynne. "Cultural Ideologies and the Political Economy of Water in the United States West: Northern Ute Indians and Rural Mormons in the Uintah Basin, Utah." Ph.D. diss., University of California at Irvine, 1987.
Leibhardt, Barbara G. "Law, Environment, and Social Change in the Columbia River Basin: The Yakima Indian Nation as a Case Study, 1840–1933." Ph.D. diss., University of California at Berkeley, 1990.
"Memoirs of William H. Hunt." William H. Hunt Papers, Montana Historical Society,1941.
"Milk River Basin Interviews." Completed by Bob Decker. 49th Parallel Institute, Montana State University, December 1989.
Shane, Ralph. *Brief History of the Fort Belknap Reservation.* Pamphlet in the collection of the Montana Historical Society, Helena, 1974.

Index

332

INDEX

United States Office of Indian Affairs.
See Indian Affairs, Office of
United States Reclamation Service. *See*
Reclamation Service
*United States v. Cedarview Irrigation
Company. See* Uintah and Ouray
Indian reservation, water rights
litigation
*United States v. Dry Gulch Irrigation
Company. See* Uintah and Ouray
Indian reservation, water rights
litigation
United States v. Hampleman (Wind River
litigation), 196, 202–205, 225, 226,
242
*United States v. Mose Anderson. See
Winters v. United States*
United States v. Parkins (Wind River
litigation), 242, 244
*United States v. Rio Grande Dam and
Irrigation Company (Rio Grande, Rio
Grande* case), 50–51, 53, 54, 69, 72,
86, 88, 91, 99, 101, 144, 154–55, 213,
275n.29
United States v. Wightman, 199–201,
287n.17
United States v. Winans, 56–60, 72–74, 98,
123, 144, 151, 153–56, 163, 208,
275n.29, 287n.17
Ute Indians. *See* Uintah and Ouray
Indian Reservation

Valentine, Robert, 191, 192
Vandalia, Mont., 29
Van Orsdel, J. A., 144

Wade, Decius, 44–45
Walsh, Thomas, 160, 217, 220, 266n.8
Ward, Ethelbert, 205–206, 226, 241–43,
276n.30, 306n.21
Water law and rights: aridity,
relationship to, 36–39, 49, 66, 92–93,
95–97, 100, 101, 124, 150, 158, 161,
216, 219, 222, 252, 261n.4; in
Arizona, 187, 188–91, 196–201;
"California" doctrine, 48, 163; in
Colorado, 89, 92, 197, 205–206, 213,
263n.8; equitable apportionment of
interstate waters, 100–101; federal

law and policy, 8, 36, 42, 43, 46, 47,
50–55, 61, 64, 74, 86–89, 92, 94, 97,
99, 100–101, 113, 145, 150, 152–56,
163, 179, 184, 192, 204–206, 212–16,
218–19, 225, 271n.6, 275n.29,
275n.30; federal property, water
necessary for beneficial use of,
50–55, 61, 62, 68–70, 72, 86, 88, 91,
99, 101, 144, 153–56, 192, 193,
205–206, 213, 271n.6, 275n.29; in
Idaho, 52–53, 162, 241; in Montana,
3–4, 7, 35, 36, 43–50, 53–55, 64, 65,
69, 72, 74, 87–90, 93, 97–99, 112, 113,
127–30, 134–36, 138–40, 144, 147,
151, 152, 154, 160, 161, 163, 186–87,
191, 196, 197, 204, 211, 213–18; in
Nevada, 199; in Oregon, 185, 197,
199, 201–202; prior appropriation
doctrine, 4, 6, 8–9, 35–54, 61–65,
68–70, 72, 74–77, 85–87, 89, 90, 92,
93, 96, 97, 99, 100, 104, 112, 113, 125,
129, 131–33, 135, 138, 140, 151–52,
157, 159, 162–64, 165–66, 175–77,
184, 187, 188, 190–91, 193, 195–99,
203–19, 221–22, 224, 225, 230–35,
238–52, 260n.3, 261n.4, 263n.8;
reserved water rights, implications
of for federal purposes other than
Indian reservations, 5, 8, 42–43, 86,
101, 167, 192, 205–206, 271n.6,
274n.28, 276n.31; riparian doctrine
(riparian rights, common-law
doctrine/rights), 37, 38, 40, 42–51,
62–64, 68–72, 85–97, 99–101, 144,
162, 163, 188, 193, 204, 261n.4,
271n.6, 276n.31; Spanish/Mexican
system, 39–40; treaty rights basis, 35,
55–61, 65, 68–70, 72–74, 87–89, 91,
92, 94, 97–100, 143–45, 152–56, 159,
162, 182–83, 190, 193, 200–205, 208,
214–15, 226, 229, 231, 242, 247,
257n.2, 267n.10, 276n.31, 284n.40,
287n.17; in Utah, 170, 175–80, 184,
191, 196, 205, 223–26, 230–50;
western state water law, 4–8, 42–43,
48, 51, 65, 86, 89–92, 97, 99–101, 113,
115, 152, 154–55, 158–59, 161–64,
165–67, 175, 184, 189–94, 196–99,
205–206, 212–14, 216–19, 221–22,